A Screen of Time

A Study of Luchino Visconti

by MONICA STIRLING

I was deeply impressed by what I saw. While it was in the great old tradition of La Scala, the production was executed through a screen of time absolutely correct in taste and judgment. Only in this way can works of the Romantic epoch come alive today.

Sandro Sequi, director at La Scala, on Visconti's staging of Donizetti's *Anna Bolena*

A Helen and Kurt Wolff Book

Harcourt Brace Jovanovich

New York and London

Requests for permission to make copies of any part of the work
should be mailed to Permissions, Harcourt Brace Jovanovich, Inc.,
757 Third Avenue, New York, N.Y. 10017.

The excerpts from the poems by Leopardi are from *Giacomo Leopardi:
Selected Prose and Poetry* by Iris Origo and John Heath-Stubbs,
copyright © 1966 by Oxford University Press, reprinted by arrangement
with The New American Library, Inc., New York, N.Y. The excerpts
from Thomas Mann's *Death in Venice*, translated by Kenneth Burke,
copyright 1924 by The Dial Publishing Co., Inc., copyright © 1970 by
Alfred A. Knopf, Inc., are reprinted by permission of Alfred A. Knopf,
Inc. The excerpt from "Ithaka" is from *The Poems of C. P. Cavafy*,
translated by John Mavrogordato, copyright 1951 by John Mavrogordato,
reprinted by permission of Deborah Rogers Ltd and The Hogarth Press Ltd.

Printed in the United States of America

Library of Congress Cataloging in Publication Data

Stirling, Monica, date
A screen of time.

"A Helen and Kurt Wolff book."
Bibliography: p.
Includes index.
1. Visconti, Luchino, 1906–1976.
2. Moving-picture producers and directors—Italy—Biography.
3. Moving-pictures—Italy.
I. Title.
PN1998.A3V5865   791.43′0233′0924   [B]   78-22273
ISBN 0-15-179684-X

First edition

B C D E

For
SUSO CECCHI D'AMICO
with gratitude and affection

Photographs are between pages 136–137 and 232–233.

For kind help, hospitality, and permission to use quotations, photographs, and information, I should like to thank:

The late Luchino Visconti.
Donna Uberta Visconti di Modrone, Suso Cecchi D'Amico, Natalia Danesi Murray, Franca Danesi Lucide, Caterina D'Amico De Carvalho, Contessa Wally Toscanini Castelbarco, Conte and Contessa Carlo di Robilant, Donna Maria Visconti Bergamasco, Contessa Violante Pasolini Dell'Onda, Enrico Medioli, the late Rina Morelli, Professor Hugo A. Krayenbühl, Anne Morrow Lindbergh, Nesta Obermer, Mrs. St. George Saunders, Jane and Bruno Sacchi, Nohabbat Malekzadeh, Carola Pajouk, Mara Pfeiffer, Anne-Marie Riedlinger, and Signor Paolo Ulivieri of the Libreria del Porcellino in Florence.

Whenever Luchino Visconti's own words are given, I am quoting from things he said to me, or that were repeated to me by close friends of his—Suso Cecchi D'Amico, Enrico Medioli, and in one or two instances by Donna Uberta Visconti—to all of whom I am deeply grateful.

Everything about him . . . gave one the impression of centuries and hidden stores of pent-up civilization.

Maurice Baring

. . . Herzen was the least snobbish of radicals—like Gandhi, he treated the rich as social equals. . . .

Dwight Macdonald

The life one leads does not amount to much, but the life one dreams, that's the great thing, because it will continue after one is dead.

Gabrielle Chanel

Art may be a game, but it's a serious game.

Kaspar David Friedrich

One

*March 17, 1976, Luchino Visconti. Un romantico
dei nostri tempi. Requiescat in pace.*

March 19. Geneva airport: unique in its tranquil combination of the
efficient with the pleasurable. At this hour, 8:30 A.M., only a few passengers are drinking coffee and unfolding newspapers. The early sunshine gives the mountains on the far side of the airfield a Lost Horizon
aspect. Eleven years ago, Luchino Visconti's film *Vaghe stelle dell'orsa*
(*Sandra*) was beginning in Geneva's comparatively safe and rational
atmosphere—from which Sandra and Andrew set out for the time-eroded
mysteries of Etruscan Volterra. Remembering the film's opening scenes:
the glittering highway, a flight of birds overhead, the gathering speed,
the signposts pointing to Italy, it seems—that eternally banal thought,
its painfulness unrelieved by its banality—impossible that *never again*
will Luchino Visconti do the work that was the center of his life.

At 9:45 the plane takes off for Rome. First come vast brilliantly
sunlit fields of rhythmically curved white clouds: Tiepolo clouds in a
Tiepolo firmament. But almost at once cloud fields make way for one of
the roofs of the world: peak after mountain peak as far as the horizon,
no longer a Tiepolo universe but, rather, that of Kaspar David Friedrich, its beauty shot with anguish. Every detail is clear, as if seen
through a giant magnifying glass. Below the snow lines, steep peat-green
or brown valleys are penciled by tracks that suggest the invisible presence of circumspect wild animals.

"On your left," says the loudspeaker's crackly but amiable voice, "you
will see the island of Elba." Very small, the island looks like a dark
semiprecious stone in the neatly scalloped Mediterranean. One hundred

3

and sixty-two years ago Napoleon was a prisoner on Elba and, back in France, Bonapartists meeting in the street would greet each other with "Do you believe in Christ?" To which the orthodox answer was "Yes and in the Resurrection." That religion, politics, and blasphemy are old acquaintances should never be forgot.

The plane curves in over the Italian coast. "Soon," says the loudspeaker, "we shall be landing in Rome." At 11:00 A.M. we are on the ground at Leonardo da Vinci Airport. Outside the airport, buttercup-colored taxis are aligned in the sunlight.

"To the Church of St. Ignatius, please."

Although it is only March, Rome—beflagged with flower stalls in its great golden bubble of light—already has "all the wild summer in her gaze." The impression of seasonal riches is heightened by the ebullient holiday crowds in the streets. Today is the Feast of St. Joseph of Nazareth, descendant of David, husband of the Virgin Mary, legal father of Jesus, patron saint of carpenters and of the universal church. The final reference to St. Joseph in the New Testament occurs when Jesus was twelve years old and his parents lost Him while they were in Jerusalem for Passover—and found Him at the Temple "sitting in the midst of the doctors, both hearing them, and asking them questions: and all that heard him were amazed at his understanding and his answers." As there is no later reference, it is generally assumed that St. Joseph died before Christ grew up. Today, nearly two thousand years later, how many of these exuberant holidaymakers—"Joseph did whistle and Mary did sing and all the bells on earth did ring"—find it odd that they should have an extra moment to make hay while the sun shines thanks to a Nazareth carpenter who, obscure in his lifetime, became the patron saint of a mighty church founded upon words he did not live long enough to hear his son speak, deeds he did not live to see his son perform, and, above all, upon a young man's death by crucifixion that, had Joseph lived to witness it, would have been to him a hideous personal tragedy?

All over the center of Rome the ancient walls are adorned with copies of two posters. One, austerely designed, black letters on a white ground, proclaims "pain and grief" for the death of

LUCHINO VISCONTI
a man of culture who by his great work
has for more than 30 years followed
the history of art, of the cinema and the theater
of our country, of Europe, of the world
and we remember him

4

as a militant anti-Fascist of the Resistance
who always showed loyal and profound solidarity
with the working classes and their struggle

For the very first time, Luchino Visconti's name, still phosphores-cently alive with the historical associations bestowed by his family, the artistic associations earned by his individual genius, is featured upon a poster that announces not a new work by him but that he will never again create a new work.

Between two copies of the mourning poster, by a poignant coinci-dence, is an umber poster, its color in harmony with the lion and desert colors of Rome, that announces the coming anniversary of the Nazi-Fascist massacres perpetrated at the Ardeatine Caves, on the outskirts of Rome, on March 24, 1944. In these caves three hundred and thirty-five hostages, kidnapped at random, were shot and left, the whole and the maimed mixed in a bleeding shambles, to die in the blackness behind the sealed entrances. This massacre was followed by a rounding up of partisans. Among those arrested was Luchino Visconti. Questioned by the infamous Pietro Koch, Visconti's attitude was so "unsatisfactory" that he was condemned to death. At the last minute he escaped. Now, his death, two days ago, at sixty-nine, stares from beside the Ardeatine victims, whose deaths he so nearly shared when he was thirty-seven. In front of one postered wall a thin but jovial scarecrow, who might have escaped from a Fellini film, marches to and fro playing a trumpet.

The taxi darts, jerks, and wobbles through ancient streets made for feet and hoofs. At last we reach the sun-drenched Piazza Ignazio. Tall umber houses form a semicircle facing the church. The people gathered at every window give the impression of being in stage boxes—and indeed the seventeenth-century Jesuit church of Sant' Ignazio has in front of it a flight of steps and what could serve as a platform leading into the church. All along this platform, on both sides of the entrances, are huge wreaths, formally beautiful, suggesting mosaics rather than flowers. Their ribbons, flags of love and friendship, bear Luchino Visconti's name and the names of their donors. The spectators at the windows gaze down, the crowd in the piazza gazes up—at the loudspeakers, from which come the voices of public figures praising and mourning Luchino Visconti.

Inside, the church appears vast. Presently, a thousand people will be there to say good-bye to Visconti. No church could be more appropriate for this than that of the soldier-saint Ignazio, militant, impatient, effica-cious. The air is full of flowers, incense, music. The service will be less

5

formal than usual, since there cannot be a Requiem Mass on St. Joseph's Day. Suddenly the church is filled by an incoming tide of people. In this context, glimpses of familiar faces increase the sense of strangeness, of unreality, that accompanies all funerals where there is much grief. There is a face often seen on sets of films directed by Visconti. Now, as in the past, director of production Lucio Trentini looks harassed lest all be not in order for the *maestro*. There is Visconti's beautiful sister Uberta, the family likeness a separate haunting presence. There is President Giovanni Leone, and there Burt Lancaster, as if in an epilogue to *The Leopard*. When the coffin is carried in, there is fervent applause.

The pain and grief expressed today by applause, as so short a while ago love and appreciation were expressed to a man more alive even in illness than are most of us in health, conjure up words recently spoken by Alberto Moravia on television. Art, said Moravia, plays the same part in social life as dreams in private life—and we die if we do not dream, even though the utility of art and of dreams may not be immediately perceptible to those unwilling to give the matter thought. "Visconti taught us," said Sandro Sequi, when he was directing at La Scala, "that you must believe what you see, but that truth must be filtered through art."

In the deep afternoon sunlight the trumpeter is still playing alongside newly postered ancient walls. As the taxi stops at Sant' Ignazio, on the way to the airport, the driver says proudly, "There was a grand funeral here today, a truly *grandiose* funeral." He clearly feels that this reflects credit on Rome. And so it does.

Two

Luchino Visconti, born in his family's palace in Milan on the evening of November 2, 1906, was the third son and fourth child of Giuseppe Visconti, Duke of Modrone, a flamboyantly handsome and gifted man whose ancestors, far from being lost in the mists of antiquity, were descended from King Desiderius, father-in-law of Charlemagne and last ruler of northern Italy's eighth-century Kingdom of the Lombards. Ever since they became *signori* of Milan in 1277, the Viscontis had performed quantities of those individual feats that are the basis of recorded history. We all have ancestors, but whereas most of us know little about them, a child like Luchino Visconti, with ancestors still moving in the tapestries all around him, is born with a sense of history's continuity into a world of vast imaginative dimensions, full of communicative ghosts with familiar faces. "Memory needs links," and Luchino Visconti inherited not only an abundance of these but also a mind capable of grappling with them.

Both Luchino Visconti's parents possessed great personal magnetism. His mother, the spellbindingly beautiful Carla Erba—"La Erba," wrote a contemporary columnist, "was spoken of by the Milanese as if she were a work of art belonging to the public eye"—came of a family of peasant stock that had acquired position and wealth through talent and energy. Her father, Luigi Erba, an accomplished musician, was the collaborator and brother-in-law of Verdi's lifelong publisher, agent, and friend, Giulio Ricordi; her uncle, pharmacologist Carlo Erba, was, in Napoleon's words, "himself an ancestor," who founded the family fortunes with what was to become Italy's second-largest pharmaceutical company.

Luigi Barzini, writer and Liberal deputy, has said that the Italian family is a citadel in hostile territory where the individual is sure of moral and physical support and of protection against loneliness. Certainly no family life could be farther than was Luchino Visconti's love-filled childhood from both André Gide's "Families, I hate you!" and Mary McCarthy's "Grinning Holy Families of the Ad-Mass." The stability of these domestic ramparts was to remain a benediction to him, since he belonged to a generation jounced by more changes in its lifetime than had occurred in all the centuries between Christ's birth and 1900.

There were four Visconti brothers and three sisters, all seven with the looks of Pisanello medallions, the kind that made Stendhal say, "There was no room for affectation in those ardent spirits." The eldest, Guido, born in 1901, the year Queen Victoria died, was killed in North Africa in 1942, fighting with extravagant bravery at El Alamein. It is said that just before he was killed, fellow paratroopers yelled to him to take cover and he yelled back, "A Visconti doesn't cringe before a Windsor"—a story that suggests a vigorously anachronistic attitude in complete harmony with that of the fourteenth-century Visconti known to readers of Marjorie Bowen as the "Viper of Milan," who "dazzled through that dim-lit time." Anna was born in 1902, the year the German armaments manufacturers the Krupps founded their Essen steelworks. Over half a century and two world wars later, Luchino Visconti's film *La caduta degli dei* (*The Damned*) was to convey with petrifying precision and glacial poetry the nightmare life-in-death quality of a comparable family's existence at the vertices of Nazi Germany. Luigi, born in 1905, the year of Léhar's *Merry Widow* and Einstein's first theory of relativity, became one of Italy's champion riders, winning four hundred twenty-five trophies and fracturing twenty-seven bones before retiring to breed superb basset hounds. Nineteen hundred and six, the year Luchino was born, saw the rehabilitation of Captain Dreyfus and the opening of the Simplon tunnel, the longest in the world, giving Italy rapid access to Switzerland and central Europe. Only chance enabled Luchino, condemned to death by Fascists, to survive the war and have the career for which we now remember him. Next came Edoardo, born in 1908, the year the Austro-Hungarian Empire annexed Bosnia and Herzegovina, whose capital was Sarajevo, and that Georges Sorel published his *Reflections on Violence*, a book advocating revolutionary syndicalism that influenced Mussolini, then a twenty-five-year-old Socialist agitator. In 1945, Edoardo parachuted into Milan with a British military mission and found the Carlo Erba company a heap of ruins in a ruined city. He had twenty-five hundred employees, no money, no materials, no markets. But he had the electrifying family energy and, starting from scratch, turned the family pharmaceutical firm into the second-largest in Italy. A gap of eight years divided Edoardo's birth from that of the first of the two "babies" of the family: Ida, born in 1916, the year Italy entered what was optimistically supposed to be the Great War to End Wars, and Uberta, born in 1918, a year after the United States entered the war and the Russian Revolution erupted. Luchino was endlessly kind to his baby sisters, playing with them, reading to them, on one occasion producing floods of tears by reading them Florence Montgomery's *Misunderstood* "with the full force of his gift for acting." Beautiful Uberta was to be his favorite sister, and beloved friend, from her nursery days until the end of his life, when it was she who closed his eyes.

The love, admiration, and loyalty that the young Viscontis felt for their parents and for each other outlasted their childhood. Luchino never turned his back on the world where he grew up. "To forget," he said, "is to lose the essence of a million experiences, encounters, voices, sounds, colors. Memories exist—and beware of forgetting them." He had a passionate admiration for Marcel Proust and Thomas Mann, both poetic archeologists of family life. His friend and collaborator Suso Cecchi D'Amico—daughter of Emilio Cecchi, whose fine erudite writing gave the Italian cinema so many letters of literary credit in the early days, when they were needed, and herself one of the great Italian scenario writers—says Visconti had a patriarchal conception of family life and that to the end, despite their very different characters, outlooks, and occupations, he and his surviving brother and sisters were indissolubly linked. They remained, too, indissolubly linked to Milan. Toward the end of his life, Visconti said, when asked in which city he would prefer to live, that he would like a house "with windows overlooking Rome and a front door opening onto Milan."

Mediolanum, the Celtic settlement from which Milan grew, was occupied by the Romans in 222 B.C., four years before Carthaginian Hannibal and his elephants crossed the Alps to invade Italy. Five centuries later Milan was the capital of the western Roman Empire, last bastion of the classical world and the place where Constantine the Great proclaimed civil rights for Christians throughout his empire. At the fall of the Roman Empire the mighty jigsaw puzzle fell apart, local patriotism flourished, and much of the history of the duchy of Milan is also the story of the Viscontis. Their family crest, a serpent, symbol of wisdom, with four coils, swallowing a Saracen, one of those whom their ancestors fought during the Crusades, is still part of the city of Milan's coat of arms.

Rome succeeded Florence as capital of united Italy in 1871, but at the time of Luchino Visconti's birth Milan remained the wealthiest city in Italy and, after Naples, the most highly populated—half a million, including the suburbs and a garrison of seven thousand. Its vigorous sense of its own identity as capital of Lombardy was neither new—"all Italy is jealous of Milan," wrote Stendhal in 1828—nor in the least modified by the recent unification of Italy. Like almost every country in Europe except France and Switzerland, the new Italy was a monarchy— with, typically, the newest monarchy and the oldest reigning house in Europe—but Italian patriotism was nevertheless essentially local, and in the case of Milan the locality was imposing. Its wealth gave it power, and the efficient transport systems that linked it directly with France, Switzerland, and Austria made it the most European of Italian cities. The "virtual capital," said the Milanese, not unreasonably.

Part of the virtual capital's prosperity came from the *navigli*, inland waterways linking Milan with lakes Maggiore and Como and the entire fertile Po valley. These waterways, begun over two thousand years ago, were developed in the thirteenth and fourteenth centuries, first by the Second Commune of Milan, then by the reigning Viscontis and Sforzas. Later, Milan's "town river" was enriched by the legend that Leonardo da Vinci himself had helped construct it when visiting the Sforza court and devising a system of hydraulic irrigation for the Lombardy plain. In Luchino Visconti's childhood the center of the city, grouped around the cathedral and the opera house, was still encircled by these waterways. His paternal grandfather's palace, right on the *naviglio*, was famous for its paulownia trees and wistaria, their resplendency doubled by their reflections in the green water. Out beyond the *navigli* was yet another circle, that of the Spanish ramparts built by Ferrante Gonzaga in 1538. Despite electric trolleys—Milan had electricity two years earlier than did New York—cabs, carts, carriages, and cavalry made horses an integral part of daily life, while canal barges carrying butter, cheese, eggs, and poultry contributed both marine and rustic touches to the city.

At the heart of all this was the Duomo. This huge Gothic cathedral— even today one of the largest in the world—was begun by Gian Galeazzo Visconti nine years before his coronation as duke of Milan. One can still read on an ancient stone there *El principio di Domo di Milano fu nel anno 1386*. Gian Galeazzo Visconti got things moving, literally, by donating marble from his mountain estates at Candoglia—marble plus exemption from customs duties for its transport via Lake Maggiore, the Ticino River, and the Milanese *navigli*, lengthened for this purpose to within a hundred yards of where the cathedral now stands. After Gian

Galeazzo Visconti's death, the work was carried on by representatives of principality, city, and bishopric, organized into the Fabbrica del Duomo, and even the poorest Milanese came to feel personally involved in *el noster Domm.*

Since 1774, a gilded copper statue of the Madonnina, the little Madonna, has stood at the summit of the highest pinnacle, presiding over the Duomo—and indeed over the entire city, to which, since 1848, the Madonnina has been not only a cherished landmark, a beacon to the homesick, but also an object of patriotic as well as religious veneration. For in 1848, on the third of the famous Five Days' War, when the poorly armed Milanese drove Marshal Radetzky and fourteen thousand Austrian troops out of their city, a young patriot seized the new Italian flag and climbed with it up to the Madonnina. This created a general impression that the Madonnina was personally responsible for the victory, and had taken Milan under her protection. Even today a serious newspaper can head a leading article about the economic crisis *La Madonnina ha freddo* (The Little Madonna is cold). Below the Madonnina, Napoleon's statue, in antique costume, is one of over two thousand marble figures that stand on the Duomo's roof, amid one hundred and thirty-five pinnacles, gazing at the stupendous views—northward across the plain of Lombardy to the Alps, ranging from Mont Blanc to the Bernese Oberland, southward to the Apennines. This prodigious roof-scape is a favorite not only with tourists but also with the Milanese themselves, who often picnic there. In 1960, Luchino Visconti was to use it as the setting for a crucial scene in his film *Rocco and His Brothers.* To foreign audiences this seemed exotic; to him it was homely.

A minute's walk from the Duomo is the opera house, the Teatro alla Scala, built—after the grand ducal opera house burned down—on the site of Santa Maria della Scala, a fourteenth-century church built by Gian Galeazzo Visconti's nephew Bernabò for his wife, Regina della Scala, daughter of a noble Veronese family who assisted Dante when he was a political exile from Florence. To understand the dismay felt in Milan when the grand ducal opera house burned down at the end of the 1776 carnival, one must realize that opera held, then and there, the place now occupied by cinema and television combined. Also, the opera house was a focal point of Milan's social life. The same could be said of the cathedral, and it is significant that the Duomo and La Scala should not only be near neighbors but also give an impression of neighborliness, of serving the same public and some of the same needs. The building of a new theater was begun immediately after the fire. During the demolition of the deconsecrated Santa Maria della Scala, workmen unearthed the marble tombstone of Pilade, one of ancient Rome's most famous mimes. This was thought an excellent omen—and considering the time it takes nowadays, everywhere, for bureaucrats to provide permits, one can easily believe that Pilade's eager ghost helped the new theater to open only two and a half years after the destruction of the old one.

Right up to 1921 the boxes rented at La Scala by regular subscribers were their private property and could be decorated according to personal tastes. Even at the beginning of this century, girls' dowries often included a box at La Scala. Luchino Visconti remembered the red damask of his family's box, fourth on the left in the first tier, just above the orchestra, to which he was taken so young that he claimed to have been "practically raised at La Scala." Each box had a small anteroom for gossiping and refreshments, and in 1820 an Irish visitor, the novelist Lady Morgan, observed:

The most scrupulous ladies of the highest rank come alone in their carriages to the opera. As soon as they have entered their box and have glanced their eye along the circles, giving or returning the Italian salutation, which has something at once infantine and coquettish in its beckoning gesture, they turn their back on the scene, and for the rest of the night hear and see nothing out of their society, except when appraised by the orchestra that some scene in the ballet, or some *aria* or *duo* in the opera, is about to be performed which it is good taste or good fashion to listen to and admire. Then indeed the most rapturous attention is lent; but the scene over, the *Crocchio ristretto* (as they call it), or private chit-chat, is resumed, and is only interrupted by the ingress and egress of visitors. Every box has its habitués, its privileged guests; and it is a tiresome rule that the last arrival is always a signal for the first to depart. The observance of this rule is so strict that it sometimes leaves a passion half-declared, a plot half-revealed, a confidence the most critical, or an opinion the most important, unfinished.

During La Scala's early years this murmurous social life was intensified by the boxowners' servants, who stood below, ready to applaud their patrons' favorites with shouts and banging of sticks. Arias that occurred when the audience was self-employed were called by the singers "sorbet [water ice] arias," and there was bitter rivalry not to sing them. When Luchino Visconti's parents made their first appearance at La Scala after their wedding, his father, who was devoted to music and always violent in his devotions, locked the door of their box, so that they could concentrate on the music. But since Giuseppe Visconti's marrying a middle-class girl—reputedly as cultivated as she was beautiful and wealthy—had provided Milan with the social sensation of the season, the locked door merely caused his young bride, already focused on by all the opera

12

glasses in the house, to be teased by more or less silent turnings of the door handle.

Only Toscanini eventually succeeded in controlling La Scala's obstreperous audiences—and this is another footnote to Milanese history that is also a Visconti story. After Italy's unification, La Scala was financially supported by a *dote*, dowry, from the commune of Milan. But in 1897 this was unexpectedly withdrawn, by 31 votes against 23 and 8 abstentions. So on the day after Christmas, 1897, La Scala was for the first time dark. At this point Luchino Visconti's grandfather Senator Guido Visconti, Duke di Modrone, headed a group of Milanese opera lovers in offering to support La Scala. After securing La Scala's livelihood, Guido Visconti then performed for it the immense service of appointing Toscanini artistic director.

This extraordinary musical genius from nearby Parma had started his professional life as a violoncellist, and as such had gone with a touring opera company to South America. There, in Rio de Janeiro, one of those dramatic emergencies so unconvincing in fiction, so frequent in fact, obliged the nineteen-year-old cellist to conduct Verdi's *Aïda* from memory without a single rehearsal. Fortunately, Verdi being his idol, Toscanini was already steeped in the music. His prodigious success in Brazil won him an engagement to conduct in Turin. But on hearing that Verdi's *Otello* was to be produced at La Scala, Toscanini begged to be allowed instead to play a second-row cello for this. La Scala was then, and forever, despite Mussolini, Toscanini's very own theater—and when, thanks to Guido Visconti, his baton first ruled there, Toscanini saw to it that the curtain rose on time, lights in the auditorium were lowered during the performance, latecomers stayed outside, and chatter and clatter were muzzled until the intermission.

Giddy though Milanese operagoers may have been, they nevertheless had a genuine passion for music. This was encouraged by their Austrian rulers, who imagined that music distracted public attention from politics —even though *Evviva Verdi* was shouted and painted on walls all over Italy, not only out of genuine enthusiasm for the composer, himself a fervent patriot, but also as a battle cry for united Italy: *Evviva Vittorio Emanuele Rè d'Italia*. When Count Federico Confalonieri was arrested in 1821 and condemned to death for conspiring against the Austrians, the Milanese deserted La Scala for three nights in protest. The death sentence was commuted to life imprisonment, in the Spielburg, a fortress that Confalonieri's fellow prisoner Silvio Pellico was to render widely infamous by his book *Le mie prigione* (*My Prisons*). When Verdi's *Norma* was given at La Scala in 1859 the audience rose to its feet to applaud, shouting for war against the Austrians. Metternich advised, "Give them a new ballerina." Far from distracting the Milanese from politics, music accompanied and excited their political passions—a fact that was to mark all Luchino Visconti's work.

In Milan one of the immediate results of the Italo-French victory over the Austrians at Magenta was the authorization of improvements for the Piazza del Duomo. Giuseppe Mengoni, a thirty-two-year-old engineer from Bologna, provided Milan with its uniquely elegant, yet cozy, central meeting place, the famous Galleria Vittorio Emanuele: a glass-domed, mosaic-floored octagonal arcade leading from the north side of the Piazza del Duomo directly into the Piazza della Scala. Once again marble from the nearby mountains sailed into the center of Milan, and by 1878 the Galleria was complete, with twenty-four statues of great men and four large frescoes representing Africa, Europe, Asia, and America.

The Galleria was lined with excellent shops, bars, and two famous restaurants: the *Caffè* Biffi, which in its early days had a garden with fountain, aquarium, and evening concerts, and Savini, where several generations of artists have eaten well, sometimes bringing along their work in progress. Often cited as Milan's social, intellectual, artistic, and, above all, musical center, the Galleria was also in its early years a meeting place for southern immigrants, who brought new, and today still unsolved, problems into Italian life. The *problema del mezzogiorno* (problem of the South) entered Italian literature in 1881 with Giovanni Verga's novel *I Malavoglia,* the story of a poor Sicilian fishing family. Half a century later both the Galleria's long-lost immigrants and Verga's Malavoglia family were to be given a new and explosive artistic life by two of Luchino Visconti's films.

Among the famous figures seen in the Galleria when Luchino Visconti was a child were the Boito brothers. The younger one, Arrigo, wrote the libretti for Verdi's *Otello* (1887) and *Falstaff* (1893), and so hero-worshipped the old man that when himself in love with young Eleonora Duse—a love that began at the incandescent first night of *Otello* at La Scala—Boito yet made her miserable by leaving her without hesitation whenever the "old magician" gave the slightest sign of needing his help. In 1955, when Visconti directed Maria Callas in Verdi's *La Traviata* at La Scala, he said, "I sought to make her a little of Duse, a little of Rachel, a little of Bernhardt. But more than anyone, I thought of Duse." The elder Boito, Camillo, was an architect, but a writer and art critic as well. In 1883, he published a collection of stories, one of which, *Senso,* was to give Visconti the idea for his film of that name.

These remembrances of things past are fundamental elements of the world that molded Luchino Visconti's character, a world in which the leading parts were played by artists who helped to make modern Italy and were emotionally linked to each other and to Milan. Alessandro Manzoni (1785–1873), who in *I promessi sposi (The Betrothed)* gave Italy its greatest novel, one that was true to the Italy of his day and is real to today's Italy, spent all but five years of his adult life in or near Milan, where his house, a minute's walk from the Duomo, is today a Manzoni museum and library. Verdi, who gave so immeasurably to La Scala, admitted, despite a peasant reserve almost as excessive as his genius, to "worshipping" Manzoni, to whom he dedicated his stupendous *Requiem Mass*. Toscanini shared his friend Arrigo Boito's hero worship of Verdi to such an extent that his daughter Wally Toscanini, Countess Castelbarco, says Verdi was her father's "model"—and indeed the two men had in common both genius and an utterly resolute moral integrity. Visconti's veneration—his own word—of Toscanini began in childhood when he, too, worked at the cello and went fervently to La Scala. Seldom is continuity so visible.

From the first, the Toscaninis seemed to Visconti part of his own family. When eight years old, Wanda Toscanini played Ophelia in Luchino's juvenile production of *Hamlet* (in which he himself played the prince, his favorite part), and at eighty-seven Toscanini asked Visconti to stage *Falstaff*, which he was to conduct for the opening of the new Piccolo Teatro. And it was through Toscanini that Visconti had his first taste of Fascist thuggery in his own home circle. On May 14, 1931, Toscanini, who had been asked to conduct a concert at Bologna in commemoration of the composer, pianist, and conductor Giuseppe Martucci, refused to begin the concert with the new Fascist hymn, "Giovinezza" (Youth, youth / Springtime of beauty / In Fascism is the Salvation / Of our liberties), a lamentable caricature of Lorenzo de' Medici's exquisite "Quant'è bella giovinezza." Assaulted by thugs who had not yet heard of Göring but instinctively reached for their revolvers when culture was mentioned, Toscanini left for New York, where the Metropolitan Opera House had been a second home to him ever since he first conducted there in 1908. Not until May 11, 1946, was he to return to La Scala. On that occasion the rebuilt opera house was white with posters proclaiming *Ritorni Toscanini* and *Evviva Toscanini*.

This little universe of history and of art, home, and beauty welcomed Luchino Visconti into the world, fed him on honeydew, wove a circle around him thrice, but opened, rather than closed, his eyes to holy dread. Years later Nicola Benois, son of the Aleksandr Benois who had created marvels of scenery for Diaghilev's Ballets Russes, was to say at

La Scala: "To collaborate with Luchino was like attending an academy. He is not only a director, he is a man of knowledge, culture, and taste. Doubtless this comes from his heritage. He is a true aristocrat, not only by title, but by nature."

Three

The epoch into which Luchino Visconti was born is known to Italian social and fashion historians as the Liberty Era, rather than, as elsewhere, that of Art Nouveau, Modern Style, or Jugendstil. This commemorates Arthur Liberty, an Englishman who in 1875 opened a shop in Regent Street, London, with one hundred fifty pounds lent him by his father-in-law, and made his fortune out of bales of stuff imported from China and Japan. The East was, for decorative purposes, very popular with the West just then, and the two met in Gilbert and Sullivan's *The Mikado* in 1885, Pierre Loti's *Madame Chrysanthème* in 1887, Lafcadio Hearn's *Glimpses of Unfamiliar Japan* in 1894, Giacomo Puccini's *Madame Butterfly* in 1904. Soon Arthur Liberty was providing not only Liberty silks, floral prints, and embroidery, but also wallpaper, carpets, furniture, and stained glass.

Liberty goods were especially popular in Milan, which had been a fashion arbiter since the days when it was as famous for its handmade lace as for its steel for swords and armor. (The word *milliner* comes from Milanese bonnets, ribbons, gloves, and finery.) After Turin's 1906 Esposizione d'Arte Decorativa Moderna, more and more elegant Italian women, including Visconti's beautiful mother, her sisters, and their friends, wore Liberty dresses based on Greek or eighteenth-century models. Once, accused by an interviewer of a taste for kitsch, Visconti said, "I was raised during the Liberty period, so obviously kitsch was in the air all around me." Liberty's supremacy ended with the war—Arthur Liberty died in 1917—but both its artifacts and its name lived on for many more years.

The Liberty label has now acquired snobbishly nostalgic value, but the Liberty world in which Visconti grew up was neither snobbish nor retro, but merely that of contemporary fashion. For a sense of the past, he turned to his mother, a born animator, who told him stories of people he had only just missed. She made Verdi, who had died in 1901, seem particularly near, for not only was his personality still omnipresent at La Scala, but Donna Carla had herself known him as a treasured family friend. Luchino was to remember her story of Verdi's funeral for the rest of his life as vividly as if he had himself been present. It took place on a damp, fog-wreathed day. Silent crowds lined the streets—Verdi had left instructions that his funeral was to be as simple as possible, without music or singing—and people were perched like ungainly mourning birds in the bare branches of the wintry trees. But as the coffin reached the cemetery, the crowd began to sing, softly at first, then with mounting intensity, "Va, pensiero," the great chorus from *Nabucco*, the opera that made Verdi famous at twenty-nine, with its story of the Israelites' sufferings under Babylonian Nebuchadnezzar's tyranny—in which Milanese audiences found perfect musical expression of their own tribulations under the Austrians. "Va, pensiero" became a Risorgimento battle hymn, and when, a month after Verdi's funeral, his coffin and that of Giuseppina, his wife, were transferred to the crypt of Casa Verdi, the musicians' home, they were accompanied by nine hundred voices singing this chorus under young Toscanini's direction.

Luchino Visconti's mother communicated her sense of history to her son, conjuring up for him the old Milan—candlelit, Hapsburg-ruled, but Risorgimento-dominated—of which a vivid documentary exists in the work of Francesco Hayez, a nineteenth-century Venetian painter admired by Stendhal. As well as fine historical paintings reflecting the Milanese passion for masked and fancy-dress balls, Hayez painted a series of romantically realistic portraits that cover the Italian struggle for unity, from Count Arese in chains to Count Cavour in office, and include speaking likenesses of Manzoni, Massimo d'Azeglio, and fiery Princess Belgioioso. Carla Visconti did not, however, concentrate exclusively on the cloak-and-sword aspect of her children's heritage. On the contrary, she made it clear to them from the start that not all crusades involve the clashing of swords and the shedding of blood.

Alongside the Visconti warriors, tyrants, art patrons, cathedral builders, princes of church and state, alongside the vast cousinage ranging from Sicily to Brazil, and the fourteenth-century alliances by marriage with the kings of France, alongside an inheritance luxuriantly, and sometimes sinisterly, brilliant as the famous illuminated medieval *Visconti Book of Hours*, Carla Visconti set her own grandmother, who had sold herbs, salves, and rustic remedies from a little cart in the Porta Garibaldi district of Milan. She told Luchino of her uncle's struggle in 1855 to build a small laboratory—and of the intellectual curiosity and compassion that had impelled him to finance a scientific expedition for the physicist and inventor Carlo Matteucci, to help Cesare Lombroso's research into pellagra, an appalling skin disease then prevalent among the peasants of Lombardy, and finally to create the Carlo Erba electrotechnical institute. These stories developed Luchino's sense of the concrete, and more than half a century later the memory of the "exciting and adventurous" smell of carbolic acid at his maternal family's laboratory was still as exhilarating to his imagination as that of La Scala.

Carla Visconti was always ready to answer Luchino's questions. She understood him, believed in his future, and made him aware of this. Although she enjoyed an extremely active and stimulating social life—Luchino adored the spectacle of her ready for a ball, glowing with beauty, glittering with jewelry—she nevertheless gave her children an amount of her time and personal care most unusual for a woman of her class and period. Aware of the dangers of privilege, she was determined her children should develop their characters through contact with the world outside their semiroyal home circle—and never be so vacuous as to boast of their titles, or loll on their wealth. She gave them unlimited love and, since she was clever, artistic, and funny, entertainment—but she insisted on discipline, especially where music was concerned. All his life Visconti retained a vivid memory of her standing at the door of her children's room pinning up the timetable she had written out for the next day's music lessons. She was herself a fine pianist, and after her death Visconti kept and used her piano. His sister Uberta says he never felt for anyone else such "total unlimited adoration."

Each child played an instrument—Luchino's was the violoncello—and both music lessons and practice had to be accomplished outside school hours. Their day began at six, and, from the first, they were taught not to shirk drudgery, whether intellectual or physical. A ubiquitous English tutor, Mr. Smith, taught them gymnastics with the help of some eccentric methods. Obsessed by the need for alertness—"never let yourself be taken by surprise" was his motto—he urged them to run after and, if possible, jump onto moving streetcars. Apart from the risk to limbs and life, this brought them amazed and furious looks from the other passengers, and during Mr. Smith's reign Luchino felt that a streetcar was lurking in wait for him around every street corner. In order to develop their agility, Mr. Smith made them come down from the third floor of the palace to the courtyard via a rope slung out the window; and he insisted that they bicycle everywhere possible, and often impossible. Milan was a mecca for bicycle enthusiasts—legend said that a Milanese champion had once victoriously raced a bicycle against Buffalo Bill on horseback—but, even so, the young Viscontis' bicycling feats caused them to be known in their neighborhood as the "crazy Modrones."

The Visconti children spent their summers either at their maternal grandmother's Villa Erba, at Cernobbio on Lake Como, or at Grazzano, a castle built originally in 1387 by Gian Galeazzo Visconti for his daughter Valentina's marriage to the Duke of Orléans, and restored, with fantasy, by their father. Visconti remembered pure happiness during those summers at Lake Como, the most southern-looking of the Italian lakes, with its superb living tapestries of olive groves and chestnut woods, palms and cypresses, magnolias and camelias, mulberries, walnuts, and pomegranates, orange and lemon groves, cedars, agaves, and cherry trees, rose laurels, azaleas, giant myrtles, oleanders like those mentioned by Pliny the Younger, who, in the first century, delighted in a villa so near Lake Como that he was able to fish "from my very bed," and, sharp among the pliant verdure, the green-gray-blue scimitars of the cactus.

Formally enclosed by the Alps, with no superhighways, buses, transistors, and few billboards, Lake Como at the turn of the century was still the Lake Como described in Stendhal's *La Chartreuse de Parme*. Here was the scene of Fabrizio del Dongo's boyhood, of which Fabrizio's enchanting young aunt, La Sanseverina, thought: "Everything is noble and tender, everything speaks of love; nothing recalls the ugliness of civilization." Here, like Fabrizio—whom, as a child, Luchino thought of as "another brother"—the Visconti children had the run of the countryside, and ran so hard all day that they almost fell asleep at the dinner table. Sixty years later Visconti remembered vast summer afternoons when, after wild lavishments of energy, he would suddenly fall asleep in the long grass amid the insistent but soothing small voices of crickets. But there were darker days when the children's plans were abruptly ruined by one of the storms that can suddenly transform this deepest lake in Europe into a dangerous sea. Then the children would stand, faces pressed against the rain-slatted windowpanes, silently raging at the elements. One particularly deadly storm killed the most beautiful tree in their garden. As summer faded, they thought with loathing of their impending return to school; and when the autumn harvests began they "harvested emotions, images and dreams."

Sounds played a significant part in that personal harvest, unadulterated sounds like those of which Stendhal wrote: "The imagination is touched by the distant sound of church bells from some little village hidden among the trees; these sounds, as they float across the water that softens their tone, take on a note of gentle melancholy and resignation, which seems to say, 'Life is fleeting, do not therefore show yourself so hard to please in face of the happiness at hand, make haste to enjoy it.' "

Make haste Luchino Visconti certainly did, in every way, but especially in developing his faculty for appreciation. In a notebook kept around 1940 he wrote that his earliest memories were of stopping at his grandmother's house at Cernobbio—where as a small child he was fascinated by the "pattern of dark-blue flowers on the porcelain washbasins"—on the way to the mountains of Engadine. He remembered with delight the drive north by automobile from Cernobbio through wild valleys to Chiavenna, the first sight of the slender bell tower of the little town's collegiate Church of St. Lorenzo, and the remains of the castle around which his Visconti ancestors had hewn a moat out of the rock. At Chiavenna the family would lunch while waiting for the carriages that took them the fifteen miles north to Maloja, in Switzerland. Beside the road, pinks, or wild carnations, grew in such profusion that the air was full of their fragrance. His mother sat up on the high seat at the back of the open carriage, and the children took turns sitting beside her.

Study, art, travel, emotions—the Visconti children were from their earliest years encouraged by their parents to fling themselves into life with total endeavor. So just as Luchino Visconti was an operagoer from infancy—asked the date of his birth, he sometimes added the hour as "soon after the curtain went up at La Scala" (on a performance of his beloved *Traviata*)—so he was taken to the cinema at an early age, and thus given the advantage of knowing its catacomb days.

The early moving pictures—the words still contain their initial magic —were hawked around by itinerant showmen who bought films outright and showed them until the reels literally fell apart. Milan had its first glimpse of them at the fair that accompanied the 1897 carnival. There, amid performing dogs, antic monkeys, the Fat Lady, and the Caribbean Mermaid, was a tent displaying the brand-new word CINEMATOGRAFI. By the time Visconti was born, Italian industrialists already thought it shrewd to invest in the nascent film companies, and some Italian aristocrats were as interested in the cinema as their ancestors had been in painting, music, opera, horses, and architecture. Before Visconti was two years old, Milan had forty-four moving-picture houses, and by June 1910, the catalogue of films offered for sale by the Milanese firm of Giovanni Pettine listed eight hundred eighty-five items, ranging from *Edward VII's Funeral* to *In Love with a Bearded Lady*.

There was great variety among Milanese movie houses. Emilio Cecchi, a writer whom Visconti was to admire extremely, had a passion for seedy "picture palaces" and wrote that this passion often led him along out-of-the-way lanes, then made him halt suddenly, as if at the touch of a hand, "always at the very same yet always new place": a little bell shrilling away desperately, crinkled posters, faded photographs, two rickety vases of bamboo grasses, a trophy of wan electric-light bulbs. Some cinemas revealed their fairground origins by having a uniformed *imbonitore* (barker) stand out front to bewitch passers-by with stentorian promises of marvels and mysteries—*Tutto è meraviglia!*

Visconti never forgot his splended first cinema. This was the Centrale, right beside the entrance to the Galleria on the Piazza del Duomo side. Its enterprising management distributed free programs of coming events, on fine paper decorated with a colored picture of the film. These included summaries of treats ahead: "The Laws of the Heart in 20 tableaux: The Doctor's Family, An Unexpected Visit, A Revealing Letter, An Urgent Call, Abandoning the Conjugal Roof, A Strange Coincidence, A Much Needed Explanation, I Forgive You for the Sake of Our Children, Reconciliation. N.B. the film is set in Paris and was really made on the spot." There were also films specially for the young, like *Two Children*, a moving and instructive masterpiece from Pathé Films, "recommended to all good mothers for the instruction of their little ones," films of adventure in serial form, and films of slapstick, soon to be transcended by Charlie Chaplin, who in 1914 entered the ring with thirty-five Keystone comedies. Above all, there were the literary and historical films, for which, from the first, Italy displayed extraordinary aptitudes.

Visconti and his brothers and older sister were often taken to the Centrale by their father on Sunday mornings, after mass at the cathedral alongside. On foggy days, of which there are so many in Milan in winter, the lights of the Centrale glittered like Aladdin's magic lamp from ten o'clock in the morning onward. From the first, Visconti was bewitched. On coming out of Fingal's cave, he would turn eagerly to a little door alongside the Centrale's entrance, from which he hoped to see the actors emerge—Buffalo Bill and Annie Oakley, Zorro and Fantomas, Maciste and Pinocchio, Captain Grant's Children and the Three Musketeers, Charlie Chaplin, the Blind Girl of Sorrento, and peerless Pearl White, still breathless from her perils, of whom Louis Delluc wrote: "Pearl White, who can do anything and does it so well that the spectators are carried away. When one comes out of her films one wants to drive cars and airplanes, ride horses, shoot like Falcon's Eye, dance, skate, swim, dive—everything."

Many of these desires to "do everything" could be satisfied by the Visconti children at their other summer home, Grazzano, a place extraordinary both in itself and as evidence of their father's violently constructive temperament. On inheriting Grazzano from his father, Giuseppe Visconti had immediately started rebuilding. The Duchess of Sermoneta wrote in 1947:

I often stayed at Grazzano near Piacenza, a fine old pile of gray stone with four massive towers at its corners. Tall poplars grew in the moat and the virginia creeper hung in garlands of flaming scarlet round the courtyard where the white pigeons fluttered near the well.

Giuseppe Visconti took great interest in his home and had rebuilt the entire village of Grazzano that stood outside the park gates. Once it had been a squalid conglomeration of ugly houses and now it was so picturesque that passing motorists constantly stopped to admire the little piazza and campanile, the inn with its signboard bearing the Visconti coat of arms, the small shops under the porticos, all this festooned with creepers and every window gay with flower pots. Visconti had established a school of drawing at Grazzano in which the village boys received training and were afterward given a start in various workshops, making furniture, wood carvings and wrought-iron work. Everybody was hammering away contentedly and earning good money; they could not execute orders fast enough.

The Duke was his own architect, and supplied designs and ideas to the various arts and crafts. When he walked about his village, so tall and handsome, with his iron-gray hair and fine features, it was remarkable to see the affection with which he was greeted on all sides. . . . He knew every soul on the place, and no decision was taken in any family without consulting him. His three daughters had many friends in the village and would walk about with them on the piazza in the evening, while their father sat in front of the inn, talking to the local men.

Giuseppe Visconti had designed a picturesque peasant costume that the women of Grazzano wore every Sunday and when there were dances at the Castle or other festive occasions. There was a delicate thought behind this rather theatrical institution; he wished his daughters and the humblest girls in the village to be dressed alike. It was the ideal relationship between a modern *grand seigneur* and his people. He looked after them when sick, amused them on festas with the pageants or lotteries he organized, and was always ready to help them with his sound common sense and wise advice and, above all, put his people in the way of earning a good living.

But life itself, let alone good living, was soon to be slashed from ten million men, over half a million of them Italians. On June 28, 1914, the Archduke Francis Ferdinand, heir apparent of his great-uncle the Austrian Emperor Francis Joseph, was assassinated at Sarajevo. On July 28, Austria-Hungary declared war on Serbia. On August 1, Germany declared war on Russia. France mobilized. Italy declared herself neutral: the Triple Alliance of 1882 bound her to assist Germany and Austria only in defensive wars, not in aggression, and Austria had already violated the clause that bound her to consult Italy before taking up arms. On August 3, Germany declared war on France and invaded neutral Belgium. On August 5, Great Britain, one of Belgium's guarantors, declared war on Germany, and the United States declared her neutrality. "They all want this war," Romain Rolland wrote despairingly in his diary, "they are happy to shed blood on its altar." The Visconti children, on holiday at Rimini, saw regiments of Bersaglieri, Italy's crack troops, marching off to mount guard at the frontier.

In Italy feelings for and against intervention on the Allied side became violent. Catholics were against it, encouraged by the pacific Pope Benedict XV, elected on September 3, 1914, and so at first were the Socialists, in the name of the International Proletariat. "Not a man, not a cent," wrote Mussolini. But before long he was saying, "Only a fool never changes. A new event may call for new conduct"—and so on, until he was expelled from the Socialist party and started a paper of his own, *Popolo d'Italia*, in which he could write: "It is a European war. The German socialists will follow the Emperor, and the Socialist International will be wrecked. But social revolution is our objective and if we fight courageously now we shall be able to take command after the war." Also for intervention were the Irredentists (from *Italia irredenta*—unredeemed Italy), who wished Italy to gain possession of those districts with a majority of Italian-speaking people of Italian culture—Trentino, Alto Adige, Venezia—retained by the Austrians after their retreat from Italy in 1866. These territories would, thought the Irredentists, assure Italy a defensive alpine frontier.

Powerful among the Irredentists was the famous poet, novelist, and dramatist Gabriele D'Annunzio, at that time a charismatic figure who could fascinate crowds, even without the mass media that can now turn almost any person into a "personality." On May 3, 1915, the fifty-two-year-old writer launched himself on a politico-military career with an inflammatory interventionist speech at Quarto, Genoa—from which Garibaldi's Thousand had embarked exactly fifty-five years earlier. D'Annunzio had an extraordinary sense of the theater, offstage, and invented many of the stage properties later adopted by the Fascists, such as black shirts, Roman salutes, and the war cry *Eia, eia, alalà*. His crusade for intervention contributed magic and prestige to emotions already in the air. Both belligerents had, from the start, pressed Italy to intervene. The Duchess of Sermoneta tells of a visit to London in March 1915, during which Winston Churchill, then Lord of the Admiralty, dined with her and insisted "it would be *disastrous* for Italy to hang back any more, she simply *must* come in immediately." Asked for a reason, Churchill said, "Damn the reason! Fly at their throats! But if you want a reason, the way they treat the Italians at Trieste is plenty." A r` nth later, on April 26, the Italian government signed the secret Treaty of London— secret even from the Italian parliament—by which Italy promised to enter the war within a month, and the Allies promised that, at the end of the war, Italy should have Trentino, Alto Adige up to the Brenner Pass, Istria, Trieste, and the islands off the Dalmatian coast. On May 3, Italy formally denounced the Triple Alliance, and on May 23, 1915, she declared war on Austria.

For eight-year-old Visconti, as for many European children, the first casualty was his German governess, who went home and was replaced by a French one, Mademoiselle Hélène. And while the *Fräuleins* disappeared, taking German verbs with them, the infantry appeared on the streets, marching with bands and banners, all as new and exhilarating as next Christmas's toy soldiers. So at first, the Visconti children viewed the war precisely as did their short-lived French contemporary Raymond Radiguet, who was to write, in his masterpiece, *Le Diable au corps*, "For many young boys the war was a four-year vacation."

But the young Viscontis were allowed to invite Allied soldiers home to meals, and one day they "collected" a young French poet, who "spouted poetry like a geyser," and told them of his friends "crouched in holes full of mud and water, trying to protect themselves from bullets and bayonets and to kill other young men crouching in similar holes with a similar desire to kill rather than be killed." The pictures conjured up by the young French poet were worlds away from Mussolini's rhetoric to "Youth" about "the fascinating word war," worlds away from the fustian attitudes of recruiting posters—but straight from the heart of a world like Dante's Inferno where, between 1915 and 1918, 600,000 Italians were to die and 950,000 to suffer wounds that would leave 250,000 of them incapacitated for life.

Visconti never forgot the impression made on him by the French poet's description of trench warfare. At eight years old, but not for the first time, he touched the very texture of life—and of death—through art. This did not prevent his feeling fervent admiration for his father and all his fighting relatives. In a world so full of contradictions, it was necessary to believe six impossible things before breakfast: which is, possibly, the beginning of creativity.

Four

By Visconti's eleventh birthday, the war was physically close to him. The French poet's grim impressions corresponded to the facts—especially in Italy, a new and not yet industrialized nation, not yet trained in modern methods of murder, and with an army composed largely of peasants to whom war appeared as a fatality to be endured, like floods, earthquakes, bad harvests, and cattle diseases. On October 25, 1917, General Luigi Cadorna telegraphed to the government in Rome: "I see disaster coming."

After the Russian Revolution exploded in February 1917, the German government permitted Lenin, in Switzerland at the time, to cross Germany in a sealed train and so return to Russia. The Germans hoped this would undermine the Russian war effort. It did. The Russian front crumbled, and, in October, Austro-Hungarian troops poured south, and broke the Italians' overextended alpine front at Caporetto. A trenchant account of this ghastly battle was to figure in young Ernest Hemingway's novel *A Farewell to Arms*. Caporetto, then at the Italian frontier, now part of Yugoslavia, is only two hundred miles from Milan, which was soon full of wounded and of ghostly walking wounded.

With Caporetto a whirlpool of 400,000 refugees and 250,000 disbanded troops, all seemed "to ruin and disaster hurled." But the seismic nature of the calamity drew from the Italians an equally phenomenal courage, and when the Austro-Hungarians, fighting their last battles as soldiers of an empire, flung sixty divisions into the slaughterhouse, the outnumbered Italians held the line on the river Piave and transformed defeat into victory. Nevertheless, the end of the war—twenty-seven "victorious" nations and ten million dead—found Italy poorer than before. In addition to her human losses in dead and mutilated, she had financial debts to her allies.

Young Antonio Gramsci, one of the future founders of the Italian Communist party, wrote that Italy had survived "ravaged by wounds and bleeding from every one of them." Among the most ravaging of these wounds, politically, was the postwar split between nation and parliament. "It is alarmingly grotesque," thundered Mussolini after Caporetto, "as if forty million Italians counted for nothing beside four hundred members of parliament." This outburst appealed particularly to the 200,000 young officers who, however different their ideals, had all shared uniformed responsibility, danger, excitement, and prestige, and were loath to retreat into civilian life as subordinate mice, very probably unemployed mice. Emphatically loath were the Arditi (from *ardito,* bold, courageous), assault troops formed in January 1917, and famous for such exploits as swimming by night, naked and painted black, across the icy Piave to cut the throats of the Austrian sentries on the opposite bank.

Back home, the Arditi were feasted and flattered—and also feared for their spontaneous acts of hooliganism—as they peacocked about with "the brisk intemperance of youth," displaying their glittering daggers, flame insignia, and tasseled black fezes. The army's spoiled children, for them the change from violence to inaction, glory to oblivion, meant that peace offered an inferior way of life. By his twelfth birthday, Luchino Visconti was accustomed to seeing Arditi lounging around the Duomo and La Scala with vague but minatory intent, muscles in splendid condition, brains less so, as threatening as semidomesticated animals in rickety cages—splendid raw material for any dictator.

In January 1919, the National Association of the Arditi of Italy was formed, and set up headquarters in a handsome building in the Via Cerva only a few hundred yards from the Visconti home. Luchino thus had a firsthand view of the Arditi's typical interior decorations. The vapory light of Milan's foggy winter gave depth and mystery to the view through the windows of the Arditi's mural arrangements of helmets, bayonets, daggers, and black flags emblazoned with crossed shinbones surmounted by a death's-head.

This wintry combination of fog with symbols of death made a highly personal impression on Visconti, who had been born on the Day of the Dead and wrote in one of his notebooks that he had "missed All Saints' Day by a delay of twenty-four hours . . . a bad start . . . November is a most depressing month in the Po valley . . . the streets are rivers of fog, in which one can easily be killed by a chance cyclist. Trains advance blindly, hooting their way along. The space between earth and sky is limited by leaden clouds that seem as if they will never move.

Every living creature forgets to search the sky and turns earthward."

Before January was over, Luchino saw death's-heads not only on his doorstep but also at his beloved Scala. The fashionable old Caffè Cova, by La Scala, was crowded day and night with demobilized Arditi, as angrily purposeful as Napoleonic officers after Waterloo—and already supplied with a putative Napoleon: "the Man from Predappio," Mussolini, champing in the wings with three bodyguards and his head shaved in compliment, possibly, to D'Annunzio, who was prematurely bald as the result of a scalp injury received when dueling. "It is necessary to dramatize life," wrote Mussolini, and one of the many occasions when he followed his own advice, was on the evening of January 11, 1919, when Leonida Bissolati-Bergamaschi, a former Socialist and cabinet minister who had volunteered for the Alpine troops at the age of fifty-eight and been wounded fighting, was to speak at La Scala in favor of the League of Nations. Cafés and restaurants in the neighborhood were packed and, as the time for Bissolati's speech came near, a crowd gathered around the statue of Leonardo da Vinci in the middle of the Piazza della Scala, while the thud of marching feet and the roar of voices singing "Il Piave mormorò / Non passa lo straniero" (The river Piave murmured / The foreigner shall not pass) heralded the groups that kept emerging from the fog in the Via Manzoni.

Inside La Scala all was heat and glitter. From his box Mussolini surveyed the Futurists yelling in the stalls, applauded by officers' widows in the boxes. When Bissolati came on stage an explosion of "Down with Croatia! Long live Italian Dalmatia!" silenced him. Yells led to insults, insults to blows, and, when chaos was come again in the manner to which they were accustomed, the Arditi linked arms and, with Mussolini and Captain Ferruchio Vecchi at their head, marched to the Galleria singing "Non passa lo straniero." Memories of these scenes were to contribute thirty-five years later, to Visconti's film *Senso,* in which a Venetian countess tells an Austrian officer that she dislikes young men who behave operatically offstage.

Visconti was only twelve when Mussolini, though still only a private, if agitating, citizen, formed the first *fasci* of Action Squads, recruiting these from among the Arditi, the unemployed, and a number of both born hooligans and those created by the war. Everywhere violence was coming to the boil. Milan schoolteachers paraded the streets with red flags. Two hundred shops were pillaged in one day. The Fascists demonstrated violently against violence in front of the Duomo. Since the Visconti palace was right in the center of Milan, the schoolboy Luchino had firsthand experience of this storm.

All that summer the French and Italian occupation troops quarreled about Fiume. This large port on the Adriatic, today part of Yugoslavia, had changed hands innumerable times since early Roman days—going from Franks, Croatian dukes, Austria, Hungary, a period as a free port, France, back to Austria, then again Hungary. After the First World War the Treaty of London assigned it to the newly formed country of Yugoslavia—but Italy refused to accept this, claiming that the majority of Fiume's population was Italian-speaking. Finally an interallied commission decided that Fiume was to be policed by English troops. The Sardinian grenadiers quit Fiume for nearby Ronchi amid the vociferous regrets of the Italian population: "Fiume or death!" From Ronchi a group of young officers sought out D'Annunzio in Venice and asked him to lead an expedition to Fiume. D'Annunzio had finished the war with the rank of lieutenant colonel and a patch over his wounded right eye, and these martial exploits, combined with his reputation as a lover, had made of him a national figure, admired as "the Poet" by even the illiterate. An exhibitionist with something to exhibit, he accepted the young officers' invitation and, on September 11, wrote to the up-and-coming Mussolini: "My dear Comrade, Tomorrow I shall take Fiume by arms . . . support our cause vigorously during the conflict."

Next day D'Annunzio did indeed lead the expedition to Fiume, where he conquered General Pittalunga's resistance by a display of showy but authentic physical courage, was greeted with ringing bells and mass enthusiasm, and made a speech appealing to Victor Hugo's France, Milton's England, and the America of Lincoln and Walt Whitman to "support the will of the Italian people in joining Fiume to Italy." He and his volunteers settled in Fiume, creating an atmosphere midway between the *Arabian Nights* and *Tom Brown's Schooldays*. For the next sixteen months they defied both the Allies and their own government with a puerility and panache that captivated adolescents of all ages and concealed from imperceptive authorities. both the real gravity and the clairvoyant aspects of the venture—which included, early on, D'Annunzio's appeal to the Arabs, Palestinians, and Irish, "the new world," to unite against "the colonization of the old world."

Even as an impressionable schoolboy, Visconti was not impressed by D'Annunzio as a man of action, but he admired his poetry. By the beginning of the nineteen-twenties Visconti was already absorbed by what would be a lifetime's voracious reading. Before long he was running up bills on his father's bookstore account, at the famous old Baldini & Castoldi's, and though his father grumbled for form's sake, he was glad to see his son's extravagance take that shape. A born book lover, Visconti said years later that rereading was among his "greatest joys," that no matter how intensely he looked forward to meeting the characters in a book again, the emotion was "fresh and different every time." He began with Shakespeare, who, with his predilection for Italian scenes and stories, was as near to an Italian- as to an English-speaking child. Indeed, to Visconti, reading *The Tempest* for the first time, the line "Twelve years since, Miranda, was your father duke of Milan" suggested that Miranda might have been a relative. Soon he was in love with Stendhal's characters, and the inexhaustible world of books meant so much to him that at fourteen he was less impressed by the fact that thirty-five Fascists, including Mussolini, had been elected to parliament, down in Rome, than he was by two French books in which he saw his father absorbed. Questioned, his father told Luchino that *Du Côté de chez Swann* (*Swann's Way*) and *A l'Ombre des Jeunes Filles in Fleurs* (*Within a Budding Grove*), the recently published first two volumes of Proust's stupendous *A la Recherche du Temps perdu* (*Remembrance of Things Past*) were so wonderful that he "hated coming to the end of a page because each one took him nearer the end of the book."

Seeing the boy's interest, his father gave him copies of the first volumes of Proust for himself, a present that suggests Giuseppe Visconti had an exceptional understanding both of the new in art and of his third son's intellectual capacities. For in 1921 the Proust whose genius Giuseppe and Luchino recognized was not the Proust we know today. Far from being an established classic, Proust was then an eccentric fifty-year-old invalid, little known, much less understood, outside his immediate Paris circle. Unlike his father and brother, both distinguished doctors, Marcel Proust had, apparently, made a career only of worldliness until 1910, when asthma drove him into a cork-lined bedroom, where he stayed, an impaled but living butterfly, writing literally for dear life. By his exceptional perspicacity, Giuseppe Visconti opened up a new world for his son, a world that not only bewitched the boy ("it was like a fever," he said later), but was to become so valuable to the man that even at the end of his life, when fighting illness with rage and reticence, he was able to forget everything else while rereading Proust.

Despite the happiness of his home life, Luchino Visconti had from the start an unquiet disposition. In nearly all his early photographs he looks sad, in some, tragic, but a sister-in-law who grew up with him says "not sad but serious," and adds that the other children always did as he wished because of this very individual seriousness that made even the craziest enterprise seem imperative—especially since it was coupled with a charm and vitality of the kind that is to a person what light is to a landscape. As was recently said of Gianni Agnelli, "The word *charisma* is, alas, unavoidable—and he already had it as a child." Vitality in every sphere often rushed Visconti into difficulties, and whenever there was "any sort of collision with the family" and, particularly, with his father, he took refuge in the Via Cerva's treetop-level attics—which may, he said, have contributed to the prevalence of attics in his films: the wide sunny Venetian granary attics of *Senso,* the vast history-cluttered Sicilian attics of *Il Gattopardo,* the Etruscan undertones of the old palace in *Sandra,* the sinister labyrinthine German attics of *The Damned,* the converted Roman attic of *Conversation Piece.*

Five

Like Gabrielle Chanel, to whom he was to be passionately devoted, Luchino Visconti as a child loathed even the mildest constraint except when self-imposed. This may be why, despite his exceptional vitality, sociability, good looks, and intelligence, he was more often than not in trouble at school. His sister Uberta says that he attended several schools and was a "pessimo studente" in all of them. "Always on the back benches" was his own comment. Possibly he found school fatally uninteresting compared with his stimulating home life. But whether at home or at school, he never failed to apply himself passionately to his musical studies. When, at thirteen, he played in a concert at Milan Conservatory, the music critic of the Milan newspaper *Sera* noted that "the juvenile Luchino Visconti di Modrone" already possessed "far more than amateur talent."

His earliest school troubles were ingenuous ones, nearer to the *Bobbsey Twins* than to *Les Amitiés particulières*. On one occasion Luchino and his brother Luigi had been packed off to a school on Lake Como. Once there, quick as cats with shrimp in the offing, they realized that their new school was not far from a famous pastry cook's shop. They at once arranged for their favorite cakes to be sent them daily—Luchino adding the stage direction that "their friend the delivery man must tell the school that he was the boys' uncle bringing them unsolicited gifts." All went well until the day when the school authorities received the pastry cook's bill. That Luigi and Luchino were immediately expelled for this peccadillo tells us even more about the period than about the boys themselves, for now, just over half a century later, teachers in Western Europe and the United States are likely to find themselves forbidden to expel students for anything less than murder or drug-taking, and even these may be ascribed to the students being "disturbed," as no doubt they are. Luigi and Luchino were not, in any modern sense, in the least "disturbed," merely cheerfully greedy, and both were to become genuine connoisseurs, applying to food the same high standards as to art and animals.

A later extravaganza, when Visconti was sixteen, was more highly colored, but equally ingenuous. He was at the family castle at Grazzano, studying to retake a failed examination. But for once he seemed unable to concentrate: he was in love with a girl with the Ogden Nashish name of Titti Masier and could think of nothing else. So much so that he decided to run off to Rome with her. From Milan to Rome may not seem much of a flit now, but in those days Italy's virtual and the legal capital were worlds apart, as in some respects they still are. Indeed, after the Second World War, when Visconti settled to work in Rome, even those very Romans who, like Suso Cecchi D'Amico, became his dearest lifelong friends, were at first slightly wary if not downright suspicious of this "aristocrat from the north." Just what, they wondered, did he want.

At sixteen, all the aristocrat from the north wanted was to impress Titti Masier, and to this end he led her to one of the finest restaurants in Rome: where, to his consternation, he found himself placed at a table alongside his father, also visiting Rome. Fortunately, Giuseppe Visconti had a highly personal sense both of humor and of tolerance. (He was once heard to say, in answer to a remark about someone's private life that should, in his opinion, have been allowed to remain private, "A chacun son hobby," everyone should be allowed a hobby.) On this occasion, catching his son astray and courting, he could not prevent himself laughing, which made indignation impossible. Then, remembering that nowhere in ancient Rome is one more than thirty yards from a work of art, Giuseppe insisted that Luchino seize the opportunity to visit San Pietro in Vincoli.

In those days the church of St. Peter in Chains—so called because the original church was built, in the fifth century to enshrine the chains that bound St. Peter when captive in Jerusalem—was still an out-of-the-way church, lapped in quiet and history. There were neither regiments of buses outside nor swarms of guided tourists inside. So Visconti had the luxury of privacy among the ancient fluted columns for his first sight of Michelangelo's *Moses*. The statue's noble *terribilità*, so satisfying to his temperament, was heightened by the satyr's horns, inspired in Michelangelo by an error in Biblical translation: *facies cornuta* (horned), instead of *coronata* (crowned) with rays of light. Once again, thanks to his father, what had started as a private emotional outburst was enlarged to include an aesthetic experience that would remain with

33

him long after he had forgotten Titti Masier (who later "fell into the arms of Malaparte").

But cakes and girls could not prevent politics from casting shadows over the adolescence of Visconti's generation. Today the calamitousness of being young is often described as if it were a new disease. But it has never been easy to be young—or middle-aged, or old. Today's only real innovation is a technical one: all ages have more information, and far more misinformation, thrust at them than ever before, together with more sophisticated weapons with which to express the usual unsophisticated sentiments. In Visconti's childhood, boys who wanted to paint inflammatory slogans in public places, for example, had to go on foot, carrying cumbersome buckets of paint, brushes, and sometimes ladders. Their gesture was that of the artisan, and they were likely to be caught by police who had never heard of "broken homes" or "diminished responsibility" in that context. Today, cars, motorcycles, and automatic paint sprays insure efficiency and immunity. But then, as now, the twin nightmares of inflation and unemployment murdered sleep. By 1920, salaries were worth less than those of 1913 had been. When Luchino was fourteen, food rationing returned, currency control was instituted, and the Italian Communist party was founded by a handful of dissident Socialists, including Palmiro Togliatti and Antonio Gramsci—of whom Mussolini was to say, when ordering his arrest seven years later, despite Gramsci's being by then a deputy, with parliamentary immunity: "That brain must be prevented from functioning for twenty years." For the first time, striking Italian workers occupied their factories. The red flag flew in Milan. Chaos, it seemed, was umpire, and chance governed all.

Visconti was fifteen when a general strike broke out as a protest against increasing Fascist violence. Mussolini immediately threatened the government that, unless the strike was stopped, the Fascists would take over and establish order. The strikers went ahead with their strike, playing into the hands of the Fascists, who also went ahead, bludgeoning and murdering. By October 1922, Mussolini was able to march, figuratively speaking, on Rome, where King Victor Emmanuel III, at his wits' end, invited him to form a cabinet. It is easy, now, to conclude that the King had not far to go to reach his wits' end, but, at the time, admiration for Mussolini was widespread, and the English, French, and American press burgeoned with references to his "virile profile, scintillating eyes, love for law and order."

Mussolini was by no means, however, the only, or even the worst, threat to the Visconti children's generation. When Luchino was just seventeen, almost through with school, a thirty-four-year-old Austrian ex-serviceman, Adolf Hitler, attempted to overthrow Germany's Weimar Republic. The *Putsch* failed. Hitler was arrested, and at his trial spoke with hysterical joy of Mussolini's struggle against the "many-headed serpents of Jewry, freemasonry and Marxism."

Seven months later the new regime's greatest scandal took place. In Rome, on May 30, 1924, a Socialist deputy Giacomo Matteotti, made a finely reasoned parliamentary speech against Fascist violence and violation of the Constitution. His arguments were strengthened by quotations from forgotten articles written by Mussolini himself in the days when he was a young anarchist. Insulted and threatened by Fascist deputies, Matteotti said afterward to parliamentary friends, "Now you can prepare my funeral oration." Eleven days later Matteotti left home at his usual time to walk to parliament. The policeman assigned to him, as to all deputies, for his protection, was absent. This was unusual. It was an exceedingly hot day and the Tiber embankment deserted. The only sign of human life was in a parked car, a Lancia. As Matteotti came alongside it, several thugs leaped out, seized and beat him, and dragged him into the car. When Matteotti managed to break a window with his foot, they stabbed him, but did not immediately kill him. For the rest of the day they drove around the countryside as aimlessly as wasps with no one left to sting. When it grew dark, they went to Quartarella, twenty-three kilometers from Rome, dug a ditch, and flung Matteotti's body into it.

By the time Matteotti's body was found, emotion throughout Italy was so violent as to suggest that Matteotti was a far greater danger to Mussolini dead than alive. It was the one moment when Fascism was almost defeated by one man. Mussolini was helped, however, by the King's incapacity to deal with the situation. When a committee of ex-servicemen brought the King proof of Fascist violence, he turned pale but found nothing to say except "This morning my daughter shot two quails," a reply beside which Pontius Pilate's hand-washing seems positively constructive. The contrast between such touches of buffoonery—so aptly coincidental with the current art movements of Surrealism and Dadaism —and the tragedy from which they sprang made a deep impression on young Visconti, an impression strengthened when Mussolini and Hitler met for the first time, that same summer, in Venice. Mussolini was tasseled, decorated, booted, spurred, and all aglitter. Hitler, in a beige raincoat, looked like a minor and not very civil servant whose wild eyes might land him in a psychiatric ward without any illicit sequestration being required. Despite expressions of admiration—it was only a few years since Hitler had written asking Mussolini for a signed photograph, which was not sent ("but tell the gentleman I appreciate his sentiments")—the meeting was not a success. Given their temperaments, it could not have been successful even had they been merely fellow Rotarians; as it was, they had divergent interests in the Balkans to justify their personal differences.

It was memories of such episodes that made Visconti say forty-five years later, when asked why he chose to portray Nazis rather than Fascists in *The Damned,* "Because of the difference between tragedy and comedy . . . of course Fascism was a tragedy in many many cases . . . but as the prototype of a given historical situation that leads to a certain form of criminality, Nazism seemed to me the more exemplary . . . because it was a tragedy that, like a dreadful bloodstain, seeped over the entire world. . . . One could make thousands of films about Italian Fascism . . . about Matteotti . . . about the death of Gramsci . . . but Nazism seems to me to reveal more about a historic reversal of values."

Even when absorbed by his adolescence, swinging from bliss to misery and back again, Visconti was unusually aware that other people existed, as is clear from the rough outline of an autobiographical novel he wrote at this time. His ivory tower always had all its doors and windows wide open, and he himself was as conscious of what was in the air as an animal before an earthquake. The last time he ran away from home, at eighteen, it was not for fun or love but because he was overwhelmed by a mood of mysticism that led him to Monte Cassino, mother house of the Benedictine monks, soon to be destroyed in the Second World War. His religious beliefs were strong—they were later to lead to political beliefs— and might easily have taken him into a monastic life. Giorgio Prosperi, describing Visconti's character in 1953, wrote that religious feelings constitute "an element one must bear in mind if one wishes to understand Visconti's character and future spiritual development: unquiet, emotional, sentimental but profoundly serious, preoccupied by the great problems, and desirous every time he takes a new path to follow it to its end. His life may contain experiences that are failures, but it contains no *half experiences.*"

He was then sent off as a boarder to a school run by the strict Calasanziani Order—and once again escaped. Another school being out of the question at this stage, he was put to work in the Erba family business. As an attempt to anchor him, this proved as useless as schools had been. The privileges he had enjoyed made him anxious that others should have better lives, and his still-incoherent rebelliousness "created an atmosphere of anarchy," said the directors, making haste to get rid of him. This brief but instructive encounter with industrial life was soon cut short by military service. It is a fact so commonplace as to have become a cliché that gifted boys inevitably detest military service. Visconti, however, enjoyed every minute of his, for the simple reason that he served in a cavalry regiment and had a passion for horses. He was stationed first in Milan, then at the cavalry school at Pinerolo, a little town near Turin founded in the tenth century and known as "the Nice of Piedmont" on account of its pleasant climate. The Man in the Iron Mask spent some time in the citadel there. Visconti was still in the old world of the cavalry in 1927 when a young American four years his senior, Charles Lindbergh, opened up a new world by flying the Atlantic.

The military flavor of this cavalry interlude was far nearer to that of Stendhal's *Lucien Leuwen* than to today's army life. Toscanini's elder daughter remembers a princess who, in love with Visconti at that time, used to fetch him from the barracks. It was, says Wally Toscanini, an enchanting picture, the beautiful woman, with her spirited horses, liveried coachman, elegant carriage, and the young soldier, so handsome that, according to a popular saying, "he would make the bread fall from your hand," displaying a highly personal mixture of fieriness and reserve. Milan was still full of gardens, carriages, the smell of horses and bakeries, the sound of swallows darting around the roofs at sunset. In the evening, as the lights came on, Visconti would think of his father saying at the family dinner table, "Now the lights are going up at La Scala."

Years later, when Visconti made *Il Gattopardo* (*The Leopard*), critics were to discern autobiographical elements in the character of Prince Salina, played by Burt Lancaster; but there is probably as much autobiography in the character of the Prince's nephew Tancred, a dashing young Garibaldian officer. Visconti once said of Alain Delon, who played Tancred, that "his fascination for women was due in part to his extraordinarily boyish personality"—and the same must have been true of himself as a young officer, and even a few years later, when he could shed tears of enthusiasm at *The Lives of a Bengal Lancer*.

The duties and delights of cavalry life in peacetime not only took Visconti back into the nineteenth century, but also so developed his passion for horses that when his military service came to an end he decided to devote himself to breeding and training them. He bought his first horses in 1929, won his first victory, with Esturgeon, at St. Moritz, soon after his twenty-third birthday, and then chose white and green as the colors of his racing stable. He adored training horses and began by riding them himself, though he later entrusted them to his older brother, Luigi, one of the greatest horsemen of his generation. In 1932, Visconti's horse Sanzio won both the Grand Prix of the City of Milan and the Grand Prix at Ostend. The fact that this prolongation of his centaur years delayed what would now be called his "search for identity" was, for Visconti as an artist, a blessing. His horses satisfied his artistic as well as his sportsman's instincts—he shared the Prophet Mohammed's belief that only horses can "fly without wings and conquer without a sword"— and had he entered theater or films on a full-time basis immediately after his military service, Fascist censorship would have crippled him. So, in a sense, his horses enabled him to take his time—something he was often reluctant to do. During this period he traveled in North Africa, England, and, above all, France, where he led the life of a young man about town and, with his sisters-in-law, Madina and Niki Arrivabene, frequented Kurt Weill, Henri Bernstein, Serge Lifar, Jean Cocteau and—far the most important from his viewpoint—Gabrielle Chanel.

All the artists Visconti met in Paris were fascinated by the cinema, and it was during this period that he bought his first movie camera and planned his first film. Having written a scenario about a boy's love for three women that ends with his suicide, Visconti gathered together a "company" that included beautiful Niki Arrivabene, who, like many young aristocrats just then, dreamed of a screen career. Nothing remains of this, since the rolls of film containing his first attempt went up in flames when the Visconti palace in Milan was bombed during the Second World War.

This visit to Paris not only increased Visconti's passion for the cinema but also roused in him a consciousness of the political situation at home. This was not in fact as strictly black or white as it can be made to appear, and included a great deal of pure muddle. The Viscontis and their friends were mostly anti-Fascist, it is true, but only passively so— as Luchino Visconti was to realize when he began working in France. Just as the Fascism of the lower middle class has been admirably described by Federico Fellini in his film *Amarcord,* so the upper classes' distaste for Fascism has been summed up by Susanna Agnelli's description of it, in *We Wore Sailor Suits,* as something "inevitable, comic and seldom mentioned," which made her grandparents shake their heads at "such nonsense." Even the Communist leader Giorgio Amendola, son of the Socialist deputy Giovanni Amendola, whom the Fascists murdered in 1926, writes of his own adolescence, spent mostly among liberal intellectuals, that although there was no lack of anti-Fascists, yet while they all talked, recriminated, and prophesied, "no one proposed doing anything." As personal friends of the royal family, the Viscontis would have found it difficult to be more royalist than the King and, in addition, they were deeply patriotic in a traditional way. Even at twenty-eight, Visconti could write to the girl he hoped to marry that he was tempted to answer the call for volunteers for Africa, since he had "done nothing yet to make his country stronger and greater," and felt that his generation was sadly inferior to his father's, which had fought the war. Part of him was still at his *Lives of a Bengal Lancer* stage.

Absorption in his horses did not lessen the passion for the theater that Visconti shared with his parents. Hitherto he had taken part only in performances given in the family theater—Teatro Casa Giuseppe Visconti di Modrone—that his father had had built in their palace for their own acting. (Wally Toscanini, who attended many of these performances, said years later, after having seen the best acting all over the world, that had Visconti's mother lived in a different social sphere she would have been acclaimed the greatest actress of her generation.) All of this had liberally prepared Visconti for his first professional job, which he performed at twenty-two—stage manager for a production of Carlo Goldoni's *The Wise Wife* given at the Eden Theater by the Milan Art Theater Company, an enterprise backed by his father.

Goldoni did not keep him long from his stables, nor did his stables prevent other forms of artistic development. From childhood Visconti had expressed himself in writing—diaries, notebooks, accounts of his travels—as instinctively as through music, painting, designing, and the theater. So at twenty-three he collaborated with a friend, Livio dell'Anna, in writing a one-act "grotesque comedy" entitled *Il gioco della verità* (*The Truth Game*), a reference to the perilous *jeux de société* of that name which Visconti always thought wickedly entertaining.

From this it was natural for him to turn to writing for the cinema. Not only had he loved films from childhood, but also the cinema had just reached the fascinating point when it acquired sound. That scenarios now required real dialogue, not captions, stimulated his instinct to write. Later all his scenarios were to be brought out in handsome well-documented volumes by Cappelli, a famous old Bologna firm founded by Licinio Cappelli, a printer's son who fought for Italian unity and published Italo Svevo long before the latter's talent was widely recognized. Visconti appreciated his publishers so much that he remained with the firm all his life. In 1935, Visconti's early efforts brought him an invitation to work with the Hungarian film director Gabriel Pascal, who had just migrated to London and was planning a film of *November*, a tragic love story written by Flaubert at the age of twenty.

Visconti leaped at this opportunity to try something new in another country, especially a country he did not know well, since he had just suffered an emotional experience that was to mark the rest of his life. At twenty-seven he had fallen deeply in love, while staying at Kitzbühel, with an Austrian girl, Princess Irma Windisch-Graetz. She adored him, finding him extraordinarily different from all the other young men she knew. He wanted to marry her, and his letters—some of which Princess Irma, now Princess Weikersheim, published in a popular magazine shortly after Visconti's death—are painfully touching and suggest a stern, mannerly young man, tender, discreet, and as vulnerable as he was protective. Once sure of his feelings, Visconti's first action was to confide in his mother; throughout his life he might rebel against society or institutions but never against family or friends. His mother was full of sympathy and approval, and his father, although unconvinced that Luchino was ready for marriage, had no desire to thwart him. Princess Irma's father, however, had reservations, expressed them in a way Visconti found offensive, and insisted that the young couple wait. Visconti asked the girl to run away with him—it would not have been a great run—to Milan and his welcoming family. But she could not bring herself to disobey her father. It was typical of Visconti that he would neither accept this state of affairs nor compromise. Relentlessly unhappy, he left the girl and made no further attempt to see her.

Twenty years later, according to his sister, he met Princess Weikersheim in Rome, and, when his sister asked him cautiously how things had gone, said only, "We always destroy ourselves." Princess Irma was not the last woman in his life, but he would also be drawn to men, a fact about which he never made either a mystery or a display. The writer and deputy Antonello Trombadori said after his death: "Rationality was the only style in which Visconti imagined his relationships both with people and with things. Added to which pride and contempt for vulgarity were the kernel of his being." All his life, despite his public position, he was a very private person.

Arriving in London immediately after giving up this girl, Visconti was fiercely determined to concentrate on the Flaubert scenario. But as soon as he met Pascal, he felt sure nothing would come of this, and that he was wasting time in London. The film was never made, and, so far as concerned Pascal, Visconti was indeed wasting his time. Nevertheless, this London visit changed his life. Having returned to Paris, he attended a race meeting with Gabrielle Chanel. In between their discussions of the horses, highly professional on both sides, Visconti told her about his fruitless trip to London. Because she adored Visconti, she was much annoyed and said scoldingly that Gabriel Pascal was "not a serious person." This, for her, was almost the worst thing she could say of anyone. But, she added, if Visconti really wanted to work in the cinema she would introduce him to a friend of hers who was "truly serious."

In order to appreciate the value of Chanel's contribution to Visconti's career, it is necessary to have an idea of her position in those days. An extraordinary character of volcanic forcefulness and energy, Gabrielle Chanel, widely known as Coco, was at fifty a slender and beautiful woman, always exquisitely dressed in the deceptively simple style created by herself. As a dressmaker she marked her period as indelibly as Arthur Liberty marked his. She had worked with Dali, Cocteau, and Balanchine on theater and ballet costumes, and was as intimate with the world of art as she was familiar with that of the Almanach de Gotha. A discerning Maecenas, she had come to Diaghilev's rescue financially. Visconti loved her mixture of "feminine beauty, masculine brain, and fantastic energy." The brilliant American photographer Horst wrote of her in *Salute to the Thirties:*

Without a doubt, the center of the circle, the star of the circus, was Chanel. She was omnipresent and omnipotent. She argued and pontificated; she set up an alarm clock on her table when Dali was present, and insisted that after he had spoken for ten minutes without interruption, she had the right to do the same. Often she would be molding jewel settings in putty between her fingers as she talked. Costume jewelry was only one of her many inventions. And best of all, she sewed. One of my most cherished memories is of Chanel at the dress rehearsal of a Cocteau play, ripping apart the costumes she had designed for the production and stitching them together again, sitting cross-legged, tailor-fashion, on the bare boards of the stage. She had notoriously declined to become an English Duchess. She preferred to remain a French dressmaker. She thought of herself as a working woman, and still did, to the end. She encouraged poets and artists, old or young, known or unknown. It was she personally who bullied an aristocratic Italian playboy of the Thirties, Luchino Visconti, into going in search of better things, with results that are now a matter of common knowledge.

Gabrielle Chanel certainly achieved one of her finest pieces of creative work the day she introduced Luchino Visconti to the great French film director Jean Renoir. Renoir promptly engaged him as an assistant, and from then on the name Visconti ceased to be, primarily, something he had inherited and became his very own, a name that, when he eventually left it behind, was enriched by all he had himself created.

Six

At a first glance, the forty-two-year-old French film director Jean Renoir and the twenty-nine-year-old Italian beginner Luchino Visconti would seem to have had little in common. But in fact they had much, and Gabrielle Chanel, with her prodigious gift for matching qualities, knew precisely what she was doing when she brought the two together.

Jean Renoir, a burly figure with the face of a benevolent tortoise, was the second son of the great Impressionist painter Auguste Renoir. Like Visconti, Renoir adored his parents, and far from being oppressed by the force of his father's personality, he rejoiced in it. His book *Renoir, My Father* contains an analysis of his father's nature—"this mixture of irony, tenderness, humor and voluptuousness"—that applies equally well to his own disposition. While Visconti's mother was the granddaughter of peasants, Renoir's was herself a Burgundian peasant, and both mothers strengthened their sons' sense of the intimate relationship between nature and art. Though both were born in great cities—Renoir in the poetically named Château des Brouillards in Montmartre, Paris—they both spent much of their childhoods in exquisite countrysides that became part of their inner landscapes. Both were captivated as children by the worlds of theater and cinema. Renoir began with the guignol (Punch and Judy show), still popular with French children today, and saw his first film, a silent burlesque, at school. But, despite their precocity as spectators, they were equally late in finding their individual paths as artists, both achieving this only at the age of thirty.

As young men, devotion to horses led both into the cavalry, but Renoir joined the cavalry in 1913 and was therefore rapidly engulfed in the war, first as a cavalry officer, later as an air force pilot. He was wounded several times—convalescing, he said, gave him time to watch his father paint—and ended the war with a permanent limp. Renoir's war service added to his prestige in Visconti's eyes, making him seem, although only twelve years older, part of the heroic generation of Visconti's father.

Both grew up in homes saturated with art. Renoir's universe was the luminous one of Impressionism. Even as a child, he found his father's pictures, which covered the walls of their apartment, "an indispensable part" of his life. And among the works of art that filled Visconti's home were differently but equally luminous pictures by the Tuscan *macchiaiuoli* painters, contemporaries of the Impressionists who are only now being discovered outside Italy. Both had from their earliest years enjoyed the intimacy of great artists, Visconti with the Toscaninis, and Renoir with the Cézannes, of whom he wrote, "the Cézanne family and our own were almost one family."

Both were highly literate and relished literacy—fifteen out of Renoir's thirty-five films have subjects taken from literature, and Visconti said at the beginning of his career: "In a recent discussion of the relationship between literature and the cinema, I found myself spontaneously on the side of those who have faith in the riches and cinematographic validity of literary inspiration." Visconti and Renoir even shared an appreciative attitude toward food, which showed in their work. Renoir, of whom his father said, when introduced to the plain baby, "Look at that mouth—he'll be a glutton," noted that "all the great events from baptism to burial are accompanied by meals," and filled his films with celebrations of the beauty of food in a series of Impressionistic meals, each one a refutation of all the schoolteachers who ever said, "You can like food, you can enjoy food, but you *cannot love* food." For Visconti, it was the ritual of meals, drawing people together, that acted as a magnet, and his films are full of formal dinners. "Life," he said, "is a beehive, with each person living in his own little cell, but everyone meets in a central nucleus around the queen bee, and that's when dramas break out."

At this time the director Visconti particularly admired was the contesting and contested Erich von Stroheim, especially his *The Wedding March*, with its masterfully un-Ruritanian Hapsburg world. Strikingly different was the world of Jean Renoir, who had then made eight silent films and nine with sound. *Toni*, one of the latter, considered by critics to mark "the beginning of Renoir's antifascist period," was inspired by a news item in a Marseilles paper about a French peasant's murder of an Italian immigrant. A working-class story was a rarity in the cinema then, and much of the film was shot in natural settings with unmade-up nonprofessional actors. But it was the emotional content that roused in Visconti feelings like those with which he had read Verga—and thereby clarified his personal aspirations. Indeed, the whole Renoir experience was for Visconti a voyage of discovery dramatized by political circumstances. For he had arrived in Paris just in time for the excitement of the Front Populaire.

The Third Republic had been shaken not only by the world-wide Depression of 1929, but also by a series of home-grown scandals, the worst of which was the Stavisky one. This culminated in the absconding swindler's death at Chamonix in January 1934—some said by suicide; others, due to a police killing. Extremists on all sides accused Camille Chautemps's Radical Socialist government of complicity and corruption, and forced it to resign. On May 3, 1936, the elections were won by a coalition of Socialists, Radical Socialists, and Communists, led by the noble-minded and idealistic Léon Blum. The Front Populaire, virtually the end of the Third Republic, aimed at stopping fascism and effecting reforms.

As Léon Blum began forming a government, popular enthusiasm grew. The July 14 celebrations that Visconti witnessed in Paris were rapturous rather than revolutionary, with dancing in the streets to the sound of accordions, red flags flying, and neither red nor blue blood flowing, only red and white wine. Strangers spoke spontaneously to strangers as they gazed together at the fireworks' ephemeral wheels reeling out messages about pie in the sky. An extraordinarily poetic, tough, and accurate evocation of this atmosphere can be found in a book of photographs, *The Front Populaire*, by Capa and Chim. Robert Capa, born in Budapest, and David Seymour (Chim), born in Warsaw, were beginners at the time of the Front Populaire, but already had the qualities that were to make them two of the greatest American reporter-photographers. Loathing war but determined not to shirk history, they were both killed by it, Capa at forty-one by a land mine in Indochina, Chim at forty-five by Egyptian machine-gun fire during a truce. But when they photographed Paris in 1936, they were as young as Wordsworth when he wrote of an earlier revolution, "Bliss was it in that dawn to be alive, / But to be young was very heaven!" In their pages one can see the vanished world of the Front Populaire as Visconti saw it: a Paris full of incense-bearing trees and without skyscrapers, a Paris where lovers, tramps, fishermen, dogs and cats occupied quays of the Seine as yet unthreatened by highways.

Years later, summing up, Visconti said that though he grew up in the Liberty era, with melodrama his first love (using the word not in the pejorative sense in which it is used today, but to signify a drama in which words and music are integrated, with Verdi its supreme exponent), still many of his basic attitudes were formed by the new world of Paris to which "the stupendous Coco Chanel" introduced him. Speaking with the calm, firm, and reasonable-sounding exaggeration peculiar to him, Visconti explained. "When I was in Paris in 1936, to work in the cinema . . . I was a kind of imbecile. Not a Fascist, but unconsciously affected by Fascism, colored by it . . . I knew nothing, understood nothing—where politics were concerned my eyes were as tightly shut as a newborn kitten's. But the friends I made there opened my eyes. They were all Communists, card-carrying Communists."

This last statement was not strictly true. But anarchists must have been indistinguishable from Communists to someone fresh from Mussolini's Italy. At this time Fascism was more popular with the Italians than ever before or since, thanks to the supposed success of the Ethiopian war, and to public exasperation at the futile sanctions imposed on Italy by a league made up of nations most of whom already had colonies safely under their belts.

"At first," continued Visconti, "as was only natural, they viewed me with suspicion. What does that titled fool want? Then . . . it was the Front Populaire. I remember it all as clearly as if it were only yesterday —the elections, the processions in the Place de la République, the enthusiasm, the vitality of that period—the vigor, the effervescence. . . . I was assistant to Jean Renoir, whom I consider my master. Renoir had been a passionate ceramist since his boyhood and he told me that ceramics and the cinema have a lot in common—writers, directors, ceramists all know what they want, what they're driving at, but once the work's in the oven you can't be sure whether it will come out as you intended or quite different. . . . That was the period when I got my aspirations into focus. . . . I remember Jean's gift for directing actors, for getting them to adhere completely to the characters they were playing. . . . He was so meticulous, had such technique."

Here, again, these two dissimilar characters had a trait in common. They both understood acting and, unlike some well-known directors, did not despise actors, but included the artists in their feeling for the art. Renoir acted himself in several films, almost as well as his brother Pierre, who was an actor by profession, and a distinguished one. Visconti never acted in public, but the performances he gave for the benefit of the actors he directed are famous in professional circles.

Looking back at that time in Paris, Visconti added, "Renoir was an extraordinary man, surrounded by militant left-wingers, and he had a great influence over me both artistically and morally. . . . I remember the richness of his humanity . . . his tenderness for people and for their work. I could talk to him as if we were brothers." Renoir's ascendance over Visconti at this period was the natural result not only of the elder man's genial gifts, warmth, fun, and fantasy, but also to the political atmosphere in which the unbigoted Renoir swam as gaily as an otter. Though vigorously anti-Nazi and in favor of reforms such as those Léon Blum did achieve—among them the forty-hour week, holidays with pay, and higher wages—Renoir's approach to politics was tender-hearted rather than vindictive, individualistic rather than doctrinaire. As for the "militant left-wingers," many of these were enthusiasts carried away by the excitement of a historic moment. In July 1936, the Spanish Frente Popular, democratically elected the previous February, was attacked by General Francisco Franco, who thus set in motion the Spanish Civil War.

Renoir, disillusioned but not embittered, could write later that dividing men into Fascists and Communists was "meaningless," since "both believed in progress and a society based on technology," but that if he had to choose all over again, he would still choose the left simply because it had "a more honorable conception of human beings." Visconti, who could be headstrong but never failed to use his head, presently committed himself to the left with far more tenacity and seriousness than most of those light-heartedly urging him that way. This choice was to make a militant partisan of him in wartime and a fighter with ideas during the approximate peace that followed. It was also a choice that would hinder his career, but that he never repudiated or regretted. Nor did he ever refrain from criticizing left-wing actions that disgusted him. In 1965, soon after his fifty-ninth birthday, he was to say that he had been wholeheartedly for Kennedy, Khrushchev, and Pope John XXIII, and feared we might be about to go back on their achievements.

While these ideas were germinating, Visconti was absorbed by his first professional experience of film making. Renoir had adapted *Une Partie de campagne* from Guy de Maupassant's story about an iron-monger's family's country excursion, during which mother and daughter are seduced by two holidaymakers. Visconti designed all the costumes as well as working as one of Renoir's assistants. The five other assistants were Claude Heyman, Yves Allegret, and Jacques Becker, all three future directors, Jacques B. Brunius, a fantastic character who had studied aero-nautics before entering the cinema, and a young photographer, Henri Cartier-Bresson. From Visconti's viewpoint the most interesting of these was Cartier-Bresson, an enigmatic young man with curious mineral-blue eyes who had studied painting with André Lhote, literature and painting at Cambridge, before being captivated by photography, thanks to the work of Man Ray and Eugène Atget. After six years spent traveling, he had returned to France specially to work with Renoir, and was to become not a merely fashionable but a truly great photographer.

Renoir had planned *Une Partie de campagne* as a short film, fifty-five minutes, with a week's shooting of exteriors in the country, near his own house at Marlotte, on the banks of the Loing, about a hundred kilometers from Paris. The summer of 1936, however, was abnormally rainy, and although Renoir started shooting on July 15, he was still waiting for the sun in September. It is a measure of Visconti's enchantment with his new work and ideas—one day, when Renoir was kept in Paris, Visconti was able to shoot a bit of the film himself, a stupendous day for him—that he admired the comradeship, one for all and all for one, around him at the very moment when that comradeship was fast dissolving. Enthralled by Jean Renoir's directing and Claude Renoir's magical camera work, which gave a *Midsummer Night's Dream* quality to the river and its banks, Visconti scarcely noticed at first that the amount of hanging around inflicted on actors and technicians by the weather was fermenting intrigues of every kind. The leading actress, Sylvia Bataille, said later that it reached a point where they could not bear the sight of each other. In addition, there were financial difficulties. Finally a morning came when Renoir arrived with the announcement that he was dropping the film and had signed a contract to make Gorki's *The Lower Depths. Une Partie de campagne* was not shown publicly until ten years later.

In the autumn of 1936, back in Italy, Visconti showed something of the authority he had gained in Paris by producing a play for the first time: Giannino Antona Traversi's *Carita mondana* (*Worldly Charity*), at Como's Teatro Sociale. This was followed by Jan Mallory's *Sweet Aloes* at Milan's Teatro Manzoni. But his time in Paris had made him want to study American film making. So in 1937, after a cruise to Greece, he went to the United States. This was the period of Charlie Chaplin's *Modern Times*, Greta Garbo's *Camille*, Gary Cooper's *Mr. Deeds Goes to Town*, William Powell and Carole Lombard in *My Man Godfrey*, Norma Shearer and Leslie Howard in *Romeo and Juliet*, the Marx brothers' hilarious *Night at the Opera*, and Janet Gaynor's *A Star Is Born*. In the growing world of the cinema, Hollywood was phosphorescently powerful, but, since Sunset Boulevard was not yet visually familiar from Cork to Katmandu, Visconti's ideas of the film capital were based chiefly on the writings of Emilio Cecchi, who was as marvelously responsive to Buster Keaton as to Giotto.

Visconti found Hollywood a smaller, greener, and more seemly town than it is now. Smog and offshore oil derricks had not yet appeared. As regards the industry itself, the studio system was at its peak, each studio having its own stable of stars, including a plethora of child stars, for whom this was the greatest period. Nine-year-old Shirley Temple, who had just made *Wee Willie Winkie*, was, for example, the most financially valuable "property" of Twentieth Century–Fox. Everything was done on a gigantic scale, even the "block-booking system," by which distributors wanting guaranteed box-office successes were obliged to make a package deal including a film unlikely to make money. Most disconcerting to Visconti was the omnipresent advertising. Paradoxically, the Depression had made glamour more desirable than ever, but it now had to be combined with respectability. This led to the most fanciful manipulations, with the studios playing up the domesticity of stars not in the least domestic, in order that fans not notably domestic themselves would "identify" with their idols. There was nothing strictly new about this— first-century Rome probably contained donkeys who really believed Nero was a peace-loving character, devoted to his mother and conscientious about violin practicing—but Visconti had never before seen braying organized on such a scale. Nevertheless, he learned things that enriched his future, made friends, and enjoyed being a Man in the Moon. Back home, his first scene designs—for the Milan Art Theater's production of Henri Bernstein's *The Voyage*—showed the influence of American scenography.

Then, suddenly, all joy ceased for him. In January 1939, he was called to Cortina d'Ampezzo, in the Dolomites, where his mother was dying. Years later he said that he and his mother had "made a pact" that if ever she was in danger in his absence she "would wait for him." He reached Cortina in time to hear her repeat his name as she died. At fifty-nine, she had been still beautiful and vital, and Visconti was overwhelmed by the most terrible grief he had ever known, the most terrible grief he ever would know. Later he said that his mother was "the being I loved most." At the time, he was suicidal, feeling that life without her held nothing for him. His memory of her never faded. Thirty-six years later he put her, young and beautiful, into his next to last film.

He was still in the state of shock that provides self-insulation for the early stages of grief when he received a telegram from Jean Renoir: "Am leaving for Rome to make *La Tosca*. Join me." For the first of many times, work provided a life line—a life line that, on this occasion, drew him from Milan to settle permanently in Rome. Since Visconti and Renoir last met, Renoir had made a great film, *La Grande Illusion* (1937), and, although it was banned in Italy, Mussolini seized a copy for his private cinema and himself suggested that Renoir should be invited to make a film in Italy and lecture at the official film center. By the time Renoir arrived he was no longer a private individual, but a lieutenant in the French army. On August 23, Nazi Germany and Soviet Russia signed a pact of friendship. On September 1, Hitler invaded Poland. On September 3, England and France declared war on Germany. For the time being, Italy was neutral, and Renoir was assigned to a French cultural mission supposed to help detach Italy from Germany.

That summer in Europe was more nonsensical than anything conjured up by Lewis Carroll. Lieutenant Renoir's *La Grande Illusion* was banned not only in Italy (for pacifism) but in France (also for pacifism), as was his *La Règle du jeu* (for demoralization); yet this demoralizing pacifist was chosen during the early months of the war, when "nothing was happening," for a cultural mission, with military aims, and was warmly welcomed by the target country. In Russia, meanwhile, Sergei Eisenstein's officially sponsored film *Alexander Nevsky* was banned. An epic with music by Prokofiev, it showed a people's army driving Teutonic hordes from Holy Russia. The ban was lifted nearly two years later when Teutonic hordes were at their work again in reality.

Renoir had never been to Rome before and, since he could not have had a more gifted and generous guide than Visconti, he was delighted with his visit. He liked all the friends to whom Visconti introduced him: Vittorio de Sica, an enchanting and successful actor with his own stage company; Cesare Zavattini, a gifted journalist and film critic who was to work as scriptwriter with both De Sica and Visconti; Roberto Rossellini, who would be made famous after the war by *Rome, Open City;* and Giuseppe de Santis, who was to collaborate on the script of Visconti's first film. All these young men had been able to express their anti-Fascist leanings at the Centro Sperimentale di Cinematografia, which was established in 1932 by director Alessandro Blasetti, as a department of the Rome Academy of Music. This center became an independent establishment in 1935, giving two-year courses in directing, production, camera work, sound, acting, scenery and costume designing, history of cinema, theater, and music. It was the first great film school in the world and published an influential film magazine, *Bianco e nero.* Renoir was delighted to lecture there and found his listeners as stimulating as they found him.

At first, too, work on *La Tosca* seemed to be going well. Renoir, Visconti, and Carl Koch had collaborated on the script, and, with the war apparently static, nothing happened to disturb the film shooting—until the day when the admirable Swiss actor Michel Simon, who was playing the wicked Scarpia and had a passion for spending his free time photographing the painted ceilings of Roman palaces, and then showing his photographs to some prostitutes, with whom he had long and instructive conversations, went to his beloved brothel and found it overrun by Germans in civilian clothes. The terrified madam hustled Simon out as quickly as she could. It was obviously time for foreigners to leave Rome.

Before they parted, Renoir gave Visconti something that was to prove an Aladdin's lamp in his hands: a French translation of an American novel, James Cain's *The Postman Always Rings Twice*. It had been passed on to Renoir by Julien Duvivier (director of *Pépé-le-Moko, Un Carnet de bal* and, after the war, the *Don Camillo* series), and now Renoir passed it on to Visconti, saying, "Perhaps this might interest you."

More than any other activity, war amputates time, allows no parting to be well made, and destroys nerves, bodies, and buildings with the same impartial imbecility. At any moment Renoir was liable to find himself in the absurd situation of an "enemy alien" among close friends. Later he wrote: "My farewells to my collaborators were sad occasions and I particularly regretted parting from Luchino Visconti because of all the things we might have done together but did not do. . . . I was never to see Luchino again, despite the great friendship between us."

So ended the prologue to Visconti's career.

*It takes twenty years or more of peace to make a man;
it takes only twenty seconds of war to destroy him.*

Baudouin I of Belgium

---

*Ah! que la victoire demeure avec ceux qui auront fait
la guerre sans l'aimer!* (May victory rest with those
who have fought without loving war!)

André Malraux, *Les Noyers de Altenburg*

". . . something is going to happen," said Moomintroll.
*"Something dreadful and unnecessary that nobody
knows much about. But there has been a strange feeling in the air lately."*

Tove Jansson, *Comet in Moominland*

Seven

In 1940, Hitler's invasions of Denmark, Belgium, Holland, Luxembourg, and France convinced Mussolini that England would soon be among the conquered. As the German army raced through the June sunshine toward Paris, he decided that Italy must have a share in this prestigious enterprise. When Marshal Pietro Badoglio warned him that intervention would be suicide—so many lives and weapons had been squandered in Ethiopia and Spain that the Italian armed forces were even less prepared in 1940 than they had been in 1915—Mussolini replied, "I need *only a few thousand dead* to sit down at the peace conference as a belligerent."

With this absurd end in view—absurd in the Ionesco sense, because had Hitler conquered he would surely have spared no consideration for any claims but his own—Mussolini declared war on France and Great Britain on June 10, 1940. The war was unpopular with the majority of Italians from the start. Even the illiterate felt in their threatened bones what the novelist Ouida had written, with extraordinary prescience, in 1882, when the new kingdom of Italy joined Germany and Austria in the Triple Alliance:

Germany has always been fatal to Italy, and always will be. The costly armaments which have made her penniless are due to Germany. Her army and navy receive annual and insulting inspection by Prussian princes. *The time will probably come when German troops will be asked to preserve "social order" in the cities and provinces of Italy.* So long as the German alliance continues in its present form, so long will this danger for Italy always exist. . . . And if the House of Savoy be driven from the Quirinal, it will ·owe this loss of power entirely to its own policy. . . ."

Alas for Visconti's youthful hopes of serving his country on Bengal Lancer lines. The call to arms found him a convinced and active anti-Fascist whose part would have to be played underground and without uniform. It also found him surviving rather than living: he was still in a state of shock from his mother's death when, in December 1941, his father died. He was buried in the little cemetery at Grazzano, and the castle was closed. It snowed on the day of the funeral, for which the villagers wore the vivid costumes Giuseppe Visconti had designed for them. Because he had left instructions that there was to be no black, the church was hung with red brocade, reminding Visconti of the family box at La Scala. This loss affected him profoundly. Although his most passionate love had been for his mother, he was nevertheless devoted to his father, saying near the end of his own life, "We seven children had *stupendous parents*. My father was, admittedly, a nobleman, but not in the least frivolous and certainly no fool. A cultivated and sensitive man who loved music and the theater, who helped us to understand and appreciate art." In 1942, Visconti's eldest brother, Guido, was killed in North Africa during the battle of El Alamein. Visconti reacted to this with a mixture of Proustian sensibility to the past and of stoicism inherited from the ancestors whose recumbent effigies, clad in marble armor or ecclesiastical robes, grasping marble swords or crosiers, adorn the tombs of ancient churches that illustrate our attempts at civilizing ourselves.

In the early stages of the war Visconti turned for support to his work. He and the friends and rebels grouped around the magazine *Cinema* longed to create what they called "Verga cinema"—films that would do for the cinema what Verga's novels had done for literature. Verga's stories of Sicily had inspired the literary term *verismo*—from which it was only a step to the cinema's Neo-Realism, a word that was to be used for the first time by Mario Serandrei, most creative of film editors, when describing Visconti's first film, *Ossessione*.

There were, however, many hurdles between Visconti and *Ossessione*. The Italian cinema's early history was magnificent, but by the twenties American films, occupying sixty-eight percent of screen time, and other foreign films, twenty-six percent, were endangering the home industry. The only Italian company that managed to keep going throughout the crises was Cines. When Emilio Cecchi was asked to take its presidency he did a great deal for Italian films, particularly by instigating the production of first-rate documentaries. Nevertheless, the most successful films from 1930 to 1942 were sentimental comedies about well-heeled characters in smart surroundings. These were known as "white telephone movies"—a name coined for them by Carlo Levi, the doctor, painter, and future author of *Christ Stopped at Eboli*. On one occasion Levi and another Turin painter, Francesco Menzio, were called to Rome to design film sets for one of these comedies. It took place in "Hungary or Czechoslovakia," so, to accentuate its "exotic" character, jovial Levi said, "Let's do it all in white—white telephones, too, even white pianos." This they did, and since the telephone played a ubiquitous part in these films, the "white telephone" label stuck.

It is unlikely that Visconti would at any time have been drawn to white telephones, but in 1941, surrounded by death, armored by grief, he wrote furiously in his first article published in *Cinema:* "When one enters the premises of certain film companies one all too often finds oneself among corpses who insist on believing they are alive . . . will we ever see the hoped-for day when the youthful forces of our cinema, nourished for the moment on hope alone, but with so much to say, will be able to decree that the place for corpses is the cemetery?"

What he himself wanted to make was a film of "L'amante di Gramigna," a short story written by Verga in 1880 around a contemporary news item. It is a very short story, less than six pages in a 1968 paperback, and reading it tells one a lot about Visconti's personal conception of art. On the first page Verga writes: "A simple human fact will always arouse thought, will always possess the efficacity of having happened, of representing real tears, fevers, sensations that were an intrinsic part of real flesh and blood . . . the science of the human heart, foremost in modern art, will develop the imagination to such an extent that in the future the only novels written will be news items." There is a curious connection between this and what André Malraux wrote shortly before his death in 1976 about the birth of an entirely new type of literature, the colloquy, or direct biography, made up of tape-recorded interviews: from Plutarch's *Lives* to *This Is Your Life,* and so into a new era with sight and sound ousting print.

"L'amante di Gramigna," written when Verga was forty, is a news item from the past that is both in tune with today's violence and also a romantic story from which Verdi might have created an opera. Peppa, a Sicilian peasant girl, is about to marry a prosperous young peasant. Her mother is rapturously preoccupied by Peppa's trousseau—"all white and four of everything"; by Peppa's good fortune—"a gold ring for every finger and earrings to touch her shoulders"; and by the satisfaction provided by the neighbors' envy. At the same period the police are chasing all over Sicily a notorious bandit, Gramigna, who has become a local folkhero—just as the bandit Giuliano was to do after the Second World War. One day Peppa tells her mother that she cannot marry her fiancé because she loves Gramigna. Gratified by this misfortune, the neighbors say that Gramigna has been visiting Peppa secretly at night. In fact Peppa has never seen him, but is passionately in love with the idea of

Gramigna. "That is a man," she says. For a time her mother keeps her locked up, a poor man's Persephone, behind the closed shutters of their small house. But Peppa manages to escape and join Gramigna just as the police are catching up with him. When, a few months later, Gramigna is captured, Peppa is pregnant. Years later she is still interested in nothing but the prison where she imagines her lover is held. Actually, he has long since been transferred to the mainland. Because the police have proved stronger than her idol, Peppa feels a kind of twisted admiration for them, and spends the rest of her life running errands and helping out at the prison, until she herself becomes an institution there, though hardly anyone any longer remembers why.

From this material Visconti could have made a magnificent film, both realistic and operatic. But the project was banned by the Minister of Popular Culture, Alessandro Pavolini, who said he wanted to hear "no more about bandits!" This was the first but not the last of Visconti's projects to be wrecked by fools. Only then, while considering other possibilities—Melville's *Billy Budd* and George Bernard Shaw's novel *Cashel Byron's Profession* among them—did Visconti think of the script Renoir had passed on to him, the French scenario of James Cain's novel *The Postman Always Rings Twice*. Because Cain was American, known in Italy for his tough crime stories, Visconti hoped the censors would not see the subversive possibilities. Using only the anecdotal aspects of the French script as a basis, Visconti, Mario Alicata, Giuseppe de Santis, Antonio Pietrangeli, and Gianni Puccini wrote the entirely Italian story of *Ossessione*. The result of this sea change was something rich and utterly strange to contemporary Italian cinema. Gino, a young truck driver in the Po valley, stops by a cheap eating place and encounters Giovanna, who runs it with her husband. Immediately attracted to each other, they decide to run away together. But the hardships of Giovanna's early life have scared her, so at the last minute, she is afraid to quit the security provided by her gross, facetious, pathetic husband. Gino and Giovanna part, their meeting having resembled a collision rather than a love affair. Yet when, later, they meet by chance, at a local fairground, their attraction for each other is as violent as ever. They decide to kill the husband in a faked automobile accident. After the murder, Gino's nomadic instincts reassert themselves. He is haunted by the murdered man and by horror of Giovanna's delight on finding insurance money is due to her. An additional character, invented by Visconti, is perhaps the most interesting one: the Spaniard, a traveling showman whose friendship offers Gino an alternative to the morass into which passion is driving him. Passion wins, however, and the film ends with Giovanna dead and Gino in prison.

From the first, Visconti reveled in directing actors. Although quick-witted, impatient, autocratic, he could be infinitely patient and considerate with those in no position to answer back. His mannerliness revealed one of the positive aspects of aristocracy often underestimated by egalitarians. Alain Delon once said that Visconti treated actors as he treated race horses—with devotion, patience, and skill, respecting their nerves and delighting in their victories for their sake. Visconti himself said, "It is sometimes painful to locate the knot in a personality deformed by professional work, but it is always worth doing, because basically *a human being can always be liberated and re-educated.*" For *Ossessione* he had wanted Anna Magnani, but when the time came she was pregnant. So he engaged Clara Calamai, and drew a magnificently feral performance from this girl who had until then been considered a conventional actress. She was the first of an army of actors who, over the next thirty-four years, were to perform under Visconti's direction as never before—and, far from being tied to his directives as to a Svengali, would use what he taught them about themselves to build careers for which he provided the impetus.

Visconti's first film audiences were as impressed by the setting as by the acting of *Ossessione*. To many in the audience the Chicago of Al Capone's gangsters, as shown in *Scarface,* was more familiar than the vast valley of the river Po, scene of so many invasions, battles, floods. After white telephones, white pianos, synthetic merriment among characters for whom taxes held no dread and inflation no horrors, it was extraordinary to see a screen taken over by provincial Italy. And every now and again characters, emotions, taverns, fairgrounds, the sumptuous and the sleazy, destiny and desolation, seemed about to be swallowed up by the sandy lowlands of the plain, which was itself threatened by asphalt tentacles.

The sight of this gaunt landscape, remote from the tourist's picture-postcard Italy—yet not completely cut off from it, since Visconti's regard for truth always made him give as much space to the dome of St. Peter's as to a gasometer—infuriated not only Fascists, but all of the much more numerous that's-not-my-idea-of-St.-Francis school of what is oddly called "thought." When Vittorio Mussolini cried out, at the first public showing of *Ossessione,* "This is not Italy!" he was raising the flag not of Fascism but of idiocy. The Fascists took up the cry, saying of *Ossessione* in wartime what many Christian Democrats would say in peacetime of Vittorio de Sica's beautiful *Bicycle Thief:* "One should wash one's dirty linen in private." The year *Ossessione* was released, objections to it were all the more aggressive because the film's terrifying, but not terrified, view of private life corresponded with what was going on in public. *Ossessione* was started in June 1942, six months after the Japanese attacked Pearl Harbor, and the very year when the Nazis worked out a "final solution" to the "Hebrew problem" and built the first gas chambers. Visconti and his collaborators were constantly spied upon, and in December 1942 Mario Alicata was arrested and imprisoned for anti-Fascism.

Now a cinema classic, *Ossessione* caused Visconti mainly trouble at first. Inevitably, it upset the censors, and brought accusations of "degeneracy" from Gaetano Polverelli, a minister whom Mussolini himself considered a fool, although he made him minister of communications in the short and ill-fated republic established at Salò. At Salsomaggiore, a watering place near Parma, a bishop was requested to bless the cinema after it had been sullied by *Ossessione,* and it provoked violent scenes in Bologna, where Toscanini had been molested by Fascists a decade earlier. Finally, when the Allies landed in Italy and the Germans took up stations on the Gothic Line, the Fascists burned the film. That would have been the end of *Ossessione* had Visconti not possessed a dupe negative. (A dupe negative is a copy of the original negative made as a protection against damage and always inferior to the original in photographic quality.) Seldom has a gifted man with, apparently, every advantage, been so malignantly obstructed in his work. But by the time *Ossessione* was burned, Visconti had turned from artistic to physical resistance and was living what he later described as the most interesting period of his life. As Togliatti, the Italian Communist leader, said of his own service in the First World War, "It was not a parenthesis but an experience."

As a member of the clandestine Committee to Help Persecuted Anti-Fascists, which included the painter Renato Guttuso and Prince Doria, Visconti used his house as a hiding place for fugitives. For a while he was with the GAP (Groups for Partisan Action) in the Abruzzi. This wild mountainous region beside the Adriatic includes the nearly ten thousand-foot-high Gran Sasso, to which Mussolini was taken as a prisoner on August 28, 1943, only to be rescued by German fliers on September 12. Visconti's commitments took him to forests inhabited by chamois, brown bears, and birds of prey, and to plateaus over three thousand feet high with an archaic population of shepherds whose silhouettes would suddenly appear against the skyline, tending their gray cows and black sheep. There he made friends, with one peasant family in particular, who continued to cherish him, as he did them, for the rest of his life. In his wartime diary he noted that he was glad to have been able to make his decision "with serenity" and succeeded in "conquering the impatience, enthusiasms, romantic impulses and sentimentality" of which he was only too well aware in his character.

In October 1943, while in the Abruzzi with his sister Uberta and two friends, Visconti decided to try to cross the lines and join the Allied armies. In his wartime diary he wrote that at this point he "regretted nothing but having to leave Uberta" but hoped to rejoin her soon. In some respects this beloved younger sister seems to have represented their mother, whom she so much resembles, in his life. His journey south was rough going and, in December, before reaching the dividing line, he met a group of Allied soldiers escaping from behind enemy lines. He promptly changed his plans, deciding to help, hide, and feed these men, with whom he witnessed the bombing of the famous Benedictine abbey of Monte Cassino. Later he was awarded official "thanks and gratitude" from both American General Joseph T. McNarney, deputy commander of the Mediterranean Theater of Operations, and Field Marshal Alexander, supreme commander of the Allied forces in the Mediterranean, for having helped Allied soldiers, sailors, and airmen to "escape capture and rejoin their units."

This period may well have been even more important to Visconti's future work than was his time with Renoir in Paris. His inbred courage and his responsiveness to people far outside his own class were exercised to the utmost in a world that, though hard, was free from mediocrity. The great Swedish director Ingmar Bergman has several times written tormentedly of his doubts about how he would have behaved had his country been occupied. This was something that Visconti did not have to worry about. He proved as brave as his parents could have wished.

In February 1944, Visconti returned to Rome under the assumed name of Alfredo Guidi, and hid partisans in the beautiful Via Salaria villa he had inherited from his father. A month later, an appalling tragedy put a stop to this. First, early in March, three German SS officers burst into the villa and arrested Paolo Ricci, a partisan who had fought in the Spanish war. Then, on March 23, an explosion was heard all over Rome. It came from the Via Rasella, a small street midway between the Barberini Palace and the Trevi Fountain, alongside the Quirinal, at that time still the royal palace. A time bomb, hidden on a trash wagon, had exploded as a detachment of German SS marched up the street. It killed thirty-two of them and wounded more. Chaos followed. The Germans fired in every direction. Everyone who lived in the street, and anyone unlucky enough to be passing by, was arrested. They were then thrust into the courtyard of the Barberini Palace, one of the glories of baroque Rome, where, back in the seventeenth-century, the young Santacroces, Massimos, and Barberinis had cavorted on horses decked out in red and blue, embroidered with gold and silver, carrying flaming torches in honor of Queen Christina of Sweden. The hostages were kept in the Barberini courtyard for hours, hands in the air, German guns pointed at them.

When Hitler heard the news he said the Italians must be taught "a lesson of terror." To this end he told General Alfred Jodl to order fifty Italians shot for every dead SS man. Jodl passed this on to Field Marshal Albert Kesselring. On his own initiative, Kesselring reduced the number from fifty to ten Italians per SS man. Despite the zeal with which the SS had made on-the-spot arrests, they did not have enough prisoners, and to pick people off other streets might, since Italy had been an ally, lead to "further unpleasantness." Kesselring passed the modified order on to General Maeltzer, who was German military governor of Rome at the time, and beside himself with rage. At this stage, the only person who could have countermanded the order was Colonel Dollmann, who, as highest-ranking SS officer in Rome, had the right to veto death sentences.

In the end the choice of victims was arbitrary. To raise the total to three hundred and twenty, a selection of "undesirable elements" from the Regina Coeli (Queen of Heaven) and Via Tasso prisons was added to those already arrested merely because they happened to be in or near the Via Rasella. The new Chief of Police, Pietro Caruso, recently sent to Rome to replace a "too humane" predecessor, picked out fifty-five instead of the forty extra prisoners requested. These included Colonel Montezemolo, an officer distinguished for bravery, who had been Visconti's instructor at Pinerolo Cavalry School; Father Pietro Pappagallo, of Santa Maria Maggiore, a priest distinguished for goodness; Count Giuseppe Celani, a patriot who had already endured a month of torture; and a partisan, Paolo Mocci, whose body Visconti later had to identify.

Next morning the prisoners were lined up in the courtyard of Regina Coeli, their arms tied behind them—except for those whose paralyzed arms would not bend back. Those unable to walk were carried into covered trucks that drove them to some disused quarries just outside Rome. These were the Fosse Ardeatine, the Ardeatine Caves, near the catacombs and the Domine, Quo Vadis? chapel, where, according to tradition, Christ appeared to St. Peter as the latter was fleeing Nero's persecutions of the Christians. "Lord, whither goest thou?" asked the amazed St. Peter. "To Rome to be crucified a second time," said Christ, and vanished. Whereupon St. Peter returned to Rome and martyrdom.

While the trucks were on their way to the Ardeatine Caves, two hundred German SS carried out orders to prepare a massacre. As soon as the hostages arrived, they were ordered into the caves, and were shot one by one as they reached the threshold. The last hostages had to clamber to their deaths over mounds of still-breathing bodies. Herbert Kappler, the SS officer in charge of the massacre, discovered too late that three hundred and thirty-five people had been shot instead of the requisite three hundred and twenty. By omitting to number his list of prisoners Pietro Caruso had upset the account.

At dawn on March 25 the Germans blocked the entrance to the caves by exploding mines. They did not even bother to post guards, so sure were they that the bodies would never be discovered. A few days later, however, a young man, Gallarelli, whose father was among the victims, dug his way into the caves with his hands and a flashlight. The stench was as abominable as the news Gallarelli took back to Rome.

With renewed frenzy, the Germans began arresting people right and left. Among them was Visconti, arrested on April 15 at a friend's house. He had a revolver on him, and so was taken for interrogation by Pietro Koch at the Pensione Jaccarino. People all over Rome shuddered at the thought of what went on at the Pensione Jaccarino in those days. In this case, Koch's first reaction was gratified excitement at having a man like Visconti in his power. This soon yielded to hysterical rage at what Koch called Visconti's "unsatisfactory attitude." Finally he condemned Visconti to be shot. Visconti was kept in a cupboardlike cell for nine days and nights, during which time Koch tried in vain to get names from him. Furiously determined not to let it stop at that, Koch then decided to hand Visconti over to the Germans.

Meanwhile, Uberta and her sister-in-law, Baroness Avanzo, made frantic efforts to help him, and succeeded just in time in getting him transferred to San Gregorio Prison. Their old housekeeper, Maria Cerutti, managed to visit him there, and his smuggled notes to her—"I am fine. But want news of Donna Uberta and all of you. . . . I need a bottle of ink, a pen and blotting paper. . . . Is it possible to have a spray of Flit? . . . and a bottle of Cognac? The plum cake was wonderful. Could you produce an encore?"—take us incongruously back to his schooldays on Lake Como. All would have been up with Visconti had the Allies not been nearing Rome. Confusion was growing inside as well as outside prisons. The Germans began pouring out of Rome and northward by the Via Flaminia. Their flight was punctuated by the last cruelties of fear, the last unnecessary shots, the last useless deaths. At this point some prison wardens connived at Visconti's escape, which he made on June 4.

At nine o'clock that evening, the American Fifth Army entered Rome.

The high command was installed in the Grand Hotel, on the Via Veneto. The bell of the Capitol began to ring. Rome was liberated. This, Uberta said, was one of the peak moments of Visconti's life. Cesare Zavattini remembers standing next day at the window of the Catholic Cinema center, and suddenly seeing Visconti, "radiant with solidarity," hand in hand with strangers in a vast chain of people dancing jubilantly around St. Peter's Square. Visconti's home on the Via Salaria was soon full of partisans, no longer in hiding, Allied soldiers, friends, relatives, and marvelous dreams of the future. As Carlo Levi said later, "Like all miracles, this active and creative liberty did not last long, but it was true, one could touch it with one's hands and see it written on men's faces." In this joyous frame of mind, Visconti returned to work—in the direction pointed out to him by the music-lesson timetables pinned to his bedroom door by his mother in the days when life and art were new.

Eight

Italian soldiers began returning to wrecked home towns and decimated families. With them came tales of savagery. Those who staggered back from the Russian snows, where sixty thousand Italians perished, had in many cases been treated even worse by their German allies than by their Russian enemies. Ghastliest of all looked the survivors from the Nazi concentration camps. Of the two thousand ninety-one Jews taken from Rome, only two hundred and one came back. Among friends of the Viscontis who did not return was the King's daughter, Princess Mafalda. She died in Buchenwald concentration camp, assisted when dying by the kindness of some prostitutes who were her fellow prisoners. Princess Mafalda was four years older than Luchino and, since the Viscontis were close friends of the royal family, she and he had known each other nearly all their lives.

It was a new world, a world of rickety prefabricated houses, mean reparations amid mighty ruins, a mass-produced future teetering among the myths of the past. Five centuries earlier, the Italian Renaissance had led Western Europe in celebrating the individual: what a piece of work, so noble in reason, so infinite in faculty, in form and movement how express and admirable. Now the century of the common man, as Henry Wallace had called it in 1942, needed fresh art forms to illuminate the individual's new relationship with society.

Visconti resumed work by collaborating with three Resistance friends and colleagues in writing *Pensione Oltremare*, a scenario about a man who acquires political consciousness through contact with his fellow prisoners and is killed at the Ardeatine Caves. Into this went some of Visconti's own experiences at the Pensione Jaccarino. For lack of backers, this remained unfilmed, but the text was published fifteen years later by *Cinema and Resistance*. Next Visconti collaborated with Michelangelo Antonioni, Antonio Pietrangeli, and Vasco Pratolini in a scenario about the Resistance. But nothing more came of this either, owing to lack of money and equipment in the war-torn cinema world. Nor did the scenario Visconti, Antonioni, and Guido Piovene wrote about the Countess Tarnowska reach the screen. Visconti was fascinated by this enigmatic and beautiful woman who had killed her husband at the beginning of this century, was the heroine-villainess of a dramatic trial in Venice, bewitched her jailers, and survived to remarry and end her life in an aura of respectability in England.

Leaving the cinema for the time being, Visconti turned to the theater, and in January 1945 produced Jean Cocteau's *Les Parents terribles*, a play that acted like a bombshell on Roman audiences, conditioned by years of Fascism's intellectually soporific official art. In casting *Les Parents terribles,* Visconti discovered Rina Morelli, who was to become one of Italy's greatest actresses. A Neapolitan two years younger than himself, she came of an illustrious theater family, had acted from child-hood with her father, and played her first leading part, at sixteen, in Molnar's *Liliom.* Filmgoers may remember her in later years as Laura, the Countess Serpieri's maid, in *Senso,* as the Princess di Salina in *Il Gattopardo,* and as Tullio's mother in Visconti's last film, *L'innocente.* Back in 1945, she was slender, large-eyed, shy as the young Audrey Hepburn, and Visconti changed her life. Not only did he reveal the extent of her talent, but also, with her and the fine actor Paolo Stoppa, who was to be her companion for over thirty years, Visconti formed a theatrical company to which he gave security as well as prestige. In Visconti's theater, thanks to his own disposition and Toscanini's example, the prompter was abolished, the curtain went up punctually, and, an even greater innovation, the actors had proper time and pay for rehearsals. Visconti's friendship with Morelli and Stoppa lasted until his death.

Two months later, Visconti directed Hemingway's play *Fifth Column,* translated by Suso Cecchi D'Amico, the brilliant and attractive daughter of the writer Emilio Cecchi. This first piece of shared work led to a life-long collaboration and friendship. (Thirty years later Visconti told me that Suso knew as much about his work, if not more, than he did himself.) The scenery for *Fifth Column* was designed by the Sicilian painter Renato Guttuso, who during the war had painted his impressive "Gott mit uns" as a testimony to the Resistance. Where *Les Parents terribles* created a moral scandal, *Fifth Column* created a political one, since it showed the Spanish war from the viewpoint of what, for Italians, had officially been the enemy side, and called for the "Internationale" to be sung on the stage. Visconti followed this with Alfred de Musset's exquisite *Le Chandelier*.

In June, a month after the end of the war in Europe, a U.S. psychological-warfare group asked Visconti to film the trials and executions of war criminals Pietro Koch and Pietro Caruso. In doing this Visconti showed an icy detachment that would have been phenomenal even had he not been in Koch's hands himself so short a while ago. But his own brush with death had in fact impressed him far less than had the Ardeatine Caves massacre, which was to remain for many people as symbolic of the vileness of war as Lidice and Oradour. Visconti's record became part of *Giorni di gloria* (*Days of Glory*), a collective documentary about the Resistance and liberation edited by Mario Serandrei. Recently revived in Rome as part of a tribute to Visconti, this film still conveys with extraordinary force the period's atmosphere of heroism and horror, asceticism and rhetoric.

Koch's execution took place on the afternoon of June 4, 1945, at the Forte Bravetta shooting range. The police had given tickets of admission to about thirty journalists and photographers. They stood around in the hot Roman sunshine, waiting to do their work. All had witnessed more harrowing scenes than the quick death of a young man who, when he was a power in Rome, had enjoyed prolonged torturing for its own sake. Soon after two o'clock the police van was heard. It drew up alongside a wooden chair by a slope where, ordinarily, life-size cardboard figures were set up for target practice. Koch got down. He was wearing handcuffs, but managed to look neat. He had always been a natty dresser, fond of uniforms. The handcuffs were removed and the death sentence read aloud. Koch showed no emotion. A priest came forward and spoke to him. Koch bent his knee and received absolution. He was told to sit astride the wooden chair. Two men came forward with a rope. There was some fumbling as he held out his hand. Only belatedly understanding what he meant, the two shook Koch's hand before tying him to the chair. His head sank between his round shoulders. The firing squad marched into position. An officer walked to the right-hand side of the firing squad. The two men who were tying Koch to the chair finished their task and moved away. The officer raised his sword. There was a burst of firing. A wooden coffin was ready, lined with sawdust. The execution was over. No grief, no pity, no vindictiveness was shown. It was as if a piece of necessary surgery had been performed. All this is apparent in the documentary. There are many strange scenes in Visconti's life, but none stranger than this picture of him standing in the Roman sunshine filming the execution of his own would-be executioner—not from revenge but in order to keep the record straight. Two months later the first atomic bomb fell, on Hiroshima; 130,000 people were killed, injured, or were later listed as missing. Individual executions began to seem old-fashioned.

That autumn Visconti produced and designed the scenery for three plays: Jean Cocteau's *La Machine à écrire*, with Vittorio Gassman, explosively gifted and nobly handsome, Jean Anouilh's *Antigone*—in which Rina Morelli gave a profoundly tragic performance, entirely free from the irritating quality that this text can elicit—and Jean-Paul Sartre's *Huis clos*. In all his scene and costume designing, Visconti showed a Renaissance level of accomplishment that was to make him into a great Italian painter who, because his maturity coincided with the mid-twentieth century, used the screen as a canvas.

After *Huis clos* Visconti was asked by Elio Vittorini to direct a film of the latter's novel about the partisans, *Uomoni e No*. This offer exhilarated Visconti, but Vittorini's project fell through, and Visconti's next production was Marcel Achard's play *Adamo*. This had a homosexual theme, though treated with Achard's usual delicacy, tact, and wit, and it was subsequently banned by local authorities in Milan and Venice. This interdiction was greeted in the theater world with mockery as well as anger, since Machiavelli's masterpiece *La mandragola* had been forbidden not long ago and, more recently, the censor had tried to ban one of Gorki's plays. Visconti then produced *Tobacco Road*, which outraged all those unaccustomed to the rumbustious quality of American indignation at social inequities. With seven productions, all of which justified the excitement they aroused, Visconti had made this a trumpeter year in the postwar theater.

Appropriately—though he could not have known this at the time—Visconti began 1946, the year that was to see the fall of the Italian monarchy, with a production of Beaumarchais's revolutionary *Le Mariage de Figaro*, of which Louis XVI had said, wisely from his viewpoint, that it must never be performed. It had been forbidden under Fascism, and this was its first performance in Italy for twenty years. To play Figaro, Visconti chose Vittorio de Sica, enchanting both as a performer and as a man. Then came Dostoevsky's *Crime and Punishment*, in which the future film director Franco Zeffirelli, then only twenty-three years old, played Dimitri, Tennessee Williams's *The Glass Menagerie* with Rina Morelli and Paolo Stoppa, and Jean Anouilh's elegiac *Eurydice*, also with Morelli. Today, a quarter of a century later, with the time machine totally altered, with styles, fashions, and fads constantly changing, and television constantly filling people's minds with tidbits ranging from

Tibet to Timbuktu, it is difficult for a new generation to imagine what a revitalizing effect these foreign plays had on a country only just emerging from the intellectual quarantine of war. It was rather, said Visconti, "like the effect on schoolchildren of the blackboard's being unexpectedly wiped clean—and having something totally unfamiliar written on it."

A service for the dead includes the sentence "The appearance of this world is altered" by the disappearance of "the dear and faithful dead," and so indeed it had been for Visconti by his mother's death, the war, his father's and brother's deaths, his own narrow escape from death. Now the liberation had restored meaning to the word *future*. Work in the theater earned Visconti artistic independence and stature, and with this he returned to the film world.

For the first time, since the world is the world, light, directed by human ingenuity, captures the ghosts of the living.

Marguerite Yourcenar, *Archives du Nord*

Ladies and gentlemen, such small morality as has helped me live has been distilled from images. The cinema has given me precious help. It is in films that I have seen justice triumph and iniquity defeated, the good rewarded and widows protected; but this would have been less impressive had films not also enabled me to see life assume a formal orderliness, strictly ruled by the laws of vision. It is therefore on the screen (and in paintings) that real life takes place, as actions and reactions reveal themselves through lights and shadows, philosophy is illuminated by the rules of artistic composition, and everything unfolds as in a prearranged dream.

Ennio Flaiano, "Autobiografia del Blu di Prussia"

Artistic growth is more than anything else a refining of the sense of truthfulness.

Willa Cather

Nine

By 1947, Visconti was living in one of the many transformation scenes that formed part of the world upheaval begun in 1914. The Italian royal family, figures who had seemed to him in his childhood as permanent as those of mythology, was sent into exile by a majority of 6 to 5 votes. Italy became a republic. The peace treaty was drawn up. It roused scant exhilaration, since, like most peace treaties, it was made largely by, for, and against bereaved people with ruined health, hopes, homes, or incomes. Yet it was peace of a sort and therefore better than war. People going to work in the morning could reasonably expect to return, physically intact, in the evening, to homes still standing, unlooted. Plans could be made with some hope of their accomplishment.

Visconti's own plan at this stage was to make a film from Verga's novel *I Malavoglia (The House by the Medlar Tree)*. He was haunted by a visit he had made to Sicily, several years earlier, and described in an article, "Traditions and Inventions," published in *Stile italiano nel cinema*, with illustrations by the Sicilian painter Renato Guttuso. On that occasion, while visiting Verga's birthplace, Catania, he fell in love all over again with the Sicilian writer's work. Catania, a spectacular port on the Ionian Sea, with the dramatic backdrop of Mt. Etna behind it, offers an architectural anthology of Mediterranean history. It has a beautiful Greek theater, a grim Hohenstaufen castle, an operatic Benedictine monastery, a wealth of eighteenth-century baroque palaces and churches, and gardens commemorating the nineteenth-century composer Bellini, a native son. In addition, it is on the Homer-haunted "giants' coast." Barely sixty miles to the north is the Strait of Messina, formerly guarded by the monster Scylla and the whirlpool Charybdis, past which Ulysses sailed three thousand years ago on his way home to Ithaca after the fall of Troy. Even nearer at hand is the fishing port of Aci Trezza, where

I Malavoglia is set. This, too, is guarded by weirdly shaped rocks, known as "the Cyclops' reef." The Cyclops were one-eyed giants who forged thunderbolts for Zeus, and the rocks at Aci Trezza are supposed to have been hurled into the sea by the Cyclops Polyphemus after Ulysses blinded him.

When Visconti saw Aci Trezza for the first time, it had changed little since Verga's day, and as he walked among the austere white houses, the black-clad women, the fishermen mending their nets to the sound of the sea, he felt grateful to Verga for having made this "primitive and gigantic world with its violent epic qualities" accessible to "a northerner raised on the limpid and rigorous style of Manzoni." This first impression had kept its hold on Visconti's imagination all through the war. By 1947, too, there were new reasons for taking an interest in Sicily.

In that year, Sicily was in the forefront of the news. There is a wounding division between northern and southern Italy, and just as Sicily had obtained few advantages from Fascism, so it received little from the Resistance, which has been called "the third of Italy's appointments with democracy" and was essentially a northern movement. Seldom can an island have been so multifariously invaded as Sicily—nameless prehistoric peoples, followed by Elymi, Sicani, Siculi, Phoenicians, Greeks, Carthaginians, Romans, Vandals, Goths, Byzantines, Saracens, Arabs, Normans, Spaniards, and so on until Garibaldi partially broke the spell. The Second World War brought Sicily new invaders, the Americans, the British, and their allies this time. No sooner had these disembarked than they were supported by the separatist movement and the Mafia, the far-ranging criminal organization that had started as a form of resistance against medieval foreign barons. As a result, postwar Sicily was chaotic. By August 1947, Sicilian peasants, hungry for the land they had been promised, were clashing violently with the police: more deaths, more mourning, more infectious desires for revenge. This chaos was made worse by the activities of a young Sicilian bandit.

Pavolini, the Fascist Minister of Popular Culture who had censored Visconti's first Verga scenario because he wanted to hear no more about bandits, had been shot in 1945, but Sicily's latest bandit, Salvatore Giuliano, was very much alive. In 1947, he was, indeed, an object of worship to many Sicilians, and even to Italians on the mainland, where children added to their usual prayers a request that Giuliano be not captured, and newspaper kiosks sold quantities of cheap booklets with titles such as *The Intimate Life of Giuliano* or *The King of Montelepre*. Giuliano's public story had begun in 1943, when he was a handsome, serious-minded peasant boy, devoted to his family, especially his mother. Because it was impossible just then to survive without the black market,

Giuliano and his brother Giuseppe smuggled grain, on their backs, since they had neither horses nor mules. One day they were halted by *carabinieri* who patrolled the boundaries between provinces. Giuliano's two sacks of grain were confiscated, and he was threatened with a bastinado unless he revealed where the grain came from. But he noticed that, alongside, other *carabinieri* were peaceably accepting bribes from another smuggler. Outraged, Giuliano made a run for it: He was fired at and wounded. He fired back and, by fluke rather than intention, killed a *carabiniere*, which made an outlaw of him. As an outlaw Giuliano soon gained an ascendency over his compatriots that was, in many respects, in the same imaginative class as that of Charlemagne, Roland, Oliver, and the paladins who dominate Sicilian marionette shows and turn the painted Sicilian wine carts into ambulatory legends. By the time he was twenty-five, Giuliano could write to President Truman as one potentate to another:

In 1944 the walls of all the most important parts of Sicily, Palermo included, were covered with pictures showing a man (myself) cutting the chain that keeps Sicily bound to Italy, while another man in America holds fast to another chain that is tied to Sicily. . . . Because of a lost war we find ourselves in a hopeless state, and will easily fall a prey to foreigners—especially the Russians who long to appear in the Mediterranean Sea. . . . In 87 years of National Unity we have been impoverished and treated as a small colony. . . . For these reasons we wish to be joined to the United States of America. . . .

Giuliano's love for America was sincere. Though born in Sicily, he had been conceived in America and heard much of its wonders from his parents. He was also a monarchist, like so many southerners, the majority of whom had voted in favor of the royal family. Unfortunately, the parties and associations manipulating Giuliano for their own purpose now gave a macabre twist to his story. This Robin Hood became a killer of his own people. After the extreme left won thirty percent of the April 1947 votes for the Sicilian regional parliament, the Communists in Giuliano's locality planned to hold their May Day celebrations at a mountain pass called Portella della Ginestra. This spot was chosen as central for villages on either side of it. Giuliano determined—or was persuaded—to try to stop the festivities and execute the popular Communist senator Li Causi. His men were to appear, shoot over the crowd's heads, then keep people quiet by covering them with machine guns. Something went horribly wrong, however. No sooner had the words "Fellow workers, we have come here to celebrate" been pronounced, than the dozen men who had turned up to support Giuliano (their names are still unknown) fired directly *into* the crowd, killing eight and wounding thirty-three, many of them women and children. They also killed nine horses, donkeys, and mules.

The Portella della Ginestra massacres horrified Visconti both in themselves and for what they revealed about political intrigue. War had not deadened his sensibilities, nor had the time yet come when television would offer violence as a condiment for every meal. He had not been able to make a full-length film about the Ardeatine Caves, but he wanted to include the Portella della Ginestra massacres in his Verga film, *La terra trema* (*The Earth Quakes*). This proved financially impossible, but he was full of praise for the film Francesco Rosi made of it thirteen years later.

André Malraux was the first person to write that the cinema is "also an industry" and the costs of this industry kept rising. Visconti had already spent much of his patrimony on his first film, *Ossessione,* and on his first stage productions. Apocryphal stories were told of the maniacal attention to detail developed in him by the clash between his own disposition and the sloppiness of Italian theater habits at this period. For example, on the night of the dress rehearsal of Anouilh's *Eurydice,* the actors are said to have waited and waited, teetering with exhaustion, for the arrival of the genuine French railroad guard's whistle without which, so the story goes, Visconti would not permit his stage train to leave for its imaginary destination. He certainly never waited till the sales were on to select his materials—but neither did he ever break a promise about costs or deadlines. In order to do as you please in the cinema, however, a personal fortune does not suffice. It requires a personal empire on Onassis, Hearst, or Getty lines.

By November 1947, Visconti was able to set out for Sicily with his team. He had provided some of the money himself and added to this a contract with Guarini Italia films. This contract broke down when he was only a quarter of the way through the picture, but he found a backer in Salvo d'Angelo, an architect and producer for Universalia films, a firm with strong Roman Catholic connections. The Italian Communist party also made a contribution. For this Visconti had to thank a D'Artagnonlike young art critic, poet, and future deputy, Antonello Trombadori and Palmiro Togliatti, then head of the Italian Communist party. Togliatti had returned from exile in 1944 and immediately urged greater independence of Russia, an attitude to be intermittently fashionable later with other Communist parties, but one held from the start by the Italian party, which has always had leaders with a sense of individual as well as collective life. Premier Alcide de Gasperi, founder of the Christian Democratic party, wrote Togliatti that he appreciated the latter's respect for the religion of the majority of Italians, and trusted that Togliatti's way of thinking would preserve the Italians from the "negative experiments and errors of the Russian system."

Visconti had great affection for Togliatti and thought him "a true intellectual, something rare in politics. So many politicians have nothing to say." Togliatti attended all Visconti's first nights and discussed artistic details with him with the same frankness he was later to show when admitting Visconti's condemnation of Russia's invasion of Hungary. Togliatti's sense of artistic values led him to say, "Often, an artist following an ideological current that some of us believe to be mistaken produces an authentic masterpiece." And later, when a Communist harshly criticized De Santis's film *Bitter Rice,* Togliatti wrote to the critic, a young man he esteemed: "I myself have not seen the film so cannot hold an aesthetic opinion, but I would like to ask you—with so many indecent and horrible films now appearing, should we go out of our way to attack our fellow Communists? Intellectuals, you see, are more often fellow travelers than militants, and if we attack them we only drive them away. You say the film is 'sham populism' . . . it seems to me that, all things considered, a film about the workers in the rice fields is preferable to the foolish films about the bourgeoisie that monopolize our screens. Criticism should not be head-on and incontrovertible." This was not Kremlin language. Togliatti understood as well as Malraux did "what a skein of dreams and discoveries are required to create a single Puss-in-Boots."

For *La terra trema* Visconti kept the expenses minimal. He not only wrote the script himself, but also, with conductor Willy Ferrero, composed the music from traditional Sicilian airs. The film was shot entirely on location, with a team of about eighteen people doing what would now require sixty or seventy, according to Francesco Rosi, who was then twenty-five and one of Visconti's two assistants, the other being Franco Zeffirelli. All the characters in *La terra trema* were acted by the people of Aci Trezza themselves: fishermen, local women, bricklayers, wholesale dealers.

"It would have been impossible," said Visconti, "to obtain from even the finest actors the truthfulness and simplicity of Sicilian fishermen—but it was perfectly possible to get Sicilian fishermen to express their own genuine feelings in their own surroundings and circumstances. . . . One often hears talk of 'actors picked up off the street.' This seems to me a contradiction in terms. It would be very difficult to transform fishermen into professional actors even after years of work. . . . They are not interpreters but real people expressing their real feelings. It is impossible to make a Neo-Realist film with previously written dialogue—nor could one make a Neo-Realist film with actors for the Burgtheater [Vienna's state theater, founded by Maria Theresa in 1741]. But it is useless to generalize, because one immediately thinks of exceptions, such as that *Rome, Open City* was acted by Anna Magnani. So it is very dangerous to set up rules. . . ."

Visconti's way of directing the fishermen was to describe a scene to them and compose the dialogue then and there from their spontaneous reactions. For example, to one he said, "You've lost your boat. You're destitute. You don't know what to do. But you're young. You want to try some other place—but your brother wants to hold you back. Tell him why you want to leave." Immediately, the fisherman said that he wanted to see the city of Naples, which to the people of Aci Trezza, in those days, seemed as remote as the moon. "But why do you want to leave here?" insisted Visconti. "Because here we are like animals. They give us nothing. I want to leave right away and see the world." When Visconti turned to the other fisherman, who was playing the brother who wanted the would-be emigrant to stay home, he found this young man so carried away by the story, as if it were indeed his own brother planning to leave for faraway Naples, that his eyes filled with tears as he burst out with "If you go farther than the Faraglioni [two local rocks] the storm will carry you away." The dialogue was entirely in Sicilian dialect, since, as Visconti said, "Italian is not the language of the poor in Sicily." He found their speech beautiful and "near to Greek."

Francesco Rosi, himself now one of Italy's finest directors, says the seven months he spent at Aci Trezza as Visconti's assistant proved "an ideal school of film making" that "revealed his true vocation" to him. At twenty-five, Rosi already had four years' varied theater experience behind him, but *La terra trema* was his first cinema engagement. He came to it as an enthusiastic frequenter of the lustrous Circolo Romano del Cinema, where postwar Italian films could be seen in all their strength and originality. There young Rosi had admired the vitality and comradeship that linked Rossellini, Visconti, De Sica, Antonioni, De Santis, Sergio Amidei, Zavattini, Suso Cecchi D'Amico, and Fellini—the last a slim young man in his twenties, still assistant to Rossellini.

Although *La terra trema* was only Visconti's second full-length film, he already possessed magnetic authority, and could obtain from peasants and fishermen both artistic discipline and a sense of personal responsibility in spheres totally unfamiliar to them. With professionals, he was as intransigent as young Toscanini had been at La Scala. Since a film set often resembles the Mad Hatter's tea party, it is easy for anyone working there to find in the surface confusion an alibi for personal negligence, but, where work was concerned, Visconti neither proffered nor accepted alibis. Rosi thought that Visconti's explosive rages were occasionally deliberate, used to force hidden talent out of people, just as an archeologist uses cutting instruments to excavate hidden treasure.

The central character in Verga's *I Malavoglia* is the obstinate patriarchal grandfather 'Ntoni, and the plot centers around 'Ntoni's Laocoönlike struggle, after his son is lost at sea, to help his grandchildren. In the end 'Ntoni is defeated by the elements, by conscription, by death, and, above all, by the Fates, who dominate Greek and Roman mythology. In the film Visconti adds to Verga's pity for the oppressed his own horror of injustice, and the dominant character is not the grandfather, caught up in old traditions like a fly in amber, but the grandson 'Ntoni, who confronts not only elements and Fates, but also the wholesale dealers who buy his fish cheaply and sell it for their own exorbitant profit. 'Ntoni decides to sell his own fish, and to this end mortgages the family house. All starts well, but a storm wrecks his boat, his cargo, and his hopes. Bailiffs seize the house. The grandfather dies. The younger brother emigrates north. To support the rest of the family 'Ntoni has to return to the exploiters' yoke.

Verga had planned *I Malavoglia* as the first of a series of novels to be grouped under the title "I vinti" (The Vanquished), but he managed to write only *Mastro don Gesualdo* (translated into English by D. H. Lawrence). Similarly, Visconti's *La terra trema* was planned as the first of a trilogy, the second film to be about workers in the Sicilian sulphur mines, the third about the land-starved peasants. But he was unable to find financial backing for the second and third Verga films. Visconti's characters differ from those of *I Malavoglia* in that they learn, agonizingly but positively, through the failure of individual efforts, how to cooperate for victory. Although almost vanquished by disaster, Visconti's young 'Ntoni can still say at the end: "One day, though, people will understand that I was right—they will realize that the things that have happened to me, the losses I have suffered, have a meaning for them, too. We must learn to help each other, to work together. It is only then that we shall be able to go forward."

Working conditions at Aci Trezza were almost as primitive cinematographically as socially and topographically. There was no walkie-talkie, so directions had to be shouted; no zoom lens, which now enables the effect of smoothly approaching or receding from a scene to be obtained without moving the camera; no dolly, the wheeled camera platform used for tracking shots. Visconti was never to make excessive use of the dolly;

in camera work, as in prose, he appreciated "the least possible adjectives, punctuation, and superlatives." In this instance Bruno Paccarella, a technician of genius, invented a wooden dolly that looked like the result of co-operation between Leonardo da Vinci and Lewis Carroll's White Knight, but functioned admirably. Much of the filming had to be done at night. They would work at sea or on the beach till dawn, then pause for coffee, served at the inn by one of the girls who acted in the film and moved unself-consciously from camera to coffeepot and back again. Visconti's own coffee, brewed in a Cona coffee maker from Paris, with three and a half ounces of coffee per cup, was considered positively dangerous by everyone else. Even young Rosi, proud to accept a cup, said that, "though a joy to the true coffee lover, it set the heart beating at an alarming rate." Nearly thirty years later, the aroma of "Luchino's terrible coffee" was to play a Proustian part in Rosi's memories of *La terra trema.*

Visconti became strongly attached to the people of Aci Trezza during the seven months he stayed there. In December 1947, he wrote to his friend and fellow director Antonioni, that he had spent Christmas with "my fishermen." He was particularly impressed by the nobility of their bearing, by the gaunt mixture of barbarity, beauty, and endurance that made them so different from the industrialized working class. He was also moved by the isolation of their lives. Against injustice, they had no one to whom to appeal. The government seemed to them infinitely farther away than the moon, and for practical purposes it well might have been. Law and order meant only a few ignorant policemen, themselves isolated by their uniforms and functions. There were no trade unions, and political parties were represented by five *qualunquisti*—members of the right-wing Common Man's party founded in 1946 by a fifty-four-year-old Neapolitan playwright and journalist, Guglielmo Giannini. The fishermen believed in God, as did Visconti himself, but they needed help now as well as for eternity. The depth of Visconti's feeling for them and their plight is evident from the way he handled their ancient landscape, so near to that of Greece and the wellsprings of our civilization, their ancient sounds—for many people the sea has the oldest sound of all—and, above all, the way he treated every single character, seizing the essential, with no patronage or paternalism, only pure artistry and fellow feeling.

Once the film was made, Visconti gave practical expression to his feelings by helping all of them find work—away from the sea, if they wanted to leave their actual conditions there, but not in the world of professional acting, where they would have been lost. Their feeling for him was expressed in a collective letter, signed by ten of them: "The 'Valastro family' of Aci Trezza feels it to be its duty to make public its thanks and gratitude to Director Luchino Visconti and all his collaborators who, through the film *The Earth Quakes*, will make our story known throughout Italy and the world. We are infinitely grateful for the experience, and for the future good that will result. Our 'family,' temporarily formed for the film, must now break up, but we shall remain united in our memories of the extraordinary adventure we shared."

La terra trema was not an immediate success. Part of the fashionable Venice Film Festival audience ferociously resented its social contestation, and although it won the second award, with the Golden Lion going to Laurence Olivier's screen *Hamlet,* Visconti felt that it was probably not the right moment for *La terra trema*. People might, he said, want to see it in ten years' time. Exactly ten years later, the critic Oreste del Buono was to write: "Only now have I understood what an immense gift Visconti offered to Italian culture with *La terra trema*. . . . It is not a question of beauty, but of greatness, of authentic greatness. . . . *La terra trema* and *Senso*—what twentieth-century novelist has given us more?" Today, some thirty years since the film was made, young audiences are astonished by its potency. Old newsreels display the skeletons in our international cupboards—consider, for example, poor Chamberlain and Daladier uttering hollow words at Munich under the hypnotic gaze of what Unity Mitford called "darling Hitler in his sweet macintosh"—but great films show us how living people experienced history.

Between completing *La terra trema* and showing it in public, Visconti, like several million other Italians, had a shock reminiscent of wartime violence. On the morning of July 14, 1948, there was a dull session at the Chamber of Deputies. Togliatti and a companion, Nilde Jotti, left at eleven-thirty. In the corridor they met the Republican Ugo La Malfa, who told them he was just off for Moscow. This was the period when Russia was outraged by Tito's "schism," so they exchanged friendly sarcasms as they made for the entrance hall. There a Sicilian, Antonio Pallante, suddenly fired three shots at Togliatti. The first merely grazed his head and crashed into an advertisement placard, but the second hit him in the nape of the neck, and the third in the back. As Togliatti fell on his knees, Jotti flung herself in front of him. Pallante had two shots left. He fired one, wide of the mark, then fled. The wounded man muttered conscientiously, "My briefcase."

Chaos followed: threat of a general strike, and a universal desire to know who had planned the assassination. A fellow prisoner broke into Pallante's prison cell, seized him by the collar and adjured him to name those who had ordered Togliatti's assassination. Pallante immediately, it is alleged, cited two highly placed Sicilians already involved in the bandit Giuliano's deeds. The prisoner who attacked Pallante was promptly condemned to thirteen more years in prison, and transferred to a criminal-lunatic asylum. His question was never really answered. To Visconti there seemed to be connecting threads leading from this attempted assassination back to the Portella della Ginestra massacres, to the Ardeatine Caves massacres, and so back to the Arditi of his childhood, with their death's-heads and crossed shinbones. On October 31, Togliatti returned to parliament, saying that "he hoped to continue, with renewed energy if possible"—words that Visconti was to remember a quarter of a century later when his own struggle against illness began.

Ten

From Sicily, Visconti returned to Rome and the theater. The best work in the postwar Italian theater was done by him, and by Giorgio Strehler and Paolo Grassi, founders of Milan's Piccolo Teatro. But it was not easy going for any of them. Rebecca West wrote in a recent book review that "English taxes make greatness hardly able to pay its way." This is true of most taxes now. So the Maecenas is replaced by the committee. It is useless to deplore this, but advisable to be aware of it as a historical fact, and a factor in the history of art.

In November 1948, the month Harry S Truman was elected president of the United States, Visconti produced *As You Like It* in Rome, with Vittorio Gassman as Orlando, Rina Morelli as Rosalind, rococo scenery by Salvador Dali, and Elizabethan music, including that of Shakespeare's friend Thomas Morley, Gentleman of the Chapel Royal. Visconti considered *As You Like It* "a fantasy, a dream, a fairy tale verging on ballet, a variation on the theme of love," deliberately set by Shakespeare in "a fabulous golden age amid the clouds of Olympus." He therefore gave his production of it an exuberantly Elizabethan mixture of fantasy and fun, elaborate courtliness and robust high spirits. The public reveled in this, but some critics berated Visconti for "deserting Neo-realism," to which he replied that Neo-Realism was not a strait jacket but merely a word used to indicate ideas inherent in a certain school of Italian film making. The theater had "employed Neo-Realistic methods ad nauseam" long before this and, though the claims of reality can no more be ignored than the fact that we are all destined to come to dust, poetry and a sense of the marvelous are essential to the theater's survival. As for those who instinctively resent displays of imagination, they probably, said Visconti, with a typical thrust, supposed social justice synonymous with the abolition of music, painting, and poetry, and were shocked by the people of Warsaw having given priority to the rebuilding of their theater.

It was in *As You Like It* that the future star Marcello Mastroianni first appeared with Visconti. Thirty years later Mastroianni said he had been "proud to enter the theater by the golden door"—though it had not been easy to begin with. Whereas young Gassman "acted magnificently" from the very first rehearsal, Mastroianni, in the small part of one of the melancholy Jacques's courtiers, was, according to his own account, "so unmagnificent" that Visconti constantly found fault with him, on one occasion roaring that he acted "like a streetcar conductor." Despite this Mastroianni became one of Visconti's favorite actors, and he says today that it was Visconti who taught him to distinguish between trash and truth, elegance and flamboyance.

In December, Visconti produced Clarence Day's comedy *Life with Father,* which had had a record run in the United States. Suso Cecchi D'Amico translated it, the Rina Morelli–Paolo Stoppa company acted it, and they enjoyed conjuring up the Old New York of Edith Wharton and Henry James, all the more because they were about to give its first Italian production to the very different America of Tennessee Williams's *A Streetcar Named Desire*. Italians found Tennessee Williams, who won a Pulitzer Prize for *A Streetcar Named Desire* in 1948, one of the most exciting of the new generation of American writers whose work was beginning to reach Europe. But as the horrors of war were forgotten, particularly by those who had not experienced them, a spurious sense of propriety returned. So *A Streetcar Named Desire* not only excited, but also shocked, causing eyebrows and tongues to wag as intemperately as they were to do a quarter of a century later at Bernardo Bertolucci's film *Last Tango in Paris*.

From Tennessee Williams's Deep South, Visconti turned to the ancient Greece of Alfieri's *Oreste*. The eighteenth-century play shocked scarcely less than the new American one, since Alfieri, a romantic figure, enamored of honor, glory, patriotism, revolution, and his soulmate, the Countess of Albany, former wife of Bonnie Prince Charlie, had applied the full force of his dramatic instincts to Orestes's murders of his mother and step-father. But this time Visconti had no trouble with censors. Possibly they thought murder "normal," as indeed it seems to be; possibly they were stunned by the magnificence of the play's setting, rococo again, with archaic lions guarding all the actors' entrances and exits.

That year Visconti was invited to take part in the annual arts festival at Florence, the Musical May of plays, music, and exhibitions. His production of Shakespeare's *Troilus and Cressida*, a play that after 1733 had not been performed in England for nearly two hundred years, was given outdoors in the beautiful terraced Boboli Gardens behind the Pitti Palace. Laid out in the sixteenth-century, after the palace was sold to Eleonora of Toledo, wife of the Medici Duke Cosimo I, these gardens had been specially planned to offer a princely setting for court theatricals.

What particularly interested Visconti was Shakespeare's picture of the siege of Troy as a struggle between not only two armies but also two worlds, the ancient Orient and the classical Occident. He knew Shakespeare had drawn on medieval sources, such as Caxton's *Recuyell of the Historyes of Troye*, the first book ever printed in English, and Chaucer's *Troilus and Criseyde*, and he directed with this in mind, but also emphasized the story's modern aspects, its bitterness, touches of anti-militarism, and the ways in which Troilus and Cressida's attitudes show that private life is forced, in every period, to be a resistance movement.

Young Franco Zeffirelli designed the scenery, and not even in the days of its Medici splendors could the Boboli Gardens have looked more magical than when they enclosed the white walls and turrets of the citadel of Troy, doubly whitened by moonlight. For incidental music, Visconti chose troubadour songs that Caxton would have heard when he was attached to the court of Edward IV's sister, the Duchess of Burgundy. Critics hailed Visconti's company as "Italy's National Theater," and this production made many Shakespeare lovers wish there might be truth in the story that between 1592 and 1594, when the London theater was in disorder, Shakespeare visited northern Italy with the Earl of Southampton.

After *Troilus and Cressida*, Visconti produced *Death of a Salesman*, a play for which Arthur Miller received a Pulitzer Prize in 1949. This tells the story of an aging traveling salesman's moral, financial, and, finally, physical defeat. Miller's Willie Loman was an antihero before the term existed. His fate is as commonplace as it is appalling, yet, as Miller says, "Willie Loman never made a lot of money. His name was never in the paper. He's not the finest character that ever lived. But he's a human being, and a terrible thing is happening to him. So attention must be paid."

Visconti then returned to the cinema, though the moment was not propitious. The cinema was doing poorly everywhere, and Hollywood itself was in a downward spin. The American government had succeeded in 1947, after nine years of litigation, in ending price-fixing, block-booking, and the big studios' monopolies, and around the same time the Un-American Activities Committee began arraigning people for Communist sympathies on the flimsiest evidence. Hollywood was a natural terrain for scapegoat hunting, and between 1947 and 1950 ten film directors and writers were imprisoned for refusing to incriminate themselves or their friends, and dozens more were blacklisted. Fear and unemployment spread through what was a major national industry, and were not dissipated by the Alger Hiss–Whittaker Chambers espionage trial, which, said Alistair Cooke, put an entire generation on trial. On top of this, the American film industry now had to face competition from that great novelty television, which between 1946 and 1950 cut film audiences by half. One of the solutions for all this appeared to be to sell more and more films abroad.

Italian film producers therefore asked their government to protect the home industry. Giulio Andreotti, Under Secretary of State, was put in charge of the matter. Full of energy, he tripled the distribution of Italian films at home. But he disapproved of Neo-Realism, considering adverse criticism of the government as synonymous with Communism—and his powers included censorship. The official view was that what people needed from films was "escape, relaxation, forgetfulness, bread and circuses." Even Vittorio de Sica's poignant films were blamed for "washing dirty linen in public"—despite the fact that the Italian ambassador in Paris had personally thanked De Sica for his film *Shoeshine,* saying, "It has made it possible for me to resume a dialogue with the French."

This explains why Visconti found himself hindered in 1951 by obstacles sadly similar to those he had faced during Fascism. In October 1951, the Ministry of the Interior's decision to refuse Bertolt Brecht's Berliner Ensemble an entry visa for the Venice Theater Festival drove Visconti to withdraw his name from the production of Diego Fabbri's *The Seducer,* which he had prepared for this occasion. In attacking these windmills, he was supported, then and for the rest of his life, by Suso Cecchi D'Amico. As daughter of the writer Emilio Cecchi and the painter Leonetta Pieraccini, wife of music critic Fidel D'Amico, and daughter-in-law of the theater historian Silvio D'Amico, Suso had grown up in and into worlds totally involved in all that interested Visconti most, and since her first play translation for him, she had made her own debut in the film world. She had begun by collaborating with Alberto Moravia and Ennio Flaiano on the screenplay of Théophile Gautier's story "Avatar," and in 1947 she won a Silver Ribbon, the first of many awards, for her contribution to *Vivere in pace.* After that she worked on the screenplays of *L'onorevole Angelina,* played by Anna Magnani, and of *Bicycle Thief* for De Sica. So she had more than competence to offer Visconti when they began their lifelong collaboration.

Visconti wanted to make a film of *Le Carrosse du Saint-Sacrement*

(*The Coach of the Blessed Sacrament*), a play by the French writer Prosper Mérimée, whose stories include the original *Carmen*. Visconti intended to make this his first color film, and was entranced by the possibilities of the South American setting—eighteenth-century Lima—and by the character of the actress, La Périchole, to be played by Anna Magnani. He and Suso had already written much of the screenplay when the project was wrecked by the imperatives of coproduction. The director, it was suddenly decreed, must not be Italian. Two years later the film was made by Jean Renoir, though not before he asked Visconti for his consent.

Immediately, Visconti embarked on another project—to film *Cronache di poveri amanti* (*Chronicle of Poor Lovers*), a recent novel by the Florentine Vasco Pratolini. As a very young writer, Pratolini had been hamstrung by poverty and Fascism, but this novel brought him international success at thirty-four. When this project fell through for technical reasons, Visconti and Suso wrote *The Wedding March,* a complex story of parallel marriages involved in the same suicide that was a tribute to Erich von Stroheim and one of Visconti's most interesting texts. It was published in the May 1953 number of *Cinema Nuovo*, but the censors saw to it that it never reached the screen. While they were working on this, a backer, Salvo d'Angelo, who had lost money with *La terra trema* without losing his belief in Visconti, suggested that Visconti direct Anna Magnani in *Bellissima*. The idea, of a working-class Roman mother who dreams of her child's becoming a film star, came from Zavattini. At first Visconti hesitated, wary of producers, whom Fellini once called "the cinema's infantile diseases." But he wanted passionately to work with Magnani, whom he thought "a stupendous actress, and extraordinary woman, with a pagan disposition." The offer of *Bellissima* came at a particularly harrowing period in Anna Magnani's personal life. She had been acting since her teens; but only in 1945, when the Fascist shutters were at last flung open, was she able to do herself justice, in Rossellini's *Rome, Open City*. In this she had seemed the very incarnation of the Roman populace. Now Rossellini had left her for Ingrid Bergman. But Magnani would not allow her work to suffer. She was as eager to work with Visconti as he with her.

He began the film with a concert of Donizetti's opera buffa *L'Elisir d'Amore* (*The Elixir of Love*) in a Roman broadcasting studio. The dowdy looks of the chorus contrast with the romantic music, which is interrupted by the announcement of a film company's contest for *la più bella bambina di Roma* (the most beautiful child in Rome). *Bellissima*, sings the unbeautiful chorus, and Maddalena (Magnani), hearing the an-

85

nouncement, is carried away by visions of her plain lisping child, Maria, becoming a film star, a latter-day Shirley Temple, and so escaping from their tenement-house world into the glorious Never Never Land created in Maddalena's imagination by the movies.

In making this, Visconti was not, as some critics supposed, bent on satirizing the Hollywood-on-the-Tiber aspects of Cinecittà. Far from having any desire to bite the hand that fed him—and, in any case, it was usually he himself who provided most of the food—he was primarily concerned with the vulgarity, demagogy, mediocrity that drove Maddalena to seek this escape route. The audition scene with the mothers, supermarket Furies urging their offspring on with current clichés, has an appalled humor. Visconti also got pure fun from the scenes with the Director, a godlike figure who moves through the studios undisturbed by the pigmies agitating themselves all around him. This part was played by director Alessandro Blasetti, who had begun his career in the days of silent films, and whose film *1860*, made in 1933, has been considered a precursor of Neo-Realism and may have influenced Bertolucci's recent *1900*. Blasetti's charming and grave performance of himself would not have been funny had Visconti not arranged for all Blasetti's appearances to be accompanied by a soft rendering of the "Charlatan's air" from *Elixir of Love*. Not being familiar with Donizetti's music, Blasetti did not realize the significance of this. When someone told him, he wrote Visconti indignantly that he would not have believed him capable of such a thing, and so on. Visconti replied, "Why? We're all charlatans, we directors. We put illusions into the heads of mothers and little girls . . . we're selling a love potion that isn't really a magic elixir. It's simply a glass of Bordeaux, the same as in opera. I'd apply this 'Charlatan's air' quite as much to myself as to you."

Similarly, Visconti used "Quanto è bella quanto è cara" ("How beautiful, how dear she is"), from the same opera, to underline the child Maria's lack of charm or talent. Maria's film test, seen by Maddalena from the projection gallery, provokes cruel laughter from all but Blasetti, who chooses Maria just because her mediocrity is so *natural* and naturalness is the fad of the moment. The audience will no doubt be able to "identify with Maria." But by this time Maddalena has seen through the dream factory. She has been defrauded of her savings by a plausible young man who professed to have "influence" with Blasetti, but when he also tries to seduce her, she realizes not only that everything about this particular operation is bogus, but also that she is damaging her child's dignity rather than putting her in the way of a glamorous destiny. So Maddalena backs out and returns to her stick-in-the-mud, underpaid, but decent husband, to whom her foray has seemed a crazy one from the start.

Years later, asked if the plot of *Bellissima* had not been "more or less a pretext," Visconti said, "Yes, the story really was a pretext. . . . My whole subject was Magnani: I wanted to create a portrait of a woman out of her, a contemporary woman, a mother, and I think we succeeded because Magnani lent me her enormous talent, her personality. That was what interested me. Not so much the cinema setting. It's been said that I wanted to make something ironic, malicious even, of this setting, but that wasn't what I had in mind."

Bellissima was not one of Visconti's own favorites, but it proved the most popular film he had yet made. One critic said that "nothing so strong or sincere had ever been seen in the cinema before." For a true comparison, another said, "one must turn to literature—to Hemingway's *To Have and Have Not* and Elio Vittorini's *Conversation in Sicily*." This was certainly a change from the days, nine years earlier, when it took a bishop's exorcism to cleanse a cinema after Visconti's *Ossessione*.

Eleven

In the Italy of 1951, led by Alcide de Gasperi, the hopes left by the Resistance were being fast dissipated by the Cold War. The Italian "economic miracle" was still to come, and finding money for the arts was a blood-out-of-a-stone enterprise. So Visconti was glad to join two young film enthusiasts, Marco Ferreri and Riccardo Ghione, in an attempt to counteract the mediocrity of the newsreels, still a regular feature of cinema programs in those last days before television entered the majority of homes. Twenty-three years old, the future film director Ferreri already had a corrosive humor, and he and Ghione, son of an actor-director who had been a Robin Hood of the silent films, planned to produce monthly documentaries on current events.

De Sica provided them with a documentary about his *Bicycle Thief*. Moravia contributed an erotic documentary, at a period when explicit eroticism was rare in the cinema and forced to base itself on allusions rather than orifices. Visconti made *Notes on a News Item* for them. This concerned a murder inflaming public opinion just then. The raped body of a child, Annarella Bracci, had been found in a well. The police immediately arrested a man recently seen with her. He confessed to the murder, but in court retracted, described the tortures that had driven him to malign himself, and was acquitted. Visconti conjured up this tragedy with a sobriety that emphasized its horror. He set his film in a miserable street with festering walls. In fading sunlight some slum children are beating a drum. At the end of this blind alley is wasteland. In the wasteland is a well, wreathed by a few flowers. A little farther on is Annarella's grave.

Notes on a News Item was a startling piece of work, proof not only of Visconti's gifts but also of his concern for others. It was promptly censored in Italy—though much admired in France, where it was shown in 1953 and immediately singled out by Anne Philipe, then a young critic, with her best-selling books still to come. So Visconti and Suso returned to *Wedding March*, only to have it turned down by Lux Films, who feared the censors' reactions. This was not surprising, considering that in 1952 Andreotti wrote De Sica an open letter about his beautiful film *Umberto D*, admonishing him "never to forget the obligation to include a minimum of sane and constructive optimism."

This checkmate was followed by a series of theater productions: Goldoni's *La locandiera* (*The Mistress of the Inn*) for the 1952 International Theater Festival at the Fenice Theater in Venice; Chekhov's *Three Sisters* in Rome; *The Evils of Tobacco*, a playlet by Chekhov, in Milan; and Euripides's *Medea*. Visconti came to love Chekhov relatively late. As a young man he once said that whereas the problems of the poorer classes are sickness, bills, heat, those of the upper classes spring from lack of interior force, "a sort of Chekhovian crying into the pillow while the orchard is being chopped down. I prefer to tell the story of protest, rather than only that of the lost floundering will. I believe in life, that is the central point. I believe in organized society. I think it has a chance." But later he was to say that if he lived long enough he would have a theater of his own where the program "would be Chekhov + Chekhov + Chekhov + Shakespeare + some music." "Chekhov is, for me, the greatest author, alongside Shakespeare and Verdi. . . . Stendhal wanted engraved on his tomb 'He adored Cimarosa, Mozart, and Shakespeare.' In the same way I would like on mine 'He adored Shakespeare, Chekhov, and Verdi.' "

After Euripides, Visconti was asked to direct Anna Magnani in a sketch for a film to be called *Siamo donne* (*We Are Women*); to act as adviser for a revue at Milan's Teatro Nuovo starring Wanda Osiris, a flamboyant variety favorite; and to direct *Come le foglie* (*As the Leaves Fall*), a play by the nineteenth-century Milanese playwright Giuseppe Giacosa. After this Visconti received what was to him a wholly fascinating offer: to direct an opera at La Scala in which Maria Callas, thirty-one and in beautiful voice, was to open the season.

The first time Visconti saw Callas she had been only twenty-five and still fat. He nevertheless thought her beautiful onstage, with thrillingly authoritative gestures all her own. Soon afterward the Associazione Anfiparnaso, a group of Roman opera lovers to which Visconti belonged, sponsored a two-week season at the Teatro Eliseo. They commissioned four new operas, including *Job* by Luigi Dallapiccola, a leading exponent of Schönberg's twelve-tone, serial, method of composition, and two revivals, one of them Rossini's *Il Turco in Italia* (*The Turk in Italy*), which had not been given at La Scala for over a hundred years. Orchestra and chorus were provided by Italian Radio, which was to broadcast the performances. The best young singers were sought out, and Maria Callas was offered the part of Donna Fiorilla in *Il Turco in Italia*. Rehearsals gave Visconti and Callas an opportunity to get to know each other. Totally committed to music, she was touched and surprised that "a man of his distinction" should attend almost all the rehearsals. There were two of these a day and they never lasted less than three or four hours each. Nevertheless, Visconti appeared totally absorbed throughout. He, too, was touched and surprised by her personality.

Maria Callas was a Greek girl, Cecilia Sophia Anna Maria Kalogeropoulos, born in New York, the child of immigrants—and a disappointment to her mother, who had wanted a boy to replace the little son who had died in Greece. At the age of eight the plump, pimply, vulnerable, and insecure child started piano lessons. From the first she showed flashes of the brilliance that was later to give her a phosphorescent quality. When she was thirteen her family returned to Greece, where, her mother having given the child's age as sixteen instead of thirteen, Callas was admitted to the National Conservatory. Surviving the war in German- and Italian-occupied Greece was difficult. Young Callas never had the right food for her developing voice. Spaghetti, spaghetti, spaghetti—and that only when in luck. In 1947, while engaged to sing Ponchielli's *La Gioconda* at Verona, she met and married Giovanni Battisto Meneghini, a Veronese industrialist, thirty years her senior, with a fanatical belief in her voice.

Then in 1953, while preparing her first performance of Cherubini's *Medea,* she suddenly decided that her appearance was not right for a character who should have a lean and hungry look. With her usual violent determination, she dieted until she had lost seventy-five pounds. So by the time Visconti directed her, she looked as beautiful as she sounded. Conductor Carlo Maria Giulini noticed a resemblance between her eyes and those of the charioteer at Delphi, and she entranced Visconti. Not only was she free from the slightest trace of banality, but as a singer she seemed to have stepped directly out of the nineteenth century, the great Italian opera period. She was nearer to the legendary soprano Giuditta Pasta, creator of Rossini, Donizetti, and Bellini roles, than to any of her contemporaries. Not only her voice but also her character beat wild on this world's shore. Visconti was to have more influence on her artistic development than anyone since Elvira de Hidalgo, her teacher in Athens, and conductor Tullio Serafin, from her Verona days. An inspired singer, who had recently become a beautiful woman, Callas enabled Visconti "to witness the birth of an extraordinary actress." Her *Traviata* and *Anna Bolena* were, he said later, "two of the greatest acting performances, quite apart from her singing."

Their first joint undertaking was *La Vestale*. Its composer, Gasparo Spontini, had qualities particularly suited to both Callas and Visconti. Born in Naples in 1774, the year Louis XV died, Spontini had as a young man gone to Paris, where his music subjugated Napoleon, who made him virtually the official First Empire court composer. The plot of *La Vestale* might have been conceived specially for Callas. It tells the story of Julia, a Roman girl who, while her fiancé Lucinius is away fighting in Gaul, is compelled by her father to become one of the priestesses of Vesta, the Roman goddess of the hearth. The vestal virgins lived austere but privileged lives, their prestige being as awesome as their doom—that of being buried alive—if they broke their vow of chastity. Their holiest duty was to keep the sacred flame alight, a perilous task in stormy weather in a small circular temple with a vent hole in the roof. They also had charge of the Palladium, a small wooden statue of Pallas Athene brought by Aeneas from Troy, and handed on to his descendants, the founders of Rome. The vestals' position was so sacrosanct that their order survived for almost a century after Christianity had become the Roman Empire's official religion. Neither prestige nor position, however, console Julia, wretched in a life she has not chosen. When Licinius, whom she still loves, returns to Rome as a triumphant young general, she is in such despair that she admits him into the temple. As they embrace, the sacred flame goes out. The High Priest condemns Julia to be buried alive. Licinius tries in vain to rescue her, begs in vain to share her fate. Then, just as Julia is about to enter her tomb, a storm breaks out. Lightning resuscitates the sacred flame. This proves that the heavens forgive Julia. She and Licinius are permitted to marry in this same vestal temple.

To this ancient Roman equivalent of a police-court scandal, Visconti brought his sense of opera and of Callas's possibilities—"Maria is possibly the most disciplined and professional material I have ever had occasion to handle," he once said—and his unusual capacity for seeing historical events in the context of their own period, without the patronage of hindsight. This was a particularly useful gift to have just then, since the fifties were the period of musical *riesumazione* (exhumation), when operas were presented as far as possible in the styles of their first performance. Visconti had an uncanny gift for this. From family recollections and traditions, from old books, prints, posters, programs, early vocal manuals, theatrical warehouses and their stock books, he would create not a mere simulacrum of the past but a renewal of it that made an old opera far more comprehensible to modern audiences than an attempt to modernize it would have done.

In the case of *La Vestale*, it was clear to Visconti that the Napoleon who applauded this opera had seemed to the Italians of that day not a loathsome dictator, midway between Attila and Hitler, but, on the contrary, a welcome liberator. Young Italians, many of them future Risorgimento heroes, entranced by the young Napoleon's "careers-open-to-talent" policy, saw him with the eyes of Stendhal, who described the Italian period as "the most pure and brilliant of Bonaparte's life." (Visconti's own ancestors had ardently supported Napoleon—and contributed fodder for his cavalry.) With this in mind, Visconti gave his *Vestale* a First Empire setting. He asked scene designer Piero Zuffi for Appianian colors, "cold as moonstruck marble." Andrea Appiani (1754–1817), a leading figure in international Neoclassicism, was celebrated for his frescoes in Lombard churches and palaces, painted an "Apotheosis of Napoleon" on the Council Room ceiling of the royal palace in Milan, and became one of Napoleon's official painters.

The singers' gestures, too, had to be of the right historical period. For these Visconti searched the pictures of the French painter Jacques Louis David (1748–1825). Devoted to ancient Rome, Corneille, and civic virtues, and to admonishing people to "read their Plutarch," David had given superb artistic expression to the Napoleonic period. In his care for detail, Visconti even had the stage of La Scala enlarged forward, because in Spontini's day singers advanced to the proscenium to sing. From the start, rehearsals went well. Visconti particularly appreciated Callas's appetite for work, her avidity to learn, her capacity to obtain more, always more, out of herself. He found her inspired and inspiring. She never failed to exceed his hopes.

Drama was added to the rehearsals by the eighty-seven-year-old Toscanini, who was to inaugurate the Piccola Scala by conducting Verdi's *Falstaff* there. He wanted Visconti to direct this. They often lunched together to discuss the plan, and at one of these lunches—in the old maestro's apartment in the Via Durini, parallel with the Via Visconti di Modrone, and leading into what is now the Via Toscanini—Toscanini asked Visconti if he might come to a rehearsal of *La Vestale*. Visconti was honored, and delighted when Toscanini praised his direction and said that he found Callas "very good, a beautiful voice and an interesting artist." Later, when Toscanini came to the performance itself, and sat in the stage box, Callas interrupted her curtsies to catch a red carnation thrown her by an admirer and offer it to Toscanini with her deepest curtsy of all.

Another kind of dramatic tension was contributed to rehearsals by the fact that whereas Visconti adored Callas's talent, Callas had begun to adore Visconti. Similar complications often occurred. According to his closest friends, Visconti never deliberately set out to charm people, but just as a born bore is irremediably boring, so a born spellbinder irremediably casts spells. One of Visconti's oldest friends has said, half sadly, half smiling, "*Oh*, the heads I have had to hold in this room."

Among the joys and satisfactions that *La Vestale* brought to all concerned, the simplest were, for Callas, that of having achieved a childhood longing to be at home at La Scala, for Visconti, that of returning to a childhood home. They were both in the rare position of Kipling's character:

> Down with the drawbridge and let him through—
> The dreamer whose dreams came true!

As Visconti's name was shouted, as he bowed from the stage, he saw beyond the footlights not only the cheering audience but also the red damask of his family box, where his love for La Scala had begun.

Twelve

Visconti's fourth full-length film, *Senso*, was shown the same year as his Scala production of *La Vestale*, but was made under very different conditions. People employed at La Scala at that time were financially secure and therefore able to concentrate on the quality of their work. The cinema, on the other hand, often meant, to a director, financial uncertainty and political skulduggery.

No profession depends to such an extent as film making on obtaining vast sums of money from people who, in many cases, know next to nothing —so much more dangerous than plain nothing—about the art in which they are investing. Whether the investors are capitalists wanting profits or totalitarians wanting propaganda, their attitude is likely to be equally trying for those who do the work, though more dangerous to life and sanity in the latter case. What backers favored most at this period were coproductions, considered the best weapon against television, which, now that a Eurovision network was being formed, threatened to keep more and more people at home with the box instead of in front of a cinema screen.

After the lavish Franco-Italian coproduction *Fabiola* (which might have surprised Cardinal Wiseman, the English prelate whose novel *Fabiola, or the Church of the Catacombs* had been published a hundred years earlier), flocks of American directors, stars, technicians, began winging their way to Cinecittà, cheap labor, and plentiful sunshine. Tales circulated of fantastic anomalies. Synthetic-rubber marble, it was said, had been brought from California, at far greater cost than would have procured genuine marble from the Carrara quarries once used by Michelangelo, and which still produce three-quarters of Italy's marble output.

Foreign competition was rendered all the more harassing by the fact that whereas the censors seldom meddled with coproductions, Italian directors still had to face a system that subsidized Julien Duvivier's *The Little World of Don Camillo*, a comedy prettifying the struggle between church and Communist party, but banned Carlo Lizzani's *Chronicle of Poor Lovers*, although the novel from which this had been made was available at bookstores all over Italy and had been translated into twenty-five languages. Visconti was therefore pleased when Lux Films, which had wanted to do *Wedding March*, invited him to make a "spectacular film on a high artistic level."

At this point Suso saw that some short stories by Camillo Boito had just been reprinted in a series edited by Giorgio Bassani, a poet, novelist, and essayist from Ferrara whom Suso and Visconti both admired. (Bassani was to become widely known abroad for his novel *The Garden of the Finzi-Continis*, filmed by Vittorio de Sica in 1970.) These stories were already part of Visconti's own life, dating back to his childhood, when the Boito brothers were pointed out to him in the Galleria.

The story that attracted Visconti most was *Senso*, published for the first time in Boito's *More Vain Stories* (1883), of which Benedetto Croce wrote in his *La letteratura della nuova Italia* that, far from being "vain," these stories were full of "Boito's dreams, his melancholy and pangs of love, with all the places and landscapes that he saw with a painter's eye." It was an account by a Venetian countess, Livia Serpieri, of a love affair she enjoyed in 1866, during the last months of Italy's revolt against Austria. Livia was twenty-two at the time, the newlywed bride of a grumpy nobleman old enough to be her grandfather. Her lover, Remigio Ruz, was a Hapsburg lieutenant only two years older than she was, and as dissolute as he was handsome. But, since Remigio roused Livia sexually as she had never been roused before, she found even his corruption entrancing—so much so that she gave him the money to bribe an army doctor to declare him unfit for further active service. When, however, Livia discovered that Remigio was spending her money on a new mistress, she promptly denounced him as a deserter, attended his execution, and, because she saw the new mistress fling herself on Remigio's dead body, felt no remorse for the revenge she had taken. The Livia who tells this story is still beautiful, and trifling with a would-be lover, who assures her repeatedly that she is "an angel." Visconti saw this story as a "news item" in the Verga sense and wanted to tell it as "part of a tableau of Italian history." What particularly interested him were the glimpses it offered—like glimpses of a play seen from the wings—of a war that, though victorious on the whole, nevertheless included a terrible defeat at the Battle of Custoza.

To understand why Visconti felt the Battle of Custoza—which occupies merely a line or two, if that, in foreign textbooks—to be so important, it is necessary to remember two facts: first, when Visconti made *Senso,* Italy had been united for less than one hundred years; second, before unity, Italy was not simply the country we know today, "occupied" by foreigners, but a collection of heterogeneous states used as counters in the power games of leading European rulers. The Hapsburg Empire had disliked the idea of an independent Italy, just as George III's England disliked the idea of her thirteen American colonies becoming independent. The Italians' struggle for *unità* and independence therefore meant to them very much what the contemporaneous Civil War meant to Americans. To Visconti this recent past seemed very near indeed. His family and relatives had played leading parts in it—among them, for example, Count Opprandino Arrivabene, the patriot, music lover, and member of parliament who was Verdi's lifelong friend. A man as close in time to Visconti as his own grandfather had, though he lived to be a senator of the new Italy, nevertheless been born in an Italy made up of independent states only two of which—the Kingdom of Sardinia (Piedmont and Sardinia) and the Papal States—were ruled by Italians.

Visconti's first choice for the part of Livia was Ingrid Bergman, but Rossellini could not stand her working for anyone but himself just then. Alida Valli, the younger actress who finally played the part, could scarcely have been bettered. Visconti noticed her "beautiful face, lost-looking eyes, stubborn lips" when she played in Mario Soldati's film of Antonio Fogazzaro's minor classic *The Little World of Yesterday.* In writing the screenplay, Visconti and Suso had the collaboration of Giorgio Bassani, Giorgio Prosperi, and Carlo Alianello, and, for some additional English dialogue, Paul Bowles and Tennessee Williams. But the original screenplay was all their own—until the censor loosed his incontinent scissors on it.

Senso begins with the words: "Venice, Spring 1866. The last month of the Austrian occupation of the Veneto. The Italian government has just made a pact of alliance with Prussia and the war of liberation is imminent." These words fade into the stage of the Fenice Theater, in Venice, where the third act of Verdi's *Il Trovatore* is ending. The most fashionable parts of the auditorium are filled with Austrian officers, in their white uniforms. *Il Trovatore,* with its romantically unbridled passions, is one of Verdi's most popular operas, and one with rousing political associations for Italians. Cavour himself was so attached to it that when writing, as prime minister, to beg Verdi to accept a seat in the first Italian parliament, he addressed the maestro as "the composer of

Il Trovatore." Also, the Risorgimento poet Giovanni Prati, who was with Cavour on the April evening in 1859 when the Austrians invaded Piedmont—thereby making French intervention and their own defeat certain—said that as Cavour read the telegram containing the news, his exhilaration was so overwhelming that he sang a few bars of the famous call to arms at the end of *Il Trovatore*'s third act. So by beginning *Senso* with "All'armi! All'armi!," Visconti roused not only the screen audience, but the cinema one. He said later that he had tried to make the emotions expressed in *Il Trovatore* "leap over the footlights and into a story of war and rebellion"—and he did precisely that.

As the tenor thunders out "All'armi," the audience applauds more and more wildly. Suddenly, from above, a girl's voice shouts, "Foreigners out of Venice!" From the top gallery rosettes and streamers in red, white, and green, the new Italy's colors, rain down on the orchestra seats amid cries of "Viva Verdi" and "Viva Lamarmora" (the head of the Italian army). During this commotion Countess Livia Serpieri, watching from a box filled with her husband's friends from the Austrian high command, sees a handsome young Austrian officer laughingly say something that makes a civilian in evening dress slap his face. Horrified, Livia recognizes the civilian as her cousin Roberto Ussoni, for whom just being there at all is dangerous. Determined to save Roberto's life, Livia begs the Austrian General to introduce her to the "hero" of this incident. With creaking gallantry, the General expresses dismay, saying that "all the Venetian ladies" are in love with Franz Mahler. Franz is sent for and presented to Livia. Handsome, fatuous, in his twenties, he makes no impression on her, since she is thinking only of her cousin's safety. She, however, makes an impression on Franz. In reply to Franz's query as to whether she likes opera, Livia says that she likes it on the stage, but dislikes young men who behave operatically in daily life. She manages to persuade Franz not to fight a duel with Roberto—all the more easily, though she does not know this, because Franz is a coward.

For the part of Franz Mahler, Visconti wanted Marlon Brando, who had made his first stage success in Tennessee Williams's *A Streetcar Named Desire*, and had just starred in Laszlo Benedek's film *The Wild One*. But Lux Films insisted on Farley Granger, from whom Visconti obtained a better performance than Granger had ever given before.

Although Livia manages to prevent the duel, she cannot prevent Roberto's being sentenced to exile. By chance, Franz sees her at the palace requisitioned by the Austrians, where she is saying good-bye to Roberto before he and his comrades are marched off under armed escort. Since her husband disapproves of Roberto's views, she is alone. Mis-

97

interpreting this, Franz accosts her as she is leaving and, after assuring her that he is not responsible for Ussoni's plight, adds that he would have acted differently had she told him frankly that Ussoni was her lover. Outraged, Livia turns her back on the Austrian and leaves the building. Franz follows her. When she orders him to leave her alone, he says with insolent humility that he must see she does not get into trouble for being out after the Austrian curfew hour. Livia's skirts rustle over the glistening cobbles, Franz's white cloak swirls above its reflections in the shot-silk waters of the canal, their footfalls are escorted by echoes. A man is following a woman through a city emptied by night where, after the uniforms, the weapons, the shouted orders of military headquarters, private life is reasserting itself. Venice, so often made banal in postcard and poster terms, appears in *Senso* with its mystery intact.

Suddenly Franz and Livia come on the body of a murdered Austrian soldier, sprawled half in the canal. Aware that they must not be found there, Franz leads the still-dignified, but shaken, Livia down side alleys.

The grim encounter with a murdered soldier reminds them that they are enemies, and, paradoxically, establishes a truce between them. Livia thinks of the dangers her young enemies have passed through, and Franz is quick to encourage her to pity them. As they drift across this sea-borne city, whose existence is a perpetual defiance of nature, it becomes apparent that the labyrinth into which they have wandered is that of passion. Franz quotes a poem of Heine's about the Day of Judgment, when the dead will be "reborn to eternal joy of suffering, but we remain locked in our embrace, caring nothing for heaven or hell." Suddenly it is morning. Franz and Livia part. From a censor's viewpoint "nothing has happened." Yet to Livia, everything seems new as the morning. As she hastens past the early vendors unloading gondolas piled with fruit and vegetables, she hears her own voice asking, "How could I have spent the night with an Austrian?"

After this strange beginning, passion takes its banal course. Livia becomes Franz's mistress and discovers sexual passion. But her joy is short-lived. Franz cannot be relied upon, and one day he disappears. Possibly he has been posted elsewhere.

The imminence of war makes Count Serpieri decide to move at once to their country estate. The rural scenes at the Serpieris' villa were a revelation of how color could be used in a film. There, one night, Livia is awakened by the dogs' insistent barking. Franz is hiding on her balcony. Her first reaction is incredulous anger. He says he has come because he could not endure her absence. She does not believe this, yet, finally, cannot resist him. All night she watches over his sleep, and in the morning gives him the partisans' funds entrusted to her for safe-keeping by Ussoni, so that he can bribe the army doctor to certify that he is unfit for further active service.

Meanwhile, near Verona, the Battle of Custoza is beginning—and it was at this point that Visconti discovered how ingenuous he and Suso had been when they assured each other "we can't have any censorship troubles with this." To Visconti, the Battle of Custoza was the heart of *Senso*, no more to be relegated to the background than was the music of Verdi and Bruckner. But—and it was from this that the trouble with the censor sprang—although the campaign as a whole was victorious, the individual Battle of Custoza had been a calamitous and unnecessary defeat for Italy. Unnecessary because when Italy made a secret alliance with Prussia in April 1866, Prussia was aiming at German unity, had decided to attack Austria, and promised Venice to Italy in case of victory. In July 1866, Prussia defeated Austria at Sadowa—and Italy could have had Venice without further bloodshed. But Lamarmora wanted blood shed for Venice, and was not alone in this. The statesman Francesco Crispi was applauded in parliament for urging that Italy be given a "baptism of blood." The army, condemned to go ahead in these circumstances, was ill-equipped—military expenses had been steadily cut down for the past four years—and the high command was faction-ridden. Above all, the regular army wanted no part of Garibaldi's volunteers.

No sooner had *Senso* been shown at the 1954 Venice Film Festival than the Ministry of Defense intervened, insisting on the elimination of a scene in which Ussoni is at the Fifth Division's headquarters talking to a staff officer, Captain Meucci. Ussoni says, "We've done the impossible to raise this company of volunteers. We're trained to harass the enemy, and now you tell me we aren't wanted. . . . Just when it's being publicly proclaimed everywhere that it's the duty of every Italian to take part in the war. . . ." Meucci says soothingly that while he understands Ussoni's feelings, past experiences have shown that volunteers using guerrilla tactics are no real help to the regular army. Finally Meucci offers Ussoni a safe-conduct for himself and his men. Ussoni brushes this aside, saying he hasn't come to ask for small favors; does Meucci realize all that the volunteers have done, have sacrificed? Indeed yes, says Meucci, all the information you gave us was perfect. Nevertheless, the argument continues. The war has changed its ideological character.

This scene, for which Visconti had historical warranty, illustrated the changes that came over the Risorgimento toward its end, and suggested parallels with 1948, when partisans were not always welcomed by what was officially their own side. Possibly for this reason, the scene upset not only the Ministry of Defense but also the Under Secretary for Entertainment, who declared that *Senso* would "soil even the Risorgimento"—which is as if a congressman were to declare that any film about the Civil War that mentioned carpetbaggers would "soil America." Visconti felt so strongly about this that, although "Senso" was the film's first provisional title, he wanted to call it either "The Defeated" or "Custoza." The producers' outcries can be imagined. Their attitude was: he only does it to annoy because he knows it teases. But this was not so. Visconti was capable of an extraordinary mixture of candor and literal-mindedness when his principles were involved.

While Ussoni is pursuing his dream at Custoza, where he is killed, Livia is pursuing her dream of Franz, from whom she has had only one letter since he fled with the partisans' money. Despite her coachman's protests, she sets off for Verona in her husband's absence. The journey is hard and frightening, and Verona is seething with Austrian troops. At the city gates, she gives her husband's name and political position. The Austrians immediately allow her to enter. The streets are packed as for a sinister carnival. At last she finds Franz's lodgings.

As she enters the main room, Franz emerges from the bedroom in the company of his mistress. Determined not to leave her even the small change of the heart, Franz taunts her for being older than he is, for bogus romanticism, and for refusing to admit to herself what he is really like: "I'm a deserter because I'm a coward—and I don't care that I'm a deserter and a coward."

Beside herself with grief, Livia rushes out into the shadowy torchlit streets of Verona, full of confusion and drunken Austrian soldiers. Like a sleepwalker, she makes her way to military headquarters and asks to see the General. Then she denounces Franz as a deserter. The General asks her if she is Austrian. No, she says, "I am Venetian." Franz is dragged, struggling and yelling, to the place of execution. Livia, meanwhile, weaves around the streets of Verona, crying out Franz's name in a voice inhuman as a bird's.

The scene of Franz's execution is awesome: a vast gloomy courtyard (a courtyard in Rome's blood-haunted Castel Sant'Angelo was used); the thudding footfalls of torchlit soldiers moving like automatons, every figure ramrod stiff except the struggling prisoner, but he is already so nearly anonymous that his struggles have no emotional impact; the minatory roll of drums, the raucously barked orders, the dry hail of shots; the crumpled figure removed as expeditiously as if it were garbage in the hands of efficient, but not personally interested, street cleaners; the automatons marching off as smartly as they came. Nothing, the scene seems to say, nothing particular has happened, merely a sordid little deserter has got his deserts. Night and silence reclaim the history-saturated courtyard. Despite its plastic beauty, this scene is as terrible as any of the pictures that were then arriving from the war in Indochina. The scene held echoes, too, of the executions filmed by Visconti for American military archives.

It was not, however, with Franz's execution that Visconti had wanted *Senso* to end. In his original screenplay, Livia fled from Franz only to lose herself in the torchlit streets of Verona, among the drunkenly celebrating Austrian soldiers. "It doesn't matter in the least," Visconti said, "whether Franz was killed or not. We leave him after the scene in Verona where he shows himself in his true colors. Pointless that he should be shot. Instead we see Livia running to denounce him and wandering the streets among the soldiers and prostitutes. It's as if she's become a sort of prostitute herself. She keeps calling Franz's name. Then we see a young soldier, one of those who really pay the price of victory. He is weeping and shouting 'Long live Austria!' "

One of the producers, who personally liked this ending, warned Visconti that it would not be permitted. Nor was it. The original ending was cut and its negative burned. Alarmed by official censorship, the producers joined in the game, and by the time all the scissors had ceased to twinkle, the copy of *Senso* for export was senselessly mutilated—all from fear of reality.

The Ministry of Defense and the Under Secretary for Entertainment were not the only ones to harass Visconti. Many of those on the right disliked his attitude toward the Risorgimento: it had not, they insisted, been an unblemished people's crusade. Above all, the right objected to comparisons being drawn between 1866 and 1943. Many of those on the left, equally vocal, suspected Visconti's attitude toward the Risorgimento, which had, they insisted, been an unblemished people's crusade. Above all, the left objected to the change from truckdrivers, fishermen, working-class housewives to nobles and officers. And, right or left, all accused Visconti of "repudiating Neo-Realism." In fact Visconti had gone beyond Neo-Realism to reality. As critic Guido Aristarco, founder of *Cinema Nuova,* wrote: "With *Senso* we see the birth of the first true and authentic Italian historical film."

When *Senso* reached Switzerland, Freddy Buache, director of the Swiss Film Library and a highly creative critic, wrote: "This masterly and original film is likely to be misunderstood, since it is an avant-garde film, the precise significance and aesthetic grandeur of which will become clear only in a few years' time." Sure enough, *Senso* did become first a success, subsequently a classic. Looking back over his career, Visconti was to say, "After *Senso* everything was easier."

Thirteen

In 1955, Visconti returned to La Scala to direct Bellini's *La Sonnambula* (*The Sleepwalker*), with Maria Callas as its sleepwalking heroine, Amina.

After the grotesque meddling to which film work was subjected, Visconti found the atmosphere at La Scala superbly liberal. In no other country does opera matter as it does, to all classes, in Italy, and during the three and a half centuries since opera was invented in Florence, it had developed, along with its other qualities, a gift for circumventing censorship. In 1849, for example, when the mere word *Italy* was forbidden to diplomats and public speakers, Verdi had a male chorus singing "Viva l'Italia" for all it was worth in *The Battle of Legnano,* an opera that he conducted himself when it opened in Rome. The audience's tumultuous reactions helped turn the Papal States into the Roman Republic a fortnight later. But only after this was *La Battaglia di Legnano* forbidden.

Nor did opera's catalytic powers vanish with the nineteenth century. When Visconti went to work at La Scala, monarchist students had formed Verdi Clubs all over the country. Questions raised in parliament elicited only the obvious answer that, as a battle cry, *Viva Verdi* could still inflame the young, even for purposes opposed to Verdi's own. But in 1955 no one harassed La Scala about Verdi Clubs. Politically the moment was a comparatively peaceful one in Italy. On the international scene, Stalin's death had modified the Cold War. At home, Togliatti had proposed an accord between Catholics and Communists to try to "save humanity from the catastrophe of a nuclear war." Alcide de Gasperi, who died in 1954, had left a miraculous economic boom under way. Thanks to this, there was enough optimism around to induce censors, addicted to fulminating at films and fussing over plays, to take opera for granted, as an integral part of life, like saints' days and soccer matches, both of which often produced agitation.

Bellini had chosen the subject of *La Sonnambula* with his eye on the censors, who had previously forbidden him to go ahead with his opera *Ernani*. Born in Catania, Sicily, in 1801, the son and grandson of organists and composers, Bellini composed his first piece of music at the age of six, had his first opera produced when he was twenty-four, and at twenty-six was invited to compose an opera for the Scala. There was a premonitory prudence about this early start, since he died two months before his thirty-fourth birthday. But he was not among those who became famous only when safely dead. When he went to London, near the end of his short life, the fourteen-year-old Princess, and future queen, Victoria noted that she liked the modern Italian school, "Rossini, Bellini, Donizetti and C," much better than "old tiresome Handel." Wagner was to write that he would never forget the impression made on him by a Bellini opera that revealed a "simple and noble melody" to him at a period when he himself was "completely exhausted with the everlastingly abstract complications used in our orchestras."

Simple and noble indeed had been the melodies for his forbidden *Ernani,* so Bellini used them for this new opera, with an innocuous story: Amina, a young Swiss village girl, is betrothed to Elvino, a local boy who loves her and whom she loves. All is happiness until a foreign count comes to stay at the local inn. One night Amina is seen entering his room by the window. The Count realizes she is sleepwalking and respects her innocence. But the woman who runs the inn provokes a scandal. The mystery is cleared up when Amina sleepwalks onto a flimsy bridge over the mill wheel. She is rescued in time, and the Count explains to Elvino what sleepwalking is; in 1831, when *La Sonnambula* was first given, somnambulism was still a mysterious phenomenon. Elvino and Amina are then reconciled.

Having Visconti direct her in this particular part put Callas in a highly emotional state. Her teacher, Elvira de Hidalgo, had triumphed as Amina at the Metropolitan Opera in New York, and when Callas herself graduated from the Athens Conservatory, singing Puccini's *Suor Angelica,* she passionately envied a fellow student who was allowed to follow in their teacher's footsteps and sing extracts from *La Sonnambula.* Now, Callas was to sing Amina herself, at La Scala. She came to it in dazzling form, not only vocally but also physically; her twenty-two-inch waist unimpaired by delicious meals. Her newly found beauty enabled Visconti to make her resemble Bellini's contemporary Maria Taglioni, prototype of the romantic ballerina. The Scala's theater museum is full of prints of this ethereal-looking creature, idolized during the first part of the nineteenth century, when ballet was as popular as it is today. Thackeray wrote in *The Newcomes*, "Young men will never see anything as graceful as Taglioni in *La Sylphide*."

Once again, Callas succeeded in creating precisely the effect Visconti desired. She had a capacity rare among divas to transcend her own personality. Offstage, Callas was tall, with a magnetic presence, yet as Amina she appeared small and fragile. Visconti suggested that she assume a ballerina's distinctive walk. She followed the suggestion at once, and when she stood still her feet instinctively fell into the dancer's fifth position. Piero Tosi, the gifted young Florentine designer who had first worked with Visconti on *Troilus and Cressida*, created scenery and costumes exquisitely suggestive of the spirits of Bellini's day, through so many of which Taglioni dances upon the air with flying feet.

Their conductor was the prodigious Leonard Bernstein, who, at thirty-seven, had conducted the New York Philharmonic-Symphony Orchestra, taught at Brandeis University, composed the Jeremiah Symphony (1944), *Age of Anxiety* (1949), and the musicals *On the Town* (1944) and *Wonderful Town* (1953). His *West Side Story* was just ahead. He was as entertaining as a person as he was fascinating as a musician, and he and Visconti worked together with exhilaration, and similar reactions to both art and humor. Seventeen years later, remembering this production, Bernstein told John Gruen (*Opera News*, September 1972):

". . . it was something marvellous, the closest to a perfect opera performance I've ever witnessed. The time expended on its preparation—the care, the choices that were made, the work Maria and I did together on cadenzas and embellishments and ornamentations—was enormous. I remember hours of sitting with Visconti in the costume warehouse of La Scala, picking feathers for the caps of the chorus! I had eighteen rehearsals for a score that is usually done in one rehearsal, because the orchestra doesn't have too much more to do than a series of arpeggios, but those arpeggios were something never to be forgotten. And Callas was just glorious."

An extraordinary moment occurred in the scene over the mill wheel. When Callas entered, in a white dress like the one worn by Taglioni for her celebrated pas de quatre, the light was so dim that for a second she appeared in outline only against the backdrop of lake and mountain. She glided across the bridge above the mill wheel—and then, suddenly, coming to a broken plank, seemed to fall. So convincing was this fall that the audience echoed the chorus's gasps of dismay, but in fact she did not move at all. The effect was created by her method of breathing. As she slowly breathed in, she seemed to move upward, then when she released her breath she seemed to fall. Just so had Taglioni appeared to hover in the air at the height of her leaps, then come slowly down.

The finale was as moving as it was magnificent. As Amina went down to the footlights to sing the joyous "A, non giunge!" Visconti had all the lights go up, not only on the stage, but also all over the auditorium, including La Scala's mighty crystalline chandelier. This sudden blaze provided a glorious climax, and a moment of apotheosis for Callas. The plump adolescent, who had longed to sing Amina at her graduation performance, was now a beauty who had La Scala's audience shouting with delight even before she finished singing. For a man as generous as Visconti, it was a joy to have had a hand in this.

A month later Suso's father-in-law, Silvio D'Amico, died. He was sixty-eight and a true loss to the theater, to which he had devoted himself with acumen and erudition. The sense of change that death arouses—so that for a second we are physically aware of living on a planet in constant motion—was stirred again in Visconti three days later when England's eighty-year-old Prime Minister, Winston Churchill, gave a party at Downing Street on the eve of his retirement. The dramatic moment when the old statesman escorted the young Queen to her car echoed Lord Melbourne's farewells to Queen Victoria. Visconti's revered Thomas Mann died this same year, as did Teilhard de Chardin and Einstein, who had said of the vast unease that accompanied postwar changes: "The release of atom power has changed everything except our way of thinking . . ."

In May, Visconti directed Verdi's *La Traviata* at La Scala. *La Traviata*, of which Proust said, "It lifts *La Dame aux camélias* into the realm of art," was Visconti's favorite of all operas, and Verdi's favorite among his own. But on this occasion Visconti's first thoughts were for his Violetta. "I did it to serve Callas, because one *must* serve a Callas."

Alexandre Dumas the younger's famous novel *La Dame aux camélias* was published when he was only twenty-three, in 1848, a year of revolutions in the arts as well as on battlefields and barricades. The story, that of the doomed love between a celebrated Paris courtesan and a young man of upper-middle-class family, had autobiographical elements. The heroine was based on Marie Duplessis, a beautiful and witty courtesan who had died of tuberculosis at the age of twenty-three, a few months before the book appeared. Her lovers included Liszt, Musset, and Dumas the younger himself. There the autobiographical element ceases—for it would not have occurred to genial Dumas the elder to interfere with his son's love affairs. In 1977, when Maria Callas herself suddenly died in

Paris of heart failure at the age of fifty-three, her ashes were buried in Montmartre cemetery, near Marie Duplessis and Stendhal.

The stage play of *La Dame aux camélias* was produced in Paris in 1852, and is often said to have inaugurated a new school of realistic playwriting—what is taken nowadays for a wildly romantic story was considered then to contain a thorny social problem. Visconti decided to set his production around 1875. The social imperatives on which the plot depends were still operative then, and Callas would look dramatically beautiful in the tight bodices, wasp waistlines, bustles, and trains of that period. Since Violetta is, when *La Traviata* opens, primarily a performer, a provider of glamour, midway between a human being and an artifact, Visconti wanted to make her "a little of Duse, a little of Rachel, a little of Bernhardt. But more than anyone I thought of Duse." Whereas Rachel died in 1858 and could be reached only through books, pictures, family memories, Visconti had seen both Bernhardt and Duse during his stage-struck childhood.

In addition, Visconti saw parallels between the elegiac mood of Dumas's story and the decadence (in the literal sense of decline or decay) of the period in French history between 1870, when Bismarck's attack on France transformed the Second Empire into the Third Republic, and 1886, when a group of French poets published a review called *Le Décadent* to express their revolt against mid-nineteenth-century realism. To create this atmosphere visually, Visconti could not have had anyone better than Lila De Nobili. A truly great scene and costume designer, she had studied painting in both Paris and Rome, and had at that time done her finest work in Paris, notably for actor-director Raymond Rouleau, including his production of *A Streetcar Named Desire*.

Conductor Carlo Maria Giulini said that when the curtain rose on the first night "my heart skipped a beat. I was overwhelmed by the beauty of what stood before me . . . the most emotional, exquisite decor I have seen in my entire life. Every detail of Lila De Nobili's extraordinary sets and costumes made me feel I was materially entering another world, a world of incredible immediacy. The illusion of art—or should I say artifice, for theater is artifice—vanished. I had the same sensation every time I conducted this production—over twenty times in two seasons. For me, reality was onstage. What stood behind me, the audience, auditorium, La Scala itself, seemed artifice. Only that which transpired on the stage was truth, life itself."

La Traviata was as familiar to Visconti as the Galleria, the Duomo, La Scala, but familiarity had bred no contempt in him. To understand his passion for this opera, it may help to consider what his contemporary the novelist Elio Vittorini had written nearly ten years earlier. In 1937, Vittorini, then a young working-class journalist and writer, obsessed by the Spanish Civil War, chanced to go to an opera for the first time—to *La Traviata* at La Scala. Ten years later, the memory still vivid, he wrote: "I had the luck to attend a performance of *La Traviata*. . . . It was the first time in my life that I saw a melodrama, and I saw it in a special way, my heart swelling with suspense over Teruel, and for the combatants in the icy mountains around Teruel, as I imagine Verdi's contemporaries felt their hearts swelling for the Risorgimento which Verdi's music epitomized. But the work itself, despite the present-day preoccupations through which I heard and saw it, showed me that melodrama—opera—has possibilities, denied to the novel, of expressing general sentiments, great sentiments, over and beyond those expressed by the specific action, characters, emotions of the work itself."

Visconti had a clear picture of Violetta as a very young woman to whom, when the opera begins, true love is not something alien, but something feared—lest it cancel her power over lovers who provide the luxury so precious to a girl raised in hardship. Her famous remark, "I like camelias because they have no scent and rich men because they have no hearts," is defiant but true. Love of pleasure does not, however, protect Violetta when she encounters Alfredo, and once she loves him she becomes capable of a self-sacrifice that leads her straight to her death. Proust says we all have, deep inside ourselves, feelings we are unaware of holding dear; we live without taking account of these, and postpone taking possession of them for fear of failure or suffering. Visconti wanted Callas to create a Violetta who, through love and at the price of death, finally takes complete possession of her own innermost resources.

In directing Callas, Visconti gave her guidelines, but complete freedom within them. He and Giulini worked alone with her for several weeks before general rehearsals began. Giulini had conducted *La Traviata* at Bergamo four years earlier when Callas replaced Renata Tebaldi at the last minute. On that difficult occasion she sang admirably, but, said Giulini, this second *Traviata* was infinitely superior, emotionally as well as musically. During these days when the three of them worked together to establish the exact relationship between text and music, Giulini was amazed by Visconti's "sensitivity to Italian opera," quite apart from his perceptiveness as "a genius of the theater."

All Callas's instincts, as singer, actress, woman, responded with passionate agreement to Visconti's suggestions. Violetta's pride, defiance, joys, and sufferings seemed to Callas integral parts of her own self and struggles. Realizing this, Visconti kept urging her to invent gestures and business for herself, but devotion to him made her eager for his ruling on even the smallest details. As before, he found that no amount of repetition or routine could dull her reactions. She did not seem to know the meaning of staleness or caprice.

De Nobili's first set, Violetta's drawing room, was black, gold, and deep red, suggesting both luxury and death. In this scene of worldly gaiety, Callas wore a black satin dress, long white gloves, carried a bouquet of violets, and moved among her guests with an air that was a reminder that the word *courtesan* had courtly origins. Watching her, Alfredo, a young man who had for some time loved her from afar, had as much reason as Romeo to think "O, she doth teach the torches to burn bright!" When all the other guests had left, Alfredo declared his love. Violetta backed down to the footlights, her white-gloved arms behind her, maneuvering her train. This attitude gave her a vulnerable air, and when Alfredo embraced her, and the violets fell to the ground, the suggestion of vulnerability became complete defenselessness. The scene was typical of both Callas and Visconti, combining as it did an air of perfect naturalness with formal beauty and high dramatic content. When she gave Alfredo a camelia, telling him to return when it was faded, she seemed to be doing something foolhardy if not downright dangerous. After Alfredo had left, Violetta wrapped herself in a shawl and crouched by the fire while her maid wandered through the room's after-the-party disorder snuffing out the candles. As Violetta let her hair down, she sang "Ah, fors' è lui" (Perhaps it is he). Finally, self-preservation making a last stand, she tried once more to resist her own emotions—straightened up, kicked off her shoes, and, for a second, looked every inch a courtesan. Visconti's idea that she should kick off her shoes when alone is considered a stroke of genius now, but created a scandal at the time.

In the second act, the garden of Alfredo's and Violetta's country villa outside Paris, everything conveyed serenity, especially the exquisite blues and greens, every scrap painted by De Nobili herself. A domestic atmosphere, strikingly in contrast with that of the first act, was provided by wicker furniture, gardening tools, a bird fountain and greenhouse. Callas wore a dress inspired by a photograph Visconti had found of Bernhardt in *La Dame aux camélias*—creamy white adorned with lace and pale-green ribbons, accompanied by a beribboned bonnet and parasol. Blissfully disarmed, totally happy, she showed the calm and beautiful lineaments of gratified desire. Visconti directed the scene in which Alfredo's father, Germont, arrives to beg Violetta to give his son up—their liaison is about to ruin the life of Alfredo's sister by preventing

109

her marriage—in such a way as to make it clear that, given the social class and historical period, there was nothing bigoted about Germont's arguments. Just so might an upper-middle-class father today discourage a love affair between a son training for the Foreign Service and a girl involved in terrorism. Instead of the conventional old hypocrite bullying a poor girl with a heart of gold who is trying to go straight, there was a well-bred middle-aged man forced by society, of which he is a supportive member, to demand a painful sacrifice from a young woman whose sincerity and dignity have impressed him from the moment he laid eyes on her. By making the scene rational, Visconti heightened its drama. The combination of the highly rational with the highly emotional was characteristic of him off- as well as onstage.

When Violetta asked Germont to give her strength by embracing her as if she, too, were his daughter, he seemed as moved as the audience indeed was. Her despair as she fell on her knees, crying out that she would die of grief, truly had the shadow of death on it. This shadow lingered when, after Germont had left, Violetta tried to write to Alfredo. Describing the scene, Visconti said, "At this moment, Violetta is all but dead. While Maria sat at the table, she made not one move we had not prepared in rehearsal—how she cried, how she grasped her brow, how she put the pen in the inkwell, how she held her hand as she wrote, everything. No singing, only acting as the orchestra accompanied the long pantomime. Some members of the audience wept as they watched Callas in this scene."

The third act was set in the winter gardens of a courtesan friend of Violetta's earlier days. A profusion of tropical plants suggested torrid heat worlds away from the summer garden of Violetta's happiness. Gambling was in progress, and Alfredo, who had not seen Violetta since she, so he thought, betrayed him, arrived early and gambled feverishly —and with luck. When Violetta arrived, on the arm of Baron Douphol, Alfredo pretended not to notice her. That Violetta was back where she had been in Act I was obvious from her dramatically beautiful red satin dress, the ruby necklace like a surrealist halter about her long neck, the ruby bracelets like costly handcuffs around her white gloved wrists—and it was equally obvious that love had incapacitated her for her old life. When, unable to bear the sight of the Baron, Alfredo hurled his winnings at her, Callas had a supreme moment. She stood absolutely still, and what critic Francisque Sarcey wrote of Bernhardt was true of Callas then: she had indeed "an artistic beauty that, like the sight of a beautiful statue, sends a shudder of admiration through one's entire body."

The scene suggested Balzac's *Splendeurs et misères des Courtisanes*, and was a perfect illustration of Visconti's belief that melodrama is "right on the frontier between life and the theater"—which was why, he said, he loved it so much.

The last act, in Violetta's bedroom, had the denudation of death. Her furniture had gone to pay her debts. Workmen could be glimpsed in the passage. Propped against the wall a ladder indicated a faded patch where formerly a picture hung. Besides the bed on which she lay dying of tuberculosis, Violetta had only a chair and a dressing table. Here Callas looked, and sounded, literally sick unto death. Several years later, discussing her pianissimo singing in this act, she said that it required a very clear throat to sustain a fatigued way of speaking, but "how could Violetta in her condition sing in big round tones? It would be ridiculous." Lying on the bed in her fleeced room, she listened to the sounds of the carnival outside, precursor of the fasting and penitence of Lent. A succession of lights washed over her windows. The revelers' shadows danced around her empty walls. So weak she could scarcely sit up, Violetta dragged herself to the dressing table, reread Germont's letter, with its viaticumlike promise that Alfredo, knowing the truth at last, was on his way to her.

One of the most harrowing moments of her whole performance was when she gazed desperately into her mirror and sang "Oh! come son mutata" (Oh! how changed I am). Germont's letter had lighted a little flame of life in her, but even so she could scarcely move when Alfredo arrived. Together they sang of their future happiness far from city life— and, stimulated by illusory hopes, as if by a drug, Violetta called to her maid for some clothes. She could hardly dress herself. Visconti, who at that time had never himself experienced a moment's serious illness, made Violetta's fumbling with her clothes, formerly as essential to her as its plumage to a bird, as heartrending as the efforts of someone half paralyzed.

Violetta's cloak hung awry, her bonnet strings eluded her, but it was her inability to push her stiffening fingers into her gloves that provoked her desperate "Ah, gran Dio!—morir si giovane" (Oh, God!—to die so young). Equally heartrending was the way in which she assured Alfredo that thanks to his presence she could feel life pouring back into her. Joy, she sang, oh joy!—and on this word she died, her eyes open, as eyes are at the dawn of death. Suddenly blind as the eyes of a statue, her huge dark eyes went on gazing through and beyond the audience as the curtain fell.

For a second there was an appalled silence. For once, catharsis had truly taken place. Then waves of applause, the beginning of a great beneficent storm, filled La Scala. Visconti never failed to draw the best out of actors, even out of those who had not previously appeared to have a best, but this time he had been dealing with a woman of genius. It was a happy and glorious moment in both their lives.

Fourteen

From this supremely Italian opera at La Scala, Visconti went to Rome for a new American play, *The Crucible*, by Arthur Miller.

This conjured up seventeenth-century witch-hunting in Salem, Massachusetts, through the historic case of the Proctors, a couple hounded and informed against by a hysterical teen-ager. It was also a satire on modern witch-hunting by the Un-American Activities Committee and Joseph McCarthy, Senator from Wisconsin, and apart from its intrinsic merits, *The Crucible* aroused special excitement through its connection with the Rosenberg case. Ethel and Julius Rosenberg, indicted in 1950, when McCarthyism was at its height, for conspiring to obtain military information for Russia, were condemned largely on the evidence of Ethel Rosenberg's brother, David Greenglass. They were the only American civilians executed for espionage, and their fate aroused feelings similar to those aroused nearly a quarter of a century earlier by the fate of Sacco and Vanzetti. In *The Crucible*, Arthur Miller changed the historic Mary Proctor's name to Elizabeth, so that the Proctors' Christian names would have the same initials as the Rosenbergs'.

Miller's indignation was fresh, fierce, and thoughtful. He truly felt, as one of the characters in *The Crucible* says, that "little children are jangling the keys of the Kingdom and common vengeance writes the law." Visconti conveyed Miller's indignation all the more corrosively because, intensely as he himself despised McCarthyism, it did not make him anti-American. Visconti knew there was nothing specifically American about this latest manifestation of stupidity and cruelty. And by November 1955, when Visconti's production of *The Crucible* was given in Rome, indignation over the Rosenbergs was turning to gall and wormwood among those who, by then, knew that while the possibly innocent, and certainly idealistic, Rosenbergs were refusing to save their lives by pleading guilty, the undoubtedly innocent (and posthumously "rehabili-tated") victims of the contemporaneous Prague and Moscow trials were being induced not only to plead guilty, but also to beg for death sentences for "crimes" that both they and their judges knew they had not committed. Alone among Western Communist parties, the Italians denounced these persecutions. In this light, *The Crucible* became an indictment of stupidity and cruelty wherever flourishing.

As always, Visconti's first concern was to situate the play for Italian audiences. While American witches were being hunted by the Spanish Inquisition's Puritan counterparts, Salem, founded when the *Mayflower* was still a memory and not yet a legend, was merely the homestead of a small group of settlers on a vast continent scarcely marked by recorded history. These settlers had little in common with the older-established Spanish settlements far away on the west coast or with the French down south, except hostility to the natives and a determination to tame the wilderness that lay about them as unexplored as the spaces labeled "Here be Lions" on ancient maps.

The best description that Visconti found of Salem as it used to be was the one given by Nathaniel Hawthorne in *The Scarlet Letter:* "So far as its physical aspect is concerned, with its flat, unvaried surface, covered chiefly with wooden houses, few or none of which pretend to architectural beauty . . . its long and lazy street lounging wearisomely through the whole extent of the peninsula, with Gallows Hill and New Guinea at one end, and a view of the almshouse at the other—such being the features of my native town, it would be quite as reasonable to form a sentimental attachment to a disarranged checkerboard."

The scenery, which Visconti designed himself, emphasized the isolation of this "disarranged checkerboard," the darkness of mind that turned Salem houses into outposts rather than homes, the fanaticism that turned windows into spy holes, and common cats into witches' familiars. His costumes, too, with their predominant grays, browns, blacks, their muffling sobriety, helped build up an atmosphere in which it seemed normal for a husband and wife to express their love only when the hangman's noose is dangling over them.

Visconti finished the year with Chekhov's *Uncle Vanya.* Although politics are never mentioned in this quietly great play, it is permeated by the aspirations, hopes, fears, discouragement of the Russian middle class, who know their country is cruelly misgoverned and are groping in limbo for a solution. Visconti said once that while he did not think it possible for any authentic work of art to be without ideological content, he nevertheless preferred art in which ideology was too well assimilated for its presence to be obvious, let alone intrusive. He thought Chekhov an "eminently ideological writer" whose incomparable pictures of a vanishing world in crisis had no need of "declarations and programs" to make them explicit. Nothing in Brecht, he thought, reached the polemical level of *The Cherry Orchard*.

This was followed by a new departure for him—a ballet, *Mario and the Magician*, at La Scala. Several years earlier he had written a libretto based on Thomas Mann's novella. The music was by Franco Mannino, a gifted young composer, pianist, and conductor who had won the Columbus Award for 1950, and first worked with Visconti on music for the film *Bellissima*. Visconti and Mannino submitted their ballet project to Thomas Mann in the summer of 1951 at Bad Gastein, in Austria. Mann was excited by the idea and encouraged them to go ahead.

Written by Thomas Mann in 1930, when Mussolini had been in power eight years and Hitler, just acquiring German citizenship, had three years to go before becoming chancellor, *Mario and the Magician* is a grim fairy tale of fascism—complete with the sexual perversity found in fairy tales as often as in daily life. When the novella opens, a German couple and their children are arriving for their summer holiday at a middle-class Italian seaside resort. Because it is not their first visit here, they notice a subtle change for the worse in the atmosphere. The series of petty annoyances they suffer seems connected with the new political regime. On the beach one day, they tell their little daughter—eight years old "but in physical development a good year younger and thin as a chicken"—to take off her bathing suit and rinse the sand out of it. She runs naked into the sea. Whereupon "a gentleman in city togs, with a not very apropos bowler hat on the back of his head," accuses them of immorality, indiscipline, and insulting the country's hospitality. They are obliged to go to the town hall, where an official says "very serious" and fines them. After this, trying to make the best of a deteriorated job, the Germans take their children to a much advertised conjuring show. The local all-purpose hall is packed with holidaymakers expecting an evening's cheerful entertainment. But the conjurer turns out to be a deformed and sinister figure—"perhaps more than anywhere else the eighteenth century is still alive in Italy, and with it the charlatan and mountebank type so characteristic of the period." The conjurer's tricks are merely a cover for a murky form of hypnotism. While "establishing contact" with his audience, he so teases, humiliates, and sexually alarms Mario, a young waiter who is there with his girl, that the boy is finally maddened to the point of shooting him.

Visconti and Mannino set to work on this novella in the summer of

1952 at the Colombaia, the villa Visconti had rented, and was to buy, on the island of Ischia. The Colombaia had quickly become a study center for artists. Guests usually included Suso Cecchi D'Amico, Rina Morelli, and Paolo Stoppa. The libretto for *Mario and the Magician* was completed there. It offered Visconti an opportunity to approach his ideal of "total theater": drama, music, acting, singing, and dancing. With four main characters (the Magician was to suggest Mussolini), and a crowd of local inhabitants, it was set in 1925 at Versilia, formerly a wild country district renowned for the pure Tuscan accents of the local inhabitants, later a fashionable seaside resort. The choreographer was Léonide Massine, who as a young man, dancing in Diaghilev's Ballets Russes, had created *La Boutique Fantasque, The Good-Humored Ladies,* and *The Three-cornered Hat.* Jean Babilée danced the waiter with feral ingenuousness. Lila De Nobili designed the scenery, and although she did not neglect the Bright Young Things aspect—obvious now, but not so obvious in 1956, when the term *retro* had not yet come into use, let alone fashion—she created a twenties decor that, like Thomas Mann's story, was subtly sinister. The world of *The Great Gatsby* and *The Constant Nymph,* of Paul Morand and Pitigrilli, of Chanel clothes and the Orient Express, shingled hair and the Charleston, was also the world in which Hitler's *Mein Kampf* was published.

Thomas Mann was particularly gratified because the ballet showed no trace of the expressionism that had been fashionable in Germany in his youth, but which he himself had always avoided in his own work. He asked Visconti to let him know the date of production well in advance, because he hoped to come to Milan for the first night. Since, however, La Scala's programs were composed far ahead, the curtain did not go up on the ballet of *Mario and the Magician* until 1956, when Mann had been dead six months. His daughter Elisabeth Mann Borgese came to the first night and wrote Visconti and Mannino that the whole spectacle had seemed to her a gift from them, "unique in its originality and suggesting vast new possibilities."

After *Mario and the Magician,* Visconti began planning a new film, taking into account the need to show film producers who were alarmed by hyperbolic stories about the costliness of *Senso* that he could make a film rapidly and without extravagance. Also, Visconti and Suso wanted to offer young Mastroianni a part more suited to his gifts than the "good-natured cabdrivers" for which he was too often cast.

Visconti was struck by the prophetic strain in Verga's short story "E andato cosi" (It Happened This Way), in which four boys end an aimlessly spent Sunday by committing a senseless crime. In a few pages

Verga covered much of the ground discovered later by Theater of the Absurd writers. "E andato cosi" touched, too, on the mindless violence described in 1955 by Pier Paolo Pasolini in his novel *Ragazzi di Vita,* on slum delinquency and boy prostitutes—a novel that looked ahead, in most uncanny fashion, to what would be labeled "typical seventies' violence," including Pasolini's own brutish murder at the hands of a *ragazzo di vita.*

Nevertheless, previous battles with the censor about Verga had slightly discouraged Visconti, and at this point Suso mentioned their problems to her father. Emilio Cecchi suggested they examine Dostoevsky's novellas. Reading these, Visconti and Suso were both struck by "White Nights," first published in André Kraïevski's *Annals of the Fatherland* in December 1948.

The plot of "White Nights" is a simple one. During one of St. Petersburg's light summer nights, a lonely young man (Mario, in Visconti's film), who has recently come to work there, meets a girl almost equally solitary. Natalia lives with her blind grandmother, and the two women support themselves by mending old carpets and renting rooms in their canalside house. Mario immediately notices something strange about Natalia. She is obsessed by her passion for one of their lodgers, a mysterious figure who said on leaving that he would return for her in a year's time. Every evening Natalia waits for the lodger at the bridge beside her home. The year has now been up for several days. Mario and Natalia meet for three evenings in a row. He tries to comfort her and, in doing so, falls in love with her himself. Grateful for a listener, Natalia seems momentarily to waver. But the lodger returns and she rushes joyously into his arms at the appointed meeting place.

Since Mario seemed to Visconti and Suso an excellent part for Mastroianni, the three of them decided to make a co-operative job of the film. Then Franco Cristaldi, a producer from Turin who had already been in the business ten years and worked with the Vides firm, became interested. The four of them—one producer, one director, one scriptwriter, and one actor—decided to form their own company, the Cinematografica Associati. Cristaldi saw in this venture the possibility of creating an Italian Associated Artists, which he felt to be just what was needed in a country where artistry and enthusiasm were far more abundant than capital. Cinecittà agreed to contribute by building the sets. The Rank Organisation, Vides, and Cinematografica Associati itself would take care of the film's distribution.

Because the cinema was experiencing one of its crises, these underpinnings took until the end of summer. Meanwhile, thanks to Khrushchev's revelations about Stalin, the political climate was becoming stormy in Italy, as elsewhere. To most of today's young it seems incredible that Stalin could ever have been thought to be anything but a monster. But to those who were young during the siege of Stalingrad—especially those who had themselves fought in resistance movements—the news that Comrade Stalin, Uncle Joe, was a modern Genghis Khan seemed earthshaking. Nor was this all. Khrushchev's report was followed by riots in the Georgian Soviet Republic, and the "rehabilitation" of Laszlo Rajk, the Hungarian minister executed for "Titoism" in 1949. The Polish Communist leader Wladyslaw Gomulka, arrested for "Titoism" in 1951, was likewise rehabilitated, and, more fortunate than Rajk, was alive to enjoy the change while it lasted. In June, there were anti-Soviet riots in Poland, where a hundred striking Polish workers were shot down. Finally, a nationwide uprising in Hungary was crushed by Soviet planes, troops, and tanks, and 190,000 refugees fled the country. Cardinal Mindszenty, Primate of Hungary, took refuge in the American legation. In his most recent book (1978), Giorgio Amendola calls 1956 "a terrible year."

More than half of the Italian left, Visconti among them, were hostile to Russia's invasion of Hungary. But it did not occur to him that to choose Dostoevsky at precisely this moment might seem deliberately provocative. Unappreciated during his lifetime by Tolstoy, Chekhov, and most of his great contemporaries, Dostoevsky was still not popular with the Soviet authorities. His "ideological contents," they said, "were negative," a remark Visconti was to hear repeated more than once. However, at the time, having completed arrangements for the financing and distribution of *Le notti bianche*, he was completely absorbed in securing Maria Schell for the part of Natalia. Visconti had been one of the jury that voted her Best Actress at the 1956 Venice Festival for her performance as the laundress Gervaise, in the film of that name made by René Clément from Emile Zola's novel *L'Assommoir*.

Like Rina Morelli and Romy Schneider, Maria Schell came of an acting family. Since it is often supposed that makers of Neo-Realistic films always preferred nonprofessional actors, it should be mentioned for the record that Visconti, on the contrary, had immense respect for professional actors, and used nonprofessional ones only once, when the nature of *La terra trema* made this obligatory. He especially liked directing actors' children—*figli d'arte*—saying that someone raised in dressing rooms, who knew Italy from top to toe through one-night stands, who had played a murdered Macduff infant and graduated via "dinner is served," was likely to have "a discipline and total dedication to the theater" seldom found in people not born to it, especially nowadays, when films and TV tempt the young before they have had time for an apprenticeship. Maria Schell was the eldest of the five children, all actors, of the Austrian poet and dramatist Herman Karl Schell. Her mother, also an actress, taught at the conservatory in Bern, Switzerland, where the family had taken refuge after Hitler invaded Austria in 1938.

Two days after the Cinematografica Associati was legally set up, Visconti telephoned Munich. Maria Schell was not there that day. Impatient, as usual, he went to Munich with a French translation of the first half of the script. Schell thought him "an extraordinary man," and "an exceptional mixture," since despite "the culture and great traditions" that must, she felt, "bind him to the past," he "seemed to understand modern life perfectly and had succeeded in rendering this story of the past actual." But, meticulous in character and training, she would agree to nothing without a thorough discussion of the story itself, the script, her own part and salary. To settle the matter, Visconti and Cristaldi went to Paris, where she was staying for the first public showing of *Gervaise*. There they found her in the happy Tower of Babel produced by success in the film world. European producers in person, Hollywood producers via the telephone, buzzed around a hotel room where screenplays lay thicker than autumn leaves in Vallombrosa. Nevertheless, Maria Schell chose *Le notti bianche*.

She thought that the ideal person to play the lodger would be the French actor Jean Marais, whose romantic appearance would add credibility to Natalia's passion for the "dream character." Neither Cristaldi nor Visconti thought it likely that Marais, who had leaped to fame in Cocteau's *Les Parents terribles* in 1938, and was by 1956 at the height of his success on both stage and screen, would accept so small a part, virtually no more than an appearance. But Marais said he would be glad to play anything that meant working with Visconti.

Visconti then returned to Rome to organize the building of the sets. Since it was impossible to shoot *Le notti bianche* in Leningrad, he decided to situate the film in Livorno. This was not a disruptive change. St. Petersburg, a port on the Gulf of Finland, possessed beautiful eighteenth-century buildings made for Peter the Great by French and Italian architects. Livorno, a Mediterranean port, was developed in the fifteenth century by the Medicis. But Livorno was to be only the model. For the first—and there was to be only one other—time, Visconti decided to film not on location but entirely in studios. He was determined to shoot *Le notti bianche* within the agreed time limit and without extravagance. Although it took one hundred and twenty artisans forty-five days to build the sets, this cost less than it would have done to film in Livorno, cordoning off streets, eliminating extraneous noise, and, above all, having to rely on unreliable weather. Nor was anything essential lost by this, since the action of Le notti bianche evolves in a small space, and the inner isolation of the characters is more important than the place in which they are isolated.

The topographical pivot of the action is a little bridge over a canal. On one side of this stands Natalia's home, on the other side the neon-lighted modern city where Mario works. Shooting was to begin at the end of January 1957, and earlier that same month Visconti produced Countess Julie at Rome's Teatro delle Arti. This was his first professional contact with the peculiar personal gloom that made Strindberg an angler in the lake of darkness.

In the scenery and costumes, which he designed himself, Visconti emphasized the atmosphere of Scandinavian midsummer madness, with its sense of supernatural beings temporarily abroad, by details such as the ethereal white summer curtains put up ritually at the moment when festive outdoor bonfires proclaim that there is no longer any need to light the stoves indoors. He also emphasized the play's insistence on the way that the social classes change places according to the Darwinian belief in the survival of the fittest, shared by Strindberg. Visconti's capacity to combine passion with precision enabled his Countess Julie to have as violent an effect on its 1957 audience as the original Lady Julia had on hers in 1888—only forty years after the first convention favoring female independence took place at Seneca Falls, New York.

Five days after the play opened in Rome, on January 16, 1957, Visconti was grief-stricken by the death of Toscanini in New York. In a sense, nothing was there for tears—certainly no weakness, no contempt, dispraise, or blame, nothing but well or fair. At eighty-nine, Toscanini had been able to look back on a fine and fiery life, during which he had shared with the whole world the genius it would have been death to hide. Like his beloved Verdi, Toscanini had played a leading part in his country's history. Born at the same time as Italian unity and the Italian monarchy, he had witnessed two world wars, victory and defeat, the rise and fall of Mussolini, the end of the monarchy, the beginnings of the Republic—and, through all the hopes and horrors, had himself steadfastly deserved Shakespeare's words "What a piece of work is man! How noble in reason! How infinite in faculties! In form and in moving how express and admirable!"

All this Visconti knew and felt. But it could not assuage his grief for a man he had known and revered since earliest childhood. With Toscanini vanished not only memories of Visconti's father and mother when they were young and beautiful and not yet parents, but also memories of the Visconti children before they were of an age to remember themselves. There vanished, too, a thousand trivial memories of their home in Milan, with its long-lost dogs and cats, its absurd athletic tutor, its ubiquitous bicycles—and all the family jokes and catchwords that are among the most poignant of death's smaller deprivations.

Nothing has more power than grief to actuate memory, our truest means of conversation, so Visconti heard again his mother's voice describing Verdi's funeral to him, saw again, what he had never seen in fact, the young Toscanini conducting nine hundred singers in "Va pensiero" as a last farewell to Verdi. Visconti remembered his mother showing him the Grand Hotel, where Verdi had died at four o'clock in the afternoon on January 21, 1901. It was, and is, in the street named after Verdi's idol Manzoni. When first Verdi stayed there, Milan was still full of street cries, and one morning the old maestro had been awakened by a chimney sweep's boy chirping like a bird, on three notes, "Spaaaz-zacamin" (chimney sweep). These three notes were transformed by Verdi into Alfredo's exquisite love song, "Di quell' amor," in *La Traviata*. And Visconti remembered Callas, radiantly beautiful as she curtsied from the stage of La Scala to the box where Toscanini, himself the "old maestro" by then, held the flower she had thrown him. Visconti remembered the Galleria, where, as a child, he had seen the Boito brothers, Camillo and Arrigo, who wrote of Verdi, "Poor Maestro, how brave and handsome he was up to the last minute."

For Visconti, the death of Toscanini meant not only the death of a man of genius, the loss of a revered friend and mentor, but also the end of a whole world of affections old and true.

Fifteen

Fortunately for Visconti, he was due to start filming *Le notti bianche* four days later, and, since he would for once be working exclusively in the studio, his rhythm would be uninterrupted by weather or other outside hindrances.

Le notti bianche starts on the city side of a canal in Livorno. It is evening. People are coming home from work. A young stranger, Mario, wanders disconsolately alone, stopping by the bridge to pat a dog as rootless as himself. In this way he meets Natalia, in tears because the mysterious lodger whom she loves has not returned, as promised, after a year's absence. The isolation of Natalia and Mario is emphasized by the sound of ships' sirens from the harbor, eerily distressing as the cries of birds trapped in the act of migrating. Mario insists on accompanying Natalia to her door. Their timid friendship begins as if it were a consultation between two invalids, both suffering from the same malady, which is solitude.

For three consecutive evenings, Natalia and Mario meet, talk, try to comfort each other. As in Dostoevsky's story, Rossini's opera *The Barber of Seville* provides a leitmotif. Natalia tells Mario how the lodger took her and her grandmother to the opera. A flashback shows the three of them there. Rossini's music, associated with the absent lodger, is later contrasted with the rock 'n' roll music that Natalia hears for the first time when Mario takes her to a café, which, though not far from the opera house, seems to be in another world.

For the modern music, Visconti called on Nino Rota, a brilliant and fluent composer whose opera *Il Cappello di Paglia di Firenze* had driven the first-night audience in Palermo nearly mad with excitement and was later to be performed all over the world. Rota had at this time composed three operas, as well as symphonies, chamber and piano music, and music for several films, including Fellini's *Lo sceicco bianco* (*The White Sheikh*, 1952) and *La strada* (1954). Rota gave his *Le notti bianche* music a Wagnerian romanticism appropriate to Natalia's mysterious love affair; Dostoevsky had written *White Nights* the year Wagner completed *Lohengrin*. Visconti understood modern music as thoroughly as he did classical. He directed the scene in the café so brilliantly that it has become an anthology piece of historical evidence as to how rock 'n' roll music and dancing sounded and looked in the mid-fifties. Natalia is so shaken by this music's deliberate assault on the nerves that she is still caught up by it at ten o'clock, the time for her tryst at the bridge. The sudden ruthlessness with which she then whirlwinds out of the café, without an instant's thought for Mario, sends him to the grasping arms of a prostitute.

The prostitute was admirably played by Clara Calamai, the Giovanna of Visconti's first film, *Ossessione*. When Alberto De Rossi, in charge of make-up, asked how she was to look, Visconti said, "Do you remember Giovanna in *Ossessione?* Well—fifteen years have gone by. Badly, for her. She's been let out of prison, has gone home, and become a prostitute." So De Rossi gave her the same hair style as in *Ossessione*, hair falling over her eyes, and accentuated her pallor, to indicate that she had been a long time shut away from the sun. Calamai herself cleverly combined a tragic version of vanished charm with a desperate, grabbing avidity.

Frightened by this avidity, Mario tries to back out. The prostitute immediately begins insulting him. Bystanders join in with the sheepish conformity and hyenalike savagery of crowds everywhere. Natalia returns. The lodger has not appeared. Mario no longer believes in his existence. Feeling angry and betrayed, Natalia is ready to fall in with Mario's suggestions. He takes a boat and rows her to a spot popular with lovers. But they find it occupied by homeless families trying to shelter from the cold. It begins to snow. Natalia is childishly delighted with the snowflakes. She and Mario get out of the boat and walk alongside the canal.

Absorbed by the snow's fluid architecture, Natalia seems to Mario so beautiful, yet so remote, that he begins to understand her romantic conception of love. At this point the bridge where they met three evenings earlier comes into sight—and by it stands a figure in a dark coat and hat who calls, "Natalia!" in a tone of authority. Natalia rushes to her lover, no dream, but a handsome man beside whom she and Mario look like children. Mario is left to solitude and a stray dog. But he is not left empty-hearted, since, in Dostoevsky's words, "One entire minute of happiness. God! What more does a human life need."

Le notti bianche was completed in eight weeks, on a low budget. Since they made it on a co-operative basis, Visconti, Suso, and Mastroianni earned next to nothing out of it but, perhaps because it was "their very own," they had never enjoyed filming so much. Nor was it financially unprofitable in the long run: by winning the Silver Lion award at the 1957 Venice Festival it attracted backers for Visconti's next film. Before this, though, Visconti did another spell at La Scala. From young Dostoevsky's dream of a minute's happiness, he turned to one of the dreadful matrimonial dreams of England's Henry VIII, as displayed in Donizetti's opera *Anna Bolena*.

Gaetano Donizetti was among the dazzling princes of his day. Although born to poor parents in the Bergamo of 1797, he got an excellent musical education at the composer Giovanni Simone Mayr's Charity Music School, wrote his first opera at nineteen, and made his debut at La Scala at twenty-five. *Anna Bolena*, composed when he was thirty-three, in a flow of inspiration so intense that he completed the entire opera in thirty days, brought him international fame. Between the ages of nineteen and forty-eight, when he was paralyzed by a stroke, from which he died three years later, Donizetti composed over sixty operas, also songs, symphonies, chamber music, oratorios, cantatas, church music. When, near the end of his working life, he offered to attend rehearsals of young Verdi's *Ernani*, Verdi wrote the "Honored Maestro" that he had no hesitation at all in accepting this courteous offer with the deepest gratitude, since "my music can gain a lot if Donizetti deigns to give it his attention."

When Visconti started work on *Anna Bolena*, it had not been performed at La Scala since 1877. Stimulus to revive it came from Donizetti's hometown, Bergamo, where a group of talented young singers performed it in 1956. Since Bergamo, home of the comedia dell'arte—the original Harlequin is said to have been based on a real-life local character—is only thirty miles from Milan, a number of Milanese attended this performance. Among them was Gianandrea Gavazzeni, conductor at La Scala as well as composer, writer, music critic, and himself born in Bergamo. It struck him that Maria Callas would be an ideal Anne Boleyn. The management of La Scala liked Gavazzeni's suggestion, and Visconti was invited to stage it. Scenery and costumes would be designed by Nicola Benois, head of La Scala's scenic department since 1936.

Before general rehearsals began, Gavazzeni and Visconti met daily for a couple of weeks' preliminary work at Visconti's Roman villa. This, with its high-walled garden—Visconti was a stubborn gardener, as patient with plants as with animals and artists—was on the Via Salaria, a road with origins literally lost in the mists of antiquity. Four and a half centuries before the birth of Christ, salt from the salt pans of Ostia, at the mouth of the Tiber, was carried along this road to the Sabine country; and our word *salary* comes from the special allowance given to Roman soldiers to buy *sale* (salt), without which it was then impossible to preserve food—which made salt as important to the ancient world as oil is to us. Here, amid dogs, flowers, books, pictures, tapestries, statues, a Maggiolini table of miniature obelisks, and a marble chess table set with miniature towers, Gavazzeni and Visconti went over the score of *Anna Bolena* again and again, discussed the libretto's tragic qualities, and endeavored to see Anne Boleyn's destiny and period as they had appeared to Donizetti in 1830.

Their documentation included pictures of Henry VIII's castles and Holbein's portraits. When Holbein went to England in 1526, his friend Erasmus introduced him to Sir Thomas More's circle and he was appointed court painter to Henry VIII the very year of Anne Boleyn's execution. But Visconti and Benois used the documentation they collected as a stimulant rather than a model.

In their superb book on Callas, John Ardoin and Gerald Fitzgerald quote Nicola Benois as saying of this production:

Callas' costumes in *Bolena* were literally sculpted on her figure. The elegance she had developed over the years so enhanced her esthetic effect that Luchino and I did everything we could to emphasize her presence onstage. How she walked in her gowns! Like a queen. All her costumes were inspired by Holbein's portraits of Anne Boleyn, but no single detail was authentic. Nor in the sets were specifics copied from any of Henry VIII's castles. Luchino gave me precise documentation from history, but he did not seek reality.

Our entire production of *Anna Bolena* became a trick of perspective, an optical illusion. Some scenes seemed very deep set, even 125 feet, but none were really more than 35. I believe illusion to be the greatest merit of the designer's art. Today, this might seem an outmoded ideal, but for me it holds true and beautiful. Consider what opera is. A totally artificial form of theater. No one speaks, they sing, and this is not life. If you say "Open the window," you are talking about a real window. But if to a beautiful melody you sing "Open the window," it has already become something else. Music transforms. It creates another sphere. And just as it gives extension to words, so it extends all the dimensions of theater. Operatic scenery must have a snug quality, must exist in another space, be doubly poetic, doubly romantic. Nothing is real in opera, however true the human values it expresses and intensifies.

Most important, scenery must capture the spirit of the music it accompanies. In *Anna Bolena,* Luchino and I discovered Henry VIII's time through Donizetti's score. Had the opera been composed by Schoenberg, Gershwin, or Britten, we would have done something quite different.

The blacks, whites, and grays of the sets contrasted dramatically with the brilliant colors of the costumes—the guards' scarlet and yellow, the red worn by Anne Boleyn's rival Jane Seymour, and, above all, the exquisite blues and immense jewels worn by Callas. The total effect had the accuracy of great poetry, which hits a mark of which we were previously unaware. Director Sandro Sequi said, "I was deeply impressed by what I saw. While it was in the great, old tradition of La Scala, the production was executed through a screen of time—absolutely correct in taste and judgment. Only in this way can works of the Romantic epoch come alive today. Imagine *Anna Bolena,* or any opera from its era, staged with historical accuracy. It would be like some cheap, fake movie." The first-night audience applauded each set as the curtain rose.

The extraordinary dignity Callas gave to the part provided a reminder that Anne Boleyn was not only a repudiated wife of Henry VIII, but also the mother of Elizabeth I of England, the Queen who said, "If thy heart fails thee, climb not at all." She confronted death as unfalteringly as she did her first entrance down the great staircase of Windsor Castle to sing "Son calde ancor le ceneri del mio primiero amore" (The embers of my first love smolder still). When she refused Jane Seymour's entreaty that she save her life by pleading guilty, a sense of doom played like lightning around both women. For Jane Seymour, lady-in-waiting to Henry VIII's first and second wives, was to become his third wife less than two weeks after Anne's execution—but would herself die the following year, after the birth of her son, who became Edward VI.

In the final scene, in the Tower of London, Callas was stupendous. The light that seeped through the barred windows gave the underground room a likeness to Rembrandt's *The Night Watch,* in which a crowd is both an entity and a collection of solitudes. As the light grew stronger, the crowd's elements could be distinguished: soldiers to help the King eliminate the obstacle to his new love, and court ladies, so that Anne Boleyn can go to her death in the state to which she is accustomed. Visconti lighted this scene so that the central figure was the last one to become visible. As the shadows lifted from around her, an anticipatory silence took possession of the entire auditorium. Callas began singing almost in a whisper. "Here," said Piero Tosi, "Visconti showed his genius, for he never intruded on this sound, so perfect, so expressive. Callas's stillness created incredible tension while her voice, human yet crystallized, seemed almost an object. What one saw and heard were indivisible." The way in which her gentle plea to be allowed to return to her own home changed into a terrible cry for vengeance, "l'estrema vendetta," was a perfect illustration of Hugo von Hofmannsthal's dictum: "Singing is near miraculous because it is the mastering of what is otherwise a pure instrument of egotism." At the end the audience rose and cheered. The applause lasted for twenty-four minutes. Artistic director Francesco Siciliani said that this production "established entirely new standards at La Scala."

Anna Bolena opened on April 14, and Visconti was to stage Gluck's *Iphigénie en Tauride* June 1. This would be his fifth production with Callas, and his first work on a foreign opera. But although Gluck was German—born in what is now Bavaria in 1714, the son of a forester—he studied in Italy and composed his first ten operas in Italian style. *Iphigénie en Tauride*, composed for the Paris Opéra, had been produced there with immense success in 1779, on the eve of the French Revolution. It tells the story of Clytemnestra and Agamemnon's daughter, Iphigenia, in what was at the time a new and revolutionary musical style that influenced Wagner, who conducted Gluck's *Iphigénie en Aulide* when composing *Lohengrin*.

The first Iphigenia tragedies were written by Euripides four and a half centuries before the birth of Christ. Gluck followed their narrative line. His first *Iphigénie* opera, *Iphigénie en Aulide*, related the first part of Iphigenia's life, when, about to be sacrificed, with her own patriotic consent, to the goddess Artemis, in order to obtain fair winds for the Greek fleet on its way to the Trojan War, she was spirited away to Tauris by Artemis. *Iphigénie en Tauride* opens with Iphigenia already in Tauris (today's Crimea) and established as High Priestess of Artemis among the wild Scythians.

Nicola Benois again designed scenery and costumes. There was to be a single set, and Benois and Visconti drew inspiration for it from the work of the Bibienas, the extraordinary seventeenth-to-eighteenth-century family of architects, scene designers, and painters who worked all over Europe and were the master scene designers of Gluck's day. The sea could be seen behind the central staircase at the back, and all around were columns, loggias, statues, and an altar to the goddess Diana: a rococo version of mythical Greece. With this went costumes inspired by Tiepolo—the Tiepolo of the Homer and Virgil frescoes in the Villa Valmarana at Vicenza.

The result was fabulously beautiful, completely in harmony with the music, always Visconti's first consideration, and uncannily reminiscent

127

of Petra—"uncannily" because no Bibiena could have seen or heard of Petra, the "rose-red city half as old as time," discovered, near the Red Sea, only in 1812. There, long before the birth of Christ, were pillared temples and palaces, carved in many-colored living rock, that suggested a link between legendary Greece and baroque Rome, in the exact style of the Bibienas' fantasy world.

When the curtain rose, a storm was in progress and a distraught Callas swept across the stage—distraught but superb, with pearls looped in her hair and around her neck, a dress of silk brocade with a long train, and a cloak of the color of Baccarà roses. At one point she had to rush down a steep staircase, which she did with a feline combination of grace and frenzy, her cloak billowing out behind her. To Visconti's delight, her co-ordination was so great that she never once failed to hit her high note precisely as her foot touched the eighth step.

Visconti thought *Iphigénie en Tauride* the most beautiful production on which Callas and he collaborated. But it was to be the last one. They had many plans for future work together. One of these was to open La Scala's 1960-1961 season with Donizetti's *Poliuto*. Benois intended using, as a point of departure for his scenery, designs by Pietro Gonzaga, a Venetian architect and scene designer who had worked at La Scala in 1775 and subsequently went to St. Petersburg, where he became head scene designer of the imperial theaters.

All was settled for *Poliuto* to be produced at La Scala in December 1960. But when the time came, Visconti had just fought a monumental battle with the censors over his production of Giovanni Testori's play *L'Arialda*. This came on top of a series of battles over his film *Rocco and His Brothers,* and the pettifogging bad faith displayed by officialdom on both occasions drove him to swear he would never again work in an Italian state-subsidized theater. On November 16, 1960, he telegraphed to Maria Callas, telling her that having to refuse to stage *Poliuto* was painful to him "above all because it prevents me working with you, which is the work that gives me the greatest gratification. Although I apologize to you, dear Maria, I am nevertheless sure that you will understand my state of mind and approve of my decision. I embrace you with all my customary admiration and immense affection."

To this Maria Callas at once replied with a long letter in which she expressed her distress "first of all because you are being tormented" and because working with him meant so much to her and she had been "counting the hours" until they started on *Poliuto*. She hoped his troubles would soon be over—but doubted that either he or she "would ever be free of troubles." She thought the censors very stupid to harass the theater yet leave complete liberty to the type of newspaper that owes its enormous sales to "obscene, inexact and defamatory" accounts of the private lives of the famous. All this "incongruity" distressed her, she wrote, since it seemed to her "so absurd, so contrary to common sense" that she found it "difficult to believe that it could exist in the world of today." Finally, she begged him to send news of himself whenever he had a free moment, not to forget her, but to continue always to care for her. All of this Visconti did. As a friend he was as loyal and supportive as he could be exacting.

The importance of Visconti's impulsive, self-sacrificing, yet reasonable, attitude in this instance was emphasized in a letter from critic Nicola Chiaromonte, who wrote at the same time as Maria Callas: "Dear Visconti, allow me to express my admiration and gratitude for your refusal to stage *Poliuto* at La Scala. It is to be hoped that your gesture will set in motion a whole movement of solidarity among the most vital part of our culture and that this will be shown by a refusal to submit to the humiliating conditions they are attempting to impose on us. In any case you have set an example. And it seems to me that the Italian theater, in particular—producers, actors, playwrights, critics—owe you gratitude and support. Gratefully, your Nicola Chiaromonte."

This did not mean the end of opera work for Visconti. He was to direct operas in Spoleto, London, Vienna, eventually Rome, but never again in Milan, never again with Callas, and, as he himself said, what he did with her "was always something apart, created for her alone."

Sixteen

That same summer, two months after Gamal Abdel Nasser, first president of the new Egyptian republic, reopened the Suez Canal, an elderly Sicilian prince died of lung cancer in a Roman nursing home. His name was Giuseppe Tomasi, Duke of Palma and Prince of Lampedusa and, at the time of his death, he was known only to his family, his animals, his friends and acquaintances. A man of exceptionally wide culture, he understood what he had lived through—the destruction of entire worlds in 1918, and of even their ruins in 1945—and he had for years hoped to rescue a fragment of the past by writing a book about his grandfather's life and landscape. Finished only at the end of the Prince's life, and published posthumously, *Il Gattopardo* (*The Leopard*) found admirers all over Italy and all over the world.

Visconti was to be among *Il Gattopardo*'s admirers, and to make from it a film of powerful beauty, historically authentic and spiritually convincing. But at the time of the Prince's death, *Il Gattopardo*, rejected by two leading publishers, seemed condemned to die with him; and Visconti was unaware of the drama so near to him in every sense. He himself was just then occupied with the scenery and costumes for Goldoni's *L'Impresario delle Smyrne*, which he was directing for the International Theater Festival in Venice, and which would be presented at the Paris International Theater Festival the following year. In addition, he was staging a ballet, *Dance Marathon*, for the seventh Berlin Theater Festival.

As a young man, a visitor from Mussolini's Italy, Visconti had seen something of the Berlin where Christopher Isherwood's Mr. Norris changed trains and Sally Bowles changed horizontal partners—a garish, inflation-wracked city soon to dissolve into the Berlin of Erich Kästner's "Know'st thou the land where the cannon blooms?" and Hitler's "All those who are not racially pure are mere chaff." Twenty years later, a distinguished artist from republican Italy, Visconti visited the prosperous half of Berlin, governed by *Der Alte* (the Old Man), as sage Chancellor Konrad Adenauer was called. The Russians had not yet built the Berlin Wall, and there was a steady flow of refugees from East to West Berlin, where the shops, niched above the ruins like paste jewels in a toad's head, were already full of consumer goods.

The music of *Maratona* (*Dance Marathon*), for which Visconti had himself composed the libretto, was by Hans Werner Henze, a young German composer who had settled in Italy after three years at the Wiesbaden state theater, of which he had been appointed artistic director in 1950 at the age of twenty-four. Henze had already composed two operas, *Boulevard Solitude* (1951) and *König Hirsch* (*King Stag*, 1955), two ballets, symphonies and concertos. The choreography was by the American dancer Dick Sanders, who had worked for Visconti on the rock 'n' roll scene in *Le notti bianche*. The soloist was the French dancer Jean Babilée, who had danced in Visconti's *Mario and the Magician* at La Scala. All Visconti's free evenings were spent at the theater. What interested him most was the famous Berliner Ensemble company from East Berlin, which Bertolt Brecht had directed himself from 1949 until his death, at fifty-eight, in 1956. Brecht's life—much of it spent, in his own words, "changing countries more often than my shoes"—had not been easy anywhere, and both his own evolution and that of the European left could be followed in his *Life of Galileo*, rewritten after the atomic bomb was dropped on Hiroshima. Visconti had just read the final version of this, published in Italian in 1957.

Despite nascent prosperity, there was little sense of security in West Berlin. Artists, including the future Nobel Prize winner Heinrich Böll, were skeptical about the German "economic miracle," and the young, including Günter Grass, were obsessed by the "absurdity" of the recent past, in which, although not responsible for it, they felt themselves entangled. At the end of Visconti's Berlin visit, the Russians performed the masterly feat of launching the first artificial satellite, Sputnik I, into space—but were unable to perform the simple feat of publishing Boris Pasternak's novel *Doctor Zhivago*, which was therefore given its first publication in Italy, by Giangiacomo Feltrinelli, publisher of *Il Gattopardo*.

Around this time Visconti had two very different projects in mind: to direct a French version of Eugene O'Neill's *Long Day's Journey into Night* on the Paris stage with Edwige Feuillère, and to go on a filming expedition to Tibet. He longed to make "some record of the extraordinarily tenacious resistance put up by that small ancient world, with its archaic traditions, against the modern world advancing on it from China." The Dalai Lama had not yet been driven out of Tibet, and little was known in Europe of the struggles underway on that lost horizon, so it is sad that Visconti was finally unable to bear witness to them. Fifteen years later the young Italian director Liliana Cavani made *Milarepa,* a film in which a Tibetan mystic, Milarepa, confronts today's world.

Back in Rome, that autumn, Visconti's first professional film, *Ossessione,* was revived, in a new version put together by Visconti from spools of film found at the National Film Library. Only fifteen years had passed since the film's first appearance, but the 1957 audiences belonged to a new world and this time *Ossessione*'s success neither provoked scandal nor brought a bishop hastening to exorcise the cinema where it was shown.

At Christmas, Visconti began rehearsals for Arthur Miller's *A View from the Bridge,* with Rina Morelli and Paolo Stoppa. He felt for the characters in this play about "submarines"—illegal Italian immigrants in an American seaport—the way he had felt for the crude defenseless characters in *Ossessione.* Miller seemed worried by the use of Sicilian dialect in the Italian translation, so Visconti wrote him a long letter, explaining that only two of the characters used a few Sicilian expressions, but that this was essential "in order to show the difference between newly arrived immigrants and Italians who have been long enough in America to adapt themselves to local ways." Visconti expressed his admiration for the "truthfulness and dignity" with which Miller had portrayed the immigrants, but said that translating it into Italian presented "linguistic problems that could not be ignored." He told Miller of how he had made *La terra trema* entirely in Sicilian—which seemed to him "the most vigorous and tragic" of Italian dialects—and he mentioned that "the two best novels of recent years, Pasolini's *Ragazzi di Vita* and Gadda's *Quer pasticciaccio bruto de via Merulana,* are written entirely in an elaborate and personal form of dialect." After quoting the work of Vittorio de Sica, Eduardo De Filippo, and Fellini, he summed up: "All that is best in the Italian theater, from the Commedia dell'Arte to Goldoni and Pirandello is based on dialect, which truly reflects Italian life. I wanted to tell you all this to show you how important it is for me to preserve the dignity you have given to your characters. I hope it will suffice to reassure you. We consider the things recounted in your play as integral parts of our national experience, and have done everything possible to present it vividly—as a drama of our own flesh and blood—with the same respect, the same devotion, compassion and understanding as you have displayed so fully in the creation of your characters." Arthur Miller understood this perfectly, and the Italian production was as successful artistically as commercially.

Next Visconti was invited to the first International Theater Festival in Paris, which was to include his production of Goldoni's *La locandiera*, the first of his theater productions to be given abroad. From Paris he went to London to direct Verdi's *Don Carlo*—and design the scenery and costumes—at Covent Garden. Visconti's Renaissance capacity to range from one form of art to another enriched all he created.

Don Carlos, as the opera was first called, was Verdi's twenty-fifth opera, written for the Paris Opéra on the occasion of France's 1867 Exposition Universelle. Inspired by Schiller's tragedy, it tells the story of Don Carlo's attempt to liberate Flanders from the tyranny of his father, Philip II of Spain. Visconti and conductor Carlo Maria Giulini, who had worked together on *Traviata,* decided to use not the French version, the first act of which had been cut after the opening night in Paris, when the devout Empress Eugénie ostentatiously turned her back as Philip II, with characteristic high-handedness and most uncharacteristic good sense, ordered the Grand Inquisitor to "Be silent, priest." Instead, they used the complete five-act Italian *Don Carlo* of 1887.

The restored first act contained enchanting music, much of the love interest—Don Carlo's requited but doomed love for Catherine de Medici's daughter, Elisabeth de Valois—and, because it was set in king-haunted Fontainebleau, it offered Visconti an opportunity to use vivid colors and a light touch on set and costumes for the Italianized French court in its full Renaissance bloom. All this rich artistic life—it was Catherine de Medici's father-in-law, François I, who invited Leonardo da Vinci to France and had the walls of Fontainebleau castle made luminous with frescoes—provided Visconti with a perfect contrast for the rest of *Don Carlo,* set in the Inquisition-polluted air of Philip II's Spain.

For the setting of the four Spanish acts, Visconti turned to El Greco, the most tormentedly spiritual painter of Philip II's world, who once said, "The glare of daylight would spoil my inner light." His convulsive lights and lines seemed to Visconti peculiarly appropriate to what he considered a "less romantic" Verdi opera, in which the composer's immense effort to "penetrate the text" had resulted in a fusion of Second Empire style with modern psychological drama. Visconti never forgot Toscanini's saying, at a rehearsal of *La Traviata,* that the audience must be able to hear the libretto, since "opera is theater, and the words are more important than the music." For a moment, Visconti had been

133

astonished; then he realized that Toscanini was merely insisting on the obligation not to mutilate art by dividing it from its context.

This was particularly important in the case of *Don Carlo*, an opera in which politics play an explicit part, and moments of high tension between the King and the Grand Inquisitor suggest Dostoevsky's *The Brothers Karamazov*, written thirteen years after the first performance of *Don Carlo*. Visconti's Covent Garden *Don Carlo* was not a fantasy world in which the characters are merely ambulant voices, but the real world of a powerful Spanish king with one foot still in the Middle Ages, who identified himself with the Counter Reformation to such an extent as to provoke revolt in the Netherlands and a new pattern of statehood in Europe.

Visconti did not know England well and had planned to make a tour of the English countryside. Instead he had to fly back to Italy for the first Festival of Two Worlds at Spoleto. This new festival, which became an annual event, featuring young painters, sculptors, composers, playwrights, actors, dancers, and singers from all over the world, owed its existence almost entirely to Gian Carlo Menotti and Thomas Schippers. One of the most popular living composers, Menotti was best known at that time for his operas *The Medium* (1946) and, especially, *The Consul* (1950), in which he succeeded in making the commercially unpromising subject of refugees from a police state appeal to the same audiences as flocked to *Carmen* or *Madame Butterfly*. Born in a village on Lake Lugano in 1911, Menotti had started composing at ten. He studied first with his mother, then at Milan Conservatory, and finally at the famous Curtis Institute in Philadelphia, where he himself later taught. Thomas Schippers, a magical conductor, only twenty-eight years old at this time, had been a child prodigy and, at nineteen, conducted the Philadelphia Orchestra in the first performance of Menotti's *The Consul*. Their enthusiasm for the festival was shared by Visconti, who said, "We Italians must help Menotti. Spoleto is wonderfully different from other festivals, freer, more independent, less academic. And the name of the festival is most important. It is truly a place where Italians and Americans can meet and work together."

Among the things that made the Spoleto Festival different from other festivals was the little Umbrian city itself, with its lime trees, fountains, Roman and Romanesque architecture. Beloved by St. Francis, it was thought by Shelley "the most romantic city" he had ever seen, with its "acqueduct of astonishing elevation, which unites two rocky mountains— there is the path of a torrent below, whitening the green dell with its broad and barren track of stones, and above there is a castle, apparently of great strength and of tremendous magnitude, which overhangs the city, and whose marble bastions are perpendicular with the precipice." Though small, Spoleto is ancient. The Etruscans were there before the Romans; Hannibal and his Carthaginians came that way, and their defeat is still marked by a city gate called the "Porta della Fuga" (Gate of Flight). Fra Filippo Lippi and his son Filippino painted frescoes, which included their own portraits, in the cathedral; and beautiful Lucrezia Borgia attracted poets and artists to Spoleto when she lived there as papal governor for her father, Pope Alexander VI.

For the opening festival, Visconti staged and Schippers conducted Verdi's *Macbeth,* first performed in Florence in 1847. Since political murder is far from being a thing of the past, Visconti decided to set his production in the nineteenth century. This intensified the horror by removing any "barbaric Scottish chieftain" excuse for Macbeth's actions. During the festival the execution was reported of Imre Nagy, Premier of Hungary during the 1956 revolt. After the Soviet tanks arrived, Nagy took refuge in the Yugoslav Embassy, and was seized leaving there with a safe-conduct provided by his executioners. Visconti was among those who signed a letter of protest.

From the Spoleto Festival, Visconti returned to Rome to supervise the film insertions for *Immagini e tempi di Eleonora Duse* (*Pictures and Times of Eleonora Duse*), a commemorative production in honor of the great Italian actress who died in 1924 while touring America. Visconti could remember her death clearly. There had been no television or radio then, and newspaper boys' voices—"Importanti notissieee"—echoed along the canals of old Milan.

Sarah Bernhardt's only rival, Duse was the child of strolling players, the last of the great romantic actresses born and raised in the theater— *figlie d'arte*—who kept their costumes in wicker property baskets, shared dressing rooms that smelled of grease paint, singed hair, and cooking, performed one-night stands on outdoor, makeshift, perilously gaslit stages, and took for granted a bone-deep professionalism of a kind rarely found nowadays outside circus and music-hall families. Duse's performance as Shakespeare's Juliet, when she was only fourteen herself, in Verona, revealed a gift not only for acting but also for suffering, which D'Annunzio was to exploit to a devastating extent.

Visconti had seen Duse's last performance in Milan, in D'Annunzio's *La città morta* (*The Dead City*), and as, thirty-five years later, he fitted pieces of old film into a commemorative tapestry for her, he remembered a simple sentence embedded in *The Dead City*'s rhetoric: "We ate oranges as if they were bread." Maybe the sixty-three-year-old Duse, whom the adolescent Visconti saw then, had, indeed, been, as Emilio Cecchi wrote of her last appearance in California, merely "a glorious shadow" of the young Duse who electrified the students packed into the cheapest seats. Yet there was still drama in every inch of her as she approached the end of the long journey that took her from her birthplace, Vigevano—a small Renaissance town with a castle begun by a fourteenth-century Luchino Visconti—across the Atlantic to America to die. Among the actors who performed for Duse on this occasion were Luise Rainer, the Viennese-born actress who was to establish a Hollywood record by winning two consecutive Oscars, for her performances in *The Great Ziegfeld* (1936) and *The Good Earth* (1937); and eighty-three-year-old Emma Gramatica, herself a *figlia d'arte,* who had acted with Duse, in D'Annunzio's *La Gioconda,* in 1899, and whom today's filmgoers have had a chance to see as the magical old woman who opens De Sica's *Miracle in Milan* (1951).

Next Visconti directed a play made from Thomas Wolf's massive novel *Look Homeward, Angel,* about his struggle to get away from his home in the rural South and make good as a writer in New York. This novel brought Wolfe success when he was twenty-nine—the year of Hemingway's *A Farewell to Arms* and Remarque's *All Quiet on the Western Front*—and, sinec he died at thirty-eight, his public image remained that of a young man who, like Scott Fitzgerald's Great Gatsby, believed in "the orgiastic future." The play was admirably translated by Suso, who, thanks to her father—Emilio Cecchi's *English and American Writers* was published a couple of years before Wolfe's death—is as responsive to American as to English writing, and can distinguish between the two.

Look Homeward, Angel opened in Rome in October, and Visconti immediately went to Paris, where he was to direct the French version of an American comedy, William Gibson's *Two for the Seesaw.* This was Visconti's first French production. A world war and twenty-two years had gone by since the Front Populaire Paris days when he was Jean Renoir's "spare wheel" assistant; and now, in a Paris violently divided over the war in Algeria, with General de Gaulle about to be elected first president of the Fifth Republic, Visconti's name on a poster was as sure a guarantee of quality as a hallmark on silver.

Two for the Seesaw had been skillfully translated by Louise de Vilmorin, a beautiful woman of the world and of letters, who resembled a Nancy Mitford character. The Egeria of former British Ambassador Duff Cooper, and the lifelong friend of prodigious André Malraux, she wrote with charm and wit, and in this case had managed to produce a soufflé

Grazzano Castle

Donna Carla Erba
Visconti di Modrone,
1905

Duke Giuseppe
Visconti di Modrone,
1905

Luchino Visconti,
shortly before his
first birthday,
1907

Luchino and
his mother,
1909

The Visconti family
in 1909 (Luchino with
his arm around his
mother's neck)

Luchino (foreground),
age 4, with Guido,
Luigi, Edoardo, and
Anna in the park
at Grazzano Castle

Visconti during
the shooting of
Death in Venice,
1971

Visconti scrutinizing a frame

Visconti during the shooting of *Conversation Piece*, 1974

Visconti in 1975

Visconti during the shooting of *The Intruder*, 1975

Visconti with Suso Cecchi D'Amico on the set, 1976

Photo by Monica Stirling

Posters on the
walls of Rome on
the day of Luchino
Visconti's funeral,
March 19, 1976

Poster for the
Visconti Exhibition
at the Galleria,
Milan; drawing by
Renato Guttuso

effect without altering the ingredients. The two parts were to be played by Jean Marais and Annie Girardot. Visconti was familiar with Marais's work but not with Girardot's. He liked her immediately and was to say later that she could "express sublime things by doing almost nothing, a half smile, a gesture."

This slight, good-looking young actress, energetic as a Stendhal hero, and with similar lapses into generosity and ingenuousness, had had her natural gifts well trained at the Paris Conservatoire. But after four years as a *pensionnaire* at the nearly three-centuries-old Comédie-Française, and on the eve of being promoted to *sociétaire* (which means life membership, with a financial stake in the company and a pension), she decided she needed a more nipping and eager air—and fled. She said later that she found precisely what she hoped for when she began work with Visconti. "I owe one of the greatest emotions in my life to Visconti. He was to direct me in *Two for the Seesaw* and he acted the entire play for me—he is a formidable actor and draws the actress on until she gradually becomes—bit by bit, imperceptibly—an extension of life itself. He works in depth, almost on one's subconsciousness, and succeeds in getting what he wants—the actress's total adhesion to the part—through her instincts rather than her intelligence. And I maintain that when a director is marvelous, terrible, and joyful, as Visconti is, then it's worth more to an actor just to *be* than to understand." One of the results of *Two for the Seesaw* was that the marvelous, terrible, and joyful Visconti —a most perceptive description, incidentally—was later to offer Annie Girardot her best part, in what would be his own favorite among his films, *Roco e i suoi fratelli* (*Rocco and His Brothers*).

From Paris Visconti returned to Rome for a Christmas production of *Mrs. Gibbon's Boys*, another American comedy, translated by Suso and acted by Rina Morelli and Paolo Stoppa. While Visconti was away a dramatic change—not immediately recognized as such—had occurred in Rome: Pope Pius XII had died, and ten days later Cardinal Roncalli, the benevolent Patriarch of Venice, was elected to succeed him. Seventy-seven at the time of his election, John XXIII was at first mistakenly considered merely an "interim pope," a good moderate man who would keep things ticking until it was time for his place to be taken by a younger man. Pope John's was the first papal coronation to be televised, and it introduced the operatic splendor and liturgical beauty of Roman Catholic ceremonies to viewers all over the world. Early in 1959, Pope John began a fresh search for Christian unity by summoning the Second Vatican Council.

Visconti next directed the Rina Morelli–Paolo Stoppa company in

Figli d'arte (*Children of Art*), by Diego Fabbri, a leading Catholic dramatist whose preoccupation with the Christian attitude to contemporary problems was to be intensified by the new pope's highly personal and positive approach to them. After being given in Rome in March, this play was taken to the Théâtre des Nations in Paris for the fourth International Drama Festival there.

Next came the second Spoleto Festival, for which Visconti was asked to direct Donizetti's *Il Duca di Alba*. This involved the kind of research that fascinated him. *Il Duca di Alba* was to have had its first performance at the Paris Opéra in 1840—the year the saxophone was invented and the moon photographed for the first time. But before completing it Donizetti was suddenly seized by the idea for his famous comic opera *The Daughter of the Regiment* and although *Il Duca di Alba* was completed by Donizetti's pupil Matteo Salvi, the score was mislaid. Found only thirty-five years later, it had its first production in Rome in 1882, the year of Wagner's *Parsifal*.

There was nothing musty, however, about *Il Duca di Alba*. Its historic plot, concerned with intolerance and tyranny, was as actual as ever. Donizetti's Duke of Alba had, unfortunately, existed and, as adviser to Philip II of Spain, set up a special court in Brussels to crush the Spanish Netherlands' desire for religious toleration and national independence. Known as the Council of Blood, this executed eighteen thousand people, including Count Egmont, publicly beheaded in 1568, about whom Goethe wrote the tragedy *Egmont*, for which Beethoven composed his sublime overture. Visconti wanted his production to have some of the atmosphere of the original one, so he went to the leading Italian theatrical warehouse and asked if they possessed any old sets for a piazza, an ale house, or an oratory. They consulted the stock books and said yes, they did, but very old ones—"made back in 1882 for something called *Il Duca di Alba*." These helped Visconti to re-create his opera's revolutionary 1840 spirit, which had been in perfect harmony with that of the rebels preparing all over Europe to rise against the Holy Alliance of Russia, Austria, and Prussia.

Although outer space was fast becoming part of all our inner worlds, and nuclear weapons, breeding faster than hamsters, made individual struggles seem useless, Visconti still believed in them. Life could seem to him cruel and unjust, but never *absurd*, that fashionably misused word. His next film, *Rocco and His Brothers*, was to center around a southern immigrant quite as determined as Count Egmont to fight against tragic circumstances. Rocco would continue what Visconti's Sicilian fisherman 'Ntoni had begun.

Seventeen

A film of great violence and beauty, *Rocco and His Brothers* is the story of an Italian peasant family, a widowed mother and her five sons, who come from the deep south to try to earn a living in Milan. The problems of southern emigration were highly topical in 1960, and now, nearly twenty years later, these problems are so far from being solved that *Rocco and His Brothers,* a favorite with film libraries, is more topical than ever.

Visconti said when asked what made him choose this subject, "In everything we do there is a grain of something that preceded it—and we are influenced, without being aware of it, by a thousand things, some of them very distant from us. So far as *Rocco* is concerned—and I had been thinking of the story for a long time—the strongest influence was that of Giovanni Verga. His novel *I Malavoglia* obsessed me from the first moment I read it. . . . So I made *La terra trema . . .* to which *Rocco* could, in a sense, be called a second chapter . . . and there were other elements. I wanted to make a film about a southern mother, strong, energetic, obstinate, a mother to whom her five sons are like the five fingers of her own hand. With her husband dead, she becomes the head of the family and is drawn by the mirage of the great northern city. She wants to exploit her sons' energy, but doesn't take into account their different characters and possibilities—she doesn't, but Milan does, and the city gives each one a different destiny. Simone, who seems the strongest, but is in fact the weakest, ruins himself and kills a prostitute. Rocco, the most sensitive and spiritually complex, wins a form of success, as a boxer, that is fundamentally only a form of self-punishment, because he feels personally responsible for Simone's misfortunes, and he loathes boxing. Once he is in the ring, face to face with his opponent, boxing releases in Rocco a hatred of everything and

139

everybody—and he recoils with horror from this hatred. Ciro, the wisest and most practical of the brothers, is the only one who will become completely urbanized, truly part of the Milanese community. Luca, the youngest, may one day return south, because by then things will have changed there, too; and Vincenzo, the eldest . . . will be satisfied with a little security."

Visconti was influenced, too, by Thomas Mann's trilogy *Joseph and His Brothers*, written when Hitler ruled Germany and the great German writer was himself an involuntary emigrant; and by the parts of Dostoevsky's *The Idiot* concerning the beauty of the "idiotic" Prince Myshkin's character, and the complex relationship between Myshkin, Rogozhin, and Nastya, which ends in the latter's murder by Rogozhin. The name Rocco was chosen in memory of Rocco Scotellaro, a southern poet whose work Visconti admired. In 1946, Scotellaro had, at the age of twenty-three, been elected mayor of Tricarico, his hilltop birthplace in the deep south, just off the last lap of the Appian Way, where it leads toward Greece and the East. As mayor, Scotellaro took part in the peasants' postwar struggle to obtain what they had been promised. He also expressed their aspirations and struggles in poems, short stories, and the outline of a novel. Four volumes of these were published after Scotellaro's death at the age of thirty, and his *Contadini del Sud* (*Peasants of the South*) gave Visconti background material for Rocco's family.

The summer of 1958, Visconti joined Suso and her family and the novelist Vasco Pratolini by the sea, at Castiglioncello, and the three of them spent the holiday period working on an outline of *Rocco*. More research led Visconti and Suso to replace some details by material from three short stories in Giovanni Testori's *Il ponte della Ghisolfa* (*The Ghisolfa Bridge*), published that same year. Testori is now a well-known Milanese art critic, poet, painter, novelist, and playwright, but was then a new writer—a Catholic, preoccupied by problems of grace and individual salvation, who applied his vigorous religious sense to social problems. Visconti was particularly impressed by Testori's descriptions of the jungle life that had sprung up in the new slums of postwar Milan, so different from the Milan of his childhood, with its artisans and its street cries, its horse traffic and canalboats. After these changes had been made in the outline of *Rocco and His Brothers*, Visconti and Suso set to work on the final scenario with Enrico Medioli, scenarist and close friend, Pasquale Festa Campanile, and Massimo Franciosa. Much of the material finally used was collected by Visconti while visiting Milan to choose exteriors and talk to *terroni* (the northern Italian's name for southerners) in workshops, housing developments, cafés, and sports centers on the outskirts of the city. Wherever he went, his interest in people made the *terroni* talk to him as readily as to one of themselves.

By 1955, interior migration was a regular feature of Italian life, with peasants who would formerly have tried for America, North Africa, or northern Europe, now seeking Eldorado in northern Italy. In 1958, over thirteen thousand southerners settled in Milan. Many of them came from worlds as archaic as that of Carlo Levi's *Christ Stopped at Eboli,* worlds full of pagan and Greek myths, superstition and witchcraft. Families accustomed to the cave dwellings of Matera or the *trulli* of Alberobello (little one-room stone houses with cone-shaped roofs, like surrealist beehives) felt lost among the skyscrapers of Milan or the Po valley, an area more industrialized than any in Europe except the Ruhr basin. Television, which would eventually provide a lingua franca, merely increased their confusion at first—characters like Mike Bongiorno, and detergents that "wash whiter," seeming far more mysterious to the *terroni* than the heroes and henbane to which they were accustomed.

In the preliminary script of *Rocco and His Brothers,* Visconti's southern family was homesick. But conversations with the *terroni* in Milan contradicted this. Once they had decided that emigration was their only means of survival, the southerners accepted it as fatalistically as they had endured their earlier existence. Visconti promptly eliminated homesickness from the script and made one of the sons say—as he himself heard said—that "it would never occur to him to do anything so fantastic as to go home again." Then, during one of his expeditions, Visconti came across a woman whose attitude was exactly that of the imaginary mother he had visualized as "a peasant Hecuba."

This woman, Rosaria T., had come north with a brood of sons, hoping to get work for all of them through a nephew already settled in Milan. But at first it looked as if they would never find lodgings. Since private citizens were free to take lodgers without registering their names with the police, it was by no means exceptional for one bed to be rented to three *terroni,* each one allowed eight hours out of twenty-four on it. Outraged, Rosaria T. led her flock to the suburbs of Milan and bullied her nephew into building a shack there for them. While he did this, she herself walked daily into Milan and hectored municipal authorities until, stunned by her assiduity, they disbursed something from the funds provided for needy immigrant families. Rosaria T. then sold the shack her nephew had built and swooped down on a district where, according to the immigrants' grapevine, blocks of working-class apartments were being put up. Sure enough, Rosaria T. found a block, completed but empty. She immediately broke a window, entered with her family, and

141

established squatters' rights. At last she and her sons had a base from which to fight for work. Other *terroni*, fifteen families in all, followed her example. When Visconti met her, Rosaria T. and her family had been living in this block for over a year, and local authorities seemed powerless to eject them.

In honor of this authentic tigress, Visconti called the mother in his film "Rosaria." As surname he chose Pafundi—partly because it is a name found all over the southern province of Lucania, among all classes, and partly because Suso had spoken with enthusiasm of an exceptionally skillful southern Italian worker, Vincenzo Pafundi, whom she had encountered in northern Germany when writing a script there for Francesco Rosi's second film. This innocent choice of name was to cause trouble later.

For *La terra trema*, Visconti had deliberately chosen a slow rhythm appropriate to lives regulated by sea and season even more than by the vicissitudes of the marketing system. *Rocco and His Brothers* required an entirely different rhythm, since it was to show peasants struggling to adjust themselves to the speed of modern life in a big city. In Sicily, 'Ntoni and his brothers stepped from their own houses directly across the beach to their own boats, and mended their nets on the beach, within sight of both home and sea. But Rocco and his brothers have to spend harassing yet vacuous hours shuttling to and fro between their dormitory homes and their workplaces. Visconti had intended to underline what the change meant to this family by beginning down in Lucania with the father's funeral. After the four older boys cast the coffin into the sea, they were to return home for a family council and decide to sell their plot of land, which would not yield a living for them, in order to get the cash required for emigration. Financial and practical obstacles made this impossible, so the film opens with Rosaria's arrival in Milan with her sons Simone, Rocco, Ciro, and little Luca. Vincenzo, the eldest, has gone ahead and is waiting for them in Milan, with a job and a fiancée.

Such families could, and still can, be seen every day arriving in Milan. Keeping close together, in domestic battle formation, the older women usually in black, these southerners clamber down from the trains dragging with them muleloads of cloth bundles, paper and plastic bags, cardboard suitcases held together by puzzles of knotted string, and battered jerry cans of oil or wine. Dazed and excited, they advance along the platform into the vast neon-lighted Babylonian cave of Milan's Central Station. Archeologists of the future, they gaze at posters extolling apéritifs, detergents, deodorants, products all more alien to them than the Pyramids, which have at least a Biblical connotation in their minds. Arrival and departure boards name places—Venice, Geneva, Paris, Munich, Avignon—as remote to them as the surface of the moon. Each newspaper stall is a little Babel of foreign headlines. Other stalls, displaying *panettoni*, candied chestnuts, gilt models of the Duomo and the Madonnina suggest luxury, religion, art. Sounding brass and tinkling cymbals, which seem plentiful, give an impression that prosperity is just around the corner.

From the moment the Pafundis set foot in Milan's station, it is plain sailing—into trouble. First, almost before they have had time to check that no one and nothing has been mislaid, comes a quarrel—Rosaria's tyrannically maternal fault—with Vincenzo's good little fiancée and her respectable Milanese family. Rosaria's combination of tragic muse and irate fishwife transforms her hosts' desire to be warm and hospitable into prim horror of "southern savages," and embitters the search for lodgings, which Rosaria approaches in the same belligerent spirit as the Rosaria from whom Visconti took her name.

Rocco is due for his military service and Ciro finds work at the Alfa-Romeo factory. Simone, his mother's favorite and potentially the black sheep, settles for boxing, since this is a poor boy's lottery ticket for fame and fortune. Attracted to gambling, drinking, women, easy money, Simone is an opportunist who lacks the capacity to assess his opportunities correctly. Yet he is courageous in the boxing ring, and his desire for Nadia, an intelligent, independent prostitute, is as genuine as it is crude. His need to "assert his virility" and squander money rapidly lead to his losing both Nadia and his boxing future. She can stand no more of him. His trainer kicks him out of the gymnasium. Heavily in debt, he takes to petty crime.

Rocco's problems are very different ones. A boy of innate goodness, Rocco is the only one of the family homesick for the south, and, alone in this, too, believes in the capacity of goodness, expiation, and self-sacrifice to change society and the world. Down in a small provincial garrison town, where he is finishing his military service, Rocco meets Nadia, who is just out of prison. The love that springs up between them is so profound that it could save them both. But once they are back in Milan, Simone discovers their feelings. Vanity, the southern myth of virility, and plain dog-in-the-manger-ism madden him. One evening, on the outskirts of Milan, Simone and some of his thuggish cronies set upon Rocco and Nadia. Simone rapes Nadia while the rest hold Rocco down.

Devastated though Rocco is, it does not occur to him to transfer his loathing of the deed to the doer. Nor does he dwell on his own humiliation. On the contrary, he blames himself for Simone's wretchedness, and takes for granted that his own devotion to Nadia, and her to him, must be immolated to save Simone. Here southern respect for family hierarchy is operative. As older brother, Simone has rights. Nadia realizes with despair that nothing she considers rational has any power in this situation. The scene in which she and Rocco discuss it, up on the roof of Milan's cathedral, is not only individually moving, but also, like the family's arrival at the station, typical of Milan, where the roof of the Duomo is seldom without lovers, picnickers, and sightseers among its forest of spires.

Up to this point, the family's troubles have been due to their situation as immigrants, and to Simone's corruptibility. Now Rocco's goodness intervenes, with catastrophic results. Not only does he persuade Nadia to return to Simone, but also, in the hope of being able to pay Simone's debts and give him a fresh start, Rocco himself becomes a boxer, although he loathes boxing. Nothing is more difficult to portray than goodness, our instinctive opinion of our fellow creatures being such that anyone saying "It's only human" is invariably referring to unpleasant behavior. But Visconti made Rocco's goodness utterly and sadly convincing—"sadly" because, as Ciro says after the final catastrophe, "Rocco is a saint, but in the world we live in there's no place for saints like Rocco. Their compassion provokes disaster."

Visconti offered the part of Rosaria to the magnificent Greek actress Katina Paxinou. To the question why a Greek, the answer was not only that Visconti thought that particular performer perfect for that particular part—Katina Paxinou had an elemental violence comparable with that of Anna Magnani—but also that Rosaria comes from a region of southern Italy colonized by the Greeks seven hundred years before the birth of Christ, a region where Greek physical types can still be seen and Greek words still heard in the local dialect. Even in plain mileage, Milan, beyond the mountains, was three times farther away from these southerners than Greece, across the sea.

Fifty-nine-year-old Katina Paxinou had trained as a singer before switching to acting. She was a member of the Greek National Theater company, had played in both Greek and English in New York and London, and had been internationally admired for her screen performances in *For Whom the Bell Tolls* (1943), *Mourning Becomes Electra* (1947), and in Orson Welles's *Confidential Report* (1955). She was in New York, playing in Brecht's *Mother Courage,* when she received a call from Rome asking if she would be free in the near future. She was about to return to Greece, where she was under contract for the the-

144

atrical season in Athens, so she gave her sailing dates and said her ship would be stopping for a couple of hours at Naples. A telegram from the Titanus Film Production Company fixed an appointment on board. When she heard who wanted her, she "jumped for joy" and said, "Tell Visconti I admire him because he is a great artist, one of the greatest in Europe, if not in the world, and that I am truly happy to work with him."

Meeting Visconti, for the first time, in Milan, Paxinou expected to find "this extraordinary being" stormy and temperamental. Instead, he seemed to her to be "gentleness personified." Few, certainly, of those who worked with the "extraordinary being," felt anything but admiration, gratitude, and affection for him. Paolo Stoppa, who, in the part of a boxers' impresario, was making his first film with Visconti, after having been directed by him on more than twenty stage plays, said that, judging by his own long experience, Visconti "possessed truly phenomenal magnetic powers" and was "an authentic director in the same sense as Toscanini was an authentic conductor." Such powers, said Stoppa, are extremely rare, but "only those who possess them can obtain from an actor exactly the performance that both desire."

The six young actors chosen for the film were Renato Salvatori, Annie Girardot, Alain Delon, Claudia Cardinale, Spiros Focas, and Max Cartier.

Renato Salvatori was at the top of his physical form. At Visconti's request, he had prepared for the part of Simone by several months of regular boxing, gymnastics, walking, jogging, and skipping. Nevertheless, he was terrified when he found himself on the set. This terror quickly made way for the conviction that Visconti was leading him, "with enormous facility," to obtain results "beyond any he had hoped for as yet." Annie Girardot, who had played in insignificant films since leaving Comédie-Française, was delighted with the part of Nadia, and had acquired complete confidence in Visconti during rehearsals in Paris of *Two for the Seesaw*. Claudia Cardinale had already appeared in thirteen films, but jumped at the small part of Vincenzo's Milanese fiancée because it offered her her first chance to work with Visconti.

Spiros Focas, a young Greek actor who had been in three films at home, could scarcely believe his luck in being engaged for *Rocco and His Brothers*. He was to play Vincenzo. On the first day he was rigid with nerves and feared this might come across as insincerity, but said later: "Visconti, who, despite his proverbial lightning flashes, possesses a persuasive kindness that only his actors and actresses truly know, literally convinced me that I *was* Vincenzo." Max Cartier, who was to play Ciro, was a gymnast who had refused previous film offers. He, too, was nervous, but said that Visconti immediately put him so much at ease that he needed only a couple of rehearsals before his first scene was shot. "Visconti never took his truly magnetic eyes off me," and everything went "so easily that it seemed to me as if it had been a scene out of my own daily life."

Most impressive of all was Alain Delon, for whom Visconti had, from the first, intended the part of Rocco. At twenty-four he already possessed most of the star qualities, including talent, and was never completely happy except when working, a fact that created an immediate bond between him and Visconti. His boyhood had been difficult but instructive. His father ran a small cinema at Sceaux, near Paris. This sounds promising but was not, since his parents separated when he was a small child, and he was then bandied between them. The effect on him can be guessed by the fact that he was six times expelled from various schools. Neither Benedictines nor Franciscans, not even Jesuits, could control him. His own comment on this intractability was that *enfants terribles* are invariably unhappy children. At seventeen, attracted by a recruiting poster, "Join the Air Force and See the World," he tried to do just that. But the last contingent was filled, so he was told to wait six months. Wildly impatient, he joined the navy, and soon found himself in Indochina, fighting in the French rear-guard action that preceded the American war in Vietnam. After demobilization, Delon took whatever jobs he could get. These included working as a market porter at Les Halles, the old food market at the center of Paris, transformed into an open-air recreation area linked underground with nearby Beaubourg, the Georges Pompidou art center.

Les Halles' porters had a centuries-old reputation for toughness, and while "weightlifting" among flowers, vegetables, and curses, Delon encountered an immense variety of people, ranging from characters who could have walked out of Balzac's or Zola's novels to jetsetters who came, as Scott Fitzgerald and the Lost Generation had done, to complete a night's amusement with the onion soup for which Les Halles was famous. Presently Delon got acquainted with contemporaries who were fascinated by the cinema. These included the future stage and screen star Jean-Claude Brialy, who suggested they go down to Cannes for the 1957 Film Festival and try to gate-crash a few previews. Delon's good looks were so noticeable that, not surprisingly, he attracted attention even in the Cannes buyers' market. When a friend dragged Delon to a film studio, he suddenly felt, for the first time in his life, like a fish in its rightful waters. He had at last found a home.

The star of the first film in which Delon appeared was Edwige Feuillère, and this gifted and benevolent actress was amused and impressed by the boy's wild desire to learn from everyone, every place, and everything he encountered. It was this passion to learn, combined with Delon's obvious but unconscious feeling that energy is eternal delight, that roused Visconti's paternal instincts and made him want to help the young actor help himself. This he certainly did. Delon had never before acted as he did in *Rocco*. The part was an extremely difficult one, because it required a touch of the saintliness that makes certain saints go momentarily out of their own finite minds in their search for the infinitude of God. Since then Delon has become an international star, and played many of the crooks and gangsters dear to box offices; so it may be difficult for those who have not seen him as Rocco to imagine the radiant innocence, sadness, and strength that Visconti guided him into giving to this part. Later Delon himself said that of all the directors he had known, "Luchino is the most understanding and sensitive—he goes to so much trouble that all the actors feel that they come first, even before the film itself."

Visconti not only developed Delon's acting ability, but also opened new cultural worlds to him. In this he was helped by Romy Schneider, at that time passionately in love with Delon, as he with her; their engagement had been publicly celebrated at her mother's villa on Lake Lugano. Romy had been raised in a home where the importance of art and culture was taken for granted. She was to become one of Visconti's favorite actresses.

The shooting of *Rocco and His Brothers* began at the end of February 1960, and went so well that it was finished in under four months—despite hindrances provoked by a municipal mixture of high-handedness and low-mindedness. As usual, it was not actors but temperamental bureaucrats who wasted the producer's money. The scene in which Simone murders Nadia was to have been shot at Milan's *idroscalo* (seaplane station), a stretch of water on the western outskirts of Milan, alongside Forlanini Airport, particularly popular with the young for outings. The area Visconti wished to use came under the jurisdiction of several authorities: Milan itself, the neighboring communes of Linate and Segrate, and the Air Ministry. For the scene in question, it would be necessary to add a small refreshment kiosk, and about a hundred lampposts alongside the water. Titanus asked the Air Ministry's permission first. The reply was prompt and courteous. The ministry asked that the lampposts be placed in another zone of the *idroscalo*, where they would not endanger gliders, and, in compensation for this shift, the ministry offered to provide lighting for the military sports ground there. The Milan Questura (Police Headquarters) and the mayors of Linate and Segrate were equally prompt with the required authorizations. So film technicians got busy at the *idroscalo*.

Only when the work was almost finished did some guards from the provincial administration suddenly ask: What is going on here? Permits were shown. The provincial administrators declared these insufficient. There existed, apparently, yet another formality that must be gone through, a formality seldom insisted upon (at least a thousand films had been made in Milan without its being even mentioned, let alone complied with) but which had now, suddenly, acquired Biblical status. Titanus sent a representative to the provincial administration's Secretary General. He was not to be seen. "Requests must be submitted in writing"—and, in this case, the request must be accompanied by a detailed description of the scene to be shot at the *idroscalo*. Written request and description were sent, along with the permits already granted, including the one from Air Ministry in Rome. Next, the provincial administrators demanded an excerpt from the scenario of *Rocco and His Brothers*. After that they forbade Titanus to use the *idroscalo*.

The scene from *Rocco and His Brothers* was, said these administrators, immoral and bore an "inopportune resemblance to reality"—this last a reference to the murder of a prostitute recently committed in these precincts intended, according to the provincial administrators, for "healthy young people devoted to sport." Murders have never been perpetrated exclusively by elderly invalids with poor athletic records, but, even apart from this solecism, the administrators' aims were not clear. Did they particularly wish to harass Titanus? Or Luchino Visconti? Did they want only to assert provincial authority over that of Rome? Were they genuinely shocked by the scene? If so, had they not led lives so sheltered as to incapacitate them for public office? Whatever the cause, their insolent obfuscation suggested the legal labyrinths that appalled Charles Dickens more than a hundred years ago: "You can't make a head and brains out of a brass knob with nothing in it. You couldn't when your uncle George was living; much less when he's dead."

Electrifyingly exasperated, Visconti wanted to hold a press conference and make the nonsensical facts public. He refrained while Titanus tried to remedy matters through official channels. But too many peoples' livelihoods were involved for the facts to remain hidden long. By mid-April the administrators had a scandal on their hands. The moment was particularly inappropriate since, as the *Associazione Industrie Cinematografiche Associate* pointed out by telegram, attempts were being made during the city's annual International Trade Fair to establish a film center in Milan—an attempt that would certainly be discouraged by arbitrary local censorship. The Associated Film Critics of Milan protested that the provincial administrators were acting illegally, against the freedom of expression guaranteed by the Constitution. Matters were not improved when a prominent member of the MSI (the neo-Fascist party founded in 1946) congratulated the provincial administrators and publicly expressed the pious hope that he had seen the last of films about "prostitutes and bicycle thieves."

Meanwhile, Visconti worked on other scenes, and at finding an alternative location for the murder. It should not, he thought, be too difficult to discover a stretch of lakeside resembling the Milan *idroscalo* in all but its provincial administrators—who had not been able to prevent him filming on the roof of the Duomo or at the Ponte delle Sirenette (the Bridge of the Little Sirens). In Visconti's childhood, this little bridge, with two statues at either end, crossed a canal just behind his home, and Visconti loved these statues, which had been there ever since an Austrian grand duke inaugurated the bridge in 1842. When water made way for wheels, this canal became a street, today's Via Visconti di Modrone, and the little bridge was removed to the park behind the Sforza castle, where, centuries earlier, Visconti's ancestors had hunted. During the war one of the sirens was stolen, but was eventually found and replaced. The Ponte delle Sirenette is only a detail in the landscape of *Rocco and His Brothers*, but Visconti's assigning the old bridge, in its new site, to the young immigrants, was a gesture of love for his hometown, and for the days when as a child he had wondered what song the sirens sang.

Visconti's feeling for places was vividly demonstrated during one of the film's final scenes. The Pafundis were packed around the table, toasting Rocco's victory in the boxing ring. Rocco was telling his little brother, Luca, about their southern home. Visconti, leaning forward, seemed to be silently willing Alain Delon–Rocco to act in a certain way. Suddenly Katina Paxinou begged Visconti to show them how he wanted this scene played. Visconti had scarcely started to act Delon's part when it seemed to everyone watching that he had literally become Rocco.

"One day," he said, "one day, even if not immediately, I want to go back to our country . . . but I don't know if I'll be able to. . . . It may be impossible for me . . . but one of us must go back—perhaps you, Luca?"

Paxinou turned pale, and the child, Luca, was moved as he answered, "I want to go back with you."

"Remember, Luca," Visconti's strong, deep, gritty voice said as it grew fainter, "that is *our* country . . . the country of olive trees and moon sickness . . . the country of rainbows." He turned to Vincenzo. "Do you remember, Vincè . . . do you remember, when the foreman began the building of a house . . . how he used to draw a stone across the shadow of the first passer-by?"

Tears were running down Paxinou's face as Luca asked, "Why?"

"Because there has to be a sacrifice so the house will stand firm."

Drawing a stone across the first passer-by's shadow is a vestige of ancient and bloody rituals to insure a building's solidity. As Visconti spoke the word *sacrifice,* Paxinou looked at him, petrified—and at precisely this moment the front doorbell rang, announcing Simone's blood-stained return from killing Nadia.

For the site of this murder, an alternative to the *idroscalo* was eventually found by chance. It is seldom feasible to make a film in chronological order, and the scene in which Rocco and Nadia meet had still to be shot. Since Rocco is just finishing his military service, Visconti had picked a garrison town for this meeting—Civitavecchia, the little town where, a hundred and thirty years earlier, Stendhal, there as French consul, had dreamed of his last love. Visconti explored the countryside there, and on Lake Fogliano, only about seventy-five miles from Civitavecchia, found a site that could easily be made to resemble the Milan *idroscalo,* but that, unlike the *idroscalo,* belonged to a private society and had among its leading administrators the son of a pioneer of the silent films.

The murder was shot there with no more ado. Visconti gave this scene both its unvarnished police-court aspect. ("Unemployed Southerner Stabs Prostitute at Idroscalo") and its Shakespearean elements: the way in which Simone is blown with restless violence into a state of mind that Nadia partly understands. Her "Don't ask me any more. You know what you know. From now on I won't say a word" echoes Iago's "Demand me nothing. What you know, you know. From this time forth I never will speak word." Her resignation provokes Simone's superfluous savagery—superfluous, that is, for an efficient murder, but not superfluous as an expression of his utter inability to deal with life in Milan. Simone cannot express himself, yet has something to express, and it was Visconti's comprehension of pent-up grievances that made him direct Simone to stab Nadia not once but again and again, in a paroxysm of protest against life itself. A child, screaming and stamping at the ground against which it has hurt itself, does not give a single scream, a single stamp, but goes on and on until it obtains the relief of exhaustion.

Everyone on the set was moved by this scene, particularly by Annie

Girardot's expression when the sudden realization that Simone has a knife merely deepens her resignation. Later, however, Visconti was to be blamed high and low for the violence of this murder. It must "sicken all healthy people," said one Paris newspaper—and this during the Algerian war. Less virulent, but sillier, the British censor reduced the number of stabbings so carefully that he made the murder look cold-blooded, and consequently even more shocking. Now, nearly twenty years later, Simone's violence seems to have been prophetic, not only of things to come in Milan, but also of the violence that is part of the entire world's way of life: vandalism, muggings, holdups, kidnappings, psychiatric clinics, labor camps, barricades, and battlefields. Not long ago an ingenuous schoolgirl was murdered at Milan's *idroscalo* by would-be kidnappers, "young, healthy, and sports-loving" men who, having a revolver, did not need the poor man's dagger.

Thanks to Visconti's drive and the co-operation of actors, scriptwriters, technicians, and producer, *Rocco and His Brothers* was finished by June 4, 1960, according to plan, despite the provincial administration. The completion of the film did not, however, mean the end of Visconti's troubles with it. Among the many Pafundis in Lucania was the son of a former prosecutor of the Supreme Court. He suddenly announced that he intended to go to law to get the name of Rocco's family changed. Titanus would have been within its legal rights in refusing to change the name, but because modern technology made it possible, though expensive, to effect the change without affecting the quality of the photography, neither time nor money was wasted on law courts, and the Pafundis became the Parondis. After this *Rocco and His Brothers* started on its public career. At the twenty-first Venice Film Festival it was received with the most violent feelings for and against, and won the Jury's Special Award. Three months later it won another award in the shape of an invitation from a group of Turin factory workers who admired the film so much that they had organized a public discussion of it—a detail that, incidentally, shows the importance of the cinema's place in Italian life. *Rocco* was the first of Visconti's films to have a huge success at the box office as well as with the critics.

But *Rocco*'s troubles with Bumbledom did not end once it was shown. First signs of squalls ahead came when the official Vatican paper, *L'Osservatore Romano*, objected to Fellini's brilliant *La dolce vita*. Cardinal Tardini appealed to the civil authorities to take action against "certain destructive films." The Cardinal named no names, but on October 17, 1960, *after* the first public performance of *Rocco and His Brothers*, the Milanese public prosecutor, Commendatore Carmelo Spagnuolo, formed a commission of police officers, *carabinieri,* and jurists to view the film. Afterward Titanus was told that unless four scenes were cut, *Rocco and His Brothers* would be confiscated and the producer, Goffredo Lombardo, would face the accusation of "disseminating an obscene object." Today's audiences, accustomed to pornography at their neighborhood cinema, can find no obscenities in *Rocco and His Brothers,* now shown regularly on television and at film libraries. But there are periods, everywhere, when governments dislike references to specific topics—in this case immigration—far more than they dislike pornography, which can be a substitute for bread and circuses.

The ensuing "discussion between the interested parties" suggested that the similarities between ecclesiastical and political censorship have never been better grasped than by Dickens in *Our Mutual Friend,* when Mr. Wegg, asked the difference between "the Rooshans and the Romans," says, "There you place me in a difficulty, Mr. Boffin. Suffice it to observe, that the difference is best postponed to some other occasion when Mrs. Boffin does not honour us with her company." The decision on *Rocco* was of a silliness without precedent in the history of the cinema: "to darken the incriminated scenes by the use of filters." The scandal was all the more explosive (it is easy to imagine Fellini's roars) because the situation was ludicrously like the one in Thomas Mann's *Mario and the Magician,* when a child's nudity on a bathing beach causes minor bureaucrats to balk at the imagined affront to their national honor. But there was nothing farcical about the fact that a film, providing a livelihood for hundreds of film workers, entertainment and art for thousands, possibly millions, of filmgoers, and providing also tax money and foreign exchange for the treasury, could be arbitrarily wrecked by bureaucrats, despite the fact that its producer had received a regular government permit to go ahead, without which the film would not have been made in the first place.

Public uproar was so loud that the censors in Rome, standing by their Milanese colleagues, demanded to re-view *Rocco and His Brothers*—after which they decreed that two of the filtered scenes must be entirely cut. As obstinate with functionaries as with Fascists, Visconti subsequently got this decision nullified by a legal declaration that a film is a work of art, which enabled him to restore the cut scenes. The Milanese magistrates then confiscated Antonioni's *L'avventura* and Mauro Bolognini's *La giornata balorda.* Italian film censorship did not lead to concentration camps or psychiatric clinics, nor were its standards quite as vicious as McCarthyism or as infantile as the Hays Code; nevertheless, it was wasteful and unsatisfactory to all concerned, except to censors with a disinterested love of coercion for its own sake. Just how wasteful was to be emphasized twenty-eight years later by a three-week exhibition of "Great Films Censored." These were shown in their complete versions in Rome by the AIACE (Associazione Italiane Amici Cinema d'Essai). Films included Antonioni's *Blow-up*, Truffaut's *Jules et Jim*, and also Lewis Milestone's *All Quiet on the Western Front* (1930); democratic censors had censored this last for antimilitarism in 1950, exactly as Fascist censors had done twenty years earlier. This exhibition coincided with the second anniversary of Visconti's death, and opened with *Rocco and His Brothers*—which seemed more topical than ever in Italy, where the number of squatters like Rocco's family had reached twenty thousand. From all sides clamor rose against grotesque forms of censorship. It was obvious that some reforms would take place—they did, two years later—and few situations are more exasperating than having to obey ridiculous laws during the last minutes before they join the scrap heap. Making the best of the time left, the censors proceeded to surround the entertainment industry with an atmosphere of tyrannical duncery. Comparatively short though this period was, it lasted long enough to wreck Visconti's next stage production.

Wartime ordeals had not troubled him. He had tumbled in and out of danger with wholehearted energy. But this kind of attack, pettifogging and fatuous, did trouble him. Wartime enemies could be hated, censors could only be despised—and since contempt is a sterile emotion, it neither suited Visconti nor came easily to him. He had, moreover, as little capacity as is humanly possible to take no for an answer. Suso said once, speaking of his tenacity, his "perpetual bet with himself," that had it occurred to him that the murder scene in *Rocco* was "excessive," he would only have gone ahead and "made it more so," determined to carry anything he undertook to the end. So it was typical of him that now, with the troops of Midian prowling around, Visconti should choose to up and smite them with a new play by the controversial Giovanni Testori.

Eighteen

L'Arialda, the play Giovanni Testori wrote in the summer of 1960, had the same setting as the *Il ponte della ghisolfa* stories drawn on for *Rocco*. Arialda, the leading woman character, is part of Milan's new proletariat, in whose harsh lives sex offers the only pleasure that appears to cost nothing. Much of the dialogue's aggressiveness was prophetic, as when Arialda warns her mother that the times are past when people could "throw open the window and allow the poor to get a glimpse of how life can be lived outside, in comfort," and then shut the window and expect them to go on enduring drudgery and hunger.

Visconti decided to produce *L'Arialda* in Rome with Rina Morelli and Paolo Stoppa. But the play was refused a government permit. It was in good company. Carlo Lizzani's excellent film *Il gobbo* (*The Hunchback*) —based on the true story of a young Roman hunchback who, after taking an active part in the Resistance, rebelled against postwar prostitution and black-marketeering, and was finally shot down by the police—was denied a permit, and three minutes were cut out of Ingmar Bergman's *The Virgin Spring*, based on a Swedish legend, showing pagan and Christian conceptions in conflict. In neither film did subversion or licentiousness exist outside the eye of the beholder. As for *L'Arialda*, it was indecent only insofar as almost all lives are indecent according to standards of probity, kindness, and courtesy that have never obtained except among very few people, in very few places, for very short periods.

Visconti found it ironic that such interdictions should occur in Rome less than a year after the U.S. courts had decreed D. H. Lawrence's *Lady Chatterley's Lover* not objectionable, and the Obscene Publications Act permitted Vladimir Nabokov's *Lolita* to be published in Britain. He decided to put the case before the President of the Republic, Giovanni Gronchi, and, accompanied by Rina Morelli and Paolo Stoppa, went to the Quirinal. The situation was embarrassing for the Christian-Democratic President, who had taken part in the Resistance as representative of the Committee of National Liberation, and been elected to the presidency in 1955 by both right and left. Visconti also gave a press conference at which he read L'Arialda to the assembled journalists so that they could judge for themselves. Finally, the permit was granted.

Visconti produced L'Arialda in Rome for Christmas, with music by Nino Rota and sets and costumes by himself. His emotionally rich style was far more effective than a kitchen-sink one in revealing what really goes on among people to whom the possession of a kitchen sink would be a miracle in itself, and L'Arialda roused vociferous applause and no protests among the audiences who packed the Teatro Eliseo during its fifty performances in Rome. But no sooner had the company moved to Milan, in February 1961, as planned, than trouble began again.

Ever vigilant, Commendatore Carmelo Spagnuolo attended the first night of L'Arialda at the Teatro Nuovo. Determined that its first should be also its last night in Milan, Spagnuolo not only forbade any future performances, declaring in his nuanced way that L'Arialda was "a sea of obscenity without a drop of art," but also ordered the confiscation of the book of the play, published by Feltrinelli. On this occasion Spagnuolo added to his achievements that of breaking up the best theatrical company in Italy. Rina Morelli, Paolo Stoppa, and their group of actors continued to work with each other whenever possible, but such a financial loss as this made it impossible for them, or Visconti, to keep their company together any longer on a permanent basis.

The capricious nature of censorship is neatly illustrated by the fact that fifteen years later, six months after Visconti's death, L'Arialda was revived in Milan in a cordial atmosphere of approval and interest—nostalgia even—for a play that "held an important place in the theater history of its period, although seen by few people." L'Arialda was not altered for the 1976 revival. The author thought that keeping the play in the period in which it was written would reveal its "premonitory quality" and underline the fact that the misery of which it showed the beginnings (what Arialda called "the misery of animals in cages") has now become a "vast slough," a national problem. All of this seemed highly proper to the Milan of 1976, almost too proper to compete successfully with freely displayed films of pornography or science-fiction horror. During this revival, a leader of the Armed Proletarian Group was shot, and police reported that many members of this group were southern immigrants, "so demoralized by unemployment or prison as to be an easy prey for the militants who take them in hand and teach them to put their violence to practical use."

Disgusted by working conditions at home, Visconti left for Paris. His search for a play "free from mediocrity, something violent and great," led him to John Ford's *'Tis Pity She's a Whore*, an Elizabethan masterpiece, although written in the reign of Charles I, and dazzlingly violent and great. A note of *Alice in Wonderland* humor was added to the enterprise by the fact that this play, published the year that Galileo was forced by the Inquisition to "abjure, curse, and abhor" his discovery that the earth revolved around the sun, had been banned in Italy in 1947. Just how and why a seventeenth-century English play came to be forbidden in the Italy of 1947 is one of the minor mysteries of bureaucratic folly.

'Tis Pity She's a Whore admittedly features incest—but this was a popular subject during the Renaissance, possibly because there is a great deal of it in Greek mythology, possibly because conditions of transport in those days made people readier than now to satisfy themselves with what they had at home. Marlowe's

> There might you see the Gods in sundry shapes,
> Committing heady riots, incest, rapes:
> Jove slyly stealing from his sister's bed
> To dally with Idalian Ganymede . . .

certainly suggests scenes beside which today's hard porn looks like very soft porn indeed. But the wartime atrocities from which the world was reviving in 1947 should have made incest look like child's play, which is often how incest begins.

Visconti understood Ford's violence and the historic reasons for it. For him, this violence was on home ground. The little city of Parma, where *'Tis Pity She's a Whore* takes place, had been ruled by Visconti's ancestors back in the fourteenth century, and he could see Parma both as it is today, the city of Verdi and Toscanini, and delicious cheese, and as a sixteenth-century city so powerful that Queen Elizabeth I, addressing her troops at Tilbury while the Spanish Armada sailed toward England, could defy "Parma or Spain, or any prince of Europe" to invade her realm. Visconti wanted to make his production "like the epoch, magnificent and terrible."

He planned to give the two leading parts to Alain Delon and Romy Schneider. Delon, no longer an unknown actor, but a young star with two dazzling performances behind him—in *Plein Soleil*, the film René

Clément made from Patricia Highsmith's brilliant novel *Mr. Ripley*, and in Visconti's own *Rocco*—was a choice agreeable to all concerned. Romy Schneider was another matter. But, since seeing her offstage during the shooting of *Rocco*, Visconti had become interested in her talent, and discerning about her possibilities.

The Romy Schneider of 1961 was not the superb international actress she has since become, but a little Austrian girl whose status as a film star was that of a teen-age Shirley Temple, the little fiancée of central Europe. As Visconti noted, however, she had the theater in her blood. She, too, was a *figlia d'arte:* not only were both her parents, Magda Schneider and Wolf Albach-Retty, superb performers, but her grandmother, Rosa Retty, the child of poor traveling actors, had been known as "the German theater's miracle child" when she made her debut in Berlin at the turn of the century. Unfortunately, Romy's own reputation, as the "miracle child" of Ernst Marischka's *Sissi* films, with their kisses-tears-and-smiles version of Elisabeth of Austria's youth, was at this point becoming a prettily painted iron curtain between her and her true future.

At fifteen Romy had made a film about Queen Victoria, *Mädchenjahre einer Königin* (*The Youth of a Queen*), followed when she was sixteen by *Sissi* (Elisabeth of Austria's family pet name). The success of *Sissi* was too great to be left alone. After it came *Sissi die junge Kaiserin* (*Sissi the Young Empress*), *Sissi Schicksalsjahre einer Kaiserin* (*Sissi Face to Face with Her Destiny*). Romy Schneider's professional position was now a tricky one. A child star can make a comeback with a new adult personality; for adolescent stars, it is far more difficult to shake the saccharin from their feet. Fortunately for Romy, she was introduced by Alain Delon at twenty-one to Visconti, who soon discerned the capacities for passion, tragedy, femininity, and sensuality that had not been required for Sissi's kitten-on-the-keys ways. *'Tis Pity She's a Whore* offered Visconti a risky but splendid opportunity to reveal Romy Schneider's true personality.

The subject of *'Tis Pity She's a Whore* was taken, as were the subjects of so many Elizabethan plays, from Italian chronicles of the kind that enthralled Stendhal. Its poetry was saturated with the atmosphere of the Renaissance—an immoderate desire for knowledge and pleasure, a vitality rendered almost paroxysmal by a sense of life's brevity: "brightness falls from the air, Queens have died young and fair." Man was the measure of all things, poised to triumph over the human situation in the new world as in the old and, through the very strength of his individuality, intensely aware of the God who cares for individual sparrows.

George Beaume's translation of this play was admirably precise and poetic. Visconti's scenery, Piero Tosi's costumes, period music and that of Nino Rota, brilliant lighting, great swags of flowers like animate jewels—all this did justice to the play itself and to the physical beauty of Giovanni and Annabella. To support the young couple, Visconti had a magnificent cast, headed by Valentine Tessier, of eighty actors, including soldiers and servants. But, having provided all this, he was determined that Giovanni and Annabella should reveal talent worthy of such support. So the six weeks of rehearsals at Elvire Popesco's glittering Théâtre de Paris had stormy moments.

Visconti could crack a whip when necessary, and was particularly severe with Romy Schneider. He knew how zealously she was working at her French diction, but he knew, too, that she was no timid beginner in need of reassurance and coaxing. She was a theater child, theater-bred, professional to the marrow of her bones. He refused, therefore, to allow her to stand for one single minute more with reluctant feet, where the brook and river meet, womanhood and childhood fleet. At the slightest suggestion of the spoiled child, he threatened with lionlike roars to send her "home to her mother." During those weeks in Paris, worlds away from her long-lost Sissiland, Romy Schneider often felt she was like a ship in a black storm driven she knew not whither—but was in fact being most carefully driven by Visconti to put all her passionate and tragic temperament into her work. When, at the end of the first night, she ran into the wings to bring Visconti on stage to acknowledge the applause, she knew that thanks to him she had made the difficult leap—the equivalent of an acrobat's first *saut périlleux*—out of the nursery into an adult career. By this time Visconti had begun to love Romy as if she were his daughter. Friends of his say she may have reminded him of the Austrian girl he had wanted to marry, but, in addition, he loved and understood Romy's theater background. His house was, up to the end of his life, full of photographs of her, and he was very distressed when she and Alain Delon parted.

Fifteen years after *'Tis Pity She's a Whore*, Romy Schneider would be toasted at the Cannes Film Festival as one of the small handful of truly international stars. On that occasion her forty-seventh film, Robert Enrico's *Le Vieux Fusil* (*The Old Rifle*), won a César (the French Oscar, awarded for the first time in 1976) as the best film of the year and its two leading actors, Philippe Noiret and Romy Schneider, were acclaimed best actor and actress of the year. When Romy Schneider received her award she dedicated it to her "master and friend, Luchino Visconti," who had died seventeen days earlier.

Having opened up a new world in Paris for Schneider and Delon, Visconti returned to Italy to stage Richard Strauss's *Salome* for the fourth Festival of Two Worlds at Spoleto. *Salome*, a musical drama inspired by a one-act play Oscar Wilde wrote in French for Sarah Bernhardt, was first performed at the Königliches Opernhaus in Dresden, then the capital of the Kingdom of Saxony, on December 9, 1905. It was conducted by Gustav Mahler, at that time conductor of the Vienna State Opera. Despite Strauss's and Mahler's fame, and the high standard of the performance, the result was a scandal, with the words *sadistic, perverse, erotic* flying around the auditorium. After his recent experiences with censorship, Visconti therefore expected trouble over *Salome*. But murder in a Biblical context apparently left the censors calm.

So Visconti was able to go ahead with a production that was not only handsome—he designed the set and the costumes himself—but also electric with suspense. He set Strauss's opera in a violent first-century Eastern court, where it was natural for Salome to dance provocatively in order to obtain the beheading of someone her mother disliked, and for Herod Antipas to order his stepdaughter to be murdered in front of her mother, himself, and the entire court.

Here, as in all his work, Visconti's sense of history inspired his poetic realism. When, that same year, the Russians built a fortified wall between East and West Berlin, Visconti was not among those wailing, with the air of discovering something, about the "dreadfulness of our times." He knew that all times have been dreadful for those experiencing them, that history goes forward only on the rare occasions when someone refuses to yield up John the Baptist's head.

By the time the curtain came down on *Salome*, Visconti's thoughts were occupied by Lampedusa's novel *Il Gattopardo* (*The Leopard*), which he was to film. But between *Salome* and *Il Gattopardo*, he was asked by producer Carlo Ponti to direct one of four episodes in a film to be called *Boccaccio 70*, the other three to be directed by De Sica, Fellini, and Monicelli.

The title, *Boccaccio 70*, was commercially effective for Italy but required explaining abroad. Boccaccio is, with Dante and Petrarch, one of the pillars of Italian literature. His most famous book, *The Decameron*—"known" to all Italians as Chaucer is "known" to all English-speaking people—is set in fourteenth-century Florence at a time when the Black Death, or plague, was arousing fears similar to those aroused in 1945 by the bombing of Hiroshima. *The Decameron* begins with seven girls and three young men coming out of mass at Santa Maria Novella in Florence. Faced by desolate streets where only funeral processions are to be seen, only funeral bells heard, the young people decide to picnic in the fresh air of the country. Once on the hills outside Florence, these medieval evacuees decide to remain there for ten days. (Hence the title, from the Greek *deka hemerai,* for ten days.) To pass the time, each of the ten tells a story a day.

Carlo Ponti, a lively Milanese who had spent twenty years in the film industry, producing both blockbusters and films of artistic value, had no wild plan to tell a hundred stories in one film. But he thought that, with four episodes, he could offer the public an anthology of work by the best directors. Unfortunately, each director was free to choose his own subject without consulting the others—"unfortunately," because this meant that, although the sketches were to be grouped together under one title, there would be no cohesion among them.

De Sica's episode, *The Lottery,* was to concern a girl—played by Carlo Ponti's delicious wife, Sophia Loren—who sells lottery tickets and is herself the prize. Fellini's *The Temptations of Doctor Antonio*—played by Peppino De Filippo and Anita Ekberg—was to be a rumbustious satire on censorship and advertising. Monicelli's *Renzo and Luciana* was the only one of the three about which Suso and Visconti were informed, since Suso had been asked to help write the screenplay for it. Renzo and Luciana, the names of Monicelli's twentieth-century working-class couple, echo those of Manzoni's seventeenth-century peasants in *I promessi sposi,* but whereas the marriage of Renzo and Lucia was threatened by the tyranny of their feudal overlord, Don Rodrigo, that of Renzo and Luciana is threatened by marriage regulations at the factory where they both work, and the foreman is their Don Rodrigo. It struck Suso that it might be possible for Visconti to use Guy de Maupassant's short story "Au bord du lit" (In the bedroom) for a sketch about marriage that would contrast with Renzo and Luciana's problems.

"Au bord du lit" is written almost entirely in dialogue, with the concision encouraged in Maupassant by his old friend and mentor Flaubert. It concerns a young married couple in the Paris of the Belle Epoque. The Count reproaches his wife for the attentions paid her by a would-be lover. She cheerfully reminds him that since he himself has had mistress after mistress, they have made a pact to keep up appearances but do as they please behind the façade. The Count reveals that he has fallen in love again with his wife. She asks him what is the most he has spent in a month on his costliest mistress, and says that if he will give her that, she, too, will become his mistress. Under its apparent levity can be discerned Maupassant's agreement with Flaubert's view that since God

160

created the female, but left it to man to make a woman of her, men get the women they deserve.

Reading this story, Visconti realized that a contemporary version of it would provide an excellent part for Romy Schneider. That summer she and Alain Delon came to visit him by the sea, at Torre San Lorenzo. As Visconti watched her on the beach, playing with some wooden serpents he had bought in Karachi, during a recent trip to India, he thought that her femininity could, because of its cerebral quality, be far more powerful on the screen than the dolly ways of the child woman fashionable at that moment. He decided to ask Chanel to take her in hand and teach her elegance. He felt sure Chanel would be delighted to bully out of hiding the modern *femme fatale* concealed behind Romy's *Sissi* façade.

Visconti's sketch, called *Il lavoro* (*Work*), the change of title underlining the change of period, was set in the Milan of the postwar economic boom. The young husband, Ottavio, is nominally an industrialist. His wife, Pupe (baby, doll), is the daughter of a rich German industrialist who considered a title for his daughter a good investment. Both Ottavio and Pupe are attractive, and the first two years of their marriage have passed suavely. But when *Il lavoro* opens, Ottavio has got himself involved in a call-girl scandal likely to outrage his father-in-law and vex Pupe. There are fashions even in scandals, and this was, in fact as well as fiction, a call-girl period. To deal with his problems Ottavio has lawyers, but Pupe merely reaches, via long-distance telephone, for her father in Bürgenstock, Switzerland, where the money is. She has suddenly decided that she is going to earn her own living. Her father, thinking her conception of work lighter than a bee's knee, has bet her ten million lire that she will not succeed in finding a job.

Throughout the discussion between husband and wife, Ottavio shows an inconsequentiality that suggests a P. G. Wodehouse character, while Pupe displays a deliberate levity. They seem to have some feeling for each other, if only of complicity, and, finally, Ottavio admits that he still desires Pupe. She says that in that case he must pay her. She has visited his call girls and knows the rates. This excites Ottavio. He agrees. As Pupe begins to undress, the telephone rings. Ottavio says, "Let it ring," but she lifts the receiver and tells the valet to inform her father that she can't speak to him "because she is at work." She will call him next day, but right now she is "on the job." This way, she has won her bet with her father.

The heart of *Il lavoro* is the young couple's palatial home—through which, when the film opens, Ottavio's Afghan hounds dart, aureoled by race and rarity. Equally rare are the furniture, the eighteenth-century French bookcases, the pictures, which range from the ancestral to Domietta Hercolani's abstract paintings, the art objects, which include a collection of marble spheres from Visconti's own home, and two marble busts sculpted by Sarah Bernhardt and lent by Sophia Loren. The value of the sets was such that three watchmen had to be engaged, and provided with special slippers to protect the tender-colored carpets. Visconti attached prime importance to the authenticity of this world of objects —in which each generation, like a receding wave, has left something on the shore—because Ottavio and Pupe are imprisoned by this "precious and cold world that lacks the soul for which they are vainly seeking." Asked to sum the film up. Visconti said it was about the playful vengeance of a young wife who is in love and betrayed "as the result of costly shares bought by her husband on the stock market of sex. There is a scandal. The value of the stock falls—and she takes her revenge, a revenge that is a mixture of angelic perfidy and intellectual abjection."

Il lavoro was shown at the fifteenth Cannes Film Festival. At that time the words *consumerism* and *consumer society* had not yet entered fashionable jargon. But conspicuous consumption is what *Il lavoro* is about: what it displays, dissects, satirizes. It is a world without love, where time is told by clocks without hands. To fill the void there is conspicuous waste of art, energy, sexual instincts, and time itself. For this alone, *Il lavoro* deserves more than a footnote among Visconti's films.

It accomplished, too, all that Visconti had hoped for Romy Schneider. It made her an international star and taught her to recognize her own capacities and work to enlarge them. She received offers from all over Europe, and from Hollywood. Walter Wanger, the independent American producer behind Garbo's *Queen Christina* and Ford's *Stagecoach*, cabled Visconti that never had an actress been so marvelously used, or so marvelously to her own advantage, as Romy Schneider in *Il lavoro*.

Visconti was pleased, but was longing for Sicily. While actually involved in a production, he was apt to be in love with its theme and characters. As soon as it was finished, he looked ahead. His temperament was not nostalgic. He had an unusual awareness that the present is not a parenthesis but history in the making: the future's past. The world of *The Leopard* was not as far as might at first appear from the world of the Aci Trezza fishermen. When Visconti went to Sicily to choose settings for his film, he felt as if he were going home.

Nineteen

At the beginning of the sixties, the Russian Pasternak's *Doctor Zhivago* and the Italian Lampedusa's *Il Gattopardo* were the recent novels most discussed in Europe and America. People were curious about the private lives of the two writers, both recently dead when Visconti began filming *The Leopard.*

Pasternak, forced to refuse the Nobel Prize for literature in 1958, two years before his death, had been a forerunner of today's Russian dissidents, with a well-recorded literary career. About Lampedusa, however, there seemed at first to be a man-in-the-iron-mask mystery. His simple and reserved way of living had offered material for the Almanach de Gotha rather than the gossip column.

Giuseppe Tomasi, Duke of Palma and Prince of Lampedusa, was born in Palermo, capital of Sicily, in 1896, the year Italian physicist Guglielmo Marconi patented his system of wireless telegraphy. After a happy, well-educated and traveled childhood—he particularly enjoyed the family visits to Paris, where he immediately made for the secondhand-book stalls along the quays of the Seine—Lampedusa was, at nineteen, plunged into the First World War. An artillery captain, he was captured by the Austrians and imprisoned in Hungary, but succeeded in escaping. After the war he married Baroness Wolff-Stormersee, the half-Italian, half-Baltic stepdaughter of his uncle Marchese Pietro Tomasi della Torretta, diplomat and senator. From the start his wife shared his intellectual interests—she was later elected president of the Italian Psychoanalytical Society—and the rest of his life was devoted to study, reading, writing, and travel. His favorite subject was history, particularly that of the Risorgimento. Early in their married life he told his wife of his wish to write a novel about that period, and the part played in it by his great-grandfather Giulio, who had been, among many other things, an astronomer of distinction.

Lampedusa did eventually succeed in transforming his great-grandfather, whose proud and princely nature he knew only from kinship and hearsay, into the fictional Prince Fabrizio di Salina. "Il Gattopardo," the book's title and Prince Fabrizio's nickname, was chosen by Lampedusa because it is a variant of leopard (*gatto*, cat, *pardo*, panther) and the Lampedusa coat of arms has a leopard rampant at its center. But between Lampedusa's first desire to write *Il Gattopardo* and the physical writing of it, years elapsed. During those years he accumulated memories, experiences, material, but old people who could remember the astronomer-prince died, and *The Leopard*'s landscape was drastically altered by the Second World War. Lampedusa was forty-seven when his beloved palace in Palermo was bombed. Eleven years later he wrote: "From the ceiling [of the ballroom] the Gods, reclining on gilded couches, gazed down smiling and inexorable as a summer sky. They thought themselves eternal; but a bomb manufactured in Pittsburgh, Penn., was to prove the contrary."

Lampedusa continued, nevertheless, to think of *Il Gattopardo*, and in the summer of 1954, when world war had been replaced by more local forms of genocide—Indochina, Algeria, Korea, Guatemala—he accompanied his cousin Baron Lucio Piccolo to a literary gathering at the spa of San Pellegrino in northern Italy. There ten literary figures were to introduce ten new writers to their potential public. The two large, quiet, mannerly cousins, dressed with the elegance of an earlier period, and accompanied by a Sicilian manservant, made a curiously strong impression on everyone there. Lucio Piccolo's poems were eulogized by the great poet Eugenio Montale. In the letter, composed for Piccolo by Lampedusa, that accompanied the poems, he said that he wished to conjure up the old world of Palermo at the very moment when it was about to vanish "without having had the good fortune to be expressed in a work of art." This was certainly Lampedusa's own aim.

In 1956, the year Khrushchev denounced Stalin's policies, Lucio Piccolo sent the typescript of his cousin's novel to a leading Italian publishing house, Mondadori. It was rejected, sent to another leading house, Einaudi, again rejected. Lampedusa accepted defeat with dignity and, in a note written shortly before his death, told his wife and adopted son that though he would like *Il Gattopardo* published, it must not be published at his own expense.

After Lampedusa's death a typescript was sent to the writer Giorgio Bassani. Had Bassani been the first to receive the manuscript, how different Lampedusa's last year would have been. Bassani showed it to Giangiacomo Feltrinelli, a rich, eccentric, anarchistic publisher. *The Leopard* was published by Feltrinelli in November 1958, with a preface by Bassani. Because it was not expected to be a commercial success, the first edition was of only three thousand copies. The reviews, however, soon changed the book's commercial status. Within six months, *Il Gattopardo* was a best seller, with foreign publishers fighting for it at that literary stock market, the annual Frankfurt Book Fair.

Visconti was fascinated by *Il Gattopardo*. He thought it completed the work of Verga, Pirandello, and De Roberto and said what they had left unsaid about Sicily during the Risorgimento. But to film it would cost a fortune and, since the cinema was just then experiencing one of its financial crises, producers were looking for King Kong rather than King Lear. Visconti accepted this fact calmly. The advantage to an artist of being also what is called a "man of the world" is that this sometimes prevents him from wasting valuable indignation. Years later, while making his last film, Visconti told a journalist who complained of the producer's conservative political views, "Your ingenuousness is touching. Films are made with money and money comes from producers—and producers are not ascetic characters preoccupied by social problems; they are businessmen." In the case of *The Leopard*, however, Visconti received vigorous support from Goffredo Lombardo, a young Neapolitan producer as cultured as he was energetic. Son of the founder of the Titanus Film Production Company, Lombardo contributed to the resurgence of the Italian cinema in the sixties, was determined that Visconti should get the backing for *The Leopard*, and obtained that backing from Twentieth Century-Fox.

While estimates were drawn up, technicians began working on plans from photographs of Sicilian sites and palaces. They also, on Visconti's instructions, performed such eccentric but essential chores as soaking red shirts in tea, drying them in the sun, burying them in the earth, and then repeating the process, so as to obtain the faded color required for shirts like those worn by Garibaldi's Italian Legion in South America. (Their color was not due to political choice but to a glut of red woolen shirts on the market in Montevideo, due to trade difficulties caused by war with Argentina. In 1843, the Uruguayan government bought these shirts cheaply and gave them to Garibaldi for the legion he was raising.)

As soon as Lombardo gave the go-ahead sign, the first group of Visconti's technicians left for Sicily: twenty electricians, one hundred and twenty make-up men, hairdressers, and tailors, one hundred and fifty masons, fifteen florists, and ten cooks. Ten cannons were required for street fighting in Palermo—and the streets themselves had to have signs of modern life, such as television aerials, removed and their 1860 aspect restored. Carriages of the period were needed, and a few were discovered employed by funeral parlors or rotting in the disused stables of half-ruined palaces. Horses were brought from Rome, but for the Bourbon soldiers to ride them, local labor was employed, and had to be taught by an army colonel to ride in 1860 style, stiffly upright and with long stirrups.

The scenario, written by Visconti with the same collaborators as for *Rocco and His Brothers*—Suso Cecchi D'Amico, Enrico Medioli, Festa Campanile, and Massimo Franciosa—was completely faithful in spirit to the novel. When the film opens in 1860, Garibaldi, already a folk-hero, and his famous thousand red-shirted volunteers have just landed in Sicily in an attempt to overthrow its feudal Neapolitan Bourbon rulers and make Sicily part of united Italy. Prominent among the onlookers is Fabrizio Corbera, Prince of Salina, the very opposite of an absentee landlord. Handsome, autocratic, patriarchally devoted to his family, his retainers, his animals, and everyone dependent upon him, he nevertheless has a detached attitude, due to the hours devoted to astronomy in his private observatory, and he is completely lucid about the long-term significance of Garibaldi's arrival. The part was a difficult one, requiring as much subtlety as power. Since this was a coproduction, Visconti had to have an American star play the Prince, and was extraordinarily fortunate with Burt Lancaster.

At forty-eight Lancaster, who began his career in show business as part of an acrobatic act for which he and his partner were paid three dollars a month, had become a fine actor with considerable intellectual interests and moral commitments. He took the risk of forming a production company, and his choice of parts was, and is, ruled by ethical as well as artistic considerations. Not long ago he said, "Movies can change things. They are no longer fairy tales, forgotten when we leave the cinema. They command respect and they inspire thought, because they reflect the surge and urgency of our time in a realistic fashion. . . . After all, the whole world is in revolution, and the movies are not excluded from this questioning and re-evaluation." After studying the scenario, the novel, and much of the history and literature of the Risorgimento, Lancaster brought to this, his thirty-ninth film, the humility and eagerness to learn of the best beginners. Visconti wholeheartedly appreciated this. He thought the Prince "a complex character, capable of being autocratic, rude, strong, romantic, understanding, sometimes stupid—but always mysterious. And," he added, "Burt is all these things, too. I sometimes think Burt is the most perfectly mysterious man I ever met." On March 19, 1976, in the church of Saint Ignatius, in Rome, the expression on Burt Lancaster's face made it seem for a second as if Prince Fabrizio himself stood beside Visconti's coffin.

In the film, as in the novel, Prince Fabrizio ceases to be a spectator when two things happen. First, at the film's opening, during family prayers at the Salina palace on the outskirts of Palermo, a young Bourbon soldier is found dead in the palace gardens. At this point Sicily is still part of the Bourbon-ruled Kingdom of the Two Sicilies, but not for much longer. Second, the Prince's orphan nephew, Tancredi Falconieri, a brilliant and handsome boy far dearer to the Prince than his own conventional sons, arrives unexpectedly, to say good-bye to his uncle. Tancredi has decided to join Garibaldi's rebels. He tells his uncle this with a mixture of enthusiasm and virility that probably reflects Visconti's own attitude as a young officer. Prince Fabrizio tells Tancredi he is crazy to join such riffraff, connected with the Mafia, too; a Falconieri "must be on our side, must be loyal to the King." Ah, but "which king," says Tancredi. Garibaldi has no wish to overthrow monarchy as such, only to expel the Bourbons so that Sicily can become part of united Italy. This is the only way, Tancredi assures his uncle, for "Italy to enter modern history without falling into the chaos of Don Peppino Mazzini's republicanism."

Lampedusa's key line occurs during this first discussion between the Prince and his nephew, when Tancredi says, "If we want everything to stay as it is, everything must change." He says this with the gaiety and energy of a Stendhal hero. His cynicism, as yet merely youthful exhibitionism, is still checked by "the noble qualities of his feudal upbringing" and "the recklessness of his spendthrift father." As the Prince is to say later to Tancredi's lower-class father-in-law, "Maybe a young man as distinguished, discriminating and fascinating as Tancredi cannot be produced without ancestors who ran through half a dozen fortunes." The part was played by Alain Delon, who, at twenty-six, possessed not only the beauty and charm ascribed to Tancredi by Lampedusa but also had learned so much from playing in *Rocco and His Brothers* that he was capable of learning more. A stubborn character with a strong capacity for loyalty, Delon has never forgotten what he owes to Visconti. The fact that their relationship was very much like the relationship between Tancredi and the Prince contributed to the creative atmosphere in which the film was made.

Lampedusa based the character of Tancredi partly on that of his own adopted son, Gioacchino Lanza di Mazzarino, the present Duke of Palma, who helped Visconti as artistic adviser, as did Lampedusa's second cousin the famous jewel designer Fulco Santostefano della Cerda, Duke of Verdura. In his recent memoirs, *The Happy Summer Days,* the Duke of Verdura says that Tancredi and Angelica are based, not very accurately, on his own grandparents. Just as Visconti put much of his own youth as a cavalry officer into Tancredi, so he contributed to Lancaster's performance his sense of the old age he himself would not live to experience. When Visconti denied that *The Leopard* was partly autobiographical, he was undoubtedly sincere, since by the time journalists asked him this, the film had been released and he was preoccupied by plans for *La Traviata* for the Spoleto Festival and *Il Trovatore* for Covent Garden. Nevertheless, lifelong friends, such as Suso Cecchi D'Amico, say that Luchino just *was* the Gattopardo. Years later, when locked in mortal combat with illness, Visconti still gave this impression and managed, despite sufferings bravely and nobly endured, to carry his extraordinarily fascinating and impressive personality intact and in triumph through the iron gates of life.

In the beginning of the film the Gattopardo is haunted by the thought of Tancredi lying dead like the soldier found in the palace gardens. Equally haunted is the Prince's daughter Concetta, who has adored her cousin since their childhood. Had it not been for the historical changes taking place, Tancredi might well have married Concetta. But when he returns from his brief Garibaldian campaign, lightly wounded, a local hero in splendid spirits and looks, just in time to accompany the Salinas to their summer palace at Donnafugata, he falls violently in love with Angelica, the voluptuously beautiful only child of Don Calogero Sedara, the newly rich Mayor of Donnafugata. Sedara is a clever lower-middle-class opportunist who, as the Prince observes, talks loudly of his revolutionary sentiments but in fact merely wants his own class to grab the aristocrats' privileges.

One of the most exquisite moments in *The Leopard* is the Salina family's carriage journey to their summer palace: the horses trotting steadily up the bare lion-colored mountain slopes ("Worse than Africa," moans the French governess); Tancredi's autocratic refusal to allow revolutionary comrades to halt the family party; the picnic lunch, a ravishing version of the *Déjeuner sur l'herbe;* the welcome awaiting the Salinas at Donnafugata, its feudal character unchanged by recent upheavals despite the "Long Live Garibaldi" and "Death to the Bourbons" slogans painted across whitewashed walls. As the Salinas' carriages come within sight, the municipal band strikes up "Noi siamo zingarelli" (We are the gypsies) from Verdi's *La Traviata.* This is a time-hallowed greeting to the Prince's family. There are cheers, bows, curtsies. The church bells peal. The Prince says, "Thanks be to God, everything seems to be as usual."

For Lampedusa's fictitious Donnafugata, Visconti chose the village of Ciminna, inland from Palermo. Its piazza and church resembled Lampedusa's invented ones, but the palace near the church was so dilapidated that it took forty-five days to reconstruct the façade. This not only provided work for local people, but also taught them new skills. The church, with its seventeenth-century stuccowork and sculpted wooden choir stalls, was perfect for the Salinas' processional entry for the Te Deum. This was accompanied by "Amami, Alfredo" from *La Traviata*, played fortissimo on the organ—not, as might be thought, inserted by Visconti for love of Verdi, but specified by Lampedusa in the novel. Milan is far from being the only place in Italy where church and opera house seem interchangeable. Verdi's music is, moreover, a special case. No other composer has such a hold on every class, not only in his country's musical life, but also on its political, civic, patriotic, amorous, and domestic emotions. Love of Verdi was a bond between Lampedusa and Visconti, and love of Verdi unites the quick and the dead in this stupendous film that shows the making of modern Italy as no other film has done.

When asked if ideological motives had predominated in the making of *The Leopard*, Visconti said no—because ideological motives are "always part of people's general feelings and can't be isolated." He did not believe in incompatibility between private and public feelings. For example, Tancredi's passion for Angelica is genuine, spontaneous, momentarily overwhelms him, yet by choosing to marry a girl from a lower social class than his own—an action far more provocative and shocking then than most of today's filmgoers realize—Tancredi is following his own earlier advice to his uncle: "If we want everything to stay the same, everything must change." Angelica is not only beautiful but sufficiently bright, shrewd, and ambitious to transform herself almost overnight into a member of the old ruling class that, thanks to the wealth and health of girls like herself, will to a large extent retain its authority. Those of Henry James's European aristocrats who married American heiresses pursued the same not necessarily ignoble aims.

The only way in which Visconti's version of *The Leopard* differed—in letter, not in spirit—from the novel was in the ending. The novel is divided into eight parts, of which the first six, occupying six-sevenths of the entire book, go from 1860 to 1862 and culminate in the great ball at the Palazzo Ponteleone. Then, after a gap of twenty years, ten pages are devoted to the death of Prince Fabrizio and, after a gap of twenty-seven years, to the old age of the Prince's spinster daughters and their sister-in-law Angelica, widow of Senator Tancredi. Visconti thought that, cinematographically, everything that happened after 1862 could be implied or foreshadowed at the ball—which occupies a third of the film and, since it is the Prince's meditation on things past, conveys the essence of Lampedusa's book.

For the fictitious Palazzo Ponteleone, Visconti used the real Palazzo Gangi, one of the few palaces in Palermo still lived in by the family for whom it was built. The heat of August in Sicily made it necessary to equip the ballrooms with air conditioning and the buffet with giant refrigerators. Candles had to be manufactured with a higher content of purified fatty acids than is usual to avoid their melting in the heat of the studio lamps. The Mayor provided servants but, since most Europeans are larger now than they were in the nineteenth century, few modern servants could get into the old liveries. Finding the guests proved easy, however; Visconti invited the owners of the Palazzo Gangi, their relatives, friends, and habitual guests, to take part in the film. They accepted with delight and the way in which they totally committed themselves to what came to seem to them yet another, if slightly eccentric, part of their social round—at which gossip flowed, friendships and enmities were renewed, flirtations and love affairs abounded—gave these scenes an authenticity unique among film balls. Because of the heat, all the filming took place at night, from eight in the evening until four in the morning. But the "guests" did not have their days to themselves. In the afternoons a dancing master taught them the mazurka, the galop, and the waltz.

One or two critics, aware that Visconti planned to film part of *Remembrance of Things Past,* called the ball scenes "Proustian." On this Visconti commented: "If anyone said that Lampedusa's personal manner of envisaging social life, and existence itself, provides a link between Verga's realism and Proust's 'memory,' I should completely agree. It was with this impression that I reread the novel many times—and it would satisfy one of my deepest ambitions if Tancredi and Angelica at the Palazzo Ponteleone ball recalled Proust's Odette and Swann, and Don Sedara's attitude toward the peasants during the plebiscite at Donnafugata recalled Verga's Mastro-Don Gesualdo."

A particularly poignant moment occurs after Prince Fabrizio, tired of wandering through the brilliant enfilade of rooms full of elderly gossips who were once young beauties he pursued, takes refuge in his host's small and seldom-used library. On the wall is a copy of Greuze's *Death of a Just Man,* an old man on his deathbed surrounded by his children and grandchildren. Prince Fabrizio is contemplating this when Tancredi and

170

Angelica join him. In answer to their affectionate queries, he speaks of death in moderate and peaceful tones uncannily like those in which Visconti himself was to speak of it fourteen years later.

Angelica, fresh yet opulent as a newly opened magnolia, draws the Prince back toward life by begging him to dance with her. She has heard so much, she says, of his prowess as a dancer. Since it is clear that this means even more to Angelica emotionally than socially, the Prince allows himself to be persuaded.

No sooner have Prince Fabrizio and Angelica taken the floor than the other guests fall back and become spectators. The music to which they dance is a waltz, previously unknown to the public, by Verdi. The score of this was a gift to Visconti from film editor Mario Serandrei, who discovered it among a pile of old manuscripts in a Roman bookshop. The beauty of the waltz emphasizes the fact that the pair dancing so exquisitely together, the resplendent girl at the beginning of her life and the noble man near the end of his, are aware that they could in other circumstances have been passionately in love with each other. After the waltz the Prince refuses Tancredi's and Angelica's warm invitation to have supper with them. He remembers his own youth too vividly, he says, not to know how irksome the presence of an old uncle would be to two young people in love. What he does not tell them is that he is suddenly exhausted.

Leaving supper table and palace, the Prince walks homeward, through the dark, narrow, cobbled streets of old Palermo. As he picks his way through the refuse that litters narrow alleys and little piazzas, he is increasingly exhausted. In his evening clothes, white scarf, and silk hat, he suddenly resembles Boldini's portrait of Verdi. Presently he meets a priest, with acolytes, hastening to a deathbed. He immediately crosses himself and humbly kneels to eternity on the dirty cobbles. This brush with death is almost immediately followed by another. He hears the sound of gunshots, and knows from talk at the ball that two royalist soldiers are being executed for having attempted to join Garibaldi. What recently led to decorations is now an error in timing that leads to death. The quick dry gunshots convey the horror of political intrigues, the inadequacy of attempts to mitigate human cruelty, so much worse than that of animals. The imminence of Prince Fabrizio's own death is clear in his listening face.

Togliatti, to whom Visconti showed *The Leopard* privately as soon as it was finished, thought the ball "a magnificent apotheosis," foresaw that distributors would say it was too long, and urged Visconti "not to cut a minute of it." The matter was not, unfortunately, in Visconti's hands.

Despite the film's success in Europe, American distributors, in a Hamlet-without-the-Prince mood, cut forty minutes off its original two hundred and five minutes' running time.

When *The Leopard* was released, Emilio Cecchi wrote that it was "extraordinarily instructive amid so much stupidity that has been written about the Risorgimento." This was typical of Cecchi's discernment. For although plenty of critics have commented on Visconti's sense of drama, music, acting, and aesthetic values, little has been written about his extraordinary sense of history. If generations of your family have played leading roles in history, you are likely to know that history exists, just as a clown's child knows that circuses exist. But only his individual gifts enabled Visconti to benefit from his inheritance, to listen, as carefully as he did as a child, to elderly relatives to whom the Risorgimento was as near, as painful, as much a subject for disagreements, as the Second World War is to elderly people today.

Twenty

While Visconti was shooting *The Leopard,* producer Franco Cristaldi offered to finance another film—provided it had a leading part for Claudia Cardinale. Both Visconti and Suso Cecchi D'Amico agreed that Claudia Cardinale had not yet been offered a part in which she could do herself justice, and it seemed to them a good omen that the offer should come from Cristaldi, who had helped them seven years earlier to give Marcello Mastroianni a good part in *Le notti bianche.* Both Mastroianni and Cardinale were to fulfill the hopes they aroused.

For days Visconti, Suso, and Medioli discussed possible parts for Claudia Cardinale. Finally, they agreed on a mythological character: Electra, daughter of the Greek king Agamemnon and Queen Clytemnestra, who conspired with her lover Aegisthus to murder Agamemnon on his return from the Trojan War. The violence with which Electra and her brother Orestes pursued their mother and, above all, their conception of violence as a duty seemed to Visconti as topical today as when the first dramatizations of the story were written by Aeschylus, Sophocles, and Euripides, over four hundred years before the birth of Christ. New versions of Electra's story had been created during the last four centuries. Of most recent ones, Visconti's favorite was Richard Strauss's opera *Elektra* (1909), with its libretto by Hofmannsthal. He had also been interested in Eugene O'Neill's *Mourning Becomes Electra* (1931) and Jean Giraudoux's *Electre* (1938).

In his own 1964 version of Electra's story, Visconti replaced the Trojan War by today's most tragic institution, the concentration camp. No concentration camp appeared in the film, but the existence of this man-made monstrosity was central to it, since Sandra-Electra is a half-Jewish Italian girl convinced that her mother and her mother's lover betrayed her father, a Jewish professor who died in Auschwitz. And since Sandra and

173

her brother Gianni are obsessed by their childhood, Visconti chose as title a quotation from the great Italian poet Leopardi's "Le Ricordanze" (Memories):

O you bright stars of the Bear, I did not think
That I should come once more, as was my custom,
To gaze upon you glittering above
My father's garden, or converse with you
From the windows of this house, where as a boy
I lived, and saw the end of happiness. . . .

There is no object here which meets my sense
Which does not bring some image back again,
Or raise some sweet remembrance—sweet in itself,
But then creeps in, with pain, thought of the present,
And so, an empty longing for the past,
Though it was sad, and these words: "I have been."

Today English-speaking readers without Italian owe their knowledge of Leopardi to Iris Origo's superb biography of him. Count Giacomo Leopardi, who was born ten years after Byron and died the same year as Pushkin, spent most of his brief life under his mother's fiercely pious tyranny in the little Adriatic town of Recanati, which "combines distinction and squalor, dignity and dreariness." Iris Origo's book throws light not only on Leopardi's own life and art but also on the art he inspired, including Visconti's film.

He had decided to set *Vaghe stelle dell'orsa* (*The Bright Stars of the Bear*), or *Sandra*, as it was called in the U.S., in Volterra. This formerly Etruscan city, founded eight hundred years before the birth of Christ, crouches around its fortress on a Tuscan hilltop, only thirty miles from the Mediterranean—and so dominated the film that Claudia Cardinale's looks seemed to acquire an Etruscan quality. Today only a third of its original size, Volterra is so eerie with history that when the winds whistle through it they seem to bring echoes of old, unhappy, far-off things and battles long ago. Time's destructiveness is as dramatically visible as in a Piranesi engraving. The famous gray-and-yellow *balze* (cliffs) on which Volterra stands are constantly menaced by landslides, which have already swept away an ancient necropolis, a church, part of the original Etruscan wall. An eleventh-century monastery, poised on the edge of the abyss, provides an architectural question mark.

Just as Visconti was about to leave Rome for Volterra, news came of Togliatti's death. As a personal friend, Visconti was among those who kept vigil by the coffin and attended the funeral—a funeral so startlingly different from the funeral of any other Communist, in any other country, that certain details seem now to have anticipated today's Italian Euro-communism. Over a million people were present as the hearse carried Togliatti's body from the Piazza Venezia, where Mussolini's thunderings had died down only twenty years earlier, to San Giovanni in Laterano, older than the Vatican itself, since the original basilica was built by the Emperor Constantine in the fourth century. As the coffin passed, many people crossed themselves, many gave the Communist salute, and many did both. On either side of the forecourt of the great baroque church where a separate building contains the Holy Staircase—supposedly from Pontius Pilate's palace, used by Christ Himself, and brought back from Palestine by Constantine's mother, Saint Helena—stood delegates from every Communist mayor in Italy. Each one carried the flag of his commune. All the flags were brilliantly colored, and almost all adorned by images of the communes' patron saints. When Togliatti's successor, Luigi Longo, one of the party's founders, addressed the vast crowd, he thanked the Pope for having asked everyone to pray for the dying Togliatti.

All this took Visconti's thoughts back to the war—and to the concentration camps that still exist in a world not, as a whole, in the least safe for democracy. Next day he was in Volterra, choosing sites and settings. Two days after that he started rehearsing Sandra and Gianni.

Twenty-four-year-old Claudia Cardinale was resplendent but terrified. Although she had worked with Visconti before, she had never had such an exacting part, and she had heard many an apocryphal story of his "implacable severity." She soon discovered, however, that she had nothing to worry about. A born teacher, Visconti knew at once the difference between those who need to be told they *can* do what is wanted, and those who need be told they *cannot*. He realized that Cardinale needed gentleness, just as Romy Schneider needed, now and again, bullying.

Sandra's brother, Gianni, was played by Jean Sorel, a handsome young French actor, married to an Italian, who had made an excellent start in Italian films in Bolognini's *La giornata balorda* (1960). Andrew, Sandra's American husband, was played by Michael Craig. With his family, who accompanied him, and his ubiquitous pipe, Craig looked typically English, and gave Andrew an appropriately Bostonian note. He was an adventurous person; born in India when it was part of the British Empire, he had joined the merchant marine at fifteen and gone around the world, before settling for the theater. He was playing golf at his club when a call came through from Rome asking if he would be free to play in *Sandra*. Did he want to read the script before deciding? No, he said, if the script was good enough for Visconti it was good enough for him.

175

For the part of the mother, a former concert pianist, now mentally deranged, Visconti had thought of Francesca Bertini, one of the great stars of the silent days—*Fedora* (1916), *The Seven Deadly Sins* (1917), *The Nude Lady* (1918). Following her marriage to a Swiss nobleman, Francesca Bertini had retired in her twenties, but, after a Sherlock Holmes-like search, Visconti learned that the Countess Cartier had a poste restante address in Geneva. Unfortunately, she wanted a hundred million lire to play the part. There was pathos of *The Old Lady Shows Her Medals* variety in her demand, which Visconti understood and did not resent. Francesca Bertini had indeed been a great beauty, a great star, and he respected her past, but he could not afford to meet her present demands. The day shooting began, she cabled Visconti, "Deeply distressed not to be working with you." Ten years later, over eighty, she played, with distinction, a tiny part in Bertolucci's *1900*.

Meanwhile, Visconti turned to a friend, the French actress Marie Bell, another big star, who had begun her career at the Comédie-Française and won international success for her performance in Duvivier's film *Un Carnet de bal* (1937). Marie Bell combines great talent with common sense and was to prove admirable as Sandra's mother. Not only was she completely convincing as a pianist, but also she gave the part precisely the ambiguity Visconti wanted. Watching a scene in which her daughter visits her, the audience feels that while she may be innocent, she just may have betrayed her husband, not with malice aforethought but merely because he happened to be in her way.

Sandra opens with a glimpse of a Geneva hotel where Sandra and her American engineer husband, Andrew, are giving a farewell reception before leaving next morning for a visit to Sandra's home, Volterra—Andrew's first visit—on their way to New York. Sandra and Andrew are a handsome and happy couple and their party flows along conventional lines. The only odd incident is Sandra's quickly suppressed distress when one of the guests goes to a piano and plays César Franck's Prélude.

Next morning Sandra and Andrew drive off in a powerful automobile, roof down in the sunshine. This scene, like the opening one, is brief: the glittering Swiss highway and landscape, a flight of birds overhead, signs changing from French to Italian, a glimpse of the Autostrada del Sole, the Tuscan landscape. From the clean modern international world of Geneva's lakeside hotels and banks to time-eroded Volterra is only a few hours' drive, yet it takes Sandra and Andrew into another world, a world apparently stagnant, yet saturated with history that is still radioactive. "See the cliffs?" says Sandra. "That's Porta San Francesco. Volterra! Look—the sea! And the Etruscan walls, look!" Andrew does look—with interest as a husband and with pleasure as a tourist. His expensive camera is ever ready. But he has no idea of the power Volterra still wields over Sandra. To Andrew it is an exotic, picturesque little place; to Sandra it is still the city of her childhood:

> . . . lordly Volaterrae,
> Where scowls the far-famed hold
> Piled by the hands of giants
> For godlike kings of old.

For Sandra's old home Visconti rented Marchese Inghirami's palace in Volterra. Its gardens are as mysterious as the ancient grove and sanctuary at Lake Nemi described in *The Golden Bough,* and give a similar impression of sheltering within them a death-dealing yet sacred form of life. In *Sandra* the disturbing presence is that of a shrouded monument to Sandra's father which stands in the garden, waiting to be unveiled. D'Annunzio set his novel *Forse che sì, Forse che no (Perhaps so, Perhaps Not)* in this very garden in 1910. The palace was arranged by Visconti to suggest semiabandonment halfway between a museum and a Sleeping Beauty's palace with no prince on the way. Andrew says wonderingly to Sandra, "This is the strangest house I've ever seen . . . and yet in a way it's like you. . . ."

They are welcomed by Fosca, the family's old housekeeper, a black-clad elderly peasant who holds herself as if carrying an invisible amphora. This part was taken with eerie effect by Amalia Troiani, a Sicilian who comes of an old acting and marionette-playing family. She mentions to Andrew that Gianni, supposedly in London and unable to get to Volterra for the unveiling ceremony—just as he was unable to get to Geneva for Sandra's wedding—often comes to Volterra. Sandra, coming into the room and overhearing this, says, "Nonsense, Fosca, Gianni was ill in London last Easter." Fosca's obstinacy suggests there is something mysterious about Gianni's visits. Just then they are interrupted by a telegram from Sandra's hated stepfather, Gilardini. He does not want to bother them the moment they arrive but expects to see them at the town hall. Sandra is going to the town hall next day to sign the papers donating the palace gardens to Volterra as a public park in memory of her father.

Sandra then takes Andrew into the garden. It is already dark and the trees are swaying in a high wind typical of Volterra. Sandra walks ahead to her father's monument, caresses the shrouded marble face. Suddenly a figure appears at a garden gate. It is Gianni, unannounced and unexpected. He and Sandra embrace. From the first there is something extravagant and strained in their attitude toward each other. Gianni is a handsome, reckless rebel without a cause. He is obsessed by the past and jealous of Andrew for having provided Sandra with an escape line from this past. So Gianni sees to it that they meet Pietro Fornari again. Son of their former overseer, Fornari was in love with Sandra during their adolescence, studied "to raise himself to her level," and is today a highly respected doctor. Here, as in many Visconti films, one sees how history calls the tune for the game of musical chairs that is one of the more peaceful forms class struggles have always assumed.

Gianni nevertheless likes Andrew, appreciates his strength and candor, shows him around Volterra at night, when it is at its most mysterious. Bemused, Andrew says, "I'm a foreigner, remember. A town like this is nothing like a provincial town back home." "That's only your impression," Gianni tells him. "Provincial life's the same everywhere . . . with its intense passions that seem incredible once one's left them behind, but that smother one all over again the minute one returns—even if one's been away a hundred years." This is precisely what the poet Leopardi thought of his own birthplace. But it is not true for Andrew, whose own provincial towns have never been sacked by foreign armies, never seen wooden crucifixes weighed down by living bodies, never heard the roar of trucks carrying people away to deportation, degradation, and death.

Visconti emphasized the lethal quality of the most recent past by showing its aftereffects on one of its victim's children. Excessive, spoiled, self-absorbed as Sandra and Gianni are, their inability to put their war-twisted childhood behind them and accept adult responsibilities comes from a refusal to forget the dead or take treachery, suffering, and murder for granted. They are therefore on the side of the angels even if they themselves are distinctly fallen angels. Hatred of their stepfather and pride in their dead father's race have strengthened the childhood bond between them. Their stepfather knows this but prefers to believe that the bond is an "unnatural" one.

Visconti makes it clear that just as Gilardini may be wrong about this, so the children's mother and stepfather may be innocent of having denounced the father. (During the war there was far less denouncing of Jews in Denmark, Holland, and Italy than in any of the other countries invaded by Germany.) Nor does Andrew believe Gilardini guilty. When Sandra tells him with passionate resentment that Gilardini ruined her and Gianni's childhood by trying to send them away to boarding schools, merely because he "couldn't stand being judged by us," Andrew says mildly, "That's understandable, you know." Sandra shakes her head vehemently. She understands perfectly why Gianni wrote his mother that he would rather die than go away to school, and then swallowed some veronal in a bungled suicide attempt, which Gilardini "is still always throwing in his face."

This attempted suicide drew brother and sister even closer together. A note of conspiracy entered their relationship. They left notes for each other in special hiding places, arranging secret meetings. "Rather a morbid game," says Andrew, still mild, but with growing uneasiness. Sandra drags him off to show him some of the old hiding places. There is one in their mother's room, in a beautiful old Cupid and Psyche clock. As Sandra leaves the room, Andrew glances inside this and finds a note there. Disturbed, he hands it to Sandra. She reads it to him: "Important! Urgent! Your faithful slave awaits you by the cistern." She laughs and says, "It can't have been all that important if it's waited all these years."

Yet soon afterward we see Sandra descending a spiral iron staircase to an underground cistern in the garden, where her brother is waiting for her. He has so much to tell her, he says, overexcitedly. "Come into the house then and tell me there." Suddenly he seizes her hand, slides off her wedding ring, and begs her to lend it to him, "just for one day." This hint at incest echoes *'Tis Pity She's a Whore:*

FLORIO   Where's the ring,
               That which your mother, in her will, bequeathed,
               And charged you on her blessing not to give it
               To any but your husband? Send back that.
ANABELLA   I have it not.
FLORIO   Ha! Have it not; where is it?
ANABELLA   My brother in the morning took it from me,
               Said he would wear it today.

The scene also echoes D'Annunzio's novel *Forse che si, Forse che no,* in which a wrongful accusation of incest provokes a suicide. Finally the hint is strengthened by a novel that Gianni tells Sandra he has written, called *The Bright Stars of the Bear.* A publisher has accepted it, and Gianni hopes it will be a best seller. As a minor he cannot touch his future inheritance without Sandra's permission but, rather than tell her the humiliating truth about his ill-paid job as a society columnist in London, he has visited Volterra secretly and taken art objects to sell them. Once again the Etruscan heritage has been drawn upon. Sitting in front of the fire in their mother's old room, Sandra reads Gianni's novel—and is outraged. Ostensibly autobiographical, it is a story of incest between brother and sister. Has anyone else read this horror? asks Sandra. The publisher, of course, and the public will. "The public will not," says Sandra; your novel is not going to be published. How much do you want, to destroy it? They quarrel like wildcats. Finally Gianni says he will

179

destroy his novel if Sandra will tell him why she wants it destroyed. "Because it could be a weapon in the hands of our enemies." The melodramatic words carry conviction in a house where betrayal and madness are as real as the ticking of the clocks.

Andrew, trying to be rational, invites Gilardini and Dr. Fornari to dinner in order to "clear up the misunderstandings." But the dinner clears nothing up. Dr. Fornari has barely arrived when he gets an emergency call from the hospital. Galardini and Sandra quarrel so violently that, finally, Gilardini cries out that Sandra and Gianni have accused their mother and himself of "monstrosities" merely in order to hide their own incestuous relationship. At last the word is out.

Andrew expects his young brother-in-law to deny this accusation immediately and categorically—and the novel fury with which he watches Gianni's supine reaction is merely the visible part of an iceberg of rage that has been forming in him ever since he began to realize that, in his wife's strange and beautiful home, he is merely a stranger in a strange land.

Beside himself with exasperation and dislike of mysteries, Andrew calls Gianni a coward and knocks him down. Sandra tries to intervene. But when she asks, "Do you believe me or them? *Answer me*," Andrew can only say that he believes in the woman he married, and would "give anything to believe in her now." Sandra swears that her stepfather's accusation is pure calumny—and she is almost certainly speaking the truth. Yet doubt subsists in the audience's mind, just as it does about the mother's and stepfather's guilt.

While making the film, Visconti said, "All the characters are ambiguous except Andrew. He would like to find a logical explanation for everything, instead of which he finds himself in a world dominated by the most profound, contradictory, and inexplicable passions. . . . It's on the same lines as those thrillers in which everything appears very clear at the beginning and very obscure by the end, as always happens when people attempt the difficult task of understanding their own reactions, feeling absolutely sure they have nothing to learn but ending up face to face with agonizing existential problems."

Andrew disappears, presumably departing in anger, and Gianni burns the manuscript of his *Bright Stars of the Bear*. The pain of this self-inflicted auto-da-fé makes him attack the one person he loves. "You see?" he exults over Sandra. "When you really need him, you can't count on your husband." Then he begs his sister to stay with him in their old home, "as if the years between didn't exist." When she refuses, telling him he disgusts her, Gianni threatens to kill himself. This makes no impression on Sandra. She has hated their stepfather for mocking at the child Gianni's attempted suicide, yet because the child survived she herself now fails to take the adult Gianni's threats seriously. So far as she is concerned, she tells her brother with Medusalike fury, he is dead already.

Andrew, however, is very much alive. Instead of departing in anger, he has left a letter telling Sandra that he is going ahead to New York only because he thinks she needs a moment's breathing space. The past has always helped him choose his future, and he prays that her past will make her choose to come back to him. Reading this, Sandra weeps desperately, torn between her vanished past in Volterra and her still-accessible future in America. This was one of Claudia Cardinale's finest scenes. Critics praised the strange admixture of Etruscan and Hebrew that Cardinale achieved in looks and expression, *the new arcane character* of her style, which recalled paintings in recently unearthed Etruscan tombs.

At last all is ready for the unveiling of the monument to the dead father. In the sunlit, wind-torn garden a small group assembles: the Rabbi, the Mayor, a handful of relatives and local notables, the dead man's children, his widow, and her second husband. But Gianni is missing. He is in his mother's room. A letter to Sandra and a handful of sleeping pills lie alongside a glass of water on the bedside table. While Sandra is fighting her way into the future, Gianni takes an overdose of sleeping pills. His gesture is a repetition of his childhood one, an act of defiance that is a cry for help. Once he has swallowed the barbiturates he is panic-stricken. Sunlight pierces the shutters, the wind rattles them, but no one answers Gianni's calls. He manages to climb off the bed, to cross the room, but in vain. "I don't want to die," cries Gianni, dying. He collapses on the floor calling, "Sandra . . . Sandra . . ."

He is alone in the house. On the desk in Sandra's empty room is her letter telling Andrew that "she has not betrayed his trust and will be with him soon—able to share his dreams, free at last from phantasmas and remorse." For her, the future has won. She is going to grow up. She has never looked as lovely as now when, in white for mourning, she runs into the wind and across the garden she has given away, toward the father who will survive as long as she lives to remember him.

It is Fosca, the old housekeeper, who finds Gianni. As she returns from shopping, she is suddenly uneasy. Parking her bulging shopping bag in a long-deserted corridor, she looks in room after room: all empty. Life as once lived by the father, now dead, the mother, now crazy, the two small children now grown, has receded forever from this haunting

181

house. Suddenly Fosca hears someone downstairs. It is Pietro Fornari. Even to Fosca's hierarchical nature, Fornari has long ceased to be the no-account local child who was the "faithful slave" of the brother and sister "up at the big house." A distinguished medical man, steady with responsibility, Fornari has stepped into the same class as Andrew, become someone to whom Fosca can appeal, as she does now, calling, "Doctor . . . Doctor . . ."

Together these two, to whom this particular fragment of the past's palimpsest is an open book, continue the search for Gianni. As they hasten down empty passages, peer into empty rooms, they might be a pair of devoted museum attendants at closing time. At last they think of the mother's former rooms, kept locked until Sandra opened them for Andrew. The door is ajar, Gianni crumpled on the marble floor. He has done with the bright stars of the bear in his father's garden, has reached the end of the Leopardi poem he loved:

> But oh, as often as I think of you,
> My early hopes, the dear imaginings
> I once possessed, then look, and see how vile
> And sorry my life is, and death alone,
> Of all I ever hoped for, now remaining,
> I feel my heart turn cold, and then I know
> Nothing can recompense me for my fate.
> When death, invoked so often, stands before me,
> And I have reached the end of my misfortunes,
> When earth seems a strange valley, and when the future
> Eludes my gaze, I know for sure that I
> Shall still remember you, my dreams; that image
> Shall make me grieve once more, with bitterness
> That I have lived in vain, and with distress
> Mingle the sweetness of my dying day.[1]

Reflected in the mirror, we see Fornari feel Gianni's pulse, gently fold Gianni's arm across his dead body. Then he runs down into the garden. But he cannot deliver the news of Gianni's death, because the memorial service has started.

The Rabbi's bronze voice proclaims "the Resurrection and the Life." Around him a dozen people are grouped. The murdered man's widow and two other elderly women are in black. Gilardini and the other men are in dark suits and hats, all except two uniformed officials who stand a few paces behind Sandra and, like her, are in white. Beside their dark

[1] Translated by John Heath Stubbs.

182

companions, these three white figures to the right of the memorial, which Sandra has just unveiled, look phosphorescent. But whether they represent darkness or light, the sunshine has given them all shadows taller than themselves, shadows so thin and elongated as to recall one of the most cherished objects in Volterra's Etruscan Museum, the little Hellenistic bronze votive figure called the "Ombra della Sera" (Shadow of the Evening). As the Rabbi's voice rises and falls with incantatory effect, this shadowy group seems momentarily to unite the imaginary world of mythology, the ancient Etruscan world, the poetic world of Leopardi, and Hitler's concentration camp world.

Fornari gazes at Sandra. Her long white chiffon scarf is billowing in the wind. Not only an individual destiny but a moment in history is finished. A new class will walk in the public park that was once a private garden. Occasionally, perhaps, someone young will glance at the name on the monument and ask who was he, what did he do, why was he deported. The Rabbi's voice continues. It is not certain that "Truth beareth away the victory." Ambiguities are integral parts of history's endless transformation scenes.

In October, when director, actors, and technicians drank a toast to the film they had just completed, Visconti was due to produce Chekhov's *The Cherry Orchard* in Rome. As he turned his back on Volterra, he thought of the aged valet who says at the end of *The Cherry Orchard*, "Life's slipped by, and one would think it had scarcely begun."

Twenty-one

Since plays are more ephemeral than films, Visconti is often thought of now as exclusively a film director; but he was just as much a man of the theater, the opera, and the ballet. Asked in 1966 which he preferred, Visconti said he truly did not know: "Cinema, theater, opera, I would say it's always the same work in spite of the immense variety of means employed." Paolo Grassi, superintendent of La Scala from 1972 to 1977 and now president of the RAI (Italian broadcasting and television corporation), writes in his 1977 autobiography, *Quarant'anni di paleoscenico* (*Forty Years of the Stage*), that Visconti's first postwar productions constituted a turning point in Italian theater history—thanks to Visconti's choice of plays, methods of production, especially of directing actors, and to the "cultural maturity" he encouraged in audiences.

After *The Cherry Orchard*, Visconti directed the French version of Arthur Miller's *After the Fall* in Paris. *The Cherry Orchard*—about which Stanislavsky had written Chekhov, after reading it in manuscript, "I hereby proclaim this play to be outside of all competition and not subject to any criticism whatsoever. Anyone who does not understand it is an idiot"—was a delight to all concerned. But a cloud of melancholy and censoriousness had gathered around *After the Fall*, which was about Marilyn Monroe. She and Arthur Miller had divorced soon after she finished making the last film Miller wrote for her—appropriately entitled *The Misfits* (1960)—and in 1962, while making *Something's Got to Give*, she committed suicide. Many of Arthur Miller's friends wished *After the Fall* unwritten, but written it was, and produced in New York by Elia Kazan. For the French version, Visconti made some alterations in the text—with the approval of Miller, who thought Visconti's version clearer than his own—and drew from Annie Girardot a subtle performance overflowing with the apparently thoughtless generosity that characterized

184

Marilyn Monroe. Although not one of Miller's best plays, *After the Fall* commemorated a Hollywood world as individual, if less mysterious, than the earlier one of *Sunset Boulevard.*

Probably no other composer appeals as does Verdi to so many emotions, including political ones. When Visconti staged *Don Carlo* at the Rome opera in 1965, television screens and newspapers had recently been full of the kidnapping of the exiled Moroccan leader Mehdi Ben Barka, in Paris, by two French police officers. So when, in *Don Carlo,* King Philip fell on his knees beside the body of his son's friend Rodrigo, murdered by the Inquisition, and cried, "Who will give this man back to me?" many in the audience thought of Ben Barka.

Next Visconti staged *Falstaff,* which seemed to him a singularly glorious monument to old age, and so to life itself—for although Verdi was nearly eighty when he wrote it, he had still been able to write to his friend and librettist Boito, "What a joy to be able to say to the public, HERE WE ARE AGAIN!! COME AND SEE US!"

After *Falstaff* came the shot-silk joys of *Der Rosenkavalier,* Visconti's third production at Covent Garden. He had been asked to provide an entirely new staging to replace the sixteen-year-old one which London's opera-loving audiences had seen too often. So he created a rococo setting exquisitely appropriate to the shimmering eroticism of Strauss's music and Hofmannsthal's words. By drawing on what he remembered of his parents' memories, he conjured up the Dresden of 1911, where *Der Rosenkavalier* was first performed—a little world of yesterday, still ruled by the King of Saxony, that vanished in 1918, a quarter of a century before Dresden itself was bombed to cinders. In this production the Yugoslavian singer Sena Jurinac, famous for her performance as the boy Octavian, exchanged her youthful part for that of the Marschallin, the no-longer-quite-young princess who, with supreme dignity, makes it easy for her beloved Octavian to leave her for a girl of his own age. Visconti helped Jurinac accomplish this conversion with superlative grace. Of all the arts, opera was the one in which he found it most natural to express tenderness.

From this happy period at Covent Garden, Visconti returned to the cinema and trouble. It is noticeable that whereas he seldom had trouble in the opera or theater worlds, apart from a brush with censors, his film career was punctuated by obstructions that would have wrecked a neurotic man. Those of 1967 were particularly trying.

That year producer Dino De Laurentiis asked Visconti to direct *La strega bruciata viva* (*The Witch Burned Alive*), the first of three sketches in the film *Le streghe* (*The Witches*). De Laurentiis, whom Visconti knew well, was, and is, an interestingly flamboyant person. A handsome and anything but last Neapolitan tycoon, born in 1919, he achieved his first big success in 1949 with *Riso amaro* (*Bitter Rice*), a Neo-Realist film directed by Giuseppe de Santis and set in the rice-growing region of the Po valley, where seasonal work is done by women who quit the city to wade in the flooded fields. Its young actors included three future stars: Vittorio Gassman, Raf Vallone, and an eighteen-year-old Roman beauty-prize winner, Silvana Mangano, whom De Laurentiis married. De Laurentiis built his own Roman film studios, Dinocittà, alongside Cinecittà, and in 1971 was to move to America with his wife and daughters—and break financial records there with his latter-day *King Kong*.

At first, Visconti welcomed De Laurentiis's suggestion. He liked the idea of working with Silvana Mangano, whom he admired for combining looks with intelligence and talent with character. The sketch De Laurentiis offered Visconti concerned a film star transformed by publicity into the sexual equivalent of a detergent reputed to wash whiter than all the other detergents it otherwise resembles.

Visconti thought something valid might be made of this since, in 1967, it was a comparatively original subject. Women's liberation had not yet come into existence, but its ideas were in the air. The early silent stars, Mary Pickford, Francesca Bertini, Lillian Gish, Lyda Borelli, enjoyed their work and status. It never occurred to them to complain of "alienation." Since then, however, the cinema had become a major industry, its stars not only admired but also envied, at a period when envy is acquiring the status of a civic duty. Visconti's personal view was that a film star is "not merely an erotic symbol, but the only modern exponent of witchcraft." Like the witch in the past she "can influence people, without their realizing it, through the sensations and emotions she arouses in them," but "like the witch, she may have to pay dearly for her success." He was fairly satisfied with his work on this—until De Laurentiis laid hands on it and, said Visconti, "completely ruined it. Because after endless fights about it, I finally gave up." De Laurentiis then asked him to make a full-length film on the subject. Visconti refused, pointing out that a sketch and a full-length film are as different as a short story and a novel. Finally *La strega bruciata viva* was released in a cut version that seemed to Visconti meaningless.

Their thoroughly articulate disagreement did not turn Visconti and De Laurentiis into enemies. So Visconti accepted another proposition from De Laurentiis this same year: to film *L'Etranger* (*The Stranger*), the famous novel by Albert Camus, who had been killed in an automobile accident in 1960.

L'Etranger was published in 1942, the year the Allies landed in North Africa, and by 1962 had been translated into twenty-one languages. Although Camus's parents were poor—his father, Lucien Camus, was a farm laborer, killed in the Battle of the Marne during the First World War, and his mother, Catherine Sintès, a servant of Spanish descent—he received a good education at the lycée in Algiers, and attended the local university, where he founded a theater group. In 1940, he joined the Resistance and, in 1942, became editor of the underground newspaper *Combat*. Immediately after the war, Camus and Sartre were the idols of young intellectuals, and in 1957, Camus became one of the youngest writers to win a Nobel Prize for literature.

The Stranger tells the story of what would now be called an antihero. Meursault is a young French Algerian who works in an office in Algiers and cares only for such simple pleasures as sunbathing, swimming, and copulation. His mother dies in an old people's home. He attends her funeral with passive rather than positive indifference. Next day he runs into Marie, a typist he used to know, goes swimming with her, sleeps with her—simply because she is there: for all her value to him she might as well be a hot dog. When Marie asks him if he will marry her, he says if she likes, it's all the same to him. In a sense, Meursault is a supreme example of absent-mindedness, never truly present in his actions. He has what E. M. Forster called "an undeveloped heart." One day a neighbor, Raymond, invites Meursault, Marie, and another couple to picnic on the beach. It is very pleasant: sun, sea, and sand. But presently, as the three men stroll along the beach, they encounter some Arabs who have a grudge against Raymond. There is a fight. Meursault watches with his customary passivity. Later he runs into one of these Arabs. Meursault has nothing against the Arab, as such, but the man happens to have a knife, and the sun happens to make the knife glitter, and Meursault happens to have Raymond's revolver in his pocket—so he uses it.

Once he is arrested, Meursault's past destroys him. People who know nothing about him, but long to see their names in newspapers, testify to his lack of feeling at his mother's funeral: He smoked, imagine! He drank coffee during the all-night vigil! He slept with a girl next day. A bad son. This condemns him. Meursault does not want to die. He still longs for sun and sea and copulation—yet, confronted by the guillotine, he behaves bravely.

When Visconti read *L'Etranger*, at the end of the war, it was a first novel by a young journalist, and both Camus and Visconti were newcomers on the postwar artistic scene. Since those days, the Algiers described by young Camus had fought a savage war for its independence.

Camus had not lived to see the end of this, but the anguish caused him by the first six years of it is reflected in his *Chroniques algériennes 1939– 1958.* Visconti had read these, and all Camus wrote; he particularly liked the lines in *The Myth of Sisyphus:* "The struggle towards the summit is enough in itself to fill a man's heart. One must imagine Sisyphus as happy." So, considering Camus's work as a whole, it seemed to Visconti that it would be ludicrous to restrict a film of *L'Etranger* to 1938. Instead, he planned to set it during the Algerian war, give screen life to the prophetic passages in the novel, and connect the senselessness of Meursault's murder of an Arab he doesn't know with the senselessness of war between French and Arab Algerians, brothers under the sun, who grew up together and love the same country. It was, he thought, a prophetic book, in which Camus had "foreseen the parachutists' excesses and the Algerians' revulsion," and the film ought therefore to have "an atmosphere of suspense, a sense that violence may erupt at any minute." Visconti wrote the scenario with Georges Conchon, a French novelist who had won the Prix Goncourt three years earlier—and both were astonished when their work was vetoed by Camus's widow. Francine Camus would accept no "modern adaptation": the scenario must adhere, line by line, to her husband's book.

Visconti explained that he had no wish to be unfaithful to the novel, but that a book cannot be turned into a film merely by a series of pictures "illustrating" the narrative—and, in this particular case, it was essential that Meursault's thoughts be "exteriorized," since they constitute the most important part of a story written in the first person. Visconti might as well have spoken to the wind. On top of this, Alain Delon, who was to have played Meursault, and would have brought an invaluable feral quality to the part, could not get free in time from a previous contract. Mastroianni was available but, though an excellent actor, had a personality far less suited to Meursault. At this point Visconti would have liked to call the whole thing off. But he had given De Laurentiis his word, and De Laurentiis was determined to produce *The Stranger* at all costs. (The film, in contrast to the book title, was called *The Outsider.*)

So for the first time in his life, Visconti found himself directing a film in which he "could not truly participate." It was he himself who was the "Outsider" on this set. He conscientiously reconstructed the Algerian coast of 1938, and managed to unearth a set of the wooden bathing cabins that, when Camus was a boy, stood beneath the lighthouse mentioned in the book. The cabins were restored to the beach, and Meursault was provided with a bathing suit with shoulder straps. As usual, Visconti enjoyed working with the actors, but his efforts were comparable with those he would have made to help a handicapped child.

When *The Outsider* was shown at the Venice Film Festival, a gaggle of critics immediately pounced on Visconti for having "stuck slavishly to the novel." He had failed, they said, to realize that "since Meursault's dilemma was a spiritual one" it would be fatal to "restrict it to a definite date." One critic said he "couldn't imagine" how Visconti could ever have thought that *The Stranger* would retain its freshness "and, above all, its impact" in a 1938 setting. Visconti was also attacked for having given the part of Meursault to "a most unsuitable actor." An English critic took him to task for "being at home in the nineteenth century and therefore incapable of entering Camus' twentieth-century world." It was typical of Visconti that he made no attempt to answer this. And today *The Outsider*, often shown at film clubs, still has the power to move us with echoes of Camus's vanished world as it was painstakingly re-created by an artist who believed what Camus wrote in *L'Homme révolté* (*The Rebel*, 1951): "In art, rebellion is consummated and perpetuated in the act of real creation, not in criticism or commentary."

Fortunately for Visconti he was not restricted to the cinema during the only year when it failed him. In April 1967 he directed his fourth opera at Covent Garden. This was *La Traviata*, but a very different one from his Scala *Traviata* with Callas. He wanted to show that it could be done in many ways, "since Verdi's music is so definite, has so much personality, that it can be fitted into any period." This time he set it at the turn of the century and, as an act of homage to England, in Beardsley sets and costumes of black and white, punctuated by splashes of color— garlands of roses, a colored scarf, a pair of scarlet gloves left lying on a table.

Beardsley's own life suited *La Traviata*'s brief and fevered story. A brilliant self-taught designer in black and white, he was born in Brighton in 1872, and became art editor of the *Yellow Book* review at twenty-two. The period being one in which permissiveness obtained only among the highest and lowest classes in England, Beardsley was harshly criticized by the middle classes for the eroticism of his drawings and for associating with Oscar Wilde. He died in the south of France, at the age of twenty-six, ravaged, like the heroine of *Traviata* herself, by tuberculosis. The Beardsley costumes were designed for Visconti by young Vera Marzot, who had designed the costumes for Visconti's Roman *Don Carlo*, his Covent Garden *Rosenkavalier*, and *Il Gattopardo*. Her husband, Nato Frascà, an abstract painter, did the sets. Visconti was extremely pleased with these, commenting, "But then I like his painting very much. If you are a good painter, and an intelligent one, you should be able to paint good sets."

This was to be Visconti's last production in London. Incredible as it would have seemed to those who saw him in Covent Garden that April—so erect and strong, so full of vitality and wit, so full, above all, of an enjoyment of life quite as vigorous as his sense of tragedy—Visconti had ahead of him only three more years of his hitherto perfect health.

Twenty-two

Two months later, Visconti produced Goethe's *Egmont* at the Pitti Palace in Florence. This tragedy about the heroic Spanish governor of the Low Countries who tried to stop persecution of the Protestants there and was beheaded, his ecumenical martyrdom causing a popular uprising against Spain, had been performed for the first time in 1791, when the French Revolution was rousing hope and hatred all over Europe. Next Visconti directed Testori's new play, *La Monaca di Monza* (*The Nun of Monza*), in Rome. By this time he was obsessed by what was to be one of his greatest films, *La caduta degli dei* (literally, The Fall of the Gods, but called in English *The Damned*).

For some time Visconti had wanted to make a film about a family—the human unit he found most interesting—powerful enough to murder with impunity. It now struck him that nowhere in the modern world had so much crime gone unpunished as in Nazi Germany, with its extraordinary mixture of banality and bloodshed. Asked later why he chose Nazism rather than Fascism, Visconti said: "Because of the difference between tragedy and comedy. Of course Fascism was a tragedy in many many cases . . . but as the perfect archetype of a given historical situation that leads to a certain type of criminality, Nazism seemed to me more exemplary—because it was a tragedy that, like a hideous blood-stain, seeped over the whole world. . . . One could make thousands of films about Italian Fascism . . . about Matteotti . . . Mussolini's Republic of Salò . . . the death of Gramsci . . . but Nazism seems to me to reveal more about a historic reversal of values."

Once he decided on the setting, Visconti realized that for years he had been unconsciously researching this very subject. Not only had he read many recent books about Hitler's Germany, but also his passion for the theater had prompted him, as a young man, to visit the Weimar Republic during a period when theater history was made there. Visconti was twenty-one when Brecht's *Die Dreigroschenoper* (*The Threepenny Opera*), with Kurt Weill's nerve-plucking music, first scandalized and haunted Germany.

When the shark has had his dinner
There is blood upon his fins
But Macheath he has his gloves on:
They say nothing of his sins.

In those Weimar days, Visconti had been not so much a young man about town as a young man about Europe, eager for achievement but still as unsure what he wanted to achieve as Stendhal's Lucien Leuwen. During Hitler's first days in power, Visconti was more interested in his horses than in politics. Nevertheless he was very much aware, during a 1934 visit to Germany, of the "night of the long knives"—so called by Hitler himself in reference to the refrain "We will sharpen our long knives" in a Storm Troopers' song. Visconti knew no more about what was happening than did anyone else around him, but he "retained precise recollections of the atmosphere of Germany in those days." He meant originally to call his film *Die Götterdämmerung* (*The Twilight of the Gods*), because Hitler doted upon Wagner's opera about the world of the Nibelungs, which ends in a blaze of death and destruction. There was nothing anti-Wagnerian about this choice of title. Wagner could not, as Visconti pointed out, help the fact that whereas Ludwig II of Bavaria's passion for his music provided support for art, artists, and opera houses, Hitler's passion for this same music contributed to anti-Semitism, mayhem, and murder.

Since industrialists were among Hitler's first satraps, Visconti decided to make his fictitious family, the Essenbecks, the latest generation of a dynasty of steel magnates. He was accused later of having portrayed the Krupps but, in fact, his portrait of the imaginary Essenbecks contained details suggested by the lives of all the industrialists who supported Hitler—not merely the four-star Krupps, but also the Kirdorfs (coal), Thyssens (steel), Voeglers (steel), Schnitzlers (I. G. Farben chemical cartel), Rostergs and Diehns (potash), Schröders (bankers). Visconti's reading about Nazi Germany had hitherto been desultory. Now it became systematic. He read everything available about Göring, Goebbels, the SA, the SS, Thyssen's *I Paid Hitler*, Alan Bullock's *Hitler, a Study in Tyranny,* and *The Night of the Long Knives,* a novel by Lorrain Kempski with considerable anecdotic value. Above all, he read and reread William L. Shirer's *The Rise and Fall of the Third Reich: A*

History of Nazi Germany, of which he was to say, "What was most important to us, our point of departure and a book in which we could always find references to all the people or episodes we needed, was Shirer's history of the Third Reich. It really became our Bible throughout the making of the film."

Visconti wanted to show the beginnings of Nazism, the brief period when it might have been possible to stop Hitler. So he limited *The Damned* to 1933–1934. This was a period of terrifying melodrama: on January 30, 1933, the National Socialist leader, Hitler, became chancellor of a panic-stricken Germany, of which eighty-five-year-old Field Marshal Paul von Hindenburg was president. On February 27 the Nazis set fire to the Reichstag in order to attribute this act of terrorism to the Communists. Thanks to arson and murder, Hitler became virtually dictator of Germany. Fifty-five concentration camps were set up that spring and, from Hitler's viewpoint, the only fly in this ointment was the rivalry between the SA and the SS.

The SA (Sturmabteilung, storm troopers, Brown Shirts) were armed gangs of street fighters, formed in 1920 to protect Nazi meetings and terrorize the opposition. Their leader was Ernst Röhm, a tough homosexual ex-officer who had done more than any other single person to help Hitler to power. He hoped to see his bully boys supplant the regular army. Once in power, however, Hitler decided with treacherous common sense that he needed a more respectable corps. Social climbing always requires sacrifices, and the SA were to be sacrificed to the SS (Schutzstaffel, defense troops, Black Shirts). Hitler's new personal bodyguard was smart and disciplined: aristocrats welcome.

Röhm provoked his own doom by shouting for a "Second Revolution." The Nazis had crushed the left and now, said the tactless Röhm, the right, big business, the aristocracy, the Prussian generals, must go. Hitler was furious; now that he was in power, he needed big business, the aristocracy, the Prussian generals to keep him there and the country solvent. So in June 1934 Hitler ordered the SA to go on leave throughout July, during which month they were neither to wear uniforms nor to hold parades. On June 7 Röhm went on sick leave to Wiessee, a charming little holiday resort near Munich: alps, cowbells, boating, and swimming. Before leaving, he asked Hitler to join him on June 30 to discuss the situation with the SA leaders. Hitler promised to do so.

On June 14 Hitler went to Venice for his first encounter with Mussolini. It was not a success. Hitler and his ubiquitous raincoat were not at their best in Venice. On June 21 Hindenburg notified Hitler that unless current agitation ceased he would proclaim martial law and put the regular army in charge of the country. Berserk at the prospect of losing power, Hitler decided to "liquidate" the SA—and called on the SS, who responded like Macbeth's Second Murderer: "We shall, my lord, perform what you command us." They descended on Wiessee on June 30. An orgy of slaughter followed. Those SA leaders not killed there were executed later. About one thousand people were murdered. Hitler was particularly determined on the death of Röhm, to whom he had written the previous Christmas, "I feel compelled to thank you, my dear Ernst Röhm, for the imperishable services which you have rendered to the National Socialist movement and the German people, and to assure you how very grateful I am to fate that I am able to call such men my friends and fellow combatants. In true friendship and grateful regard, your Adolf Hitler." On July 2 President Hindenburg thanked Hitler for his "determined and gallant personal intervention which nipped treason in the bud." On August 2 Hindenburg died. He had hoped that after his death the monarchy would be restored. Instead, Hitler assumed the trinitarian position of chancellor, president, and head of the armed forces, henceforth to be known as the Führer. Here the melodramatic gothic prologue ended and a world tragedy began.

Against this sinister background, Visconti's and Medioli's first outline of their Essenbeck story resembled an Elizabethan drama in modern setting. *The Damned* is an apocalyptic film because it is realistic, and this really is an apocalyptic period. As one of the characters in *The Damned* observes: "Private morality is dead. We are an elite society to whom everything is permitted—those are Hitler's very words, my dear cousin." In November 1967, their outline was read by the directors of the film-distributing firm Italnoleggio and accepted with enthusiasm. But since films on this scale were financially impossible without international co-operation, Italnoleggio set up arrangements with Warner Brothers–Seven Arts and the production companies of Pegaso Film (Rome) and Praesidens Film (Zurich).

The film opens with preparations for a family dinner party at the Essenbecks' Bavarian castle. This deliberately evokes the first chapter of *Buddenbrooks*, the novel, subtitled *The Decadence of a Family*, that made Thomas Mann famous in 1901. A stately butler superintends preparations. Place cards slide into dragon-shaped silver holders, each one a little work of art. We glimpse names: Baron Joachim von Essenbeck, Mr. Herbert Thalmann, Baroness Sophie von Essenbeck, Baron Konstantin von Essenbeck, and so on. The dinner is in honor of Baron Joachim's birthday. Head of the family and of the family's gigantic steelworks, he is about to retire. Since his only son was killed in the First World War, and his only grandson, Martin, appears to be about as suited to industry as Dorian Gray to alpine climbing, a battle for the succession is already underway.

Baron Joachim is a distinguished-looking old man with something of the pathos of an ancient bloodhound about to be put away for its own good. As he finishes dressing he pauses to pick up and kiss a framed photograph of his dead son in air force uniform. Next we see Baron Joachim's nephew. Fifty-year-old Baron Konstantin is in his bath, talking jovially to Yanek, a young manservant whom he orders to scrub his back. An enthusiastic SA officer, Konstantin is gross and rumbustious, but has the charm bestowed by energy and is so self-indulgent as to give an impression of good nature. The part was admirably played by Albrecht Schönhals, who gave it a touch of Göring in the early days when Göring still had his beautiful Swedish first wife, was still known primarily as a First World War flying ace, and still had some worldly social life apart from that of the growing Nazi party.

Has everyone arrived, Konstantin asks Yanek. No—Mr. Bruckman and Hauptsturmführer Aschenbach have not yet arrived from Munich. Next we see this pair driving toward the castle. Friedrich Bruckman is general manager of the family steelworks, and also the lover of Sophie, the beautiful and aristocratic widow of Joachim's son and mother of the heir apparent, Martin. Sophie means to gain control of the steelworks for Bruckman while Martin is still a minor. In this she is supported by Aschenbach, a distant relative of the Essenbecks, who is a brilliant SS officer, determined to use Bruckman's ambitions to wreck those of Konstantin.

Visconti asked Dirk Bogarde to play Bruckman because he had been impressed by the cynicism and geniality that the actor put into his performance as Charlie Hook in the British film *Our Mother's House* (1967). Bogarde—who, far from being too "typically English," as one or two critics fancied, is of Dutch parentage (Derek van den Bogaard)—made the most of his entry onto the international film scene, creating a poor man's Macbeth, a go-getter who is also a worrier, and would worry himself into panic-stricken immobility if he were not propped up by a bona-fide Lady Macbeth. Aschenbach, the *diabolus ex machina*, was played by the German actor Helmut Griem, who gave a dazzling performance. As charming as he is wicked, Aschenbach is still his own man, thinks *Mein Kampf* a touch common and prefers Nietzsche, whom he misinterprets for his own purposes: "Man is a tightrope between the animal and the superman—a tightrope over an abyss." When Visconti made *The Damned,* Albert Speer's secret diaries, written in Spandau Prison, had not yet been published, so Aschenbach was one of the very first portraits of an SS whose manners and culture rendered him more dangerous than obvious brutes.

Back at the castle, another relative, Herbert Thalmann, also on the steelworks' board of directors, but known to be hostile to Hitler, is dressing for dinner. Both he and his wife, Elisabeth, are uneasy. But, after all, says Elisabeth soothingly, Uncle Joachim has run the firm smoothly for forty years and he doesn't like "a certain gentleman." That, says Herbert, is merely because Uncle Joachim is a snob; if Hitler weren't the son of a customs' man and a servant, *Baron* von Essenbeck would have been all for him long before this.

Finally we see the entire family, except Martin, assembled for the birthday entertainment in a large room with a small stage at the end. Thilde and Erika, Thalmann's young daughters, curtsy to Baron Joachim and kiss his hand. Günther, Konstantin's musical son, plays Bach and, much to his father's irritation, is praised by his great-uncle. Meanwhile the curtain of the little stage rises on a girl who is a perfect copy of Marlene Dietrich.

Top-hatted and silky-legged, this girl sits astride a chair and sings "Kinder, heut Abend, da such' ich mir was aus" (Boys, tonight I'm going to choose one). Unlike the real Marlene Dietrich, she has an artificial insolence, devoid of hilarity and indefinably offensive. Her song is roughly interrupted by Konstantin, charging back from the telephone with the news "in Berlin the Reichstag is in flames . . . a conspiracy—no doubt about that—but it seems the culprit's already been arrested, a Dutch Communist." Oh, naturally, says Thalmann ironically, naturally a Communist. Talking heatedly, the Essenbecks leave the room. Alone on the stage, the girl snatches off her blond wig, and reveals herself as Martin, in full drag. "Pack of idiots," he says furiously.

From then on violence dominates the Essenbecks' lives. Baron Joachim's birthday dinner is spoiled, the admirable food, admirably served, is toyed with by people whose minds are elsewhere. Joachim rises to make his speech of thanks. His dignified anxiety is for the family firm rather than for the Third Reich. Much as he deplores the fact, it is essential "in the present circumstances" that he have at his side as vice-president a man "in good odor with the regime." This means by-passing Thalmann and appointing Konstantin vice-president.

But no matter what Konstantin's official status, Aschenbach intends to control the steelworks through Bruckman. Sophie can always, she says, control Martin: "He has no sense of reality; owning the steelworks or owning a Rolls-Royce, it's all the same to him." Here, however, Sophie is mistaken. At the beginning of the film he is a handsome degenerate boy, immersed in ugly sexual fantasies destined to have political consequences. After the party he plays erotically with his little cousin Thilde, and a few days later he seduces the child of a Jewish dressmaker. Traumatized, the child kills herself. Since Martin is "important," and the death of a working-class Jewish child "unimportant," the police are prepared to keep their suspicions to themselves. But this gives Konstantin, who as an SA officer has friends in the police, an opportunity to blackmail Martin.

Spoiled, neurotic, a drug addict, Martin has been equipped with nothing but money by his family, for whom his personal contemptibility is annulled by his quasi-mystical status as future president of the industry that keeps them all in luxury. This difficult part was played by a young Austrian beginner, Helmut Berger. Born in Salzburg, where his father ran a hotel, Berger spent much of his boyhood in Stuttgart and felt more German than Austrian. After studying Italian in Perugia, French in Paris, and English in London, to fit himself for the hotel business, he decided he wanted instead to be an actor. He began in a small way; then a meeting with Visconti gave him one of those improbable a-star-is-born chances. Guided by Visconti, who saw Martin as the complex result of "a profound dis-education," Berger gave the vicious little crown prince a touch of soon-to-be-lost vulnerability, as well as tyrannically willful petulance.

After the gloom-laden birthday dinner, Sophie and Bruckman plan their own path to power. They are interrupted by Aschenbach, who tells them, with his customary urbanity, that "poor Herbert" is about to be arrested—and to think, adds Aschenbach meditatively, that the frontier is so near.

Bruckman goes to the Thalmanns' room to warn Herbert to flee, insisting that he leave his revolver behind so that, if worst comes to worst, he will not be caught armed. By then the footsteps of police and SS can be heard on the stairs. Thalmann leaps from the window. Aschenbach is determined that Bruckman seize this opportunity to kill Baron Joachim. We do not see the killing, but we know Bruckman has done it—with Thalmann's revolver, which thus provides both police and SS with proof that Thalmann is a murderer as well as a traitor.

A midnight family gathering follows. This time the central figure is Martin, who in his smart dressing gown looks incongruously like a character in Noel Coward's *Private Lives*, which hit the London theater in

1930. He intends to revenge himself on all those who have hitherto treated him as negligible. Since the majority of the shares belong to him now, it's up to him to decide—and, disregarding his dead grandfather's wishes, he nominates Friederich Bruckman president of the board of directors and general manager of the steelworks and all the other companies associated with the firm.

"Oh, I see it all now," cries Konstantin, "Thalmann's revolver, Aschenbach's evidence, the arrival of the SS. Perfect!" and he walks out with his shaken son, Günther.

Joachim's funeral unites them all again. Beneath a lowering sky, and to the sound of Chopin's Funeral March, the hearse passes among the workers and the smokestacks of the steelworks. Martin walks alone directly behind the hearse. He looks very young. Behind him come the family, then a herd of political and business figures—top hats, bowler hats, black gloves. The funeral march fades into the din of the steelworks.

A few days later, Martin summons a board meeting, then disappears. Frantic, Sophie manages to track him down. He confesses hysterically that Konstantin is blackmailing him over a Jewish child's death and will hand him over to the Gestapo unless he forces Bruckman to cede the management of the steelworks to Konstantin. Sophie reassures her son. Aschenbach has told her to call on him should she ever need him.

The devastative Sophie was played by the Swedish actress Ingrid Thulin. The originality of her personality had proved a hindrance at the beginning of her career, when she studied at Stockholm's Dramaten acting school and worked at the Lilla Theater in Finland. So when she married an Austrian engineer and film critic, Harry Schein, she decided to give up acting, although only in her twenties. At this point she and her husband met Ingmar Bergman, who was interested in Schein's reviews of his films. Bergman immediately sensed Thulin's unusual qualities and persuaded her to play in his film *Wild Strawberries* (1957), and in *Nära livet* (*So Close to Life*, 1958), for which she won the best-actress award at Cannes. He also persuaded her to join the repertory company at Malmö's civic theater. When, ten years later, she came to work with Visconti, she was in full command of her beauty and talent, and her mixture of abnormal strength with equally abnormal fragility made her an ideal choice for Sophie—who is in many respects a perfect illustration of Goethe's dictum that, in Germany, romanticism "ought to be classified as a notifiable disease."

Aschenbach does not fail Sophie: he assures her she need not worry about Konstantin's power as an SA officer. "The SA had their uses when it was a matter of getting control of Germany, but to conquer the world Hitler will need the army, and the army loathes the SA and SA commander Röhm."

Meanwhile, Konstantin continues to grapple with his son. Shaken by the way in which his uncle was framed, Günther has been further disgusted by Nazi book burnings at his school. He wants to leave Germany and study music in Salzburg. Konstantin says they will settle the matter when he himself returns from the SA rally at Wiessee.

This leads to the Hanslbauer Hotel, Wiessee, so *gemütlich*, with its cozy corners and flowering window boxes, where the SA are arriving with rowdy joviality. After a day spent swimming, boating, yelling, eating, drinking, and every now and again bursting out with accumulated resentments—"if our boots were good enough to kick democracy in the pants, they ought to be good enough for the Chancellery carpets"—the SA devoted most of the night to an unimaginative orgy. Here Visconti created one of the film's most stunning moments. At last the lights are low, the noise drops from hiccup level into silence. On the lakeside terrace in front of the hotel, palely lit by the last of the moonlight and the flickering of a festoon of electric-light bulbs, are two handsome young SA members, half naked, half in drag. One of them lolls at a metal table littered with empty beer bottles. The other, who is Konstantin's young servant Yanek, stands gazing across the lake at one of Bavaria's loveliest views. The lull is as effective as a pause in music. Suddenly Yanek hears a sound. He stiffens. The sound becomes sounds. Faint at first, these sounds resolve themselves into the chugging of a motorboat, or motorboats. With the first cold light the SS are on their way, bringing death and damnation. The SS leap ashore and enter the inn, and the manhunt blasts its way through bedrooms, passages, bathrooms. Bruckman is forced by Aschenbach to shoot Konstantin as he shot Joachim.

Everything in this scene, in which the men who helped Hitler to power are butchered, on Hitler's orders, by men whom he expects to make him even more powerful, is not only true but under- rather than overstated. This needs to be said because today, less than a decade since *The Damned* was released, Nazi sadism, buttocks, blood, boots, and whips, have become regular features of the current pornographic scene. As a Hollywood public-relations man announced in 1977: "Today sex is out and violence is the new bit."

Sophie and Bruckman are now the only obstacles to Aschenbach's control of the steelworks. So Aschenbach concentrates upon Martin, and

Martin is soon confiding that he hates his mother: she has always pushed him aside, always humiliated him, he longs to see her ruined, he will do anything Aschenbach wants, *anything*.

This brings us for the second and last time to the family dinner table. Martin is still crown prince, but the congregation has shrunk. Survivors Bruckman, Sophie, Günther, look hagridden. Only Aschenbach, no survivor but a precursor, is himself: radiantly and courteously threatening. Bruckman announces his forthcoming marriage to Sophie. From now on, he says, with ill-assumed assurance, he will feel responsible not only for the steelworks but also for the family. In the midst of this, Herbert Thalmann enters, startling as Banquo's ghost.

Drained of everything but courage and despair, Thalmann knows that his wife has died in a concentration camp and wants to give himself up to the Gestapo in exchange for his children's lives. Günther longs to throw in his lot with Thalmann, but is stopped by Martin, who now tells him that it was Bruckman who killed Günther's father, Konstantin, during the night of the long knives. When Bruckman cries, "You'll pay for this," Martin answers icily, "Don't you realize that things have changed? I'm no longer afraid of you, Friederich—and, incredible as it may seem to you, you're the one who ought to be frightened—and you, too, Mother." For the first time in her dealings with her son, Sophie is panic-stricken. What do you want from Friederich? she asks Martin. *Everything*, says Martin, and for once he is speaking the truth.

To Aschenbach's satisfaction, confusion now makes one of its innumerable masterpieces. Up in Baron Joachim's old room, Martin is seen giving himself an injection of morphine; he is already under the influence of the drug when his mother comes in. Martin's resentment breaks through all inhibitions. It's not Aschenbach I'm afraid of, or Friederich . . . it's you, Mother—you've always been my nightmare . . . You've never loved me—you've always preferred Friederich— you've given him *everything that belongs to me—my* factory, *my* money, *my* home. You've no idea how much I hate you—how I'll destroy you. . . ."

Martin flings himself on his mother and rapes her on the great bed in which Joachim was murdered. Sophie scarcely resists. Her eyes suggest the windows of an empty house. It is the world of both Greek mythology and police-court news. While Sophie is being destroyed by her son, Aschenbach is more subtly destroying Günther through the boy's remorseful reaction to the news of his father's murder. I'll kill Friederich, cries Günther. Tactfully, with the charm that is his secret weapon, Aschenbach tells Günther that his "precious capital of pure youthful hatred" is far too valuable to be "wasted on a private vendetta." "We," says Aschenbach, meaning himself and the SS, will teach you "how to make the best use of your gifts." (Anyone who thinks such talk of hatred too melodramatic to be plausible should note what John Tyndall, chairman of the British neo-fascist National Front party, wrote as recently as September 1975: "The day our followers lose their ability to hate, will be the day that they lose their power and their will to achieve anything worth-while at all.")

In Martin and Günther, we see true Nazis in the making. For, as Visconti shows, Joachim, Konstantin, and Thalmann were linked to the past: Joachim to the Kaiser's Germany, Konstantin to the Kaiser's war, Thalmann to the hopes of the Weimar Republic; but Günther, who begins with Bach and ends with the *Horst Wessel song,* and Martin, who begins by pawing little girls and becomes a rapist and murderer, belong to the generation that will lead Germany through barbarism to a suicidal war. With their support, the Third Reich, designed to last a thousand years, will end after twelve years and four months, with Hitler dead in his bunker and the Russian flag flying over the smoking ruins of Berlin.

Physical cruelty did not interest Visconti, except as one of the appalling facts of life. So he never dwelt on it for its own sake. There was, however, a violent element in his character that made him turn instinctively to what he called "extreme situations in which people are caught up in moments of exceptional tension that reveal their inmost truth." His films do, therefore, contain "moral and aesthetic cruelty," which interested him profoundly. He would have liked, for example, to film Robert Musil's novel *Young Törless,* because this Austrian story of German schoolboys, written in 1906, seemed to him "to contain the seeds of sadism and blind cruelty that were perhaps the origins of Nazism."

Financial difficulties made *The Damned* an exhausting film for Visconti. "Times are bad," said producers. While *The Damned* was being made there were earthquakes in Sicily, Soviet tanks in Czechoslovakia, the assassinations of Dr. Martin Luther King, Jr. and Senator Robert Kennedy, continuing war in Vietnam, war and famine in Biafra. So while Visconti and his team were on location in Germany or Austria, money for their hotel bills often failed to arrive. On one occasion the crew were locked in their rooms as a reprisal. Sometimes the delay was due to Italnoleggio's own difficulties, sometimes to bad postal services. Nevertheless, *The Damned* was to prove as successful with the public as with the critics. In November 1969, it established box-office records in

Rome, Milan, Turin, Bologna, Florence, Naples, and Genoa, and did so well abroad that Italnoleggio considered it a triumph—a triumph that was to bring Visconti the backing to complete, at last, a trilogy.

His thoughts turned back now to the Germany of Thomas Mann's books. Once more he saw in imagination the Munich of 1911, with rococo lingering in the cultural atmosphere as well as in the architecture. Despite the rising tide of militarism, the prevalence of military bands, the music in the air was that of Richard Strauss's *Der Rosenkavalier* and Irving Berlin's "Alexander's Ragtime Band." It was in these streets that Thomas Mann's hero Gustav von Aschenbach had walked, planning the trip south that was to become death in Venice.

Visconti had longed for years to film *Death in Venice*, and, now that he could at last do so, gladly turned back from the murderous worlds set in motion by a handful of fanatics in a Munich beer cellar to what the great French writer Marguerite Yourcenar has called "perhaps the most beautiful allegory of death ever produced by the tragic genius of Germany."

*. . . places and ruins so sacred that although we have
never seen them they have a place in our memory.*

Ennio Flaiano, *Diario Notturno*

All I can say is—I saw it!

Byron, "Natural Magic"

Twenty-three

The last words spoken by Martin in *The Damned* are "Come on, light the candles"—and the year this film was released began with the death of Jan Palach, a twenty-one-year-old Czech philosophy student who set fire to himself in Prague as a protest against the Soviet invasion of his country. Palach's deed lit such a candle that half a million people followed his funeral procession. Visconti was among those who protested against the invasion of Czechoslovakia; and eight years later, when Visconti himself was dead, the French film director Robert Bresson won the second Visconti Award for his film *Probably the Devil*, in which a young man's suicide is shown as a heroic act, committed in order to draw people's attention to crimes against our environment.

Despite the commercial success of *The Damned*, all but one of the Italian producers to whom Visconti first suggested *Death in Venice* thought his project "absurd and dangerous"—and the one exception wanted to turn the fourteen-year-old boy who bewitches the hero into a girl. Nymphets, said this producer, had become fashionable since the success of Vladimir Nabokov's *Lolita*—a comment that reminded Visconti of the old story about a Hollywood nabob who when warned that the leading part in a play he had just bought was a lesbian said, "What the hell, we'll make her a Rumanian." But, at last, Visconti came across Mario Gallo, an executive producer full of sense and sensibility, who had started producing four years earlier with Florestano Vancini's *The Seasons of Our Love*, "a difficult film about an ideological and intellectual crisis in a man's life."

From the start Gallo had been interested by what are so oddly labeled "quality" films—oddly, because nothing can exist without quality of some kind, be it only that of idiocy. He agreed to "organize the financing" of *Death in Venice*, and expected the fact Visconti was ready to share in production costs and risks to facilitate their task. Instead, Gallo tried one Italian producer after another in vain. What they needed, said Visconti, was a man like Scott Fitzgerald's Last Tycoon to say, "It's time we made a picture that'll lose some money. Write it off as good will —this'll bring in new customers." Finally the president of Warner Brothers, who not only had made money out of *The Damned,* but also had read Thomas Mann, decided that the combination of Visconti with Mann might bring in both prestige and money. He therefore promised Gallo that Visconti would have a free hand with *Death in Venice,* and kept his promise, just as Visconti kept his not to spend more than the sum allotted the film by Warner.

While the contract was being negotiated, Visconti directed a play in Milan and an opera in Vienna. The play, *L'inserzione,* was by Natalia Ginzburg, one of Italy's best contemporary writers. The child of intellectual anti-Fascists, she was only nine when Filippo Turati, one of the founders of the Italian Socialist party, hid in her parents' apartment in Turin while his escape to France was organized by Ferruccio Parri, today a senator, and Carlo Rosselli, who, with his brother Nello, was murdered in France in 1937. At twenty-one she married Leone Ginzburg, a distinguished scholar and anti-Fascist, whom she accompanied into exile in the Abruzzi when war broke out. Her husband was arrested in 1943 and died in Regina Coeli prison a few weeks before the Ardeatine Caves massacre. *L'inserzione* won the international Marzotto Award and was directed by Laurence Olivier at the Old Vic in London and by Visconti at the San Babila Theater in Milan. The play's desperate leading character, Teresa, has something in common with Stevie Smith's swimmer who, far out at sea, is "not waving but drowning," and the author's verbal aggressiveness about the problems created by the inability to communicate reminded critics in both London and Milan of Harold Pinter.

From this Visconti returned to the world of opera, where people may have devastating problems but are seldom unable to communicate. He agreed completely with Maria Callas when she said, "Communication is the most important thing in life. It is what makes the human predicament bearable. Art is the most profound way in which one person can communicate with another, and music is the highest way of saying things." A curious footnote to Visconti's staging of Verdi's *Simon Boccanegra,* in Vienna, was his personal connection with the principal character. For the historic Simon Boccanegra, elected first doge of Genoa in 1339, had tried in vain to keep the peace between patricians and plebeians, gone into voluntary exile in Pisa and returned to Genoa only when he learned that the patricians were planning a coup d'état with the aid of the Viscontis of Milan.

Work on the scenario of *Death in Venice* was enhanced for Visconti and his collaborator, Nicola Bandalucco, by the helpfulness of the Mann family. Visconti once advised De Sica to stick to dead authors, "especially ones with no descendants," if he wanted to stay out of trouble, but this never applied to Visconti's own relations with the Mann family.

The plot of *Death in Venice* is simple: shortly before the First World War a famous German writer who has recently had a heart attack is prompted by a curious encounter in his hometown, Munich, to convalesce in Venice. There he conceives a platonic passion for a fourteen-year-old Polish boy. Although he never exchanges a word with the child, this passion revolutionizes the conceptions of art on which he has built his life. Before the season is over, a cholera epidemic begins to empty the city of visitors. Obsessed by his passion, the writer dies within sound of the sea only a few hours before the boy and his family leave for Poland.

Visconti's transformation of Thomas Mann's hero, Gustav von Aschen-bach, from a German writer into a composer born in Bohemia was ascribed by some critics either to complex psychological or metaphysical motives or to mere caprice. In fact Visconti made this change for two simple reasons. Mann's Aschenbach is primarily an artist and his story is primarily one of artistic development. A writer is perfectly suitable for this if his story is told in writing. But in a film, where the artist needs to be seen at work, the only alternatives are either to show him in the act of writing—and from the spectator's viewpoint it is all one whether he is writing *War and Peace* or a check for his dentist—or to have passages from his work read by a voice, a tedious device that invites an "I don't think much of that" reaction. But a composer can be heard composing, and a conductor seen conducting, with dramatic effect. Second, and even more important, was the fact that Thomas Mann had the composer and conductor Gustav Mahler in mind when writing *Death in Venice*. Mann's entire work is, moreover, filled with echoes of music, thoughts of music, references to music; he himself said, ten years before *Death in Venice*, that he had "learned to use music to mold his style and form."

Visconti had read what Erika Mann, so close to her father, wrote in her preface to Mann's correspondence: "The two [Mann and Mahler] knew each other: after the dress rehearsal of a Mahler concert, Mahler and his wife had tea with Thomas Mann and his wife Katia. The latter reported that as they returned home, Thomas Mann said it was the first time in his life that he had had the impression of meeting a truly great man." Katia Mann's parents also knew Mahler, and her twin brother, Klaus, himself a musician, admired Mahler passionately and served him for a year as assistant and teacher at the Vienna State Opera. After this first meeting, Mann wrote Mahler that he considered him to "embody the most sacred and severe artistic will power of our time." On September 12, 1910, Mann went to Munich for Mahler's Eighth Symphony. "But," writes Erika Mann, "the indelible impression that the musician's personality made on Thomas Mann was only later fully revealed." On the report of Mahler's death, in 1911, Mann noted: "Gustav von Aschenbach not only bears his Christian name, but the author of *Death in Venice* has given him the face of Mahler." In a letter of 1921 to the painter Wolfgang Born, in whose illustrations for *Death in Venice* Aschenbach resembles Mahler, Mann wrote: "The conception of my story was influenced, in the spring of 1911, by the death of Gustav Mahler, whom I had previously known in Munich, and whose personality, full of such intense ardor, had impressed me beyond measure."

Originally, Visconti intended the film to begin, as Thomas Mann's story does, in Munich, so as to introduce Gustav von Aschenbach against his own background. This is an essentially middle-class one, at a period when class distinctions were often mistaken for acts of God. Aschenbach's father was "a higher law official," his mother the daughter of "a Bohemian bandmaster," but he himself has been ennobled by the Kaiser on his fiftieth birthday, hence the *von* in his name. His wife and child are dead, and age is making him increasingly conservative: "Like Louis XIV he omits every common word from his vocabulary." When the story opens, Aschenbach is going for a walk after a tiring spell of writing. Absorbed by his thoughts, he ends up at the North Cemetery, on the outskirts of Munich. While waiting for a streetcar to take him back to the center of town, he gazes idly at the stonemason's yard, with its crosses, monuments, funeral tablets. Suddenly he notices an odd-looking red-haired man, with a knapsack on his back, obviously a foreigner, on the steps of the "Byzantine-looking Funeral Hall." This arouses in Aschenbach "a youthful longing for far-off places."

No sooner had Visconti outlined the opening scene than he was dissatisfied with what he had done. As he said: "Transformed into a film, the beginning of the novella did not work. Just imagine, 'one spring afternoon in the year 19—,' Professor von Aschenbach goes out for 'rather a long walk,' goes to the cemetery, sees a red-haired traveler whom he calls 'the nomad.' This gives him the idea of making a trip himself. He visualizes jungles, exotic countries, tigers—then goes home, orders train tickets for a short journey inside Europe, to be comfortably made in a sleeper. He goes only to Trieste, then moves on to Pola, then to Brioni. But he finds Brioni too noisy, so goes on to Venice. Well, you can't put all this into film—and then reveal at the end that it's only the *prelude*—without synthetizing the whole thing to such an extent as to deform it completely. So then I tried starting with Aschenbach on the boat for Venice—using flashbacks to show the cemetery in Munich, the chance encounter with the red-haired stranger, and a glimpse of Aschenbach at home, overwhelmed by packing but telling his friend Alfried that he must have a holiday so as to get well, and also to get a grip on himself, to understand himself better. This, too, looked fine on paper, but would have been disastrous on the screen. Because it would have made the beginning of the film completely fragmentary—and therefore incomprehensible to everyone in the audience who hadn't read the book. Because just the sight of the red-haired stranger isn't enough, doesn't automatically explain Aschenbach's sudden impulse to travel. The fact is, the reasons Mann gives in his story cannot be reproduced mechanically."

Instead, Visconti started the film with Aschenbach's crossing to Venice, but without the flashbacks. In the end he was even more faithful to the story than he could have known at the time—because Katia Mann's fascinating and honest *My Unwritten Memoirs* had not been composed. They were published five years later and, in them, Thomas Mann's widow says that her husband's plans often had results very different from those he expected, and that this had been particularly true in the case of *Death in Venice*.

When the Manns went to Dalmatia in the spring of 1911, Thomas Mann was planning a novella about Goethe. They went first to a hotel at Brioni warmly recommended by friends. But they soon discovered that not only was there no sandy beach but, even more vexatious, their fellow guests included an archduchess, mother of the future, and last, emperor of Austria. This personage made a habit of entering the dining room just after the other guests had sat down to their meal. In accordance with the etiquette of the period, everyone then had to stand up. She would repeat this performance, in reverse, by leaving just before other people had finished their meal. Mann found this particularly irritating, since he had wished—as he was presently to make Aschenbach wish— "for far-off places," and therefore found both hotel and archduchess too Austrian by half. Paul Morand, describing the Venice of that period, mentions the prevalence of Austrians who "gave a faint scent of *Cuir de Russie*" to a little world that was to vanish at the fall of "that ancient forest tree," the Emperor Francis Joseph.

Mann was, in addition, already upset by Mahler's illness. Health bulletins were being issued for the composer as for royalty, and Mann followed their ups and downs with intense emotion. He said later that these bulletins, published in daily papers for which he waited suspensefully, "led me to give the hero of my story the severe and passionate features of that artist so prized by me." Mahler died May 18, two months before what would have been his fifty-first birthday. On May 26 the Manns left for Venice. From there to the Lido they were ferried by a gondolier who took them by a roundabout way and seemed unaccountably sinister. In fact he was merely a gondolier without a license who had grabbed them when he saw that they had too much luggage for the *vaporetto*, the regular steam ferry.

Visconti gave the opening of the film a fabulous beauty in which the lagoons appear as ephemeral as sound and light. Thomas Mann would surely have rejoiced had he known that, thanks to a film inspired by a story he himself wrote while grieving for Mahler's death, millions of spectators would, over half a century later, hear Mahler's music for the first time while watching Venetian seascapes, and would, as a result, contribute to the popularity of Mahler's music, which began spreading soon after *Death in Venice* was released.

Among the passengers aboard the steamship *Esmeralda*, on which Aschenbach travels to Venice, is a group of noisy young men, clerks on an outing. Always laughing shrilly in the midst of them is a man who, despite his youthful clothes, natty summer suit, red tie, and Panama hat tilted at a rakish angle, turns out to be a raddled old dandy with a painted face and insinuating manner. Aschenbach dislikes the sight of him and recoils when, as the passengers for Venice are about to go ashore, the old dandy sweeps off his Panama and, addressing Aschenbach as "Your Excellency," wishes him a happy stay in Venice. On this jarring note, Aschenbach is taken possession of by a disconcerting gondolier.

Dirk Bogarde said that being asked by Visconti to play Aschenbach in *Death in Venice* was "like being asked by Laurence Olivier to play Hamlet, only better." But he added that when he was asked, by a long-distance telephone call, "I was kind of stupid and slow-minded, because in *The Damned* there is also a character called Aschenbach. 'We've done that already,' I told him. He was irritated—Visconti hates to talk on the telephone—but mainly I suppose because he couldn't understand that I didn't realize he was speaking of Thomas Mann. I couldn't believe at first that I was being asked, and I couldn't understand why."

The answer was supplied by Bogarde's performance. Made up and dressed to look like a cross between Mahler and Mann himself, he combined the pedantry and rigidity ascribed to Aschenbach's mannerisms in the novella with the "immoderate will power and passion" observed in Mahler by Katia Mann. Visconti made the gondolier who takes Aschenbach from Venice to the Lido tauntingly ambiguous. This increases the isolation and foreboding that seems to surround Aschenbach as he sits haunched below the Charonlike figure who ferries him across a seascape as beautiful and mysterious as any painted by Kaspar David Friedrich.

In his novella, Mann called Aschenbach's hotel the Excelsior, and today there is indeed a palatial Excelsior at the Lido, but it did not exist in 1911, when the Manns stayed at the Grand Hotel des Bains. This still exists, and Visconti rented it from March to May of 1970, hoping to accomplish his work there before the hotel opened on May 15 for its usual six months' season. The hotel's modern face was lovingly de-lifted, its Edwardian atmosphere restored, and its old bathing cabins laid out on the smooth sand between the hotel and the Adriatic. An ironic touch, of the kind often found in Mann's books, was provided by the fact that this decorative retrogression was accomplished at a moment when the Grand Hotel des Bains was about to be modernized. Engineers waited impatiently to install air conditioning while copies of the London Times dated May 24, 1911, and wine bottles labeled Vino Merlo Cantonadine 1904 and Beaujolais Richevel 1906 were carried into the hotel.

Visconti gave the restored hotel a manager as overpoweringly unctuous as the manager of the Grand Hotel de la Plage at Balbec in *Remembrance of Things Past*. The contemporaneity of Marcel Proust (1871–1922) and Thomas Mann (1875–1955) seemed to Visconti a particularly interesting feature of "the whole complex of cultural changes and revolutions that characterized those prewar years and that one must understand in order to follow our own history." It was during the period when Proust was writing his masterpiece and Mann going from *Death in Venice* toward *The Magic Mountain* that, said Visconti, "the whole of European bourgeois culture underwent radical changes, began combing out its knots and setting itself new objectives—all this just as the First World War was about to sweep away every old solution and illusion."

The moment he crosses the hotel's threshold Aschenbach is greeted by the manager and escorted by him, with many a social genuflexion and "Your Excellency," to a room the size of a minor motel, its view of beach and sea limited by nothing but his own eyesight. Visconti took great trouble over characters who make only fleeting appearances at the beginning of the story. They all seemed to him to be "devil's advocates, each one giving Aschenbach a little push toward the angel of death."

Once the hotel manager withdraws, it is clear that Aschenbach's bad temper is due to tension. Mann made a friend say of him, " 'You see, Aschenbach has always lived like this,' contracting the fingers of his left hand into a fish, 'never like this,' and he let his right hand drop comfortably from the arm of his chair." It is while Aschenbach is in this state that the first flashback occurs. A younger-looking Aschenbach is lying on a divan, in pain and barely conscious. A doctor checks his pulse. Across the room are three men and a woman in evening dress. The doctor turns to Alfried, the nearest of them, and says, "He is coming round." Alfried, who is Aschenbach's closest friend and alter ego, asks when he will be able to start work again. Difficult to say, admits the doctor—with a heart in that condition, he will need to be very careful. He must have a long holiday, "a period of absolute rest."

Still in the world of the flashback, we see Alfried at a piano, playing the beginning of the Adagietto from Mahler's Fifth Symphony. When Mahler began composing this symphony in 1901, he was forty, had been a conductor of the Vienna State Opera since 1897, and was dangerously ill, his heart already damaged. That summer he went to rest at Maiernigg on the Wörthersee, where he began his Fifth Symphony. While Alfried plays, Aschenbach sits listening and smoking. On a table to the right is an hourglass. Aschenbach murmurs, "I remember . . . there was an hourglass like that in my father's house. The hole the sand runs through is so small that . . . at first . . . there seems no change in the upper part. . . . Then we begin to see that the sands are running out. We used to want so much . . . it's no use thinking about it. . . . It's only at the last minute . . . when it's too late . . . that one realizes it's too late . . . too late even to think about it."

From this, which explains Aschenbach's exhaustion, we return to his room at the Grand Hotel des Bains. Aschenbach goes downstairs, where, in Mann's words, a "wide and inclusive horizon" confronts him. "Sounds of all the principal languages formed a subdued murmur. The accepted evening dress, a uniform of good manners, brought all human varieties into a fitting unity." An orchestra is playing Franz Lehár's *The Merry Widow,* the great hit of 1905. Among the guests sitting in the hall, with

212

its potted palms and Liberty elegance, Aschenbach observes Americans, English ladies, large Russian families, German children with French nurses. But the "Slavic element" dominates, and Aschenbach's attention is suddenly drawn to a Polish family—three young girls, their governess, and a boy of amazing beauty. Pale and slim, with an oval face, classical features, honey-colored hair and "an expression of sweet and godlike seriousness," he reminds Aschenbach of "Greek sculpture of the noblest period." The child's beauty is heightened by such "rare personal charm" that Aschenbach feels he "has never encountered anything equally felicitous in nature or the plastic arts." Whereas all three young girls are dressed with nunlike severity, their straight hair brushed tightly back, the boy's "hyacinth curls" are shoulder length and he wears a white English sailor suit.

The part of the Polish boy, Tadzio, was extremely difficult to cast, requiring as it did an androgynous beauty evocative of the early Greek world. All his hard-working life Aschenbach has believed that absolute beauty can be created only by an artist whose imagination is rigorously disciplined—and now he is confronted by a child who, without having made the slightest effort, possesses absolute beauty in himself. After an intensive search, a fourteen-year-old Swedish boy was found in Stockholm. Björn Andresen's delicate, well-bred looks could easily be made to suggest Verrocchio's statue of David, and the fact that he had never appeared in a film before was an advantage.

At last the Polish children's mother appears. Like her son, she is beautiful: a cross between a Boldini and a Madonna from an icon. She is dressed in a costly version of what Mann called "the simplicity that signifies taste in those quarters where devoutness is taken as one element of dignity," but an *Arabian Nights'* touch is introduced by her triple ropes of pearls and her earrings "as large as cherries." Casting this part was easy for Visconti. As Tadzio's mother, Silvana Mangano was herself so exquisite a work of art as to suggest there was just a chance that her son's beauty might prove more than skin deep.

At the sight of the countess, children and governess rise, the girls curtsy, the boy kisses his mother's hand, she lightly caresses his hair. The mother moves toward the dining room, followed by her three daughters, in order of age, the governess, and, last, her son. At the door he suddenly turns and gazes at Aschenbach, who is by now the only person left in the hall. On the composer, who was only recently deploring his own lack of the "fiery and fluctuating emotionalism" so useful to artistic creativeness, the boy's graceful attitude and feral gaze have the effect of *Tamburlaine's*

213

Now walk the angels on the walls of heaven,
As sentinels to warn th' immortal souls,
To entertain divine Zenocrate.

They also sharpen Aschenbach's painful doubts about the value of his life's work, and his awareness of nearing old age.

Since Aschenbach's feeling for Tadzio is the heart of the story, it is unfortunate that sexual permissiveness led some spectators to misinterpret it. For *Death in Venice* is in no sense a "gay" story—and neither Mann nor Visconti would have understood people's giving their private sexual tastes a label suggesting mass hilarity. At first sight of the boy, Aschenbach is stirred, wrote Mann, "by the paternal feelings, the profound leaning which those who have devoted their thoughts to the creation of beauty feel towards those who possess beauty itself." As for Tadzio, he is still young enough to retain the power children and animals possess to sense what they can neither express nor understand. His first reaction to his own effect upon Aschenbach is the one so beautifully circumscribed by the Austrian philosopher Martin Buber in *I and Thou* (1923): "An animal's eyes have the power to speak a great language. Independently, without needing cooperation of sounds and gestures, most forcibly when they rely wholly on their glance, the eyes express the mystery in its natural prison, the anxiety of becoming. The condition of the mystery is known only to the animal, it alone can disclose it to us— and this condition only lets itself be disclosed, not fully revealed. The language in which it is uttered is what it says—anxiety, the movement of the creature between the realms of vegetable security and spiritual venture. This language is the stammering of nature at the first touch of spirit, before it yields to spirit's cosmic venture that we call man. But no speech will ever repeat what that stammering knows and can proclaim."

The origin of this literary relationship was Thomas Mann's own admiration for a Polish boy at the Grand Hotel des Bains whom Katia Mann described, sixty-four years later, as a "most beautiful and delicious child," for whom her husband "had had a weakness." No one, thought Katia Mann, but her husband could have created a magnificent story of extreme and morbid passion out of such simple and unconcealed feelings of admiration and sympathy. This transposition had a curious little sequel. About ten years after Thomas Mann's death, his daughter Erika received a letter from an elderly Polish nobleman, Count Vladislav Moes, saying that friends had recently given him the Polish translation of a novella in which he himself, his sisters, all his family, were minutely described.

Even Tadzio, Mann's name for him in *Death in Venice,* is almost his own, since as a boy he was often called "Vladzio." He was, says Katia Mann, very amused and curious, but not in the least offended.

In 1975, the same year as Katia Mann's memoirs, the first volume of Peter de Mendelssohn's biography of Thomas Mann appeared. Entitled *Der Zauberer* ("The Magician" was the Mann children's affectionate nickname for their father), it includes Count Vladislav Moes's recollections of his family's stay at the Grand Hotel des Bains in 1911. With them was another Polish family, whose son, Jan Fudakowski, was the Count's friend and contemporary. As a child Jan was nicknamed "Jasciu," the name Mann overheard while watching the boys playing on the beach. A lifetime later Fudakowski could still remember how he and Tadzio used to nudge each other and say, "Look, there's the old gentleman who's always staring at us." (Thomas Mann was at this time thirty-six.) Count Vladislav said he had indeed been a beautiful child, as family portraits showed. Mann had certainly "adored" him, but, as far as he could remember, he had accepted the famous writer's admiration with "the indifference of a precocious and spoiled child." The elderly "Tadzio" added that not only had Mann described the child Tadzio's clothes in the smallest details, but also he had given a "deliciously poetic and ironic picture" of the entire family and their habits, "old-fashioned even then"—such as their way of walking single file, first the three girls, in order of age, then their French governess, with himself, the one proud male, bringing up the rear. He remembered, too, the lightning departures from Venice provoked by cholera.

Dirk Bogarde made Aschenbach seem already ill as he sits for the first time in the hotel dining room, glancing around every now and again at the Polish family. Absorbed in his new sensations, he suddenly hears the voice of his friend and colleague Alfried ask ironically, "And what is your personal notion of beauty?" Aschenbach's inner voice answers, "You want to deny the artist the power to create beauty out of his own spirit?" Alfried retorts that beauty is born spontaneously, regardless of artists. For the arguments about art, Visconti drew not only on *Death in Venice* but—since he believed that "every work of art contains elements that reveal its creator's past and prophesy his future work"—on Thomas Mann's *Doctor Faustus* (1947), a novel that the French composer-conductor Pierre Boulez cited, a quarter of a century after its publication, as "one of only two novels in which music is truly and profoundly discussed." (The other one Boulez selected was Balzac's *Gambara.*) The musician hero of Mann's *Doctor Faustus* employed a new twelve-tone serial method of composition, which brought Mann protests from Arnold

215

Schönberg. Visconti made Alfried echo Schönberg as Aschenbach echoes Mahler.

Although Aschenbach continues to be enchanted by Tadzio, it does not occur to him to make the acquaintance of the Polish family—although, as a famous artist, he could easily do so. He is satisfied to work at a wooden table in front of the bathing cabin provided for him on the hotel's private beach and watch Tadzio playing with other children. The spectable inspires in him a "sense of myth." It seems to him like "some poet's recovery of time and its beginning, of the origins of forms and the birth of gods." He even derives satisfaction from Tadzio's look of fragility: if Tadzio does not live long, this unique beauty will escape time's ravages.

Proof that Aschenbach is not yet tormented by his admiration for this human "art object" is shown by his deciding to leave Venice when the sirocco upsets his health. After breakfast, on the day he is to leave the Lido, Aschenbach sees the boy and thinks, "Good-bye Tadzio . . . It was too short. . . . God bless you." There is a fuss about Aschenbach's departure from the Lido, just as there was about his arrival. He misses the hotel boat and has to take the public one. Then, arriving at the station in Venice with only a few minutes to spare, Aschenbach discovers that his trunk has been sent by mistake to Como. He insists it be sent back, and pretends to lose his temper, but is in fact overjoyed at having a legitimate excuse to return to the Grand Hotel des Bains.

In an autobiographical essay written nearly twenty years later, Mann says: "Nothing in *Death in Venice* is invented: The traveler in the cemetery in Munich, the gloomy boat from Pola, the old dandy, the suspect gondolier, Tadzio and his family, the departure that went wrong because luggage was mislaid . . . all the facts were true and had only to be put in place to reveal the interpretative power of composition in an astounding manner." Katia Mann adds in her memoirs that it was her brother-in-law Heinrich's trunk that had been sent astray and so obliged them—to her husband's delight—to return to the Lido.

Back in the shelter of his bathing cabin, once more watching Tadzio on the beach, Aschenbach thinks of August von Platen's lines: "For we dream when we live, / And we live when we dream." As he sits there, dreaming between sea and sky, a woman's voice calls, "Gustav! Gustav!" and we see a much younger Aschenbach with his young wife and small child in an alpine field. The small part of Aschenbach's wife was played by Bernard Berenson's niece Marisa Berenson, who looked marvelously like lovely Alma Mahler in her youth. Aschenbach is drawn back to the present by the voice of the French governess calling, "Tadzio! Tadzio!"

Gripped once more by his longing "to be at rest in the face of perfection," Aschenbach "sees Tadzio come running out of the sea, radiant with happiness and well-being." The governess wraps him in a bath towel. Watching the boy lying in the deck chair his sister has promptly vacated for him, Aschenbach pulls a sheet of music paper toward him. As he writes we hear a woman's voice singing in German, to Mahler's Third Symphony, Nietzsche's lines from *Thus Spoke Zarathustra:*

> O man! O man!
> Beware, beware,
> What does midnight say?
> I slept, I slept,
> I woke from the depths of a dream. . . .

During one of these hours on the beach, to which Visconti gives the sense both of timelessness and of evanescence, Aschenbach finds himself walking behind Tadzio under the awning over the path from the hotel to the bathing cabins. The boy is wearing a striped bathing suit and a straw hat shaped like the bronze one of Donatello's *David.* He glances at Aschenbach, hesitates as if on the brink of speech, then, with his right hand clasping one of the poles that support the awning, swings slowly around it. Some spectators thought this unduly provocative, but there is not a detail in this little scene that is not in Mann's text, and the provocativeness is of the kind that a child or an animal displays when over-excited by adult attention.

Aschenbach's aesthetic admiration is gradually transformed into an obsessive passion. Mann is specific about this: "Aschenbach saw the boy Tadzio frequently, almost constantly. Owing to the limited range of territory and the regularity of their lives, the beautiful boy was near him at short intervals throughout the day. He saw him, met him, everywhere —in the lower rooms of the hotel, on the cooling water trips to the city and back, in the arcades of the square, and at times when he was especially lucky ran across him in the streets. But principally, and with the most gratifying regularity, the forenoon on the beach allowed him to admire and study the rare spectacle at his leisure. Yes, it was this guaranty of happiness, the daily recurrence of good fortune, which made his stay here so precious, and gave him such pleasure in the constant procession of sunny days."

One evening Aschenbach is crossing the hotel's lamplit and apparently deserted public rooms. Suddenly, from somewhere on his right, he hears Beethoven's "Für Elise" haltingly played. Drawn to the music, Aschenbach finds Tadzio in a side room, seated negligently at a grand piano.

They gaze at each other, then Aschenbach looks away. Tadzio resumes playing. ("Für Elise" was, incidentally, the boy's own choice when Visconti sat him at the piano and asked him to play something.) The hotel manager happens to pass by just then. Aschenbach expresses some of his agitation by questioning the man about the rumored cholera epidemic in Venice. The manager brushes this aside. It's the same every year, he says loftily: naturally the police have to take certain precautions during the heat, in the interest of public hygiene, but there's absolutely nothing to worry about.

As the manager offers false reassurance, "Für Elise" is heard again, but played more professionally this time—which introduces a flashback in which young Aschenbach is visiting a brothel where a prostitute, whose charming face faintly suggests Tadzio's, is playing "Für Elise" on an upright piano. Her name, Esmeralda, is the same as that of the steamship on which the elderly Aschenbach came to Venice. The girl Esmeralda mocks the young Aschenbach for his impotence. For this scene, Visconti drew on an incident in *Doctor Faustus* for which Mann had used a catastrophic moment in the life of Nietzsche. Mahler, Wagner, and Nietzsche were catalytic figures in Thomas Mann's imaginative life—and all three were important to each other. When Visconti was asked if it had not struck him that by putting Tadzio's piano playing and the brothel scene side by side he might seem to be suggesting that Tadzio and Esmeralda have something in common, he replied that he had done so intentionally, to emphasize the growing ambiguity of the mute relationship between Tadzio and Aschenbach.

This ambiguity is stressed on an evening when Aschenbach sees the Polish family disembark from a trip to Venice. It is already dark, and the Polish children walk as usual in single file, with Tadzio bringing up the rear. Suddenly the boy turns and gives Aschenbach what Mann describes as "a Narcissus smile, coquettish, inquisitive, slightly tortured, infatuated and infatuating." With spellbound consternation, Aschenbach mutters to himself, "You should never smile like that . . . you must never smile at anyone like that"—and then, at last, "*I love you.*" But, even at that stage, Aschenbach's declaration, made only to himself, reveals not so much a straightforward yearning for Tadzio as the emotion expressed by Platen in lines Mann quotes here and elsewhere: "Whoever has seen beauty with his own eyes is already consecrated to death."

Feeling that his time is running out, Aschenbach does little but follow the Polish family about Venice. As he crosses waterways, back alleys, tiny decaying piazzas, Aschenbach is indeed, in today's idiom, on a trip —and so far gone that when he begins to suspect that there really is a cholera epidemic, he feels something like gratification: "For passion, like crime, is not suited to the secure and daily rounds of order and well-being. . . ."

Increasingly hallucinated, Aschenbach only just manages to go through the motions of daily life. These include his usual visit to the hotel barber. But Aschenbach's mood is not his usual one. In front of the barber's mirror, he is suddenly appalled by the sight of his gray hair and wrinkles. The barber, a fluent persuader, lectures Aschenbach on the moral obligation to keep up appearances. In no time Aschenbach is allowing the barber to dye his hair, eyebrows, mustache, to make up his face. When the barber has finished, Aschenbach resembles the raddled old dandy from whom, so short a while ago, he shrank in disgust. Delighted by his own talent, the barber says happily, "Now, sir, you can even fall in love without qualms." Aschenbach gives a cozy satisfied smile as replusive as it is pathetic—and presently we see him, in a white summer suit and panama, a flower in his buttonhole, still darting after the Polish children. In his new clothes and make-up, he looks like a regular voyeur.

This time Tadzio senses that he is being shadowed. So at one point he deliberately lingers behind his sisters and governess. Tall and slim in his dark-blue sailor suit and Donatello straw hat, gazing back from the entrance to a small shadowy alley, Tadzio suggests the angel of death beckoning as ambiguously as Leonardo's juvenile John the Baptist. Finally, outdistanced by the children, overcome by heat and misery, Aschenbach collapses in a tiny piazza where history has left a few scraps of litter and moved on. The walls are daubed with disinfectant and tattered posters. As Aschenbach lolls, physically and morally at the end of his tether, against the parapet of a crumbling wellhead, a flashback shows him his younger self conducting one of his own symphonies—and being shouted down by a hostile audience that includes Alfried, who tells him that "nothing remains of his famous morality now," that "his music is still-born." Aschenbach's sense of failure, explicit here, implicit at the beginning of the film, corresponds with Mahler's fight for the acceptance of his symphonies.

By this time visitors are fleeing the Lido. One morning Aschenbach notices a pile of luggage in the hall. He asks whose it is. The Polish family's. When are they leaving? After lunch. Aschenbach goes to the beach. It is almost empty. A Russian woman is singing a Mussorgsky lullaby. The beach attendant, still making the rounds of the empty bathing cabins, brings Aschenbach a deck chair. Far away, two small children are building a sand castle. Farther still, at the sea's edge, Tadzio and his friend Jasciu are wrestling like puppies. Suddenly Jasciu goes too far for Tadzio's dignity. Offended, Tadzio shakes him off and moves away, alone, into the sea. Aschenbach is gazing at this distant vision when suddenly Tadzio pauses: "as though at some recollection, some impulse, with one hand on his hip, he turned the upper part of his body in a beautiful twist which began from the base—and he looked over his shoulder towards the shore."

Using Mann's description as a stage direction, Visconti gave Tadzio the attitude of Verrocchio's bronze *David*. He made the small radiant figure an integral part of a vast and dazzling entity composed of sky and ocean, light and music. So when Aschenbach, struggling to leave his chair and answer what seems to him to be Tadzio's mysterious summons, collapses—not from cholera but from the failure of his exhausted heart— it seems as if he has at long last assuaged his yearning "to be at rest in the face of perfection."

In making his German trilogy in reverse, Visconti had gone from Hitler's Germany to that of Thomas Mann. Now he was to go farther still, back to Munich's Residenz Theater in the days of the kings of Bavaria. In that little jewel box of a theater—built by François de Cuvilliés in the mid-eighteenth century—with its crimson seats, white and gold carved woodwork, caryatids, cherubs, swags of flowers and fruit, the handsome eighteen-year-old Ludwig II of Bavaria had for a brief spell adorned his function and roused the hopes of his subjects. Resplendent in the royal box, framed by garlanded palm trees and draperies that met overhead in a golden crown only slightly more elaborate than the crowns worn by the two carved swans above the proscenium arch, young Ludwig sat dreaming of Wagner's music. The fact that the boy's natural habitat was one of dreams would create his personal tragedy and contribute to the trials and errors of a Germany on the eve of unification.

From Thomas Mann's world to that of the Wittelsbach dynasty and the swan legends was only a step, and it was in this king-haunted country that Visconti was to make not his last film, but his last film as a man in good health.

A Louis II de Bavière

Roi, le seul vrai roi de ce siècle, salut, Sire,
Qui voulûtes mourir vengeant votre raison
Des choses de la politique, et du délire
De cette Science intruse dans la maison. . . .

Vous fûtes un poète, un soldat, le seul Roi
De ce siècle où les rois se font si peu de choses,
Et le Martyr de la Raison selon la Foi.

Salut à votre très unique apothéose,
Et que votre âme ait son fier cortège, or et fer,
Sur un air magnifique et joyeux de Wagner.

Paul Verlaine

Twenty-four

When *Death in Venice* was completed, Visconti's hopes of filming part of Proust's *Remembrance of Things Past* seemed at last about to be fulfilled. No plan meant more to him than this. There is in Proust an extravagance of the heart that had made the adolescent Visconti wonder: How can this Frenchman, whom I've never seen, understand me so well? Since those days Visconti had read *Remembrance of Things Past* again and again, seeing Proust's world anew as his own world changed, just as one sees differently at different periods those few people one has the good fortune to love throughout one's life. So now, in his vigorous early sixties, Visconti wanted to put a lifetime's appreciation into a film.

Together he and Suso had written a superb scenario, approved by the Proust family, which was published in May 1978, with four hundred illustrations. It begins with the little train to Balbec ambling across the sunny countryside where "nothing seems to move except the little train flying its flag of black smoke." Visconti spent weeks choosing locations in Paris and Normandy, and persuaded the authorities at Cabourg, Proust's Balbec, to postpone the demolition of the old Grand Hotel, where Proust used to stay. The actors were bespoken, and the wind seemed set fair for France. Nevertheless, this project was destined to join the list of films that Visconti planned but did not make: a list as tantalizing as the opening chapters of the ten novels Balzac left unfinished, like dancers' leaps immobilized forever in midair. In this case the initial obstacle was entirely financial: to film Proust would require vast sums, and these the producers had still to find. So, since Visconti loathed wasting time, he decided to film *Ludwig* while the gold rush was in progress. Of Visconti's vanished projects none seems more of a loss today than his view of Proust's world, this and the film of Nijinsky's life that he wanted to make with Rudolf Nureyev.

But *Ludwig*, too, encountered financial difficulties. It was becoming harder and harder to find money for unpornographic films. Italy's economic boom was over and many people who might have been moved by artistic sensibility, or even common sense, to invest in a Visconti film, could no longer afford to do so. At last four companies combined to back *Ludwig*—one Italian, one French, and two German. This meant a plethora of paperwork and constant juggling with inconstant rates of exchange. The executive producer, Robert Gordon Edwards, went far beyond the call of duty in helpfulness to all concerned, but could not prevent a six months' tug-of-war during which the project was one day on, one day off. As Visconti found vacillation infinitely more trying than overwork, his health suffered.

That summer he went to his villa on Ischia. One evening, just as he was about to dine out with friends, he had a slight stroke: so slight that he felt the nightmare effects for only a second or two, then dismissed the matter and continued according to plan—his own plan. He dined with his friends, ate well, smoked too much, as usual, and walked home. When the doctor pointed out that he was "no longer twenty"—Visconti was then sixty-four—and ought to "take things more easily," he agreed but, for all his intelligence, had not the faintest idea how to take anything easily. He had always been stronger, more energetic, more resistant than others and no more believed this could change than the average child believes it will die. He accepted a prescription of Hydergine with every intention of taking it regularly. Unfortunately, this excellent preventive medicine was in liquid form and, since he had to take it around with him, frequently spilled in his pocket. This was too much for both his patience and his fastidiousness. So he tossed the bottle away. A line of E. M. Forster's comes to mind: "I consider not to be frightened the height of folly"—it can, however, be a moving and beautiful folly.

As an instance of Visconti's personal brand of this folly, Suso Cecchi D'Amico remembers an occasion when she accompanied him to an old half-abandoned country house to see if it would be possible to rescue some frescoes from there. As they entered the attic they were talking quietly. Suddenly something above them moved. For a second Suso thought it was a swallow, nesting in the decrepit roof and disturbed by their voices. Then she looked up, and saw bats, a swarm of tiny downward-hanging heads, not quite motionless. She understood, then and there, precisely what people mean when they say they "just don't know what came over them." Because, next thing, she was outside, at the bottom of the steps to the attic, without any idea how she got there. Returning, she found Visconti methodically examining frescoes. That he

224

made no comment on her disappearance could have been due to either courtesy or absorption in the matter in hand. I have myself seen Visconti remain completely relaxed, on location, when a loud report, which sounded like a shot, but was probably a light bulb exploding, made everyone else jump.

Back from Ischia, Visconti seemed as well as ever, and completely absorbed by *Ludwig*, for which he himself, Enrico Medioli, and Suso wrote a scenario as thoroughly researched as it was imaginative. As soon as the producers' doubts permitted, he went location-hunting in Germany and Austria. Given the wintry weather, this was too much for a man who had just had a stroke, however slight. But Visconti was unaware of this, the more so because both the Wittelsbach family and the Bavarian authorities put themselves out to help him, offering loans of family treasures and permission to film in Ludwig's fabulous castles, now state property. Visconti discovered that although Ludwig II died in 1886 he was still vividly remembered in his former kingdom—not only by artists, intellectuals, and his own relatives, but also by young Bavarians of every class, who belonged to Ludwig Clubs. To Germans born after Hitler's death, Ludwig's generosity, fantasy, hatred of war, love of solitude and dreaming seemed the exact opposite of Nazism. What drew Visconti to the young King was the way he combined an inability to manage what is generally called reality with an uncanny ability to put his dreams to creative purpose. Without Ludwig, Wagner's greatest operas might never have been composed, let alone performed in his lifetime. Without Ludwig's castle-building, modern Bavaria would lack the income provided by the half a million tourists who visit these castles every year.

Prince Ludwig Friedrich Wilhelm, son of Crown Prince Maximilian and Crown Princess Marie, was born at Nymphenburg, summer residence of the kings of Bavaria, on August 25, 1845. He was to have been called Otto, but his grandfather, reigning King Ludwig I, was so pleased at his grandson's being born on his own birthday, and at the same hour even as himself, that he requested the boy be named after him. It was from this grandfather that Ludwig II inherited both his love of building and his extravagance in love. In 1848, King Ludwig I's passion for a dancer, Lola Montez, led to his abdication, so his grandson became crown prince before his third birthday.

Everything about Ludwig's upbringing might have been specifically designed to encourage the passion for Wagner's music that was to pervade the future conjured up by Visconti in this film. As a child, Ludwig often spent the summer at Hohenschwangau, a Bavarian castle at the heart of the swan country and, according to medieval German legends, once the home of Parsifal's son Lohengrin, the knight of the Holy Grail. Its walls were frescoed with pictures of the Lohengrin and Tannhäuser stories, and swans abounded—painted, carved, stuffed, woven, embroidered, of gold, papier-mâché, precious stones, porcelain, straw, and glass. There were even swan-shaped ink pots. One of Ludwig's earliest recollections was of feeding live swans on the lake below. One of his earliest drawings shows a swan almost as big as the castle behind it. As soon as he could write he signed his letters with a swan and a cross.

At thirteen Ludwig was given a copy of Wagner's recently published *Opera and Drama,* and he knew the libretti of *Lohengrin* and *Tannhäuser* by heart well before February 1861, when he heard his first Wagner opera, *Lohengrin.* So he was already spellbound when, at seventeen, he read the preface to *The Ring of the Nibelung,* in which Wagner insisted on the need for a total reform of opera production in Germany. These reforms, wrote Wagner, would be so costly as to require a prince to carry them out. "Will such a prince be found?" Already absorbed by art, Ludwig became obsessed by an artist. War disgusted and politics bored him. Ludwig's father, King Maximilian II, was only fifty-three when, a Schleswig-Holstein crisis having brought him back, against his doctors' advice, from a rheumatism cure in Italy, he died in Munich. At eighteen Ludwig became king.

Visconti's film opens the morning before Ludwig's coronation. His confessor, Father Hoffmann, is urging humility upon him—thanks to his new position, he will from now on "find the path to salvation increasingly arduous." Handsome, tense, an overbred animal liable to bite, Ludwig says that, after awaiting his coronation with anguish, he has suddenly understood "how to use the power entrusted to him." He will be able to gather around him scholars, artists, men of genius to provide his reign with its memorials.

To play Ludwig, Visconti chose Helmut Berger, whom he had already directed in *The Damned.* All actors either display their own personalities or portray those of others—and although some achieve wonders without ever going beyond their own personalities, it is a thrilling moment when a performer crosses the frontier of self. As a beginner, Berger seemed likely to rely on looks and contentious charm, but in this instance Visconti tapped genuine acting ability.

The coronation ceremonies begin with a swarm of academicians, courtiers, officers, lackeys, hairdressers. At the heart of the cyclone stands Ludwig, in military uniform, solemn and dazzled as a young bullfighter. The Queen Mother enters in gala attire, curtsies deeply to her son, who kisses her forehead in a chilly manner. Love is completely lost between

Ludwig and his mother, a Prussian princess by birth. Later he will refer to her as "my predecessor's widow." Behind the Queen Mother comes Ludwig's younger brother, Otto, their uncle Prince Luitpold von Bayern, and more dignitaries. Cabinet Secretary Franz von Pfistermeister hands Ludwig a roll of parchment: his coronation speech. With juvenile majesty, Ludwig steps toward the reign that he envisages as a private matter between himself and the arts. Presently we hear his voice making his coronation speech.

This is followed by a flash forward to 1886 at Neuschwanstein castle, where a pallid, red-eyed, prematurely aged Ludwig is told by a distraught royal coachman that three carriage loads of officials have arrived from Munich to arrest the King. From this sinister glimpse of the future we return to the newly crowned boy, handsome, headstrong—and outraged because Wagner, for whom an invitation was ready within five weeks of the coronation, has not yet been located. Brushing aside Cabinet Secretary Pfistermeister's explanations, Ludwig threatens to go to Wagner himself to "request the honor of a visit." Whereupon Pfistermeister cautiously reminds the King that the Prime Minister has "most warmly" recommended a royal visit to Bad Ischl, where the Emperor and Empress of Austria, the Crown Prince of Prussia, and the Tsarina are staying—but here Pfistermeister is halted by the obstinacy on the royal face.

Having established that fifty-one-year-old Wagner is the most important figure in the young King's imaginative life, Visconti immediately introduces Wagner's only possible rival in this sphere: Ludwig's cousin Elisabeth of Austria.

Visconti knew from the start whom he wanted for Elisabeth. When, at the May 1971 Film Festival in Turin, Romy Schneider was asked, as guest of honor, to hand him the award for his work as a whole, he whispered to her, "I want to offer you a part you're already familiar with. Can you guess what it is?" Thinking of *'Tis Pity She's a Whore* and *Il lavoro,* Schneider laughed, "A whore?" "Not at all," said Visconti. "It's Elisabeth." His choice was both obvious and adventurous. Gifted, beautiful, temperamental, an international star, Romy Schneider was, at thirty-three, very different from the Austrian teen-ager idolized as *Sissi* —and Visconti had been partly responsible for her metamorphosis.

When Elisabeth and Ludwig meet at Bad Ischl, to which Ludwig has finally been coaxed, they have not seen each other for five and a half years, and Elisabeth finds Ludwig very changed—"the handsomest king in Europe." There is narcissism, as well as a family likeness, in the looks they exchange. What is he doing here, asks Elisabeth. She knows there is a plan for Ludwig to marry the Tsar's daughter.

Next day, in the garden of her house, the Kaiservilla, Elisabeth picks up the conversation as if there had been no interruption, and advises him not to marry the Tsar's daughter. Elisabeth has only to speak to be obeyed, says Ludwig. Why then, she asks, is he in such a hurry to get back to Munich? What is he hiding from her? He is hiding Wagner—and it is Wagner whom we see next.

In casting this part Visconti was lucky as well as perspicacious. Not only is Trevor Howard an admirable actor, but with only a little make-up he looked uncannily like Franz von Lenbach's portrait of Wagner at precisely the right age. Trevor Howard's successful career—begun in the theater, where he played leading Shakespearean parts before making over forty films, including *Brief Encounter* (1946), *The Third Man* (1949), *Mutiny on the Bounty* (1962), *The Charge of the Light Brigade* (1968), *Ryan's Daughter* (1970)—had left intact his total freedom from pretentiousness and a suggestion of hilarity repressed with difficulty. This gave his Wagner a disarming quality that made it easy to understand why people remained devoted to the composer even when he betrayed them for his work's, or even his comfort's, sake. Visconti said he could not bring himself to show the composer in "an exclusively mean light"; he admired Ludwig for having, even as a boy, "understood that Wagner was Wagner; that was quite an achievement."

Wagner appears for the first time in the Munich house given him by Ludwig. The room is crowded with signs of riches of the kind portrayed by the contemporary Austrian painter Hans Makart: bibelots, draperies, potted palms, bouquets of thistles, bulrushes, peacocks' tails. Wagner is wearing a quilted and frogged silk jacket. Every now and again he strokes it appreciatively. Lying near him is a white sheepdog from the Pyrenees. Visconti liked this dog actor so much that he immediately bought a puppy of the same breed. His own passion for animals made it easy for him to sympathize with Wagner's need for them even when he was on the run from creditors.

As Wagner plays with the dog he seems overexcited. Even his arrogance has a pathetic note, a suggestion of famishment very natural considering that, although he is one of the greatest composers of the century to which he and Verdi will give its musical profile, he is still, at fifty-one, a financial failure. So he boasts about the house and urges his friend Hans von Bülow to settle in Munich with him.

Across the room from the two men sits Bülow's wife, Cosima, quiet as still waters. The half-Hungarian, half-French daughter of Franz Liszt and the Comtesse d'Agoult is twenty-seven. She has known Wagner since she was fifteen and idolizes him, as do her father and husband. Since music is sacred to all three of them, they may be said to commune in Wagner. In this part Silvana Mangano was even more striking than in *Death in Venice*. As Tadzio's mother she provided an exquisitely decorative symbol of a Polish aristocracy that, with its country partitioned, could oppose only beautifully stiff necks to Russian, Prussian, and Austrian tyranny. But the part of Cosima required more acting. Mangano's non-film-star beauty, non-fashion-magazine elegance, and non-bluestocking intelligence coalesced in a superb portrait of the woman of whom Liszt said that as Wagner's wife she "surpassed even herself," and whom Stefan Zweig was to remember in her old age, when "her white head reached upward into the heroic and Olympian world," as "hard, strong, and yet majestic with her pathetic gestures."

Silently Cosima listens to Wagner's attempts to persuade her husband that the Bülow family must join him in Munich. Wagner moves toward Cosima. "Can we consider it settled?" Wagner asks her. For the first time Cosima speaks. Very softly she tells Wagner that she is expecting another child. His expression is emotional and questioning. Her lips scarcely move, yet it is as if she cried aloud with joy that this child is his. He clasps her hand tightly. Their first child will be born the day the Munich orchestra rehearses *Tristan and Isolde* for the first time.

Back at Bad Ischl, Ludwig is asked by Elisabeth to dine with her, informally. But his reception at the Kaiservilla turns out to be a large family gathering—for which Visconti created an exquisite Winterhalter "conversation piece," comparable with the scenes of aristocratic domesticity in *The Leopard*. To Ludwig, however, this Wittelsbach onslaught seems anything but exquisite—and when Elisabeth urges her seventeen-year-old sister, Sophie, forward, telling him that Sophie loves Wagner's music as much as he does, Ludwig immediately freezes. He has come only to say good-bye; he is expected in Munich next day. Elisabeth accompanies him to the staircase. He thanks her for their happy days at Bad Ischl and adds that she *must* come to him for the first night of *Tristan*: Wagner's music will "help her understand what he has been trying to tell her."

Elisabeth remains, however, refractory to Wagner. So much so that when she visits her cousin at his Island of Roses—and Visconti makes her landing there as mysteriously beautiful as a Kaspar David Friedrich painting—her only answer to Ludwig's laments at her absence from the first night of *Tristan* is "What did it all cost?" Crowned heads, she tells him, have no personal life: "We're on parade and quickly forgotten—unless someone gives us a little extra importance by assassinating us." This scene beside Lake Starnberg, where Ludwig will drown twenty years later, dissolves into Elisabeth's own death chamber at the Hotel Beau-Rivage, in Geneva. Thirty-two years have passed since she spoke to Ludwig of assassination and now her body lies under a white veil, stabbed by an anarchist who went to Evian to murder the Duke of Orléans and, having missed him, turned to Geneva to make do with Elisabeth, Empress of Austria.

From one impossible love to another, Ludwig returns to the house in Munich. Wagner is at the piano playing Offenbach, whose *La Vie Parisienne* is one of the hits of 1866. *This* is what the Germans really like, grumbles Wagner, not my music—"not a day goes by without the critics attacking me." "Don't read them then," says the King. "I shall give orders that the newspapers are to be hidden from you." But he speaks charmingly, not despotically. In this scene, for the first and only time, we see Ludwig happy, his creative instincts satisfied by designing an opera house, his hero worship steadied by the joy of assisting genius. Later on Ludwig's homosexuality will develop—and the film indicates this—along conventional lines, among young men; nevertheless, the middle-aged Wagner was the great love of his imagination and enabled him to make the only contribution to the arts of which he was capable. Visconti thought Ludwig showed the mind of an architect in the castles he built. "Herrenchiemsee and Linderhof are beautiful," said Visconti, "although they represent eighteenth-century dreams in the nineteenth century. . . . As an architect Ludwig had quite advanced concepts. Being a man who loved spectacle, he built for a pomp that he would enjoy in solitude. He wanted to be a Medici, but had no Michelangelo to work for him. And he didn't live in the Renaissance, but in a kitsch period, at a moment when Europe was bourgeois and busy with conquests and supremacy, not with sublimation of thought."

Back at the palace Ludwig is berating Master of the Horse Holnstein, who has been reading Wagner's private correspondence on the grounds that the composer is "listed as a revolutionary." "A revolutionary!" explodes Ludwig. "Why, if Wagner were not an artist he would be a saint. His art redeems us—is an antidote to the corruption of our society. His name will be handed on for centuries"—and so on, much of it true, despite Ludwig's manner. But Holnstein has a deadly blow in reserve: it may be unwise for the law to make exceptions, since in the eyes of ordinary people Richard Wagner is simply a man who squanders the taxpayers' money, and Madame von Bülow "an adulteress." Slander, says Ludwig frantically. *"No,"* says Holnstein, who would have been a telephone-tapper at a later period, which does not make his facts necessarily untrue, "it is the truth, as these letters clearly show." Next day Minister of Justice Freiherr von Lutz gives Wagner an order to quit Munich and a letter:

Dear Friend,

Painful though this is to me, I must ask you to act in accordance with the message Freiherr von Lutz will give you. My love for you will remain eternally unchanged and I conjure you to preserve our friendship intact. It was not possible for me to do otherwise. Until death your faithful

Ludwig

One of the consequences of this episode is shown by a flash forward to twenty years later, with Holnstein testifying to the King's "mental instability," as proved by his attitude toward the 1866 Austro-Prussian war. In 1864 Prussia and Austria had invaded Denmark and seized the duchy of Schleswig-Holstein. Bismarck was determined, however, to expel Austria from the German Confederation in the interests of Prussian hegemony. Realizing that any threat to Austria threatened Bavarian independence, Ludwig tried for a defensive alliance with Napoleon III. But France wanted too much in exchange. Ludwig then tried to keep Bavaria neutral, and for this was accused of insanity. Finally, on June 10, Bavaria undertook to help Austria and her allies against Prussia should need arise. The Seven Weeks War broke out a week later. Refusing to lead his troops in person, Ludwig retired to Schloss Berg.

Ludwig's solitude deepens. One night he wanders down to the lake, hears faint splashes, calls, "Who's there?" A young groom, Volk, emerges from the water naked as a Triton. Ludwig asks irascibly who gave him permission to go out? Terrified, Volk says he couldn't sleep and thought he wasn't needed at that hour. Ludwig tosses his cloak to the shivering boy and walks rapidly away. This fades into the villa at Roseninsel, where Ludwig is kneeling in front of a sacred image, beating his breast with clenched fists as he prays aloud for help to "resist temptation." Finally, he falls asleep, only to be roused by the voice of his aide-de-camp, Count Dürckheim, who has come from the front and greets the unkempt Ludwig as respectfully as if they were on parade. Etiquette punctuates the film, as it punctuated the lives of all these people for whom even tragedy was accompanied by the rustle of curtsies and the snapping of clicked heels: sounds that seemed to courtiers as natural as the sound of the sea to sailors.

Dürckheim has come to announce defeat. Are our losses heavy? asks Ludwig. No, but our troops were so outnumbered that to continue fighting would only have meant more useless slaughter. How is Prince Otto? He has returned to Munich in desperately low spirits. One day, says

231

Ludwig abruptly, his brother will be king—soon perhaps, since he himself desires only liberty to act in accordance with his ideas, his instincts. This military catastrophe galvanizes Ludwig, however, into eccentric action.

Back at the Residenz in Munich he announces to his mother that he is going to get married and requests her to ask Duchess Ludovica for the hand of her daughter Sophie. Sophie! cries his mother. The ideal wife for you! The Queen Mother's epithalamium is repeated by Duchess Ludovica in one of Visconti's most felicitous family conversation pieces. Otto, though pleased by his brother's engagement, looks haunted, and Elisabeth is tender only to him. Toward Ludwig—"dear brother-in-law"— she is slightly mocking. Ludwig's attentions to pretty Sophie—played by Sonia Petrova, a young ballet dancer so like the real Sophie that she and Helmut Berger looked as if they had stepped out of a Wittelsbach family album—are so perfunctory that she already has an orphaned air.

Ludwig's solitude is fast becoming isolation. As he arrives at Rosen-insel, his island hideaway, a handsome, gentle-looking boy appears with an open umbrella. This is Hornig, a new servant whom Ludwig has not seen before. At the villa, Ludwig asks Hornig to light the fire. As the flames illumine his face, framed by softly curling hair, he looks like a young Fire King. Rising, he asks respectfully if His Majesty has any further orders. Ludwig tells Hornig he may sleep there that night—if he wishes to. Later, when Hornig is asleep, Ludwig returns and stands gazing down at him. Presently he surrenders to himself, bends and kisses Hornig.

Ludwig now tells his confessor that he does not want to marry Sophie. "A king cannot cause a scandal," says Father Hoffmann, majestically disregarding centuries of evidence to the contrary. Although his subjects know the king to be more powerful and privileged than themselves—since he is touched by Divine Providence—they will not allow him to differ from themselves in "certain essentials." Wagner was driven out because he was a genius and therefore "different." Ludwig is "different" in another sense, but must not give way to this. The scene dissolves into a flash forward in which Head Groom Hornig is testifying that he has been in the King's service for ten years and "nothing in the King's manner has ever been unsuitable to the dignity of a sovereign." Here Hornig's voice fades into that of a priest, a member of the now converted Queen Mother's retinue, speaking of Ludwig's expulsion of the Jesuits from Bavaria. Visconti attributed great importance to the Protestant Queen Mother's conversion to Catholicism, being convinced that this encouraged the Jesuits to conspire against Ludwig.

As episode after episode shows Ludwig's retreat from reality, while he builds his dream castles Linderhof and Neuschwanstein, and the

Ossessione, 1942

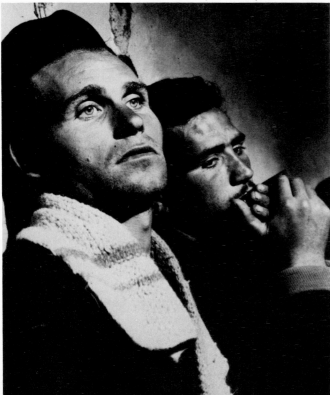

La terra trema, 1947

La terra trema

Bellissima, 1951

Senso, 1954

White Nights (Le notti bianche), 1957

Rocco and His Brothers (Rocco e i suoi fratelli), 1960

Rocco and His Brothers

The Leopard (Il Gattopardo), 1962/63

Sandra (Vaghe stelle dell'orsa), 1965

The Leopard

The Damned (La caduta degli dei), 1970

Death in Venice (Morte a Venezia), 1971

Photo Mario Tursi

Ludwig, 1972

Photo Mario Tursi

Ludwig

Photo Mario Tursi

Conversation Piece (Gruppo di famiglia in un interno), 1974

Photo Mario Tursi

Photo Mario Tursi

The Intruder (L'innocente), 1975

Photo Mario Tursi

Photo Mario Tursi

The Intruder

Bavarian Versailles, Herrenchiemsee, we see him deteriorating pitifully. In one of his hunting lodges, disheveled and unkempt, he watches a gaggle of lackeys and grooms playing blindman's buff amid raucous laughter. From this it is only a short step to Dr. Bernhard von Gudden's declaration that "the King is in an advanced state of paranoia." Gudden has not examined the King but, since he is the most fashionable alienist of the period, and head of Munich's Psychiatric Institute, his declaration suits all those who want Ludwig out of the way. Ludwig is still too popular for either a coup d'état or his assassination to be accepted by the country as a whole, but the Bavarian Constitution permits the deposition of any monarch "incapable of reigning for at least a year." A medical commission is set up.

Ludwig is at Neuschwanstein when the royal coachman brings the news that the carriages of this commission are at the castle gates. Arrest them! Shoot them! cries Ludwig—and the sentries on duty do indeed threaten to shoot the intruders. Ludwig is about to barricade himself in one of the castle towers when his faithful aide-de-camp Dürckheim arrives. He begs Ludwig to return to Munich at once. The army is loyal and will rally to him. "Munich?" says Ludwig disgustedly. "Munich? Eight elephants couldn't drag me back to that city I hate!" This reply explains many of Ludwig's difficulties—it is frivolous at a tragic moment, it combines the attitudes of a spoiled child and an absolute monarch, and the eight elephants give it a touch of absurd poetry. In just such a suicidal way did Oscar Wilde answer at his trial.

Dürckheim insists that to return to Munich is the only solution—unless the King wants to escape the country via the Tyrol? Ludwig insists he has no desire to travel—"What would I do in the Tyrol?"—and wants only to be left in peace. But before he can barricade himself in the tower he is trapped by the medical commission, told that his uncle, Prince Luitpold, is regent, and escorted to Schloss Berg. As a prisoner Ludwig displays perfect dignity; the most moving moment in Helmut Berger's performance was his repressed consternation at seeing the constraints of a lunatic asylum set up in this castle, with its painted stargazers' ceiling, from where as a child he had gazed across the lake toward his cousin Elisabeth's home country.

When Ludwig asks to be allowed out for a walk, Dr. von Gudden acquiesces and offers to accompany him. "I see he's made a conquest of you, too, Professor," says Ludwig's equerry. "You'd better watch out" —words that dissolve into Ludwig's voice, addressing Gudden as they begin their walk in the rain: "Prison makes me *hear* the silence, the night . . . there's nothing more beautiful than night. They say that the cult of the night . . . the moon . . . is a feminine one . . . while the cult of the day, of the sun, is masculine. . . . But for me the mystery of night, its grandeur, have always been connected with the boundless realms of heroes. . . ."

This lifelong passion for the night suggests the German Romantics whose dissatisfaction with reality, yearning to reconcile the immensity of nature with that of the human soul, and obsession with night, darkness, and death all found an echo in Ludwig. *Night* is a key word in Visconti's German trilogy: the darkness gathering around Ludwig of Bavaria presages the night of the long knives that culminates in the *night and fog* of concentration camps, where, as in Novalis's "Hymn to the Night," "the reign of night knows neither time nor space."

Suddenly emerging from his dreams of night, Ludwig stops and gazes at the alienist: "Poor Dr. Gudden. Obliged to study me day and night, night and day . . . But I'm an enigma, and I want to remain one, not only to others but to myself. . . ." Rain is falling heavily now. Their umbrellas, their dark stiffly conventional clothes, render this ill-assorted pair as enigmatic as Douanier Rousseau figures, enclosed in veils of rain among the great trees. Then they vanish from sight.

The murmurous silence that swallows up Ludwig's last words is replaced by sounds of official agitation: "Dr. Gudden said they wouldn't be gone more than an hour. . . . No, they're alone. Dr. Gudden didn't want the nurses with them. . . . But His Majesty seemed very quiet"—capped by an outraged shout from Holnstein: "Have I got to teach you that lunatics are cunning?" Orders are rapped out. Darkness falls. Soldiers come running with torches. Whoever finds the King is to fire a shot into the air. The torches flare to and fro in the darkness. Men shout to each other. Dogs bark. The telegraph operator repeats messages in a monotonous voice, ending with "Still no news. The search continues." Presently, however, there is news. Boats glide among the reeds at the edge of the lake, where once the child Ludwig fed the swans and dreamed of Lohengrin. Summer rain continues to fall as the dead King and the doctor are carried ashore.

The film was shot, but not edited, when an appalling tragedy befell Visconti himself.

Una casa pensile in aria sospesa con funi a una stella.
(A house floating in the air held by ropes to a star.)

Leopardi

Be quite old when you anchor at the island,
Rich with all you have gained on the way,
Not expecting Ithaka to give you riches.
Ithaka has given you your lovely journey.
Without Ithaka you would not have set out.

C. P. Cavafy

How dull it is to pause, to make an end,
To rust unburnish'd, not to shine in use!
As tho' to breathe were life! Life piled on life
Were all too little, and of one to me
Little remains; but every hour is saved
From that eternal silence, something more,
A bringer of new things.

Tennyson, *Ulysses*

Twenty-five

On July 27, 1972, Visconti spent a "normal working day" in his house in Rome. The shooting of *Ludwig* was finished, but there remained the dubbing and recording the music for the sound track. His high-walled garden served as a moat between him and the city, and what he particularly remembered about that day was the heat, which had seemed to him abnormal even for a Roman summer. The entire lion-colored city was drenched by waterfalls of light that vibrated in every cranny, offering visible proof that, far from being solid, as it usually looks, matter is composed of dancing molecules.

At this stage Visconti had no idea how badly *Ludwig* had exhausted him. Photographs of this period show Visconti radiating energy and looking, in his fur coat, cap, muffler, and snow boots, uncannily like Pisanello's medallion of his fifteenth-century ancestor Filippo Maria Visconti, himself a notably energetic character. After three months of filming in Bavaria, with temperatures of twelve degrees below zero, and many all-night sessions in the snow, the rest was done at the Cinecittà studios outside Rome; this meant that snow was exchanged for Turkish-bath heat, and Visconti's exhaustion increased all the more easily for being ignored by him.

On the evening of July 27, Visconti and Suso Cecchi D'Amico were to dine with two producers to discuss his next film. They went to the Eden Hotel. By chance, Visconti had never been there, and he liked its rooftop restaurant, overlooking the Villa Medici and the Borghese Gardens. Champagne was brought as they stood savoring the vast view over Rome.

Visconti took a sip from his glass, remarked with surprise that it wasn't properly chilled—and at that very instant was, in his own words, "struck by lightning." His left arm suddenly ceased to belong to him, except as an inanimate burden. By grasping the back of his chair with his right hand, he managed not to fall. Suso, appalled by his sudden pallor, cried out, "Luchino, what's the matter?" Although the stroke was a massive one, Visconti did not lose consciousness, and so, then and there, hearing his friends saying "He must be moved," he had his first experience of the helplessness that is one of the most abominable features of grave illness.

Presently he was carried to a bedroom in the hotel to await his doctor; and from there was taken to a clinic. He remembered the heat, the sound of voices in the corridor as well as in his room. At one moment he heard music: Wagner, then Mozart's *Magic Flute*. Friends came to see him one at a time and he talked to them. Most of his working life had been spent with people all around him, and this professional habit joined his natural dignity and courage in helping him confront doom in public without faltering. So strong was his personality, he seemed to be in charge of his own physical defeat.

Meanwhile, Visconti's Italian doctor, Professor Simone, got in touch with the great Swiss neurologist Professor Hugo A. Krayenbühl, and, on August 14, Visconti flew to Zurich. He could not have been given a better chance of recovery. For although strokes are a common affliction, they are far from being skillfully treated everywhere. There are, indeed, places where the only treatment available is likely to prove positively harmful. Switzerland is not, however, among these—and Professor Krayenbühl is part of the very best Switzerland has to offer, which is saying a great deal.

A cultured, handsome man, son of a Swiss psychiatrist, Professor Krayenbühl studied medicine in Geneva, Kiel, Paris, and Zurich, and has an international outlook. In 1948, Zurich University gave him the first Swiss chair in neurological surgery. In 1966, he was visiting professor at the Neurosurgical Service of Massachusetts General Hospital, in Boston, and this was followed by spells as visiting professor at Methodist Hospital and Baylor College of Medicine, Houston, Texas, and at the University of Texas's Division of Neurosurgery. The year Visconti went to him, Professor Krayenbühl was elected honorary member of the Accadèmia Lancisiana of Rome, and in 1977 he was selected Neurosurgeon of the Year by *Surgical Neurology*.

Being remarkable himself, Professor Krayenbühl had no difficulty in recognizing Visconti's exceptional qualities. The doctor's courtesy, common sense, and culture appealed to Visconti, as did everything about his treatment in Zurich, a city beloved by Thomas Mann. He found Swiss doctors "very congenial, very able," and particularly respected the professionalism, one of his favorite qualities, behind the Zurich doctors', nurses', and therapists' habit of telling him the truth, and how they proposed to help him deal with it. He was determined to recover, and their attitude made recovery seem feasible.

Nevertheless, Visconti's first days in Zurich were a season in hell for him. He could do nothing for himself and, whether lying in bed or propped in a chair, had a permanent sensation of being about to fall. It was as if his body had become that of a rag doll in a world without gravity. As hard to endure as his physical state was his fury against himself. His condemnation to death during the war had been the result of his having willingly assumed his responsibilities as an Italian citizen, deliberately chosen resistance. But this second condemnation, possibly to a vegetable, living death was, he thought, the result of nothing but his own heedlessness. Why had he not heeded the warning given him two years earlier at Ischia? Why had he continued living at top speed? Why had he smoked pack after pack of the cigarettes that had damaged his strong heart? The answer to all this lay, precisely, in the immense vigor of a man who had ideal blood pressure and slept so easily that he would not have recognized a sleeping pill had he seen one.

Fortunately, Visconti cared more about *Ludwig* than about what seemed to him his own idiocy. Determination to complete this film helped him to co-operate in his treatment with a stoicism and discipline that were the admiration of everyone who nursed him. Retrospectively, he was to say that at this point the desire to work had been of greater assistance to him than the will to live. Also, Professor Krayenbühl's interests include music and modern painting. He understands not only the brain as an organism, but the artist's brain as a phenomenon. He had seen *Death in Venice* four times, with such enjoyment that, he told Visconti, he now shared his patient's determination that *Ludwig* should be finished.

Within a fortnight of his arrival in Zurich, Visconti began to feel better, was able to get up, to sit at a table and start tackling the piles of mail awaiting him. Next he began walking, with the help of a therapist. The therapy for hemiplegia employed by Professor Krayenbühl is the Bobath method, invented by Dr. Bobath, of the Cerebral Palsy Clinic in London. This form of re-education often produces stupendous results, and has only one drawback—it requires intelligence on the part of both therapist and patient. As he left his room for the first time, Visconti watched everyone he met in the hospital with the same warm interest as had originally impelled him to make films of which "man would be the center," and to say: "A man's most humble gestures, his way of walking, his hesi-

239

tations, his smallest impulses, suffice to confer vibration and poetry on the objects around him. The weight of a human presence is the only *thing* that really fills a film frame. The film's atmosphere is created by human beings, by their living presence, by the passions that agitate them, and acquire veracity by being thrown into relief in this context. When man is absent from the luminous rectangle, everything there takes on an inanimate aspect."

There were many Italian immigrants at the Zurich hospital, and, when they heard Visconti was there, they all wanted to see him. So did the relatives who came to visit them, often suffering themselves from the fatigue of long uncomfortable journeys from the deep south. But many of the immigrants had no visitors, and it was this that struck Visconti, surrounded as he himself was by loving friends and relatives, and with Enrico Medioli acting as an extra nurse-cum-secretary. "It must be terrible to be abandoned in the hospital," Visconti said, and his reaction provides a clue to his political beliefs. These had no connection with envy or egalitarianism, and did not preclude a profound belief in God—"without which," he said, "life would make no sense." But he did belong among those, listed by Keats in *Hyperion*, "to whom the miseries of the world are misery and will not let them rest"—and, although he prided himself on his logic and reason, his reactions to injustice had the immediacy of an animal-loving child's toward vivisection.

As his health improved, Visconti began thinking of what he meant to do next. This revived his anger against himself. For no matter what he might say, out of pure contradictoriness, to the long-suffering Medioli, he was well aware that crowd scenes might never again be within his reach: the beach and fishing fleet scenes in *The Earth Quakes*, the battle scenes in *Senso*, the boxing match in *Rocco and His Brothers*, the battle scenes and the ball in *The Leopard*, the night of the long knives in *The Damned*, the coronation of *Ludwig* and the soldiers' torchlit search for the King's body. Nevertheless, he still had moments when he was determined to film Thomas Mann's *The Magic Mountain*, regardless of the fact that it would indeed require magic to keep his heart beating at Davos, 5,118 feet up a mountain. What made it particularly difficult for him to relinquish this project was that his understanding of *The Magic Mountain* had been deepened by his personal experience of invalid life in a Swiss clinic. He was impressed, too, by the fact that Thomas Mann had had a stroke in Zurich and died there—perhaps, thought Visconti, in the room he himself now occupied. He remembered hearing that Thomas Mann's last words, to his wife, had been to ask her to put his book and spectacles within reach.

Now and again Visconti would drop his plans to film *The Magic Mountain* in favor of a strange novel, *The Holy Sinner,* published by Thomas Mann in 1951. In his last years Thomas Mann thought a great deal about German myths and legends, and *The Holy Sinner* is based on a poem by a medieval poet, Hartmann von Aue. Visconti was fascinated by the juxtaposition of myths in this story, and by the picture of medieval Rome, which would—as Medioli refrained from pointing out—mean Visconti's having to direct vast medieval crowds.

On one occasion, however, in answer to Medioli's question as to what kind of film he would make if suddenly offered unlimited money and resources, Visconti promptly said that he would make an *intimiste* film —two characters only, and all the action in one room. This piece of contrariness had the constructive effect of reminding both Medioli and Visconti himself of a film they had planned to make after reading *Scene di Conversazione* (1970) by Mario Praz, a brilliant Italian writer, scholar, and art critic, famous in America and England for *The Romantic Agony,* which Edmund Wilson described as "one of the most truly original as well as one of the most fascinating works of our time." In art history, "conversation pieces" are pictures, of a kind particularly popular in the eighteenth century, that show a group of people, usually a family, in a domestic or landscape setting, engaged either in conversation or in "social activity of a not very vigorous character." As first planned, this film was to have only half a dozen characters and be set entirely in two Roman apartments.

After six weeks in Zurich, Visconti could walk with a cane. So he prepared to return to Italy and work. Film technicians were already busy at his sister Ida's house—their childhood holiday home at Cernobbio, on Lake Como—turning their grandmother's stables into a cutting and projection room so that he could edit *Ludwig* there. Krayenbühl approved this hunger for work. He thought Visconti had made "a remarkable, a splendid recovery, in which will power had played a far from negligible part," and that the work he loved was exactly what he needed.

Down in Cernobbio, *Ludwig* was not the only task awaiting Visconti. A mountain of mail included letters about the villa he had bought at Castel Gandolfo, in the Alban hills, outside Rome, to replace his house in the Via Salaria, which he had sold, because it was too big, and lacked the elevators now essential to him. While this villa was being readied, an apartment was found for him in Rome. He planned to work there on staging Wagner's tetralogy for La Scala, since his doctors insisted that he must do this without going to Milan.

Although alarmed by so much activity, Medioli and Suso thought that

241

at least it would quench Visconti's impatience. But not at all. Every now and again he let his glasses slide down his nose, looked sharply over the top of them, and said, "Well? *Conversation Piece?* Have you written anything yet?" Less than two months after being "struck by lightning," Visconti was back at work.

Twenty-six

Stendhal once said that if life ceased to be a search it became nothing. Visconti thought this, too, and put all his energy into the search for health with which to resume work. A Swedish physiotherapist, Christina, accompanied him to Cernobbio, where, as in Zurich, his day began with painful exercises into which he flung himself with the zest of a boxer at the punching bag or a dancer at the barre. Christina was "gentle but exacting," he said approvingly. Walks in the beautiful lakeside garden helped him morally as well as physically, not only on account of the flowers—Visconti loved flowers and always lavished them upon his friends, his houses, his stage and screen productions—but also because he could not remember a time when this garden was not part of his life.

Artists often anticipate in their work emotions that they will experience personally only years later. In 1965, when Visconti called his eighth full-length film *Vaghe stelle dell'orsa*, he had long loved the Leopardi poem from which this title came; but after a stroke had traced a before and after frontier line across the map of his life, he was more viscerally moved by Leopardi's lines:

> There is no object here that meets my sense
> Which does not bring some image back again,
> Or raise some sweet remembrance.

Visconti's remembrances in this garden included the voices of his mother and father, echoing down to him from childhood days when the world was still all before him and providence his guide. Here he could go through the looking glass into the past, could walk along paths he had taken as a child, among trees, flowers, fruit almost as familiar to him as his mother's face. Reopening the books he read here as a boy, he heard echoes of the seemingly endless conversations, now ended, that he had shared with his brothers and sisters in days made to seem more remote than they really are by the world wars that stand between them and us like great walls topped with barbed wire. Everything about Cernobbio revivified his sense of continuity, and he was able to finish his work on *Ludwig* as planned. There is something uncanny, as well as moving, in the picture of Visconti watching the doom-haunted Ludwig's sleigh horses leap in incorporeal slow-motion beauty among the ghosts of horses he himself had loved as a child.

It seemed miraculous that he could accomplish exacting intellectual work so soon after leaving Zurich, but he was helped by the fact that he had always been a self-disciplined editor of his own work. Already, in the early stages of *Ludwig,* he had cut a dozen episodes he would like to have included. Among these were a scene in which Ludwig's Cabinet Secretary found Wagner in Stuttgart and presented him with Ludwig's invitation and the gift of a ruby ring; a scene in which Ludwig, bewitched by his cousin Elisabeth, listened to a private performance of *Tristan and Isolde;* the Queen Mother's reception into the Roman Catholic church; Wagner's death in Venice, three years before Ludwig's own death; a scene in which Wagner's coffin traversed Munich's torchlit railroad station, while an army of mourners listened to Beethoven's *Eroica* funeral march and the Siegfried funeral march from *Götterdämmerung.* Visconti also cut the scene in which Elisabeth, hearing of Ludwig's death, cried out, "They've killed him! Traitors! Assassins!" Elisabeth did indeed say this. She also denied that Ludwig had been mad, and for the remaining twelve years of her life she always kept by her a photograph of her cousin's death mask.

But in no part of his editing did Visconti show more restraint than in the finale. For despite the many variations on the theory that Ludwig had strangled the doctor, then either committed suicide or suffered a heart attack, Visconti was himself convinced that Ludwig had been murdered. At the time of the King's death, there had been talk of a bullet hole in his jacket—removed and spirited away, with the rest of his clothes, immediately after Ludwig's body was taken from the lake. But Visconti never deliberately portrayed possibilities as facts and, in this case, he knew that if a solution to the enigma still existed, it must be buried in royal archives, themselves probably scattered by war.

He cut, therefore, the finale in which an old servant at Schloss Berg was to have told a young one that he knew the King had been murdered because he had seen the jacket—"They fired at the heart. One shot was enough, but the King's body wasn't in the water long enough to soak out the singeing of his jacket. . . . We will never know what happened.

There was only one witness—the assassin. And you can be sure he'll take the secret to his grave. The only evidence against him is this little hole . . . that lets a glimmer of the truth through." Without this scene Visconti thought it pointless to include, as he originally intended, a glimpse of Ludwig's tomb, virtually lost in the crypt of the Jesuit Church of St. Michael in Munich. The day Visconti had gone there, the key to the crypt proved hard to find and the neglected tomb, ermined with dust, suggested to him nothing so much as "a trunk abandoned in the unclaimed luggage department of a railway station." So Visconti let the end of his film remain an open question, with torches flaring to and fro in the rain-swept night as soldiers hunt for Ludwig and find only his drowned body, together with that of Gudden, the alienist hoist with his own petard.

Ludwig was to prove successful with both public and critics, many of whom singled out Visconti's "mediumlike" gift for "summoning up the past." A telegram of congratulations from the Italian President, Giovanni Leone, offered a token of national recognition.

While Visconti was putting the finishing touches to *Ludwig,* a Roman apartment was being prepared for him by his sister Uberta in the Via Fleming, a quiet leafy residential street named after the Scotsman who discovered penicillin. The apartment was on the top floor in the same building as his sister's own apartment, and Visconti called it his "attic," in allusion to the fascination that attics exerted over his childhood. From it he had a stupendous view over Rome, with the dome of St Peter's on the horizon. Inadequate as a home for Visconti's animals—his sheepdog, spaniel, mongrel, and cat—the Via Fleming apartment was intended only as a waiting room until his Castel Gandolfo villa would be ready.

But belongings from the Via Salaria made the new apartment recognizably his own. These ranged from white Valentino curtains to the books that invaded any room occupied by Visconti for more than twenty-four hours. Books, bibelots, art objects, Lalique glass, theater posters, photographs of actors and actresses, were all surrounded by flowers. His sister kept him supplied with armfuls of these from the nearby flower market. They were such a pleasure to him that, after his death, nothing in Visconti's last attic seemed more shocking than the emptiness of the flower vases scattered all around.

In Rome, Visconti and his physiotherapist continued to collaborate so well that he was soon able to take walks, with a cane, in the Roman Campagna. Rome's power to keep history alive, like Jonah inside the whale, is so potent that out in the Campagna the early Christians in the catacombs seem almost as near as the victims in the Ardeatine Caves.

245

Aware that his being able to walk there in 1972 was miraculous, Visconti remembered the days, back in 1944, that he spent in prison under sentence of death. At that time, he had heard that when the bodies were taken from the Ardeatine Caves for burial, the smell of jasmine flowers was for a moment stronger than that of death.

In November 1972, Visconti had his sixty-sixth birthday. Professor Krayenbühl, who paid a Christmas visit to Rome, was delighted with his progress and said that at this rate there should be no ill effects upon Visconti's work. This reassurance from a contemporary at the summit of his own profession was to prove particularly valuable to Visconti in the spring when, immediately after his return to the theater, a totally unnecessary strain was imposed upon him.

For his first stage production after his illness, Visconti had chosen *Old Times,* the fourth full-length play by British dramatist Harold Pinter. An extremely talented writer, obsessed by the problem of communication, Pinter was in 1962 cited in Martin Esslin's book *The Theatre of the Absurd* as one of the group of dramatists, headed by the Irish Samuel Beckett and Roumanian Eugene Ionesco, who share the belief that human life is essentially meaningless and human beings cannot communicate with each other—a puzzling definition, since it seems unlikely that anyone who really believes there is no communication would take the trouble to write a play merely to communicate this therefore incommunicable fact. Visconti, who believed precisely the opposite, was nevertheless absorbed by *Old Times'* poetic use of tautology to explore emotions camouflaged by incoherence.

Visconti's talk in Zurich of making a film with "only two characters and one set" seemed less of a boutade now that he was directing a play with only three characters and two sets, a sitting room and a bedroom. *Old Times'* three characters, all in their early forties, are a husband and wife, Kate and Deeley, and Kate's girlhood friend Anna. When the play opens, in a converted farmhouse in England, Kate and Deeley are discussing the forthcoming visit of Anna, who now lives in Italy. Kate has not seen her for twenty years, and Deeley has never met her. Once Anna arrives, the play becomes a verbal fight between Anna and Deeley over Kate, who at one point says they both talk about her as if she were dead.

In view of the play's verbal boxing matches, Visconti decided to produce *Old Times* in the round. Some of the Teatro Argentina's orchestra seats were removed to make way for a platform. The design for this platform, with its white brickwork and pastel-colored couch beds, was inspired by a picture by Balthus (Balthazar Klossowski), a French painter of Polish extraction, who had become a part of Roman life, and whose

246

work and integrity Visconti admired. Born into a family of artists, Balthus spent part of his childhood in Switzerland, where his desire to paint was encouraged by a family friend, the poet Rainer Maria Rilke. Although internationally appreciated—Cyril Connolly prefaced the catalogue to his 1949 London exhibition, and Albert Camus the one for his 1952 New York show—Balthus belonged to no group, followed no fashion, and was living an isolated life of painting, in the French countryside, when André Malraux, then Minister of Cultural Affairs, appointed him head of the Villa Medici, the French Academy in Rome. Since Balthus's work has ambiguous and obsessional aspects, combined with exquisite coloring and lucidity, Visconti thought it particularly appropriate to Pinter's play.

Rehearsals began in Visconti's apartment and were well advanced when they moved to the theater in April. It was four years since Visconti last produced a play, and he had a glorious sense of homecoming. Not for a second did it occur to him that a cloud considerably larger than a man's hand was advancing on his and his actors' horizon.

Pinter's Italian agent had supplied a translation of *Old Times* that Visconti considered inadequate, and therefore unfair to play and author. In particular, he thought, this translation lagged—a dangerous drawback in a play punctuated by pauses that should be as significant as those in music. So he used another version, by Gerardo Guerrieri, a fellow director who had previously translated O'Neill, Thornton Wilder, and Tennessee Williams, all extremely well. The press flocked to the dress rehearsal on May 3, and only after the first public performance had been given did Pinter's agent obtain an injunction forbidding the continuation of the play. Scandal and indignation were enormous in Rome, and the incident was exploited by a group of the MSI (the neo-Fascist party). They managed to get a question asked in parliament about "the deformation" of *Old Times*—and, although they themselves were undoubtedly expert at deforming the past, their support cannot have been agreeable to Pinter, who had often, as a boy, opposed Oswald Mosley's ridiculous but brutal British fascists in London's East End. Finally Visconti modified the production, and the play continued its run. The incident was deplorable—several critics, impressed by Visconti's production and horrified by the possible effect on his health of all this, spoke of "mental cruelty"—but Visconti reacted with dignity and learned from it something he would turn to use in the scenario of his next film.

Certainly it aroused no bitterness in him about the theater, for when asked that summer by the International Theater Institute for a message for World Theater Day 1973, Visconti's reply included these words:

247

Thinking of the theater's history in this century, all over the world, it seems to me that what has happened—apart from the appearance of new theories, forms of creativity, and technology—is that the theater has been forced, by a phase when it seemed pushed into the background and completely over-shadowed by the powerful mass media, to question its own existence and deepest values. The result of this questioning has been the rediscovery of the theater's position as a place where human values and relationships dominate.

Even the theater's weaknesses, its fragility and irreversibility, the variable-ness of stage performances and the deterioration that threatens them from the very first moment the curtain rises—the vulnerability that infuriates and distresses me when I compare it with the definite final versions of films—all this gives the theater its essentially human dimensions. Here I agree with Camus. . . .

Today the mass media, with which the theater used mistakenly to think it needed to compete, have largely taken over light entertainment, amusement, and other forms of escapism. Far from being a detriment to the theater, this has in fact enriched it. Freed from trivial obligations and forced to tackle subjects of vital importance, today's theater is no longer in any danger of becoming marginal but stands firmly at the very center of our collective ex-perience.

Among the favorite pictures Visconti took to the Via Fleming was one showing Icarus plummeting into the sea. This is by Galileo Chini, a Tuscan painter who was a friend of Puccini's and designed the scenery for the first performance of *Manon Lescaut*—an opera that Visconti was to stage for the 1973 Spoleto Festival.

One of the most popular imaginary characters, Manon Lescaut made her first appearance in 1731, in the seventh volume of *Memoirs of a Man of Quality Now Retired from the World* by a former Benedictine monk who was to become famous as the Abbé Prévost. Manon's temperament is summed up by the Victorian chorus, "I am so fond of pleasure that I cannot be a nun." At sixteen she is snatched from incarceration in a convent by the seventeen-year-old Chevalier des Grieux, whom she loves and betrays. Honor and fidelity are as alien to her as to a kitten, but the Abbé Prévost nevertheless made her so alive and seductive that, for over two hundred years, streams of tears have been shed over her sad fate.

Of the many dramatizations of Manon Lescaut's story, Visconti pre-ferred Puccini's opera, with its emphasis on the flight motif: from the very first moment, in Amiens, when the youthful Des Grieux sees Manon getting down from a stagecoach, until the very last moment, in New Orleans, when she dies in his arms, the star-crossed lovers spend more time fleeing the troubles provoked by their love than on love itself. In Visconti's production this gave their love scenes a particular intensity and brilliance. In the second act, when Manon, by this time mistress of the elderly Geronte, whose wealth she could not resist, decides to run away with Des Grieux, Visconti placed the delinquent lovers in an alcove occupied by a bed piled with pale, fragile, lacy cushions, half hidden by heavy drapes of embroidered curtains. Delicacy of color and softness of outline suggested that Manon and Des Grieux were about to embark for Watteau's Cythera; so when they slipped away from these exquisitely yielding surfaces, on which they could gain no foothold, it was as if Cythera itself rejected them. The contrast between their surroundings and their despair, between the purity and the perversity both present in their emotions, harmonized perfectly with Puccini's drumrolling emphasis of the moment when eighteenth-century frivolity began to yield to the romanticism just ahead.

The scenery was designed by Lila De Nobili and E. Carcano, the costumes by Tosi and Gabriella Pescucci, and working with them was as satisfactory for Visconti as working with the singers, and with the genial Thomas Schippers, a great friend of his. Visconti had particularly admired Schippers's conducting of Cherubini's *Medea* at La Scala on the famous occasion when Callas shook her fist at a hostile gallery to such effect that those who came to hiss remained to cheer her.

So successful was this *Manon Lescaut* that it was repeated at Spoleto the following year, when William Weaver wrote in the *International Herald Tribune* (July 2, 1974):

Although the Festival of Two Worlds continues for another week, the past few days can be considered its climax. A series of premieres has presented the remainder of Spoleto's major productions for this year.

Actually, the greatest success was a production revived from last year: Puccini's *Manon Lescaut*, thrillingly conducted by Thomas Schippers and superbly staged by Luchino Visconti.

On occasions such as this, Visconti made meticulous timetables for himself, planning the drive from Rome to wherever he was going so as to arrive at least half an hour before other people and be in his place, hedged in by friends, before the rest of the audience arrived. He who had directed so many tempestuous plays, films, operas, now stage-managed his own physical handicap with dignity and common sense, good manners always dominant. After this masterly return to opera, Visconti set to work, with Medioli and Suso, on the scenario of *Gruppo di famiglia in un interno* (*Conversation Piece*).

These savage acts are not acts that we can accept, encourage, and imitate. In a word, we ought to be inspired and guided by love for all men. Hate does not produce love, one cannot renovate the world through hate; and revolution inspired by hate will either fail completely or lead to a new form of oppression.

"A Little Theory," an article written in 1892 by Enrico Malatesta, an anarchist wanted by the police. Quoted, in an article on terrorism by Paolo Spriano in *Il Giorno*, March 4, 1978

Twenty-seven

Conversation Piece was, as Suso Cecchi D'Amico called it, "a small conspiracy of friendship." Feeling that only work could save him, but knowing producers might hesitate now to gamble on Visconti's health, his closest friends gathered around him in a creative bodyguard.

Enrico Medioli and Suso collaborated with Visconti on the scenario. It was a straightforward contemporary story: a well-off American scientist, art critic, and scholar in his sixties—called only "the professor" throughout the film—is enjoying his retirement in a Roman palace inherited from his Italian mother. His seclusion is interrupted by a jet-set family determined to rent an apartment from him. Contact between the two dissimilar worlds ends in tragedy. Even before the scenario was completed, Burt Lancaster, Silvana Mangano, and Helmut Berger were refusing all other offers in order to be free the moment a producer was found. This certainly encouraged a new producer, Rusconi, to come forward with an offer to back not only this but also "as many more Visconti films as possible."

Since the professor lives in a baroque palace in the heart of Rome, the sets required craftsmanship of a rare kind. His apartment, full of books and objects of art, its walls hung with his collection of conversation pieces, had to suggest a lair fit for Bernard Berenson. The attic apartment coveted by the intruders had to be shown first empty, then being renovated, and finally in the ice-cream and traffic-lights colors of a smart modern interior. The views from the terrace of the roofs of Rome required stuccowork that could be done only by sculptors expert at modeling in baroque style. All this work was taken in hand by Mario Garbuglia, a scenographer equally at home on stage or film set. He had worked with Visconti in the theater, made his cinema debut with the sets of *White Nights*, contributed to *Rocco and His Brothers*, *The Leop-*

ard, and *The Outsider*, and, in the spring of 1971, accompanied Visconti to France to choose locations for the Proust film. Garbuglia took great pride in his craftsmen, knowing that, thanks to the industrialization of the cinema, their skills would soon be as irrevocably part of the past as those of the professional magicians and automaton makers with whom cinema pioneers like George Méliès started their careers.

On April 8, 1974—less than two years after his stroke, and having already, since then, directed a play and staged an opera—Visconti was back on the set at Cinecittà. There is always an atmosphere of excitement on the first day of shooting a film, but when Visconti was the director everyone involved felt a special exhilaration, a sense of being part of a life-enhancing enterprise. On this occasion the excitement was graver than usual and had a poignant element. When Visconti walked onto the set he appeared to be using his cane less to support himself than to make the ground keep its distance. He had the fierce concentration of a dancer taught young that the floor is his enemy, to be pushed away, and kept away as long as possible. Among the messages awaiting him was a mass of roses from Fellini: "Mio caro amico con commozione e gioia ti abbraccio. Andrà tutto benissimo vedrai! Evviva il cinema! tuo Federico" (My dear friend I embrace you with joy and emotion. All will go well you will see! Long live the cinema! your Federico).

In some respects Visconti thought of films as Stendhal thought of novels, as "a mirror walking along a main road," and *Conversation Piece* reflects contemporary violence. Ten days before Visconti's return to Cinecittà, terrorists threw a bomb into an anti-Fascist meeting in Brescia, killing eight people. Three weeks after the film was made, a bomb killed twelve people and wounded forty-eight in a train near San Benedetto Val di Sangro station. Since firearms had become almost as cheap and accessible as pocket cameras, this new violence threatened old and young, rich and poor, leftists, rightists, centrists, cranks, and, above all, people who had the misfortune to work or shop "where the action was."

The film begins with the throb of a cardiac monitor at the professor's bedside. This fades into the professor's study, where two art dealers are showing him a conversation piece. Their discussion is watched by a woman sitting across the room. She is in her early forties, her striking good looks underlined by fashion-model clothes. The professor supposes she came with the art dealers. They assume she is part of the professor's household. In fact, Marchesa Bianca Brumonti is there because she wants to rent the professor's attic apartment. She happened to share the elevator with the art dealers, so she followed them in. When she fails to follow them out—after he has regretfully refused the conversation piece as too expensive—the professor is taken aback, and the first words they exchange foreshadow the misunderstandings ahead.

Out comes Bianca with her plan to rent the professor's attic apartment. She has been assured that it *is* empty—by the caretaker "*and* by Erminia."

The brash way in which Bianca names his housekeeper astounds the professor. It is quite a while since he has had to practice self-defense. A childless man whose marriage went awry years ago, he abandoned his career in America after deciding that "science cannot be neutral, technology is likelier to enslave than liberate, and the price of progress is destruction." Since then he has created for himself an ivory tower of art in which he lives with his elderly housekeeper, who spoils him with deference and formality. He is not misanthropic, merely withdrawn and cautious, in once-bitten-twice-shy style.

One of the most interesting aspects of the professor is the manner in which he reveals his American qualities. This is not due merely to the part being played by Burt Lancaster, but also to the fact that although Visconti was profoundly Italian, extremely European, he was also strongly aware of America and American values. This awareness had been increased by his participation in Spoleto's annual Italo-American Festival of Two Worlds. So instead of making the professor stereotypically naïve, Visconti gave him the kind of stalwart intellectual decency so common among American scholars and artists who went to Italy in the nineteenth centry—men like Nathaniel Hawthorne, William Whetmore Story, William Dean Howells.

Against Bianca's onslaught it is useless for the professor to say he needs the attic for his overflow of books. She immediately advises him to arrange his books better right here in his own apartment. The professor tries to explain that, quite apart from his books, he does not want strangers living overhead. Treating this as irrelevant, Bianca explains, as if to a backward child, that she *needs* this apartment for her eighteen-year-old daughter, Lietta, who is setting up house with her fiancé, Stefano, "so they can see whether marriage is likely to work out in their case." At this point Lietta herself arrives, a pretty, flighty girl in loden coat and ankle-length muffler—and the professor finds himself accompanying mother and daughter to the attic apartment, where piles of books and isolated pieces of furniture lie amid a tideless sea of dust.

Bianca opens the shutters and steps out onto the terrace. There are flower tubs and boxes and, along the broad top of the balustrade, large two-headed baroque marble busts. From there Bianca sees a superb Roman roofscape. Nacreous cupolas rise above a sea of ocher, bronze, chestnut, cinnamon, and faded-apricot tiles. Cats dart to and fro like feline fish among coralline rooftop plants, and here and there pennons of washing dance in the sunlight. "Perfect! Bianca, you're a genius," says Lietta's fiancé, Stefano, a somberly supercilious boy, who has just entered. When Konrad, a young German wearing a Nureyev-style peaked cap and leather jacket, joins them, it becomes clear this is a family of jet-set cuckoos, determined to grab the best nest available. At first the professor's good manners yield automatically to the cuckoos' bad ones, so he unwillingly but irrevocably becomes involved with them. Selfish, avid, and trivial as they are, they have the power to make him feel guilty. He wonders whether his own generation's failure "to create a balance between politics and morality" is partly responsible for their indifference to everything but having a good time.

Proof that the intruders have taken over upstairs is presently furnished by plaster and water showing down below, to the terror of Erminia. The professor snatches a flashlight and goes upstairs. In the attic he finds Konrad, sleeping on a camp bed. The professor tells him this is unpardonable, it's a wonder the place is still standing, they must be mad.

"I can do what I like in my own home," says Konrad. The deed of sale is to be made out in his, Konrad's, name. There was never, says the horrified professor, any question of a deed of sale, or of anything except a year's lease, nonrenewable. Taut with suspicion, Konrad asks if he may telephone; he accompanies the professor downstairs, then settles to the telephone calls that are one of the intruders' favorite hobbies—calls that parody the "white telephone" films of the thirties. Beside herself with fury, Bianca can be heard not only by Konrad but also by the professor. She has clearly been taking for granted that she would steamroll the professor into selling her the attic, and now Konrad, by his premature disclosure, has ruined her plans.

The professor is horrified by her tone, which Konrad shrugs off with "the richer they are, the worse they get." As he prepares to leave, he suddenly notices a conversation piece hanging by the telephone. "Isn't that an Arthur Devis?"

Surprised that Konrad has heard of Arthur Devis, an eighteenth-century English artist, the professor, his manner as discreet as that of a bird watcher, asks if Konrad is interested in painting. Not really, says Konrad, and then, providing a superb example of bathos, adds, "I know a picture of his backward, because it hangs by the telephone of friends of mine."

Surely, the professor says, you must have studied art. Yes, in Berlin, at the university. Why didn't he go on with it? "It was a difficult time," says Konrad, "1968. I hurled myself into the student movement, had to get out to escape the police—and here I am, landed *with people like this.*"

It was typical of Visconti's acumen that he made his rebellious student a German. For the German student revolts of the sixties, polarized later by the Baader-Meinhof terrorists, were far fiercer, physically and ideologically, than May 1968 in Paris, although the latter, thanks to accretions of folklore, has gained artistic priority as the very prototype of modern student rebellion.

Konrad and the professor become aware that communication between them is possible. Their absorption in art contains the seeds of a personal relationship that, although denied time to develop, is present throughout the rest of the film. So although the professor is disturbed, exasperated, at times appalled by the intruders, a part of him is grateful for this Indian summer of the heart.

In Konrad, Helmut Berger had a part as exciting as that of Ludwig. Neither Konrad's present existence in Rome, nor his past in Berlin, is stereotyped. His physical feeling for Bianca is genuine, but so is his loathing of his position as her social and financial inferior. In order to get money without asking Bianca, he is ready for squalid deals over Etruscan vases or murderous ones involving drugs. Yet his love-hate attitude toward the rich is, at moments, as romantic as that of Scott Fitzgerald's Gatsby.

Visconti had already shot a quarter of the film when Liliana Cavani paid him a visit on the set to thank him for supporting her fight against the magistrates who intended to sequestrate her new film, *The Night Porter.* One of the most brilliant women film directors, Cavani never chooses facility. This was one of the reasons Visconti admired her work. *The Night Porter,* which told the story of an obsessive sexual relationship between a former SS officer and a former concentration-camp victim, was to be virulently attacked, particularly by people who spent the war in safety. Yet much of the material for *The Night Porter* had been discovered by Cavani while she was doing research for *History of the Third Reich* (1962), commissioned by Italian television.

Everyone working on *Conversation Piece* was indignant at the sequestration of *The Night Porter,* and a telegram was sent expressing the entire company's "complete adhesion to and solidarity with" the protest strike to be observed by the film profession. After this *The Night Porter* was released. Barely two years later, so mysterious are the ways of fashion and censorship, the very same people who had reviled Liliana Cavani were to extol Lina Wertmuller, another gifted Italian woman director, for her film *Pasqualino Settebellezze* (*Seven Beauties*), a death-house comedy with a hero ready to shoot fellow prisoners and fornicate with the female camp commander to insure his personal survival.

Liliana Cavani watched the shooting of the scene in which the professor's lethal lodgers return after a month's unexplained absence. Lietta, Stefano, and Konrad come flying to the professor, sure of their welcome, unaware anything is wrong, and bringing him as a "surprise" an Indian bird that keeps repeating "Thank you, old man." During their visit, the restlessly roaming Konrad accidentally opens the camouflaged door of a secret room behind the professor's bookshelves.

The professor quietly explains that this room was built by his Italian mother when she was trapped in Rome by the outbreak of war. She used it to hide people on the run, anti-Fascists, partisans, Jews. The professor knows very little about his mother's life in those days. She died before the war ended.

That night the professor is reading in bed when he hears a noise upstairs. As he investigates two youths tear past. Running up to the attic, he finds Konrad on the floor, so weak from loss of blood that the professor has almost to carry him downstairs. He puts him to bed in the secret room and wants to call the police. But Konrad insists he did not recognize his assailants, and says that "the police have more than enough to do with their daily dose of murders, rapes, strikes, demonstrations." The professor insists on cleaning the bloodstains off the stairs himself. There is a curious parallel between the professor kneeling on the staircase with bucket and cloth, mopping up the blood shed by terrorists, and the professor in his study tending his pictures with rags and varnish.

Opening up his mother's secret room and using it, as she did, to hide someone in trouble has turned the professor's thoughts to the past. Only half awake after his agitating night, he sees his study as it was when he entered it for the first time, over half a century ago, as a small child holding his mother's hand. It is full of flowers, and the bookshelves that hide the entrance to the secret room have vanished. The conversation pieces have gone, too, and the pictures on the walls include two then very modern ones, a Morandi and a Scipione, and a portrait of the professor's mother. As the professor gazes at this he hears servants' voices. A beautiful young woman enters the room. At last, says a maid, our little American has arrived. "Say something," says the professor's mother, bending to an invisible child. "Greet Luisa. Don't you like my home?"

The portrait of the professor's mother was copied from one of Visconti's own mother. The part was played by Dominique Sanda, who was already beginning to be called the modern Garbo. She had been internationally admired for her performances in Bertolucci's *The Conformist* and De Sica's *The Garden of the Finzi-Continis*. She made this brief appearance in *Conversation Piece* as an act of affectionate homage to Visconti. Similarly, Claudia Cardinale made an appearance as the professor's wife —her way of giving thanks for Visconti's recovery.

Not until the next evening, when the professor is busy restoring a picture, does he hear the sound of the shower in Konrad's bathroom. Sixteen hours of sleep have restored Konrad and, when he emerges into the professor's room, he admits that he lied about not recognizing his assailants. "I never doubted it," says the professor drily. But as the professor lies in bed later, he hears music in his study. Opening the door, he finds Lietta, Stefano, and Konrad dancing naked. Far from making any attempt at fashionable pornography disguised as philosophy, Visconti directed this scene with a discretion and sophistication that, by leaving something to the audience's imagination, increased its impact. The comely young trio in the half light has something of the mysterious charm of pleasure-seeking Etruscan figures. As they move dreamily in time with the music, wreaths of smoke from their shared cigarette increase the hallucinatory atmosphere. Lietta, turning affectionately to the professor, says that they'll soon be off, all this is just a game, quite harmless, really; wasn't he just like them when he was young?

The professor's regard for truth forces him to say, "No. Absolutely not." "What a shame," says Lietta artlessly. "You missed something. Still you must have enjoyed yourself—you were rich and handsome. What *did* you do?" "I studied," says the professor slowly, as if struggling to understand himself. "I traveled, fought in the war, married. . . . And when at last I had time to look around, I found myself surrounded by people I couldn't understand." Burt Lancaster's exquisitely controlled bewilderment—suggesting less *King Lear* than Turgenev's *Fathers and Sons*—gave to the relationship between young and old a depth and gravity far removed from smart aphorisms about the generation gap.

The attic apartment is shown ready for its new tenants. It is aggressively modern: outsize couches, huge cushions, Indian and Thai objects that suggest an art gallery. Explosions of violent colors punctuate the chic black and white. Lietta invites the professor to a housewarming—"no one but the family, a little music, a little dancing, and talking." The professor compromises by inviting them to dinner the next day. And so we see Lietta, Stefano, and Konrad, formally dressed in evening clothes, seated around the professor's table, a family dinner party at last. The conversation is a trifle stiff, as if the young people are struggling to button it, too, into evening dress. When Stefano comments on this, Lietta says it's because everyone's on tenterhooks; wherever one goes nowadays there's a tragic atmosphere. From this they go on to talk of the professor's "peaceful family of conversation pieces."

"The old are strange animals," says the professor, "irritable, intolerant . . . afraid sometimes of the solitude they've deliberately created for themselves—the solitude they will fight for if it's threatened. It was during one of those moments of fear that I let you in."

The festive dinner party ends in violence. Konrad accuses Bianca's husband—just gone to Madrid—of belonging to a group that has been caught planning the assassination of Communist deputies and ministers in preparation for a coup d'état. Stefano in turn accuses Konrad of having betrayed the conspirators to the police—as indeed he had. As the two start to fight, the professor separates them, and is admonished by Konrad: "Keep out of it, keep among your pictures of the dead—they are the only people safe from the violence these clowns want to unleash."

Here Visconti drew on melodramatic facts that spoke for themselves. In December 1970, a real coup d'état was prepared by Prince Junio Valerio Borghese, a wartime hero, who joined the neo-Fascist MSI party, and was known as the Black Prince. This plot was foiled by the weather, but two months later the Black Prince fled to Franco's Spain. He was there when *Conversation Piece* was being made, and died in Spain six weeks after the completion of the film.

The morning after the party, an explosion is heard in the room upstairs. Before that, the professor had received a cryptic note: "I hope I am wrong, but I don't think we shall see each other again." When he rushes upstairs, he finds Konrad's dead body. As he tries to lift it, the porter, who heard the noise and has followed him, cries out: "Don't touch him. Wait till the police come. . . ."

The year after Visconti shot this scene, which he thought typical of our times, a nineteen-year-old Milanese student, Sergio Ramelli, died in a hospital, after six weeks of agony, as the result of being beaten with iron bars by schoolfellows who disapproved of an essay he had written in class. Konrad's death was indeed a typically contemporary way for golden lads and girls to come to dust.

"Wait till the police arrive": the porter's voice fades into that of a doctor saying "Breathe slowly." The professor is regaining consciousness after a heart attack. The sound we hear is that of the cardiac monitor with which the film began. The sight of the professor alone, with his own death, completes this portrait of an artist as an old man.

When *Conversation Piece* was finished, on July 15, 1974, all those who had worked on it gathered on the set to drink Visconti's health. To Suso

Cecchi D'Amico, Enrico Medioli, Burt Lancaster, Silvana Mangano, and Helmut Berger, the making of no other film had given deeper satisfaction. Visconti, too, was happy, and grateful. Despite his physical handicaps, his mind still had all its wonted fires, and, having managed this, he hoped to accomplish more.

Twenty-eight

Once in his new apartment in Rome, Visconti watched television with more interest than ever, and with the particular objectivity that age and illness can confer. Nowadays television seems to most viewers as natural a part of daily life as tap water—yet as late as 1962 television was described as "likely to cause a world-wide anthropological revolution." To Visconti, sitting very upright in front of the box, like an old lion gazing between the bars of his cage, television seemed as rich in possibilities as the cinema when he was a child in Milan, bewitched by *The Perils of Pauline*.

But one difference struck him. In a cinema, no matter how small or shabby, the spectators are all swallowed up in the same vast-seeming darkness. Even the ill-mannered speak in whispers, candy is unwrapped stealthily, every face is ghostly in the dim light, and, apart from a few faces engaged in embracing other faces, all are concentrating on screen figures they have paid to see. The result is an atmosphere of mystery, unobtainable in domestic surroundings, where viewers are eating, drinking, telephoning, shouting comments, and able to change channels by pressing a button.

As Visconti brought to bear on television the power to dream constructively that he had devoted to theater, opera, and cinema, he was soon invited to direct four television productions, two in Italy, two in England.

For Italian television he was to produce, first, a Pirandello play, *Questa sera si recita a soggetto* (*Tonight We Improvise*). This is the third of Pirandello's trilogy of plays set in the world of the theater. Written in 1929 in a Berlin that, although still, artistically, the dynamic city of Toller, Kästner, Brückner, Horvath, and the young Brecht, was already politically overshadowed by Hitler's approach, *Tonight We Improvise* was first performed at Koenigsberg, in 1930. Pirandello had known Germany well—as a young man he spent two years studying philology at Bonn University—and Visconti intended to set *Tonight We Improvise* there in the period when it was written.

Visconti's second Italian television program was to be a reading of poems of Carlo Porta (1776–1821). One of the familiar figures of Visconti's childhood had been a statue of this poet on a tiny island in the Public Gardens in the center of Milan. This showed Porta, with a clever, humorous nose, voluminous cloak, tasseled boots, and his left forefinger marking his place in the book he held. Sixty years later Visconti remembered the pelicans that lingered beside the statue, "stamping their feet with a flumpy sound." In August 1943, Porta's statue had been bombed to bits, but in 1966 a new statue was unveiled in the Via Verziere, just around the corner from Toscanini's home. As so often in Italy, the unveiling was both a historic and a family affair, attended by the standard-bearers of Milan's six city gates wearing their regulation uniforms of fourteenth-century design. Several of Porta's characters were as popular in Italy as Sancho Panzo in Spain, and Visconti loved both them and their vanished Milan.

For British television, Visconti's first project was a film about Scott Fitzgerald's wife, Zelda. The extravagance of her character, near to that of Tennessee Williams's early heroines, fascinated him. He did not share the widespread view that Fitzgerald was ruined by his wife. Reading Zelda Fitzgerald's only novel, *Save Me the Waltz,* published in 1932, when she was thirty-two and had already spent two years in clinics, Visconti thought that there was truth in Fitzgerald's observation, "Possibly she would have been a genius if we had never met . . . she was a great original in her way with perhaps a more intense flame, at its highest, than I ever had." The second project was for a film about the composer Puccini's lifelong amorous friendship with an Englishwoman, Sybil Seligman, whom he met in London, just after the success of his opera *Madame Butterfly,* at the house of Francesco Paolo Tosti, singing master to the royal family and professor at the Royal Academy of Music, with whom Mrs. Seligman had studied singing. Sybil Seligman was a woman of great culture—D'Annunzio called her the "Sibyl of the North" —and, after passionate beginnings, her relationship with Puccini became a deep friendship throughout which she never failed to give him excellent advice about his career. Puccini had been an important figure in the lives of Visconti's parents, and in Visconti's own life. He was just eighteen when Puccini died of cancer in Brussels before he had time to complete his last opera, *Turandot*. It was finished, from Puccini's notes, by the Neapolitan composer Franco Alfano. Toscanini conducted *Turandot* for the first time on April 25, 1926, and well Visconti remembered the moment when Toscanini interrupted the performance and, turning to the audience, said, "Here the Maestro died."

Partial physical paralysis did not lessen Visconti's mental energy. He had to try to keep his thoughts from racing as they had during the making of *Ludwig*—about which he now admitted, "Ludwig nearly killed me. Germany was freezing, Rome was stifling, and everywhere there was so much to do that I couldn't take time to think, just kept going at top speed."

Vittorio de Sica, in particular, understood Visconti's longing to work. One of Italy's most beloved public figures, De Sica was himself too unwell to work just then. To him, too, workless days seemed "cold and empty." But, thanks to the devotion of his wife, children, friends, and doctors, De Sica did not know he was dying of cancer, and his concern on this occasion was all for Visconti. De Sica was curiously impressed to find his "Wagnerian, neo-Gothic, romantically creative" colleague absorbed in the work of Dürer, that strange half-Hungarian, half-German genius whose armored knight on horseback, confronted by Death and the Devil, wears on his unvisored face an expression that combines a distinct look of Visconti with a suggestion of Ignatius of Loyola in his military days. De Sica said afterward that he felt Visconti to be terribly lonely. Perhaps this was why he told Visconti that he himself had never been able to "communicate his feelings" completely in a film. Not even at the end of his career, when he was an acknowledged master, could he find a producer for a film of Flaubert's *Un Coeur simple* (*A Simple Heart*). "Are you crazy?" was the first producer's reaction to De Sica's proposal that he make what would probably have been a masterpiece.

All this Visconti understood only too well. The workmen in his own *Ossessione*, the fishermen in *La terra trema*, the Roman housewife in *Bellissima*, the immigrants in *Rocco and His Brothers* could all be cousins of De Sica's shoeshine boys and bicycle thieves, his workmen in search of jobs, young couples in search of homes, and elderly employees on starvation pensions searching to find a reason for staying alive. The most divisive line between people is not economic, social, historic, religious, political, temperamental, geographic, but the line between those who enjoy their work and those who do not. As De Sica said, "Happy is the man who gets pleasure and satisfaction from his work," and in this he and Visconti were alike. They were not to meet again. De Sica died at the American Hospital in Paris on November 13, 1974, the day his last film *Il viaggio* (*The Voyage*) was released in France. He was to make one more screen appearance the year after his death, in Ettore Scola's *C'eravamo tanti amati* (*We Loved Each Other So Much*). This is dedicated to De Sica, and near the end of it someone says, "The future's gone by without our even noticing it."

All the actors who had worked with Visconti surrounded him with affection, Romy Schneider and Alain Delon coming great distances to be with him. Especially welcome were visits from Romolo Valli, one of the finest actors in Italy and today artistic director of the Spoleto Festival. Asked recently about his new production of Pirandello's *Henry IV*, Valli said that over the years an actor's personal experience alters his interpretation of certain lines; for example, when, nowadays, he himself speaks Henry IV's words about "all those who are dead and gone," he "instinctively thinks of Luchino Visconti, Rina Morelli, and Nora Ricci" (another actor's child who often worked with Visconti). Valli added that when he recently played Molière's *Le Malade imaginaire* at Spoleto several people told him that, at moments, a sudden fixed intensity in his expression reminded them of Visconti during the last months of his life. This, Valli said, was undoubtedly the result of the hours he spent with Visconti during that period, full of concern, friendship, and memories of shared work.

For the moment Visconti's own future looked so much healthier that by Christmas of 1974, he began to think once more of his plan to film *The Magic Mountain*. He had got as far as discussing his adaptation of it with Thomas Mann's second son, the historian Golo Mann, and deciding that he wanted the leading parts of Hans Castorp and Madame Chauchat played by Helmut Berger and Charlotte Rampling, when he was asked to direct a film of D'Annunzio's *Il piacere* (*Pleasure*), a project that interested him. Then, the film rights of this proving unavailable, Rusconi Producers asked him to direct instead D'Annunzio's *L'innocente* (*The Intruder*). Suso and Medioli, knowing how essential work was to him, urged him to accept, and together the three of them wrote the scenario for it.

As the time to begin shooting drew near, Visconti became more and more determined not to walk with a cane, as he had been obliged to do while directing *Conversation Piece*. Up till then he had been making a miraculous recovery, his brain intact and his creative powers unimpaired. Now his determination to walk unaided made him overdo self-therapy, just as he had always overdone everything else. He neglected no opportunity for exercise—which was why, having seized a rare moment when he was alone in his apartment to practice, he slipped, fell, and fractured his right leg and shoulder. As soon as it became clear that he was going to live, it also became clear that the cane had been merely the forerunner of a wheelchair.

Ogni cosa è fatta con misterio e per amore.
(All things are done with mystery and by love.)

Saint Catherine of Siena

Twenty-nine

The heat of a Roman summer, in a clinic without air conditioning, added discomfort to pain. Visconti's courage surprised no one who knew him well, but his patience did. He complained only of his own carelessness in falling, but even toward himself never took a crushed-worm attitude, always a stand-up-and-be-counted one: "Certainly I see life differently. It's my enemy now, whereas before it was my friend. I used to rule my life, now it rules me. For a while only. Then I shall get control again, shall be as I used to be. And I was lucky. Suppose I'd been a pianist. Life wants me to die, but I say no, not yet, I still have work to do."

His fight against pain made Visconti lose weight at a frightening rate. People who had not seen him for several years said incredulously: "But he used to be such a large, imposing figure. . . ." Imposing he still was, morally, but whereas he ought, for artistic coherence, to have had ahead of him a nobly hale old age, a cross between Lampedusa's Leopard and the brilliant-eyed sarcasm of Picasso's concluding years, Visconti was now honed down by illness into a figure as fragile as the aged Bernard Berenson. Nevertheless, he retained his ferruginous quality, and his resemblance to Tullio Lombardo's sixteenth-century warrior, who lies on his tomb in Ravenna with a carved lion's head clasping his armored shoulder.

His instinct never to give in was supported by family and friends, particularly by Suso and Medioli, who stayed in Rome all summer to visit him daily at the clinic. As soon as he was able to, he even interviewed possible actors for *L'innocente,* and these work sessions in the clinic enabled him, bedridden and in pain, to follow Verdi's advice to Falstaff: "Go on your way as long as you can."

D'Annunzio wrote *L'innocente* in 1892, when he was a young poet, joyously riding the waves of early fame and already pursued by women and creditors. It was a triumphal success, translated into French, German, Portuguese, Polish, American, English, Danish, Czechoslovak, Swedish, Russian, and Bulgarian before the turn of the century. Among perceptive critics who gave it serious praise were the Austrian Hugo von Hofmannsthal and the French Remy de Gourmont.

The plot is a simple one. Tullio Hermil, a well-born, worldly, and sexually insatiable man about town—a *Who's Who* version of Nietzsche's Superman—has been constantly unfaithful to his wife, Giuliana, whom he nevertheless loves tenderly but "only as a sister." Hitherto Tullio's flittings have been light-minded. But his real mistress, Teresa Raffo, has captivated him. His neglect of Giuliana has driven her to yield to the passion felt for her by Filippo Arborio, a famous writer whose books she admires. To Giuliana, this moment's folly in no way affects her passionate love for her husband. At precisely this point, Tullio decides to break with his mistress and make a fresh start with his wife. He and Giuliana go to their country house, where they are blissfully happy. Then Giuliana discovers she is pregnant—by Filippo Arborio. She confesses to Tullio, who has the grace —and in 1892, in that place and class, it was grace—not to blame her for yielding once to a lover's passion, while he himself indulged in his own whims again and again. Nevertheless, Tullio's vanity is injured—and his imagination is stirred to such an extent that he falls passionately in love with his own wife: rather as Proust's Swann falls in love with Odette only when he sees in her a resemblance to Botticelli's Zephora and can therefore love her "as a work of art." Tullio so loathes the coming child, "the innocent intruder," that he tries to persuade Giuliana to have an abortion—that this could have been taken for granted as a possibility among rich people in 1892 provides an interesting footnote to today's infuriated debates on the subject—but Giuliana refuses on religious grounds. Tullio's loathing for the child increases when its father, Arborio, dies as the result of a tropical disease caught during the travels that have made him a glamorous literary figure. When the child is born, Tullio's jealousy becomes more than he can bear, so, while Giuliana and the rest of the family are at church—which Tullio as a nonbelieving superman does not attend—he exposes the child to the cold, and it dies. Anyone who considers this incredibly melodramatic might consider the fact that the novelist Joseph Conrad, D'Annunzio's contemporary, was so jealous lest his own children take some of his devoted wife's love from him that on one occasion he flung all the second child's baby clothes out of the window of a moving train.

Visconti thought *L'innocente* "the least D'Annunzian" of D'Annunzio's novels, devoid of the rhetoric that developed in his work after 1910. The

film must therefore, he said, be realistic, not symbolic—as realistic as
The Confession, a story by Guy de Maupassant, published seven years
earlier than *L'innocente,* in which a dying man confesses to having
killed a child by exposing it to the night air. The only change Visconti
made in D'Annunzio's story line was its end: D'Annunzio has Tullio live
on "at a level of experience beyond conventional standards of good and
evil"; Visconti made Tullio commit suicide, having propelled himself into
an emotional void. "Belief in supermen," said Visconti, "has been killed
by extermination camps."

As soon as the news that Visconti was to direct *L'innocente* became
public, many a typewriter began to clack. Why D'Annunzio? Had D'Annunzio influenced Visconti in his youth? Did this show a predilection for
decadence? Wasn't D'Annunzio the originator of fascism? What were
Visconti's ideological motives? It occurred to no one apparently that,
because of the story's geographical limitations, *L'innocente* could be
directed from a wheelchair. The real trouble, in the public mind, was
that D'Annunzio's status had changed drastically in the past half century.
L'innocente was written fourteen years before Visconti was born, and
by the time Visconti was twelve D'Annunzio had the prestige of Lawrence
of Arabia and Rudolph Valentino combined. But by 1975, D'Annunzio
had been dead for thirty-seven years and was criticized as a "friend of
fascism." Visconti considered accusations that D'Annunzio had been "the
founder of fascism"—like accusations that Wagner and Nietzsche had
been the "founders of Nazism"—as an oversimplification, "merely an
attempt to visit the sins of the children on the fathers."

Visconti disliked D'Annunzio as a man but perceived the value of
his writing and disagreed with Moravia and Pasolini, who dismissed
D'Annunzio as valueless. "I admire the poet and writer. I've always
profoundly detested the man, his rhetoric, his cult of Nietzsche and the
Superman." He thought D'Annunzio had been unjustly neglected for
years, was a fine poet and, often, an excellent prose writer, whose books
offered a fount of ideas for films. Visconti deplored only D'Annunzio's
work for the theater—"a disaster."

It was decided to shoot the film partly in Rome, partly in Tuscany. To
play Tullio and Giuliana, Visconti wanted Alain Delon and Romy
Schneider, but Delon was tied for five films to a French producer who
would release him only for a million dollars and twenty-five percent of
the world takings, and Romy Schneider was pregnant. So for Tullio he
chose Giancarlo Giannini, an actor who had not yet been able to display
to the full abilities that included great physical dignity and clear cat's
eyes. For the part of Giuliana, Visconti engaged Laura Antonelli. This

was a risky choice, liable to arouse inverted snobbery in critics. A former gymnasium teacher, she had become Italy's latest sex symbol at a period when such symbols were far more pyrogenous than in the days of Marilyn Monroe.

What Visconti first noticed about Laura Antonelli, however, was that her face sometimes resembles Duse's—in certain scenes in the film she was to look uncannily like Duse—and she possessed a body that, for all its rating on the current stock market of sex, was as old-fashioned as it was beautiful: "a figure that D'Annunzio would have been mad about." Above all, Visconti thought she had hitherto unexploited possibilities as an actress. When journalists asked him if La Antonelli's performance would "owe everything to his direction," Visconti replied with the imaginative precision that made some people find him forbidding (and he did forbid stupidity): "To get something out of a person there must be juice in the fruit. You can press a pear as hard as you like, but to get juice you need a lemon."

Visconti's fall occurred in April and by September 1975, he was ready to start directing. The first part of the film was to be shot near Lucca, an exquisite little Tuscan city midway between Florence and the Mediterranean, encircled by massive seventeenth-century ramparts. Visconti settled, with his team and his therapist, in the Hotel Villa La Principessa, an eighteenth-century villa, renovated in 1800 and set in a park three miles outside Lucca. This had only recently been transformed into a hotel and was still full of quietness, privacy, and beauty. "De Lux Suites," said a disarming brochure, "are available for the most exacting guests," and in these Visconti and his team were settled.

It was fortunate that he could have his usual colleagues about him at this juncture. While a film is being made, all concerned are so closely united in their efforts to "look in the same direction"—Saint-Exupéry's definition of love—that their business and professional relationships are automatically transformed into personal ones. During this comparatively brief period the outside world seems remote—and then, suddenly, the film is over, its little world dispersed. Visconti had never suffered from this sea change, since the same people worked with him again and again and became his second, his chosen, family. It was therefore of the greatest importance to him now, when he had for the first time to work as an invalid—to find out, in Robert Frost's words, "what to make of a diminished thing"—to have this chosen family around him, coming and going, chattering, smoking, rushing in with photographs and bits of news, behaving in the normal film way, just what the doctor did not order, but just as they had behaved throughout the years when Visconti was,

272

physically as well as mentally, king of the castle—as, morally and intellectually, he still seemed to be.

When I left for Lucca, a Swiss-Italian friend who had known Visconti during his brilliant maturity, said: "I do wonder what you will find—that extraordinary personality intact? All that fire and energy? Or an old man? An invalid?" I imagined I might find all four. When I reached the Principessa, I found that his famous impatience was unchanged: no sooner was I in my room than the telephone rang and I was asked to come down to his suite "as soon as possible." There I received an immediate answer to my friend's conjectures. Seated in an armchair by a coffee table, Visconti dominated the room. His personality was still extraordinary, he was still improvident of his energy. Although thin, he looked young for sixty-eight, his eyes still brilliant, his hair still brown, and, superficially, nothing about him suggested an invalid. This amazed me. Gifted people do not necessarily have characters to match their gifts, but he had. It was as if his life had been a relay race, and his will power had taken charge of the last lap.

On the hot sunny morning of September 27, 1975, the shooting of L'innocente began at the Villa Badioli, just outside Lucca. The camera was set up in the gardens in front of the villa, and Visconti was obviously anxious about whether he would be able, with only one hand, to break the traditional bottle of champagne on the camera. He managed it. Toasts were drunk. And the shooting started with the sound of horses' hoofs as Tullio's carriage drove up to the villa. Visconti found it trying not to be able to show the actors what he wanted from them, but they sat by him as he explained to them—and this change, too, he managed. Rooms had been arranged there where he could rest and invite guests to meals—and so lively were his mind, eyes, and tongue that it was impossible to remember his handicap.

Particularly difficult was it to remember this when he gave a press conference in the Villa Badioli's big ground-floor room. "Here I am," he said in his beautiful harsh voice, "ready to make another film even if I do need a wheelchair. Next time it'll be a stretcher, but I shall never give up." The conference was crowded and he was questioned and photographed as intensively as before his illness. Friends were concerned lest he be tired, but his answers shot back, clear and thoughtful about L'innocente and the acting, and with a growling humor about himself. In mediocre novels, heroes and heroines are frequently distinguished by a lack of self-pity verging on idiocy. Visconti wasted no one's time going through a no-one-need-pity-me routine. He knew his situation was bad, but pitied himself no more—and no less—than he would have pitied someone else in a similar situation. He never dwelt on it because, like Teilhard de Chardin, he still wanted always to be "going ahead." One or two of the journalists covering the shooting arrived wondering whether he would really be capable of directing, if it would not be, rather, a matter of his loyal team carrying on for him. These doubts were dissipated by the very first morning's work.

Visconti spent his sixty-ninth birthday at Lucca, filming, surrounded by friends and love. Among the friends was Rina Morelli, who was playing Tullio's mother. It was an artistic treat to see her take Visconti's direction, the understanding between them so perfect, after thirty years of working together, that at moments it sufficed for him to raise his thick eyebrows. "She was a good actress when I first knew her," Visconti said, "a fine actress, but still relegated to supporting parts. Such upheavals there were when I insisted on her playing the lead in *Les Parents terribles* in 1945. But with her exceptional interpretive gifts she became the greatest actress in Italy. Films, too—the part of the princess in *The Leopard* was only a small one, but when Burt Lancaster saw what she did with it he kept saying, 'She's wonderful.' " Her work was still wonderful in *L'innocente,* but she was not at all well, and distraught at the thought that this might cause delays in filming. "Luchino has enough trouble without that." In fact, she was worn out, and was to die three months after Visconti, depriving the Italian theater of one of its greatest actresses and leaving her companion, Paolo Stoppa, feeling "All, all are gone, the old familiar faces."

From Lucca, Visconti returned to finish *L'innocente* in Rome, partly at Cinecittà and partly at the Palazzo Colonna. The scenes in which Tullio and Giuliana attend a concert in a princely home were shot at the Palazzo Colonna—and Visconti had his nephews and nieces, and great-nephews and -nieces, supply the concert's audience, thereby giving those scenes an authenticity similar to that of the ball scenes in *The Leopard.*

While he was making *L'innocente,* his previous film, *Conversation Piece,* was shown in New York. Whereas it had been much admired all over Europe—never, said the exacting Paris *L'Express,* had he been "more lucid and sublime"—it received shrilly bad notices in New York. This puzzled him. He was not upset by adverse criticism, nor did he pretend to ignore it; he always wanted to know "exactly what they meant" so that "we artisans can learn from it." On this occasion, along with the objections, he was sent the comment of New York's *Village Voice.* The critic of this paper said that he had looked at those who hissed Visconti's film, and they "were the same stupid faces as had hissed the Danish Carl Theodor Dreyer's *Gertrud* (1964), John Ford's *Seven Women* (1965) and Renoir's *Une Partie de campagne* (1946)." Since Visconti could truly say of Renoir's *Une Partie de campagne*, "That is where I came in," the singling out of this particular film gave a special value for him to the critic's remark that *Conversation Piece* was "not a film by an old man but an artist's film about old age."

Superficially, *L'innocente* appeared to be a period piece, a luxurious helping of retro, but in fact it was also about the violence erupting all over Italy, a violence just as selfish for all its pseudo-patriotic slogans as Tullio's personal and sexual violence, and far less honest. In this instance Visconti's glance was prophetic, since violence had not then assumed its present scale—though he had a taste of the future on his last birthday, when the fifty-three-year-old poet, writer, and film director Pier Paolo Pasolini was found murdered, by louts, on the beach at Ostia, near Rome. This murder produced emotional statements from all over, but when Visconti was asked for a statement he emphasized not the personality of Pasolini, whom he had known only slightly, but his contempt for violence. He had the horror of cruelty that is most deeply felt by those who have had to fight physically for their principles.

Back in Rome, Visconti worked on his film, and enchanted friends and family by his intellectual vigor. But though he still made plans, a great exhaustion was taking possession of him. When his film was finished, except for the cutting, he caught the flu. On March 17, 1975, he listened several times to Brahms's Second Symphony, then suddenly turned to his sister Uberta and said "Enough now." Then he laid his head back to rest—and presently was dead.

Today, as Visconti's work takes its place on the map of Italian culture, people talk of his affinities with Verga, Verdi, Toscanini. But one name equally close to his imaginative life has not yet been mentioned—that of Ippolito Nievo, an extraordinary young man from Padua who served with Garibaldi's army, wrote a masterpiece, *The Confessions of an Italian*, at twenty-six, and was drowned at the age of thirty, while carrying out a mission for Garibaldi, the very year Italian unity was won. Emilio Cecchi cited Nievo in his *Notebooks* as one of those writers who, like Manzoni and Tolstoy, enter so completely into an event that their personal creativity and the historical facts of life are "perfectly juxtaposed: Manzoni with the Plague in Milan, Tolstoy with the battle of Austerlitz, and Nievo with the Risorgimento."

Le confessioni d'un Italiano, published posthumously in 1867, conjured up the entire Risorgimento period in all its belligerence and beauty. It opens with: "I was born a Venetian . . . and by the grace of God shall die an Italian": lines Visconti adapted in his film *Senso* for the Venetian countess who calls herself Italian when devoted to the cause of Italian unity, but reverts to calling herself Venetian when passion for an Austrian officer has driven her to treachery. Nievo threw himself uncompromisingly into all the struggles of his period—as a private person, as a soldier, and as an artist, and so, too, did Visconti. Today Visconti's power to translate history into art derives a particular value from the fact that Italy's story, from the Risorgimento until now, provides in its drama and violence a microcosm of what is happening all over the world. So in entering his world we learn about our own.

Soon after Visconti's death, Suso Cecchi D'Amico's younger daughter, Caterina D'Amico De Carvalho, organized a richly comprehensive exhibition of photographs, paintings, and documents illustrating Visconti's life and work. When this was shown, first in Spoleto, then in South America, Japan, and Charleston, South Carolina, Caterina noticed that even those of the young who arrived expecting anyone of an older generation to be, automatically, "reactionary," left the exhibition full of astonished admiration for the elderly man whose face they had just seen. Asked why she had provided personal and family photographs of his childhood and adolescence, but expressed the rest of his life in terms of his work, Caterina said, "Because as an adult, Visconti lived entirely for his work." Was he, then, a solitary character? At this Caterina—who had known him all her life—looked amazed. "If there is one thing I have learned while researching for this exhibition it is that Visconti was a profoundly happy man, who made a choice and stuck to it, that of obeying his own creativeness and never undertaking anything in which he did not completely believe. He was both happy and a born conqueror—*this* is what must be remembered, *not* the 'pathetic figure struggling against illness' that everyone evokes now—and I believe that, having finished his last film, he died only when he realized that the time had come when he could no longer conquer illness."

When that time came, in March 1976, the ancient walls of Rome bore new posters mourning Visconti's death. Two years later, in June 1978, the walls of Milan were adorned with La Scala's traditionally buff-colored posters, announcing a celebration of his life: Caterina's Visconti exhibition, "Mostra Visconti," was opening at La Scala's famous Theater Museum. There, in the opera house that gave him such joy from his earliest childhood, and in the museum that contains such treasures as the little spinet on which the eight-year-old Verdi practiced in 1821, were set out records that take Visconti from the days when he was an infant in a white bonnet, beaming because he could stand on his feet unaided, to the indomitable-looking man of sixty-nine facing the fact that his walking days were over.

In between are the child Visconti beginning as he was to go on—in his family's box at La Scala; in the family theater at home, playing Hamlet to little Wanda Toscanini's Ophelia; a boy rising early to practice the cello and to bicycle along the waterways of old Milan; a young cavalry officer, "so handsome he'd make the bread drop from your hand"; a young man about town, absorbed by horses, scolded into Jean Renoir's film world by Gabrielle Chanel, who leans on the arm of the thirty-year-old Visconti and looks up at him with a young girl's devotion; a man stricken by the death of the mother he so closely resembled; the wartime Visconti, the prisoner condemned to death for refusing to yield up any names; and, above all, Visconti the artist—Visconti with Suso and Medioli, with Rina Morelli and Paola Stoppa, with Romy Schneider and Alain Delon, with Annie Girardot and Burt Lancaster, and with Callas: "happy and conquering."

On the whitewashed wall beside the little staircase that leads to La Scala's Theater Museum someone had written "Viva Callas," and someone else "Viva Visconti." He seemed, indeed, very much alive there, his work bearing witness to the fact that although the human race produces so much cruelty, ugliness, and mediocrity, it can also produce individuals who, like Luchino Visconti, are in themselves triumphant works of art, integrity, and courage.

277

Bibliography

All of Visconti's scenarios have been handsomely published, together with photographs, interviews, and critical essays, by Casa Editrice Licinio Cappelli, Bologna. In their Dal soggetto al film series, edited by Renzo Renzi, are:
  Senso (1955)
  Le notti bianche (1957)
  Rocco e i suoi fratelli (1960)
  Boccaccio 70 (1962)
  Il Gattopardo (1963)
  Vaghe stelle dell'orsa (1965)
  La caduta degli dei (1969)
  Morte a Venezia (1971)
  Ludwig (1973)
  Gruppo di famiglia in un interno (1974).
In the same publisher's Nuovo Universale paperbacks are:
  Ossessione (1977)
  La terra trema (1977)
  Bellissima (1978).
White Nights, Rocco and His Brothers, and *The Job* were published, in English translation, in *Three Screenplays; La terra trema* and *Senso,* in *Two Screenplays;* all translated by Judith Green, by Orion Press (now Viking Penguin Inc.) in 1970. These translations are not quoted in the text.
More of Visconti's own writing is included in *Leggere Visconti: scritti, interviste, testimonianze e documenti con una biografia critica generale a cura di Giuliano Callegari e Nuccio Lodato,* published by the Amministrazione Provinciale di Pavia, 1976.
Books about Visconti:
  Visconti, l'histoire et l'esthétique, published in numbers 26 and 27 of *Etudes Cinématographiques,* edited by G.-A. Astre and M. Estève. Paris, Autumn 1963.
  Visconti, number 17 of *Premier Plan,* edited by Bernard Chardere. Lyon, 1961.

Baldelli, Pio, *Luchino Visconti*. Milan: Gabriele Mazzotta, 1973.

Ferrara, Giuseppe. *Visconti*. Paris: Seghers, 1963.

Other books consulted:

Alicata, Mario. *Lettere e taccuini di Regina Coeli*. Turin: Einaudi, 1977.

Ardoin, John, and Fitzgerald, Gerald. *Callas*. New York: Holt, Rinehart & Winston, 1974.

Arruga, Lorenzo. *La Scala*. Milan: Electa, 1975.

Bianchi, Pietro. *Maestri del cinema*. Milan: Garzanti, 1977.

Bolton, J. R. Glorney. *Roman Century, 1870–1970*. London: Hamish Hamilton, 1970.

Buache, Freddy. *Le Cinéma Italien d'Antonioni à Rosi*. Paris: Editions Thièle, Yverdon & Maspero, 1969.

Carocci, Gianpiero. *Storia d'Italia dall'unità ad oggi*. Milan: Feltrinelli, 1975.

Castellaneta, Carlo. *Storia di Milano*. Milan: Rizzoli, 1975.

Cecchi, Emilio. *Letteratura italiana del novecento, a cura di Pietro Citati*. Milan: Mondadori, 1972.

———. *Taccuini*. Milan: Mondadori, 1976.

Chabod, Federigo. *L'Italia contemporanea, 1918–48*. Turin: Piccola Biblioteca Einaudi, 1961.

Colquhoun, Archibald. *Manzoni and His Times*. London: Dent, 1954.

Dickinson, Thorold. *A Discovery of Cinema*. London, New York, Toronto: Oxford University Press, 1971.

Encyclopedia dello spettacolo. Milan: Garzanti, 1976.

Grassi, Paolo. *Quarant'anni di paleoscenico*. Milan: Mursia, 1977.

Grazzini, Giovanni. *Gli anni sessanta in cento film*. Rome-Bari: Laterza, 1977.

———. *Gli anni settanta in cento film*. Rome-Bari: Laterza, 1976.

Horst, Horst P. *Salute to the Thirties*. London: The Bodley Head, 1971.

Ledeen, Michael A. *D'Annunzio a Fiume*. Rome-Bari: Laterza, 1975.

Linati, Carlo. *Milano d'allora*. Milan: Longanesi, 1975.

Lorenzi, Alberto. *Milano, il nostro secolo*. Milan: Bramante, 1969.

———. *I cinematografi di Milano*. Milan: Mursia, 1970.

Mack Smith, D. Victor Emanuel. *Cavour and the Risorgimento*. London, New York, Toronto: Oxford University Press, 1971.

Mann, Katia. *Unwritten Memories*. New York: Knopf, 1975.

Manzella, Domenico, and Pozzi, Emilio. *I teatri di Milano*. Milan: Mursia, 1971.

Milan, i navigli. Comune di Milano: Ripartizione Cultura, 1977.

Moravia, Alberto. *Al Cinema*. Milan: Bompiani, 1975.

Praz, Mario. *An Illustrated History of Interior Decoration from Pompeii to Art Nouveau*. New York: George Braziller; London: Thames and Hudson, 1964.

———. *Scene di conversazione*. Rome: Ugo Bozzi, 1971.

Romano, Sergio. *Histoire de l'Italie du Risorgimento à nos jours*. Paris: Le Seuil, 1977.

Rondi, Gian Luigi. *7 domande a 49 registi*. Turin: Società Editrice Internazionale, 1975.

Sadoul, Georges. *Histoire du cinéma mondial des origines à nos jours*. Paris: Flammarion, 1949.

Sermoneta, Vittoria. *Sparkle Distant Worlds*. London: Hutchinson, 1947.

Thomas, Tony. *Burt Lancaster*. New York, Pyramid, 1975.

Vittorini, Elio. *Diario in pubblico*. Milan: Bompiani, 1957.

Wallman, Margarita. *Balconate del cielo*. Milan: Garzanti, 1976.

Zavattini, Cesare. *Opere*. Milan: Bompiani, 1974.

Index

Achard, Marcel, 66
Adenauer, Konrad, 131
Aeschylus, 173
Agnelli, Gianni, 31
Agnelli, Susanna, 38
Agoult, Marie, Comtesse d', 228
Albach-Retty, Wolf, 157
Albany, Countess of, 82
Alexander, Field Marshal Harold, 59
Alexander VI, Pope, 135
Alfano, Franco, 264
Alfieri, Count Vittorio, 82
Alianello, Carlo, 96
Alicata, Mario, 56, 58
Allegret, Yves, 46
Amendola, Giorgio, 38, 118
Amendola, Giovanni, 38
Amico, Fidel D', 84
Amico, Silvio D', 14, 106
Amico, Suso Cecchi D', 116, 173, 269
  collaboration with, 9
    on *Boccaccio 70*, 160
    on *The Coach of the Blessed Sacrament*, 85
    on *Conversation Piece*, 249, 253, 260–61
    on *Fifth Column*, 64
    on *The Intruder*, 265
    on *The Leopard*, 166, 168
    on *Life with Father*, 82
    on *Look Homeward, Angel*, 136
    on *Ludwig*, 225
    on *Mrs. Gibbon's Boys*, 137

    on *Remembrance of Things Past*, 223
    on *Rocco and His Brothers*, 140, 142, 153
    on *Senso*, 95, 96
    on *Wedding March*, 89
    on *White Nights*, 117, 124
  friendship with, 33, 76
  nature of relationship with, 84
  in Visconti exhibit, 277
  Visconti's brand of folly and, 224–25
  and Visconti's second stroke, 237–38, 241
Amidei, Sergio, 76
Andreotti, Giulio, 84, 89
Andresen, Björn, 213
Angelo, Salvo d', 74, 85
Anna, Livio dell', 39
Annunzio, Gabriele D', 28, 135, 177, 178, 263
  directing works of, 265, 269–75
  in World War I, 24, 29
Anouilh, Jean, 66
Antonelli, Laura, 271–72
Antonioni, Michelangelo, 63–64, 76, 152–53
Appiani, Andrea, 92
Ardoin, John, 125
Arese, Count, 18
Aristarco, Guido, 101
Arrivabene, Count Opprandino, 96
Arrivabene, Madina (sister-in-law), 38

Arrivabene, Niki (sister-in-law), 38
Atget, Eugène, 46
Aue, Hartmann von, 241
Avanzo, Baroness, 61
Azeglio, Massimo d', 18

Babilée, Jean, 116, 131
Bach, Johann Sebastian, 201
Badoglio, Marshal Pietro, 53
Balanchine, George, 41
Ballet productions
    Dance Marathon (Maratona), 130–
        31
    Mario and the Magician, 115–16, 131
Balthus (Balthazar Klossowski), 246–
    47
Balzac, Honoré de, 111, 146, 215, 223
Bandulacco, Nicola, 207
Barzini, Luigi, 7
Bassani, Giorgio, 95, 96, 164–65
Bataille, Sylvia, 47
Beardsley, Aubrey, 189
Beaumarchais, Pierre Augustin Caron,
    66
Beaume, Georges, 158
Becker, Jacques, 46
Beckett, Samuel, 244
Beethoven, Ludwig van, 138, 217, 244
Belgioioso, Princess, 18
Bell, Marie, 176
Bellini, Vincenzo, 90, 103–5
Bellissima (film; Visconti), 85–87, 115,
    264
Ben Barka, Ahmed, 185
Benedict XV, Pope, 24
Benois, Aleksandr, 15–16
Benois, Nicola, 15, 124, 125, 127, 128
Berenson, Bernard, 216, 253, 269
Berenson, Marisa, 216
Berger, Helmut, 197, 226, 232, 233, 253,
    257, 261, 267
Bergman, Ingmar, 59, 154, 198
Bergman, Ingrid, 85, 96
Berlin, Irving, 202
Bernhardt, Sarah, 14, 107, 109, 110,
    135, 159, 162
Bernstein, Henri, 38, 48
Bernstein, Leonard, 105

Bertini, Francesca, Countess Cartier,
    176, 186
Bertolucci, Bernardo, 82, 176, 259
Billy Budd (Melville; Visconti film
    project), 56
Bismarck, Otto von, 231
Bissolati-Bergamaschi, Leonida, 28
Blasetti, Alessandro, 49, 86
Blum, Léon, 44, 46
Bobath (doctor), 239
Boccaccio, 159
Boccaccio 70 (film; Fellini, Monicelli,
    Visconti, De Sica), 159
Boccanegra, Simon, 206–7
Bogarde, Dirk, 195, 210–11, 215
Boito, Arrigo, 14, 15, 120
Boito, Camillo, 14, 95, 120
Boldini, Giovanni, 171
Böll, Heinrich, 131
Bolognini, Mauro, 152, 175
Bonnie Prince Charlie, 82
Borelli, Lyda, 186
Borgese, Elisabeth Mann, 116
Borghese, Prince Junio Valerio (Black
    Prince), 260
Borgia, Lucrezia, 135
Born, Wolfgang, 208
Boulez, Pierre, 215
Bowen, Marjorie, 8
Bowles, Paul, 96
Brahms, Johannes, 275
Brando, Marlon, 97
Brecht, Bertolt, 84, 115, 131, 144, 191
Bresson, Robert, 205
Brialy, Jean-Claude, 146
Britten, Benjamin, 126
Brunius, Jacques B., 46
Buache, Freddy, 101–2
Buber, Martin, 214
Bullock, Alan, 192
Bülow, Cosima von, 228–30
Bülow, Hans von, 228
Buono, Oreste del, 79
Byron, George Gordon, Lord, 174

Cadorna, Gen. Luigi, 26
Cain, James, 50, 56
Calamai, Clara, 57, 123

Callas, Maria (Cecilia Sophia Anna Maria Kalogeropoulos), 89, 107, 121, 206, 249, 277
  in *Anna Bolena*, 91, 124–27
  in *Iphigénie en Tauride*, 127, 128
  in *La Traviata*, 91, 106–12, 189
  in *La Vestale*, 91–94
  Poliuto project and, 128–29
  in *The Sleepwalker*, 103–6
Campanile, Pasquale Festa, 140, 166
Camus, Albert, 186–89
Camus, Catherine Sintès, 187
Camus, Francine, 188
Camus, Lucien, 187
Capa, Robert, 44
Capelli, Licinio, 39
Carcano, E., 249
Cardinale, Claudia, 145, 173, 175, 181, 259
Carroll, Lewis, 78
Cartier, Max, 145–46
Cartier-Bresson, Henri, 46–47
Caruso, Pietro, 60, 61, 65
Carvalho, Caterina D'Amico De, 276
Cashel Byron's Profession (Shaw; Visconti film project), 56
Causi, Li, 73
Cavani, Liliana, 132, 257–58
Cavour, Count Camillo Benso di, 18, 96–97
Caxton, William, 83
Cecchi, Emilio, 9, 21–22, 47, 54, 64, 84
  on Duse, 136
  on *The Leopard*, 172
  on Nievo, 275
Celani, Count Giuseppe, 60
Cerda, Fulco Santostefano della, Duke of Verdura, 167–68
Cerutti, Maria, 61
Chamberlain, Neville, 79
Chambers, Whittaker, 84
Chanel, Gabrielle (Coco), 32, 38, 40–42, 45, 116, 161, 277
Chaplin, Charlie, 22, 47
Charlemagne, 7, 73
Charles I, King of England, 156
Chaucer, Geoffrey, 83, 159
Chautemps, Camille, 44

Chekhov, Anton, 89, 115
  See also Theater productions
Cherubini, Maria Luigi, 90, 249
Chiaramonte, Nicola, 129
Chini, Galileo, 248
Chopin, Frédéric, 198
Christina (physiotherapist), 243
Christina, Queen of Sweden, 60
Chronicle of Poor Lovers (*Cronache di poveri amanti*; Pratolini; Visconti film project), 85
Churchill, Winston, 24–25, 106
Cimarosa, Domenico, 89
Clément, René, 118
Coach of the Blessed Sacrament, The (*Le Carosse du Saint-Sacrement*; Mérimée; Visconti film project), 84–85
Cocteau, Jean, 38, 41, 64, 66, 119
Conchon, Georges, 188
Confalonieri, Count Federico, 13
Connolly, Cyril, 247
Conrad, Joseph, 270
Conversation Piece (*Scene di conversazione*; Praz; Visconti film), 241, 253–61, 265
  attics in, 31
  cast of, 253, 254, 257, 258
  reactions to, 274–75
  scenario for, 253
  starting work on, 249
  story of, 254–60
Cooke, Alistair, 84
Cooper, Alfred Duff, 136
Cooper, Gary, 47
Corneille, Pierre, 92
Cosimo I, Duke, 83
Coward, Noel, 197
Craig, Michael, 175
Cristaldi, Franco, 117, 119, 173
Croce, Benedetto, 95
Cuvilliés, François de, 220

Daladier, Edouard, 79
Dali, Salvador, 41, 81
Dallapiccola, Luigi, 89
Damned, The (*La caduta degli dei*; Visconti film), 8, 31, 36, 191–206, 210, 240

Damned, The (cont.)
cast of, 195, 197–98, 226, 229
historical setting for, 193–94
preparatory reading for, 191, 192
story of, 194–201
success of, 201–2, 205, 206
Dante, 11, 25, 159
David, Jacques Louis, 92
Day, Clarence, 82
Days of Glory (Giorni di gloria; Visconti film), 65–66
Death in Venice (Mann; Visconti film), 205–23, 239
cast of, 210–11, 213, 215
financing of, 205–6
preparing scenario for, 207–10
story of, 211–20
De Gaulle, Charles, 136
Delluc, Louis, 22
Delon, Alain, 37, 57, 265, 277
The Intruder and, 271
in *The Leopard*, 167
in *Rocco and His Brothers*, 145–47, 149
in *'Tis Pity She's a Whore*, 156–58
in *Work*, 161
Desiderius (Lombard king), 7
Diaghilev, Sergei, 15, 41, 116
Dickens, Charles, 148, 152
Dietrich, Marlene, 196
Dollmann, Colonel, 60
Donatello, 217
Donizetti, Gaetano, 85–86, 90, 104, 124, 126, 128, 138
Dostoevsky, Fëdor, 66, 134, 140
See also White Nights
Dreyer, Carl Theodor, 274
Dreyfus, Capt. Alfred, 8
Dumas, Alexandre, fils, 106, 107
Duplessis, Marie, 106–7
Dürckheim, Count, 231–33
Dürer, Albrecht, 264
Duse, Eleonora, 14, 107, 135–36, 272
Duvivier, Julien, 50, 95, 176

Earth Quakes, The (La terra trema; Visconti film), 74–79, 118, 132, 139, 142, 240
characters in, compared to De Sica's, 264
directing, 76–77
financial loss with, 85
reactions to, 79
working conditions for shooting of, 77–78
Edward VI, King of England, 83, 126
Edwards, Robert Gordon, 224
Einstein, Albert, 8, 106
Eisenstein, Sergei, 49
Ekberg, Anita, 160
Eleonora of Toledo, 83
El Greco, 133
Elisabeth of Austria, 227–30, 232, 244
Elizabeth I, Queen of England, 126
Elizabeth II, Queen of England, 106
Enrico, Robert, 158
Erba, Carla, *see* Visconti, Carla Erba
Erba, Carlo (great-uncle), 7
Erba, Luigi (grandfather), 7
Esslin, Martin, 246
Euripides, 89, 127, 173

Fabbri, Diego, 138
Fellini, Federico, 76, 152, 254
works of, 5, 38, 123, 132, 151, 159, 160
Feltrinelli, Giangiacomo, 131, 165
Ferreri, Marco, 88
Ferrero, Willy, 75
Feuillère, Edwige, 131, 146–47
Filippo, Eduardo de, 132
Filippo, Peppino de, 160
Fitzgerald, F. Scott, 136, 146, 206, 263
Fitzgerald, Gerald, 125
Fitzgerald, Zelda, 263
Flaiano, Ennio, 84
Flaubert, Gustave, 160, 264
Focas, Spiro, 145
Fogazzaro, Antonio, 96
Ford, John (dramatist), 156
Ford, John (film director), 162, 274
Forster, E. M., 224
Franciosa, Massimo, 140, 166
Francis, Saint, 134
Francis Ferdinand, Archduke of Austria, 23

Franco, Gen. Francisco, 46
Francis Joseph, Emperor of Austria, 210
François I, King of France, 133
Frank, César, 176
Friedrich, Kaspar David, 211, 229
Frost, Robert, 275
Fudakowski, Jan, 215

Gadda, Emilio, 132
Galileo, 156
Gallo, Mario, 205–6
Garbo, Greta, 47, 162
Garbuglia, Mario, 253–54
Garibaldi, Giuseppe, 24, 165–68, 171, 275
Gasperi, Alcide de, 74, 88, 103
Gassman, Vittorio, 66, 81, 82, 186
Gauthier, Théophile, 84
Gavazzeni, Gianandrea, 124–25
Gaynor, Janet, 47
George III, King of England, 96
Gershwin, George, 126
Ghione, Riccardo, 88
Giacosa, Giuseppe, 89
Giannini, Giancarlo, 271
Giannini, Guglielmo, 78
Gibson, William, 136
Gide, André, 8
Gilbert, William, 17
Ginzburg, Leone, 206
Ginzburg, Natalia, 206
Giotto, 47
Girardot, Annie, 137, 184, 250–51, 277
Giraudoux, Jean, 173
Gish, Lillian, 186
Giuliano, Giuseppe, 73
Giuliano, Salvatore, 72–74, 80
Giulini, Carlo Maria, 90, 107–8, 133
Gluck, Christoph Willibald, 126
Goebbels, Joseph, 192
Goethe, Johann Wolfgang von, 138, 209
Goldoni, Carlo, 39, 89, 130, 132, 133
Gomulka, Wladyslaw, 118
Gonzaga, Ferrante, 10
Gonzaga, Pietro, 128
Göring, Hermann, 15, 192
Gorki, Maxim, 47, 66

Gourmont, Remy de, 270
Gramatica, Emma, 136
Gramsci, Antonio, 27, 32, 36, 191
Granger, Farley, 97
Grass, Günter, 131
Grassi, Paolo, 81, 184
Greenglass, David, 113
Griem, Helmut, 195
Gruen, John, 105
Gudden, Bernhard von, 233, 234
Guerrieri, Gerardo, 247
Guttuso, Renato, 58, 64, 71

Handel, Georg Friedrich, 104
Hannibal, 135
Hawthorne, Nathaniel, 114, 255
Hayez, Francesco, 18
Hearn, Lafcadio, 17
Heine, Heinrich, 98
Hélène, Mademoiselle (governess), 25
Hemingway, Ernest, 26, 87, 136
Henry VIII, King of England, 124–46
Henze, Hans Werner, 131
Hepburn, Audrey, 64
Heyman, Claude, 46
Hidalgo, Elvira de, 90, 104
Hindenburg, Field Marshal Paul von, 193–94
Hiss, Alger, 94
Hitler, Adolf, 53, 116, 119, 140, 183, 191, 196, 199
    and Ardeatine Caves massacre, 60
    meets with Mussolini (1934), 35, 192
    at Munich, 79
    racism and, 130–31
    takes power, 193–94
    in World War II, 53
Hofmannsthal, Hugo von, 127, 173, 185, 270
Holbein, Hans, 125
Holy Sinner, The (Mann; Visconti film project), 241
Homer, 127
Horst (photographer), 41
House by the Medlar Tree, The (I Malavoglia; Verga; Visconti film project), 71–72
Howard, Leslie, 47

Howard, Trevor, 228
Howells, William Dean, 255

Intruder, The (*L'innocente*; D'Annunzio; Visconti film), 64, 265, 269–75
Ionesco, Eugene, 246
Isherwood, Christopher, 130

James, Henry, 82, 169
Jodl, Gen. Alfred, 60
John XXIII, Pope, 46, 137
Jotti, Nilde, 79
Jurinac, Sena, 185

Kapler, Herbert, 61
Kästner, Erich, 130
Kazan, Elia, 184
Keaton, Buster, 47
Keats, John, 240
Kempski, Lorrain, 192
Kennedy, John F., 46
Kennedy, Robert F., 201
Kesselring, Field Marshal Albert, 60
Khrushchev, Nikita, 46, 117–18, 164
King, Martin Luther, Jr., 201
Kipling, Rudyard, 93
Koch, Carl, 49
Koch, Pietro, 5, 61, 65
Kraïevski, André, 117
Krayenbühl, Hugo A., 238–39, 241, 246

La Malfa, Ugo, 79
"L'amante di Gramigna" (Verga; Visconti film project), 55–56
Lamb, William, Lord Melbourne, 106
Lampedusa, Prince of (Tomasi Giuseppe; Duke of Palma), 130, 159, 163–64, 169–70, 269
  See also Leopard, The
Lancaster, Burt, 6, 37, 166–68, 253–54, 259, 261
La Tosca (Renoir and Visconti film), 48–50
Laurentiis, Dino de, 185–86
Lawrence, D. H., 76, 154
Lawrence, T. E., 271
Lehár, Franz, 8, 212
Lenbach, Franz von, 228

Lenin, Vladimir I., 26
Leone, Giovanni, 6
Leopard, The (*Il Gattopardo*; Lampedusa; Visconti film), 6, 130–31, 159–73, 229, 240, 253–54
  attics in, 31
  biographical elements in, 37
  cast of, 63, 166–68, 274
  Cecchi on, 172
  costume designer for, 189
  publication of, 164–65
  setting for, 169–70
  shooting, 165
  story of, 168–69
  writing of, 163–64
Leopardi, Count Giacomo, 174, 183, 243
Levi, Carlo, 54–55, 62, 141
Lhote, André, 46
Liberty, Arthur, 17
Lifar, Serge, 38
Lindbergh, Charles, 37
Lippi, Fra Filippo, 135
Liszt, Franz, 106, 228, 229
Lizzani, Carlo, 95, 154
Lombard, Carole, 47
Lombardo, Goffredo, 152, 165
Lombardo, Tullio, 269
Lombroso, Cesare, 19
Longo, Luigi, 175
Loren, Sophia, 160, 162
Loti, Pierre, 17
Loyola, Saint Ignatius of, 264
Ludwig (Visconti film), 223–37, 240, 264
  cast of, 226–28, 232, 233
  editing of, 241, 244–45
  financing, 224
  scenario for, 225
  story of, 226–34
Ludwig I, King of Bavaria, 225
Ludwig II, King of Bavaria (earlier Duke of Bavaria), 192, 220, 225–34, 244–45
Luitpold, Prince, 233
Lutz, Freiherr von, 231

McCarthy, Joseph, 113
McCarthy, Mary, 8
Machiavelli, Niccolò, 66

McNarney, Gen. Joseph T., 59
Maeltzer, General, 60
Mafalda, Princess of Savoy, 63
Magic Mountain, The (Mann; Visconti film project), 240–41, 265
Magnani, Anna, 57, 76, 84, 85, 87, 144
Mahler, Anna, 216
Mahler, Gustav, 159, 207–8, 210–12, 216–19
Makart, Hans, 228
Mallory, Jan, 47
Malraux, André, 55, 74, 75, 247
Mangano, Silvana, 186, 213, 229, 253, 261
Mann, Erika, 207, 208, 214
Mann, Golo, 265
Mann, Katia, 207–11, 214–16
Mann, Klaus, 208
Mann, Thomas, 9, 106, 140, 152, 194, 238
    Visconti and works of, see Ballet productions; Death in Venice; Holy Sinner, The; Magic Mountain, The
Mannino, Franco, 115–16
Manzoni, Alessandro, 15, 18, 72, 121, 275
Marais, Jean, 119, 137
Marie, Crown Princess, 225
Marischka, Ernst, 157
Marx brothers, 47
Marzot, Vera, 189
Masier, Titti, 33–34
Massine, Léonide, 116
Mastroianni, Marcello, 83, 116, 124, 173
Matteotti, Giacomo, 35–36, 191
Matteucci, Carlo (great-uncle), 19
Maupassant, Guy de, 46, 160
Maximilian II, King of Bavaria (earlier Crown Prince Maximilian), 225, 226
Mazzarino, Gioacchino Lanza di, Duke of Palma, 167
Medici, Catherine de, 133
Medioli, Enrico, 240–41, 269, 277
    collaboration with
        on Conversation Piece, 249, 253, 261
        on The Damned, 194
    on The Intruder, 265
    on Ludwig, 225
    on Rocco and His Brothers, 140, 166
    on White Nights, 173
Méliès, Georges, 254
Melville, Herman, 56
Mendelssohn, Peter de, 215
Meneghini, Giovanni Battista, 90
Menotti, Gian Carlo, 134
Menzio, Francesco, 54
Metternich, Prince Klemens von, 41
Michelangelo, 33, 230
Milestone, Lewis, 153
Miller, Arthur, 83, 113, 132, 184–85
Mindszenty, Cardinal, 118
Mitford, Unity, 79
Moes, Count Vladislav, 214–15
Mohammed (prophet), 38
Mocci, Paolo, 60
Molière, 265
Molnár, 64
Monicelli, Mario, 159, 160
Monroe, Marilyn, 184–85, 272
Montale, Eugenio, 164
Montez, Lola, 225
Montezemolo, Colonel, 60
Montgomery, Florence, 9
Morand, Paul, 116, 209
Moravia, Alberto, 6, 84
More, Thomas, 125
Morelli, Rina, 64, 116, 118, 265, 277
    in Antigone, 66
    in As You Like It, 81
    in Eurydice, 66
    in The Glass Menagerie, 66
    in The Intruder, 274
    in L'Arialda, 154–55
    in Life with Father, 82
    in Mrs. Gibbon's Boys, 137
    in A View from the Bridge, 132
Morgan, Lady, 12
Morley, Thomas, 81
Mosley, Oswald, 247
Mozart, Wolfgang Amadeus von, 89, 238
Musil, Robert, 201
Musset, Alfred de, 65, 106

Mussolini, Benito, 8, 13, 27–30, 45, 116, 120, 175, 191
and death of Matteotti, 35
on Gramsci, 34
Hitler's first encounter with (1934), 35, 192
Renoir and, 48
takes power, 34
and World War I, 24
in World War II, 53, 58
Mussolini, Vittorio, 57
Mussorgsky, Modest, 219

Nabokov, Vladimir, 154, 205
Napoleon I, 4, 7, 11, 91, 92
Napoleon III, 231
Nasser, Gamal Abdel, 130
Nietzsche, Friedrich, 195, 217, 218, 271
Nievo, Ippolito, 275
Nijinsky, Waslaw, 223
Nobili, Lila De, 107, 116, 249
Noiret, Philippe, 158
Notes on a News Item (documentary; Visconti), 88–89
Novalis (Friedrich von Hardenburg), 234
Nureyev, Rudolf, 223

Offenbach, Jacques, 230
Olivier, Laurence, 79, 206, 210
O'Neill, Eugene, 131, 173, 247
Opera stagings
Anna Bolena, 91, 124–27
Der Rosenkavalier, 185, 189
Don Carlo, 133–34, 185, 189
Egmont, 191
Falstaff, 15, 92, 185
Il Duca di Alba, 138
Il Trovatore, 168
Iphigénie en Tauride, 127–28
La Traviata, 14, 91, 106–12, 133, 168, 189–90
La Vestale, 91–94
Macbeth, 135
Manon Lescaut, 248–49
plans for Wagner tetralogy, 241
project for Poliuto, 128–29
Salome, 159
Simon Boccanegra, 206–7

The Sleepwalker (La Sonnambula), 103–6
Origo, Iris, 174
Orléans, Duke of (Louis I), 20
Osiris, Wanda, 89
Ossessione (Visconti film), 54–58, 87, 123
actors in, 57
characters of, compared to De Sica's, 264
cost of, 74
reactions to, 57–58
revival of, 132
story of, 56
Otto, Prince of Bavaria, 231–32
Outsider, The (Visconti film version of Camus's The Stranger), 186–89, 254

Paccarella, Bruno, 78
Pafundi, Vincenzo, 142
Palach, Jan, 205
Pallante, Antonio, 79–80
Papagallo, Pietro, 60
Pari, Ferrucio, 206
Paris, influence of, on Visconti (1936), 44–45
Pascal, Gabriel, 39
Pasolini, Pier Paolo, 117, 132, 275
Pasta, Giuditta, 90
Pasternak, Boris, 131, 163
Pavolini, Alessandro, 56, 72
Paxinou, Katina, 144–45, 149–50
Pellico, Silvio, 13
Pensione Oltremare (scenario; Visconti), 63
Pescucci, Gabriella, 249
Petrarch, 159
Petrova, Sonia, 232
Pettine, Giovanni, 21
Pfistermeister, Franz von, 227
Philip II, King of Spain, 133, 185
Philipe, Anne, 89
Picasso, Pablo, 269
Piccolo, Baron Lucio, 164
Pickford, Mary, 186
Pictures and Times of Eleonora Duse (Imagini e tempi di Eleonora Duse; Visconti film), 135–36

Pieraccini, Leonetta, 84
Pietrangeli, Antonio, 56, 64
Pilade (Roman mime), 12
Pinter, Harold, 206, 246–47
Piovene, Guido, 64
Pirandello, Luigi, 132, 165, 263, 265
Pisanello, 8, 237
Pitigrilli, 116
Pittalunga, General, 29
Pius XII, Pope, 137
Pliny the Younger, 20
Plutarch, 55, 92
Polverelli, Gaetano, 58
Ponchielli, Amilcare, 90
Ponti, Carlo, 159, 160
Popesco, Elvire, 158
Porta, Carlo, 263
Powell, William, 47
Prati, Giovanni, 97
Pratolini, Vasco, 64, 85, 140
Praz, Mario, 241
Prévost, Abbé, 248
Prokofiev, Sergei, 49
Prosperi, Giorgio, 36, 96
Proust, Marcel, 9, 30, 106, 108, 170, 211, 223, 254
Puccini, Giacomo, 17, 104, 248–49, 263, 264
Pushkin, Aleksandr, 174

Rachel (actress), 14, 107
Radetzky, Marshal Fëdor, 11
Radiguet, Raymond, 25
Rajk, Laszlo, 118
Rainer, Luise, 136
Ramelli, Sergio, 260
Rampling, Charlotte, 265
Ray, Man, 46
Remarque, Erich Maria, 136
Rembrandt, 126
Remembrance of Things Past (Proust; Visconti film project), 223
Renoir, Auguste, 42
Renoir, Claude, 47
Renoir, Jean, 85, 275, 277
  Visconti and, 41–50, 59, 136
    influence of Renoir's political ideas, 46
    similarities between, 42–43, 45

work on La Tosca, 48–50
work on Une Partie de campagne, 46–47
Retty, Rosa, 157
Ricci, Nora, 265
Ricci, Paolo, 59
Ricordi, Giulio, 7
Rilke, Rainer Maria, 247
Roberto, Federico de, 165
Rocco and His Brothers (Rocco e i suoi fratelli; Visconti film), 11, 128, 128, 137–54, 166, 240, 253
  cast of, 137, 144–47, 149–51, 167
  characters in, compared with De Sica's, 264
  obscenity charges against, 151–53
  preparing outline for, 140–42
  shooting of, 147–51
  story of, 142–44
Röhm, Ernst, 193–94
Rolland, Romain, 24
Rosaria, T., 141–42
Rosenberg, Ethel, 113
Rosenberg, Julius, 113
Rosi, Francesco, 74–77, 142
Rosselli, Carlo, 206
Rosselli, Nello, 206
Rossellini, Roberto, 49, 76, 85, 89, 96, 104, 122
Rossi, Alberto de, 123
Rossini, Gioacchino, 90
Rota, Nino, 122–23, 155, 158
Rouleau, Raymond, 107
Rousseau, Henri, 234
Rusconi (producer), 253

Sacco, Nicola, 113
Saint-Exupéry, Antoine de, 272
Salvatori, Renato, 145
Salvi, Matteo, 138
Sanda, Dominique, 258–59
Sanders, Dick, 131
Sandra (Vaghe stelle dell'orsa; Visconti film), 3, 31, 173–83, 243
Santis, Giuseppe de, 49, 56, 75, 76, 186
Sarcey, Francisque, 110
Sartre, Jean-Paul, 66, 187
Scala, Regina della, 11
Schein, Harry, 198

Schell, Herman Karl, 119
Schell, Maria, 118
Schiller, Friedrich, 133
Schippers, Thomas, 134–35, 249
Schneider, Magda, 157
Schneider, Romy, 147, 156–58, 161–62, 227, 265, 271, 277
Schönberg, Arnold, 89, 126, 215–16
Scola, Ettore, 265
Scotellaro, Rocco, 140
Seligman, Sybil, 263
Senso (C. Boito; film by Visconti), 28, 31, 79, 94–102, 116, 240
    actors in, 64, 96, 97
    first shown, 94
    reactions to, 101–2
    story of, 95–101
Sequi, Sandro, 6, 126
Serafin, Tullio, 90
Serandrei, Mario, 54, 65, 171
Sermoneta, Duchess of, 23, 24
Seymour, David (Chim), 44
Seymour, Jane, 127
Shakespeare, William, 30, 89, 120, 135
Shaw, George Bernard, 56
Shearer, Norma, 47
Shelley, Percy Bysshe, 134
Shirer, William L., 192–93
Sica, Vittorio de, 49, 66, 207
    death of, 265
    friendship with, 76
    last meeting with, 264
    works of, 58, 84, 88, 89, 95, 132, 159, 160, 259
Siciliani, Francesco, 127
Simon, Michel, 49–50
Simone (doctor), 238
Simple Heart, A (Un Coeur simple; Flaubert; Visconti film project), 264
Smith, Mr. (tutor), 19
Soldati, Mario, 96
Sophocles, 173
Sorel, Georges, 8
Sorel, Jean, 175
Spagnuolo, Carmelo, 151–52, 155
Speer, Albert, 195
Spontini, Gasparo, 91, 92
Stalin, Joseph, 118, 164

Stanislavsky, Konstantin, 184
Stavisky, Serge, 44
Stendhal (Henri Beyle), 8, 18, 92, 243, 254
    burial place of, 89, 107
    characters of, 30, 37, 167, 192
    on quality of sounds, 20–21
Stoppa, Paolo, 64, 116, 274, 277
    in The Glass Menagerie, 66
    in L'Arialda, 154–55
    in Life with Father, 82
    in Mrs. Gibbon's Boys, 137
    in Rocco and His Brothers, 145
    in A View from the Bridge, 132
Story, William Whetmore, 255
Strauss, Richard, 159, 173, 185, 202
Strehler, Giorgio, 81
Strindberg, Leopold, 120
Stroheim, Erich von, 43, 85
Sullivan, Arthur, 17
Svevo, Italo, 39

Taglioni, Maria, 104–6
Tardini, Cardinal, 151
Tarnowska, Countess, 64
Tebaldi, Renata, 108
Teilhard de Chardin, Pierre, 106, 274
Television productions
    projected, 263
    Tonight We Improvise (Questa sera si recita a soggetto), 262–63
Temple, Shirley, 48, 157
Tessier, Valentine, 158
Testori, Giovanni, 128, 140, 153–54, 191
Thackeray, William Makepeace, 105
Theater productions
    Adamo, 66
    After the Fall, 184
    Antigone, 66
    As the Leaves Fall (Come le foglie), 89
    As You Like It, 81–82
    The Cherry Orchard, 183, 184
    Children of Art (Figli d'arte), 138
    Countess Julie, 120
    Crime and Punishment, 66
    The Crucible, 113–14
    Death of a Salesman, 83
    Eurydice, 66, 74

The Evils of Tobacco, 89
Fifth Column, 64
The Glass Menagerie, 66
Hamlet, 15
Huis clos, 66
La Machine à écrire, 66
L'Arialda, 128, 154–55
Le Chandelier, 65
Le Mariage de Figaro, 66
Les Parents terribles, 64
Life with Father, 82
L'Impresario delle Smyrne, 130
L'Inserzione, 206
Long Day's Journey into Night (projected), 131
Look Homeward, Angel, 136
Medea, 89
Mistress of the Inn (*La locandiera*), 89, 133
Mrs. Gibbon's Boys, 137
The Nun of Monza (*La Monaca di Monza*), 191
Old Times, 245–47
Oreste, 82
The Seducer, 84
A Streetcar Named Desire, 82
Sweet Aloes, 47
Three Sisters, 89
'Tis Pity She's a Whore, 156–58
Tobacco Road, 66
Troilus and Cressida, 82–83, 105
Two for the Seesaw, 136–37
Uncle Vanya, 114
A View from the Bridge, 132
The Voyage, 48
The Wise Wife, 39
Worldly Charity (*Carita mondana*), 47
Thulin, Ingrid, 198
Thyssen, Fritz, 192
Togliatti, Palmiro, 34, 58, 74–75, 103
    assassination attempt on, 79–80
    death of, 174–75
    The Leopard and, 171
Tolstoy, Leo, 118, 275
Tomasi, Giulio, 164
Toretta, Marchese Pietro Tomasi della, 163

Toscanini, Arturo, 15, 58, 64, 145, 275
    Callas and, 92–93
    death of, 120–21
    early career of, 13
    on opera, 133–34
    Turandot first conducted by, 264
Toscanini, Wally, Countess Castelbarco, 15, 37, 39
Toscanini, Wanda, 15, 277
Tosi, Piero, 105, 126, 158, 249
"Traditions and Inventions" (article; Visconti), 71
Traversi, Giannino Antona, 47
Trentini, Lucio, 6
Trombadori, Antonello, 40, 74
Truffaut, François, 153
Truman, Harry S, 73, 81
Truth Game, The (*Il gioco della verità*; Visconti and dell'Anna film), 39
Turati, Filippo, 206
Turgenev, Ivan, 259

Une Partie de campagne (Maupassant; film by Renoir; assisted by Visconti), 46–47
Uomoni e No (Vittorini; Visconti film project), 66

Valentino, Rudolph, 271
Valli, Alida, 96
Valli, Romolo, 265
Vallone, Raf, 186
Valois, Elisabeth de, 133
Vancini, Florestano, 205
Vanzetti, Bartolomeo, 113
Vecchi, Capt. Ferruchio, 28
Verdi, Giuseppe, 7, 13–15, 55, 103, 206, 228, 275, 276
    favorite opera of, 106
    funeral of, 18, 121
    influence of, 44
    music of, in *The Leopard*, 168, 169, 171
    music of, in *Senso*, 96, 97
    Toscanini compared with, 120
    veneration for, 13, 15, 89
Verdi, Giuseppina, 18
Verga, Giovanni, 43, 165, 170, 275
    influence of, 54, 77, 116–17, 139

293

Verga, Giovanni (*cont.*)
  problem of Southern Italy in works of, 4
  projected films based on works of, 55–56, 71–72
Verrocchio, Andrea del, 213, 220
Victor Emmanuel III, King of Italy, 13, 34, 35, 38
Victoria, Queen of England, 8, 104, 106
Vilmorin, Louise de, 136–37
Vinci, Leonardo Da, 10, 78, 219
Virgil, 127
Visconti, Anna (sister), 8
Visconti, Bernabò, 11
Visconti, Carla Erba (mother), 7, 12–13, 17–19, 39
  death of, 48, 54, 67
  and Luchino
    Luchino's adoration for, 19
    and Luchino's romances, 40
    sense of history communicated to Luchino, 18–19, 121
Visconti, Edoardo (brother), 8–9
Visconti, Filippo Maria, 237
Visconti, Gian Galeazzo, 10–11, 20
Visconti, Giuseppe, Duke of Modrone (father), 7, 12–13
  death of, 54, 67
  Luchino and, 30, 31, 33
  marriage of, 12
  rebuilding of Grazzano by, 23
Visconti, Guido (brother), 8, 54, 67
Visconti, Guido (grandfather; Duke of Modrone), 13
Visconti, Ida (sister), 9, 241
Visconti, Luchino
  adolescence of
    first love of, 33
    first sight of Michelangelo's *Moses*, 33
    and Mussolini's takeover, 34; *see also* Mussolini, Benito
  ancestry of, 7
  birth of, 7, 8, 17
  career of
    Chanel's role in, 38, 40–42, 45
    first offer to work in films, 39–40
    first theatrical production, 39
    Renoir's role in, *see* Renoir, Jean

  scenarios written, 63–64
    see also Ballet productions; Opera stagings; Television productions; Theater productions; *and specific films*
  characteristics of, 30–31, 40
    as musician, 32
    passion for horses, 37–39
    reading, 29–30, 191–93
  childhood of, 8–10
    and birth of Fascism, 27–28
    at Cernobbio, 20–21
    at Grazzano, 22–23
    interest in cinema, 21–22
    in Milan, 9–15
    and World War I, 24–26
  D'Annunzio's poetry admired by, 29
  death of, 3–6, 275
  education of, 19, 36
    school problems faced by, 32–33
  father of, *see* Visconti, Giuseppe
  health of
    first stroke suffered by, 224
    fracture suffered by, 266, 269
    physiotherapy following second stroke, 243, 245
    recovers from second stroke, 241–42
    second stroke suffered by, 237–41
  military service of, 37
  mother of, *see* Visconti, Carla Erba
  music and politics in works of, 14
  place of, in Italian culture, 275–76
  religious beliefs of, 36
  visits Hollywood (1937), 47–48
  in West Berlin (1950s), 130–31
  in World War II, 53–54, 61
    and liberation of Rome, 62
    opposes Fascism, 5, 15, 58–59
Visconti, Luigi (brother), 32–33, 37
Visconti, Uberta (sister), 6, 245
  death of Luchino and, 275
  as favorite sister, 9
  and liberation of Rome, 62
  and Luchino's arrest, 61
  on Luchino's problems in school, 32
  on Luchino's relationship to their mother, 19
  in World War II, 59

Visconti, Valentina, 20
Vittorini, Elio, 66, 87, 108

Wagner, Richard, 123, 138, 271
   Bellini's influence on, 104
   Gluck's influence on, 127
   Hitler and, 192
   in *Ludwig*, 227–32, 244
   Ludwig II and, 220, 225–26
   Mann and, 218
   plans for staging tetralogy of, 241
Wanger, Walter, 162
We Are Women (*Siamo donne;* Visconti film), 89
Weaver, William, 249
Wedding March (Visconti film), 85, 89, 95
Weill, Kurt, 38, 191
Welles, Orson, 144
Wertmuller, Lina, 257
West, Rebecca, 81
Wharton, Edith, 82
White Nights (*Le notti bianche;* Dostoevsky; Visconti film), 117–24, 131, 173, 253
   cast of, 118–19, 123

setting for, 119–20
story of, 122–24
Wilde, Oscar, 159, 189
Wilder, Thornton, 247
Williams, Tennessee, 66, 82, 96, 97, 247, 263
Wilson, Edmund, 241
Windisch-Graetz, Princess Irma (Princess Irma Weikersheim), 40
Wiseman, Cardinal, 94
Witch Burned Alive, The (*La strega bruciata viva;* Visconti film), 185–86
Wolfe, Thomas, 136
Wolff-Stormersee, Baroness, 163
Work (*Il lavoro;* Visconti film), 161–62

Yourcenar, Marguerite, 202

Zavattini, Cesare, 49, 62, 76, 85
Zeffirelli, Franco, 66, 75, 83
Zola, Emile, 118, 146
Zuffi, Piero, 92
Zweig, Stefan, 229